Othello. Basic setting consisting of three archways in the back, one on either side, and platforms stretching across the stage.

Theatre Scenecraft

For the backstage technician and artist

by

Vern Adix

Associate Professor of Speech
and Art Director of the Theatre
University of Utah

Illustrated by the Author with Drawings and Photographs of
University of Utah Theatre Productions.   Additional
Drawings by Robert W. Weideman.

PRINTED IN THE UNITED STATES OF AMERICA

In memory of
my father
Jack-of-all-trades.

FOREWORD

Not many possess the ability to write in a concise manner when they must describe various technical processes; fewer still have the ability to illustrate their work, and only a very few indeed have the years of experience necessary to make what they have written about and illustrated of any great value to the reader. Yet this is the happy combination of facts found in Vern Adix's book *Theatre Scenecraft*. Some fifteen years of practical theatre work have been combined with a natural, easily read style of writing and with clean-cut illustrations, that have resulted in a text that should prove a boon to all those organizations whose business or pleasure it is to produce plays.

Of greatest value to the inexperienced designer-technician are the innumerable suggestions and methods described by Mr. Adix that, if followed, will result in the saving of many hours of time in construction, painting, rigging, and shifting of scenery. Of equal importance is the fact that these suggestions will not only lead to a saving of time and a reduction of probable cost, but to a higher standard of production as well.

—ARNOLD S. GILLETTE, *Managing Director*
The University Theatre
State University of Iowa

Acknowledgments

This book is a compilation of some of the thoughts and ideas of one lonely non-professional theatre designer and technician. The loneliness has come from the pressures and strains of as many as 20 "opening nights" a year for a period of 15 years. Out of this "Sturm and Drang" experience have come some "short cuts", simplified processes and economical means of production that may be of value to others. Since continuously working against time that is always too short, trying to stretch budgets that are too rigid, and maintaining amiable relations with directors whose "opening night tempers" are too quick seem to be the lot of the non-professional theatre worker, it is hoped that the material in this book will provide a few helpful suggestions for overcoming these "opening nightmares."

A factual crafts book is either the result of years of thought, research and experience or the careful compilation of the ideas of others. The material of this book is, in a sense, a combination of both of these processes. The material has been accumulated piecemeal over the years as the productions have been planned, built, painted, lighted, staged and "struck." The facts, figures and information of this book have been collected, assimilated and now put together in a new form. The source of most of this material is so varied and nebulous that it would be all but impossible to state specifically where much of it came from.

In general I am indebted to groups of people: to everyone for whom I have ever staged a play, to everyone who has ever answered a question regarding the multitudinous list of supplies and materials that are used on the stage, to the authors of all of the books I have ever read, to the editors of the pictorial magazines that I have thumbed through, to the builders of the private and public buildings that I have seen, to the curators of the museums I have visited, to the authors of the plays I have staged, and to all of the students who have worked with me and given me an infinite collection of new ideas.

More specifically an author is indebted to those who have given freely of their time and energy to help collect and collate the material of his text. For this I am deeply indebted to:

PATRICIA CHRISTIANSEN, whose invaluable assistance and forbearance in reading, correcting, editing and retyping the material made it possible to complete this text.

ROBERT WEIDEMAN, whose drawings in the furniture section, and on the chapter headings contribute so much to the finished format.

JOHN C. CLEGG, who carefully checked many of the facts of the electrical sections of the book.

ROBERT HYDE WILSON, who read the text carefully and provided numerous helpful suggestions.

C. LOWELL LEES, who has tolerated me as a member of his theatre staff for so many years.

SARA SPENCER, who encouraged me to write this book, and her printers who have been so kind and understanding in preparing and printing the text.

NELLIE HARVEY, who first gave me a healthy interest in drama many years ago when I was a student in her junior high school literature class.

ARNOLD GILLETTE, who contributed the foreword. As a student in his classes I gained much of my technical theatre knowledge.

To all of these people and many others I extend my heartfelt thanks.

VERN ADIX

CONTENTS

INDEX OF PHOTOGRAPHS

INDEX OF LINE ILLUSTRATIONS

xix

Theatre Scenecraft

Introduction

"All the world's a stage,
And all the men and women merely players;
They have their exits and their entrances;
And one man in his time plays many parts,
His acts being seven ages."

These words, spoken by Jacques in Shakespeare's *As You Like It,* have become an immortal description of the vastness of the stage. Shakespeare's concept of the stage may have differed from ours, but his words were never truer than they are today if we think of the vast utilization of dramatic production. The idea that all men and women, yes, and even children, are literally players is obvious when we look about. The stage includes professional and non-professional companies; civic and private theatrical organizations; adult, adolescent and child players.

This stage may be almost anywhere in the world. It may be in the corner of a backyard, in a musty basement, in New York's Radio City Music Hall, in the church around the corner, in a school house, in the center of a large room. The chosen place may become a stage the moment play activity begins, or it may take months to prepare it with elaborate machinery and equipment. The stage may be wide or narrow, deep or shallow, raised or on the ground, with or without proscenium. It may have revolving stages, traps and wagons; it may be a sylvan area consisting of a flat grassy space surrounded by trees; or it may be the end of a room with only the doors and windows normal to the living space of a home. But wherever it is, and whatever it is, the stage serves one major purpose: it is the realm of the actor, the place of the play's action.

The stage may be decorated or plain. It may be covered with acres of scenery or decorated only by human forms in motion. More often than not there is at least a minimum of decorative background for the action of the play. This may be a simple screen merely to suggest the locale of the action or it may be an entire enclosure describing the scene in detail.

Regardless of how simple or how complex the setting, the producer of a play should know how to design, build, paint, erect and light the scenery that is to provide the visual environment for the actors. He should know how to

1

achieve satisfactory scenic effects with a minimum expenditure of materials and effort. To do this he must know the raw materials of the scene crafts. From these raw materials he must be able to form the scenic units which, when manipulated, produce the structure that is assembled and lighted to provide the environment for the actor and the stage picture for the audience.

Large or small, simple or complex, the stage setting is usually made up from the same types of basic units of scenery. And with a supply of standardized units it is possible to create any imaginable type of stage setting.

Designing the setting is the refined process of the stage decorator. Before it is possible to design a stage setting it is necessary to learn about the raw materials of the arts and crafts of the stage. It is necessary to know the construction of the basic units of scenery; to know something about the various painting techniques; to know the effects of colored light on colored pigment; to know basic electric wiring and the fundamentals of stage lighting; to know something about the operation of the physical theatre plant; and to know something about tools, lumber, wood joints, perspective drawing, stage properties and other paraphernalia used on the stage. In this book it seems logical to discuss all of these matters first, since they are basic to the planning and decoration of the stage setting, and then to discuss stage design as the culmination of all of the other assembled information.

A book of this nature is not, and should not be, a rule book. At best it can only be a helpful stimulant. It should point toward ideas and techniques that have been found to be helpful and practical in the past. There is no ONE way to stage a play and there is no ONE color for a stage setting just as there is no ONE way to build a stage tree. There may be procedures that have been tried and found to be workable, and there may be ideas that seem to be the best for a specific play in a specific situation. This does not mean that you or I should limit ourselves to this procedure. Our situation may allow us to try new ideas that will work better, or our budget may restrict us and force us to use simpler, more economical procedures, or our budget may be limitless so that there are no restrictions to imagination or cost and our wildest wishes stagewise can have full rein.

The Stage House

Today there are so many sizes, shapes and varieties of theatres that it is difficult to describe one and state specifically that it is typical. However, for the sake of convenience in discussing the various parts of the backstage area and its operation, it will be assumed that the theatre in question is flexible enough that it may have any or all of the facilities that are used in normal productions. There actually are buildings having all of the equipment that is mentioned here. However, such theatre plants are in the minority. Most of them have only a meager amount of equipment. Fortunately, a building need not have elaborate equipment before plays can be presented. However, it is worthwhile to know what can be done to improve the existing theatre, and what is available if improvements are to be made.

STAGE—The term "stage" refers to that portion of the theatre used by the actors. In an arena type theatre this is the area not occupied by the members of the audience. Frequently this is interpreted so literally that the actors practically walk on the toes of the audience and sit in their laps. In the conventional theatre there is usually a narrow chasm separating the audience from the actors. This space just in front of the block of seats is the orchestra pit. It may be dropped down lower than the auditorium floor so that the name "pit" is logical, or it may be flush with the auditorium floor. This pit in a sense separates the audience from the performers.

The stage rises up just beyond the orchestra pit. The amount of its elevation above the audience level varies from one theatre to another. It may be one step or four feet. It is inadvisable for it to be higher than the eye level of the members of the audience who sit in the front row.

PROSCENIUM—The enlarged hole cut through the wall to allow the audience to view the stage is the Proscenium Arch, or simply the proscenium. This archway is, in a sense, the frame for the action of the stage. Conven-

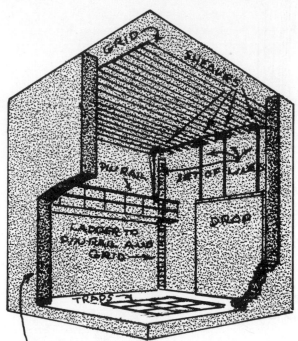

PROSCENIUM ARCH

tional staging is, for this reason, frequently referred to as picture frame staging.

The arena type theatre has nothing to correspond to the proscenium unless it is the lighted area of the action into which the audience peers. The audience is separated only by its own lack of illumination. The separation of the actor and audience here is more hypothetical than real.

APRON—If the stage projects out beyond the curtain and proscenium toward the audience, the projection is called the Apron of the stage. Sometimes this area is found convenient to use with the curtains closed in order to cut off the rest of the stage for meetings, for lectures and for scenes that require a minimum of space. In complex stage productions it is sometimes difficult to move scenery rapidly enough to keep the play flowing along and if apron scenes can be contrived to cover while

scenery is being shifted behind the act curtain this problem can be partially solved at least.

FIRE CURTAIN—Immediately next to the proscenium arch on the stage side is a fire curtain composed of a fabric woven from asbestos thread. This fireproof curtain raises and lowers in channel iron slots mounted to the sides of the proscenium. It is usually counterweighted and rigged so that the excess heat of a fire causes a low melting point metal link to melt, automatically dropping the asbestos curtain.

Masking Devices

ACT CURTAIN—The proscenium arch is usually provided with a curtain large enough to fill its opening. This curtain can be opened and closed to reveal or conceal the stage beyond. This is the Act Curtain, or Front Curtain.

GRAND DRAPE—An overhead height adjustment curtain known as the Grand Drape is mounted either immediately in front of or

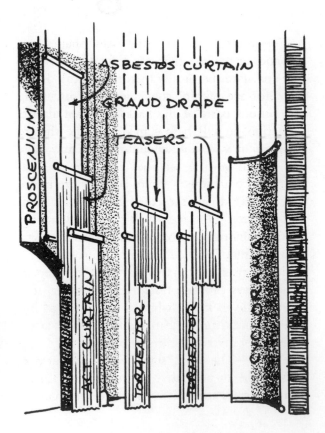

behind the Act Curtain. This curtain makes it possible to increase or decrease the height of the proscenium arch.

TEASERS—Overhead masking drapes upstage of the Grand Drape and also operated to increase or decrease the height of the stage revealed are referred to as Teasers.

TORMENTORS—Curtains installed at the sides of the stage and used to cut down the width of the stage are referred to as Tormentors.

Stage Floor

ACTING AREA—The space where the action of the play takes place on the stage is logically named the Acting Area. This area usually extends across approximately the width of the proscenium arch and runs upstage approximately two-thirds the depth of the stage. Of course the acting area proportions will not only vary from stage to stage but from production to production on the same stage. When a stage setting is in place, the acting area is within its confines. Usually the acting area is the stage space that is visible to most of the members of the audience.

FLOORING—The stage, at least that portion of it known as the acting area, should be floored with relatively soft wood so that scenery can be anchored in place easily. Fir is frequently used. When this section becomes worn it can be refloored without having to cover the entire stage area.

TRAPS—The stage floor may be equipped with removable sections, or trap doors. There are times, in *Faust* for instance, when it is convenient for an actor to rise through the floor as if coming from the steam heated world. At other times people may descend into lower levels—into the sewers of Paris in Act II of *The Madwoman of Chaillot;* into the store below in Act I of *The Merchant of Yonkers;* or into the subway in *My Sister Eileen.* For such scenes it is convenient to have "traps" in the floor.

REVOLVING STAGES—Some of the more elaborately equipped theatres have revolving discs cut into the floor of the acting area. It is possible to set up a series of scenes on the disc and change from one to another by a simple turn of the disc.

TRACKS FOR HEAVY WAGONS—The stage of the University of Iowa theatre has tracks recessed in the floor that extend across the stage parallel to the curtain. Large wagons, the full width of the stage and half its depth, can be rolled onto the stage complete with setting, properties and furnishings. A revolving disc makes it possible to switch the wagon upstage or downstage onto another set of tracks where it can be rolled into a storage dock. This is an unusual innovation that may be used to quickly shift the settings of complex productions, otherwise difficult to move.

ELEVATOR STAGES—On another type of mechanized stage, portions of the floor may be raised or lowered by hydraulic lifts similar to those used for grease racks in service stations. Spectacular vertical movement, as well as simple floor level arrangements, can be achieved with equipment of this variety.

Stage Directions

STAGE RIGHT—STAGE LEFT—To clarify directions on the stage, stage right and stage

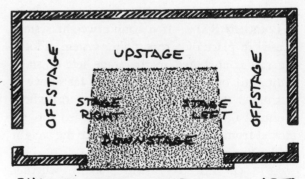

SHADED SPACE IS THE ACTING AREA

left have been set up as right and left of the actor as he stands facing the audience.

UPSTAGE—DOWNSTAGE—In like manner to the rear of the stage is referred to as upstage and to the front of the stage as downstage.

5

Anywhere on a line running through the center of the stage from front to rear is referred to as center stage. By using combinations of these directions it is easy to find one's way about the acting area of the stage.

OFFSTAGE—When one moves out of the acting area to the sides of the stage he is moving offstage.

WINGS—The offstage portions of the stage are the wings.

Flying Systems

FLYWELL—The acting area of the stage is usually provided with an extremely high roof. The space between the floor and the strut work of wood, steel or wood and steel suspended about 5 or 6 feet below the roof is called the flywell.

GRID—The strut work referred to is the grid. The grid supports pulleys through which ropes or cables are threaded to support scenery, lights, drops, draperies and other paraphernalia of the stage that are suspended in the flywell.

PIN RAIL—If a rope flying system is used to raise, lower and suspend the scenery above the stage, then the ropes are tied off on a railing which is anchored near the wall on stage right or left, either on the floor level or part way up into the flywell. It should never be more than half way to the grid.

LOCKING RAIL—If a counterweight system is used in place of a rope flying system, a locking rail is anchored to the stage left or stage right wall on the floor level and far above it just under the grid is a loading platform where counter-balancing weights are added or removed from the carriages to balance the weight of the flown units of scenery.

SETS OF LINES—Flying systems, whether rope or counterweight, ordinarily have 3 or more lines evenly spaced across the stage in each set. The ropes are located so that battens as long, or slightly longer than, the width of the proscenium may be used to fasten back-drops, draperies and scenery preparatory to suspending them in the flywell. In the 3 line

set the one nearest the operator on the rail is called the short line; the center one is logically the center line, and the one farthest away is the long line. If there are 5 lines in the set, these names hold but two more are added: the line between the short and center lines is the short center line and, of course, the one between the center and the long lines is the long center line.

ROPE SYSTEM—In a rope flying system Manila or hemp ropes may be tied directly to the objects being flown. On a unit of scenery they may be tied to ceiling plates or hanger

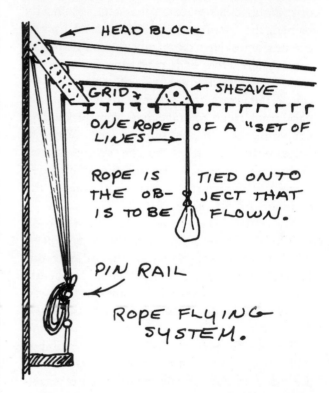

irons that have been mounted on the framework with screws and bolts. Or the ropes may be tied onto a long wooden or pipe batten and the scenery then tied onto this.

The ropes in the flying system extend up to the grid where they pass over loft blocks. The ropes of an entire set of lines cross the stage to a position above the pin rail and there pass through a multiple pulley, consisting of several sheaves (pulleys) mounted side by side

6

called a head block, and from there the ropes drop down to the pin rail where they are tied off on pegs, or belaying pins, that are mounted in a pipe or rail that runs from the front to the back of the stage against or near one of the side walls of the flywell. To raise or lower scenery, one, two or more men grasp the set of 3 or 5 lines and "take up" or "let in" on the lines. Many times it helps if these men are on the "beefy" side so that their weight can be thrown onto the lines to balance the weight on the other end.

SANDBAGS—To make the job a little easier bags filled or partially filled with sand are fastened to the lines by means of a rope lock. Usually the weight on the stage end of the lines is lifted into the air so that the sandbag may be mounted at the pin rail level. Ordinarily it is advisable to put slightly less than enough weight to balance the load in the sandbag so that the stage load will tend to sink down by itself when the ropes are released. One man will then be able to raise the scenic unit without any trouble.

BLOCK AND TACKLE—If the load on a set of lines is extremely heavy it is possible to attach a block and tackle to the lines. The block and tackle is a means of achieving a mechanical advantage, at the sacrifice of speed, in lifting objects. The number of pulleys determines the amount of advantage gained. (See appendix for details.)

SELF LEVELLING SANDBAG—If the weight on a set of lines is evenly distributed across the stage a simple self levelling device can be made. If there are 3 lines in a set, the center one, at the pin rail end, is securely tied to a sandbag. A pulley or block is tied on at the connection of the line and sandbag. One of the other lines is led through the pulley and the other tied to it. The lines are then adjusted so that the object being flown is in "trim" (level) when the ropes are tied. Thereafter it is possible to level the load by simply slipping the rope that goes around the pulley one way or the other. Since the long and short

lines are tied together, making one continuous line around the pulley, pulling one side down pushes the other side up and vice versa. This

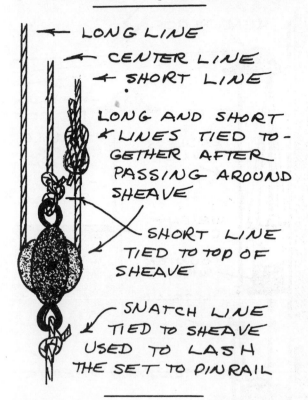

LONG LINE
CENTER LINE
SHORT LINE

LONG AND SHORT LINES TIED TOGETHER AFTER PASSING AROUND SHEAVE

SHORT LINE TIED TO TOP OF SHEAVE

SNATCH LINE TIED TO SHEAVE USED TO LASH THE SET TO PIN RAIL

is an excellent device to use since rope tends to slip through rope locks sometimes and the entire set gets slightly out of "trim."

COUNTERWEIGHT SYSTEMS—The counterweight system uses cables in place of ropes and the cables are permanently fastened on the stage end to pipe battens. On the wall end the cables are fastened to weight carriers called cradles. The cradle is governed in its up and down movement by wire or angle iron guides, secured to or near one of the side walls of the flywell. The weights for the system are stored on a catwalk or platform just under the grid. Enough weights are loaded onto the cradle from there to balance the weight of the scenery. To raise and lower a set of lines together with the scenery and the counterweight, a line is fastened to the top of the cradle, run up to the grid over a pulley, extended back down to the floor under a spring tension pulley and extended

7

back up to the bottom of the cradle where it is attached. This is rightly named the endless

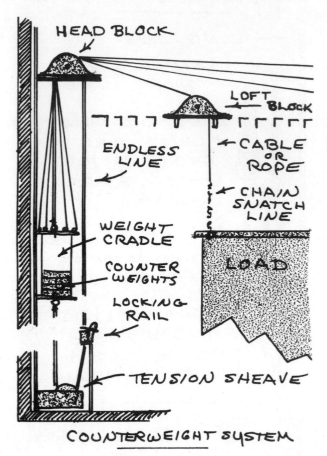

COUNTERWEIGHT SYSTEM

operator can handle heavy loads when the carriage is correctly loaded with weights; and last, but far from least, there are no great coils of rope ends under the operator's feet.

DOUBLE PURCHASE COUNTERWEIGHTS— The regular counterweight sets mentioned above require the full height of the grid in order to operate correctly. The weights must move just as far up as the battens do down in coming to the stage floor. A special type of counterweight called the double purchase is designed so that the weights need travel only half the distance of the objects they are used to lift. The locking rail can be mounted up on the wall slightly less than half way to the grid and objects can still be lifted from the

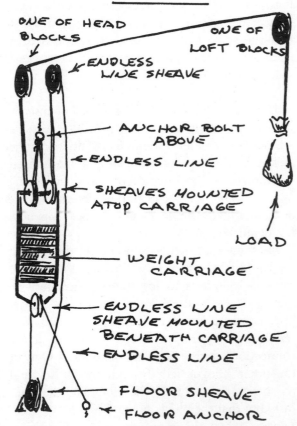

ONE LINE OF SYSTEM TO SHOW DOUBLE PURCHASE COUNTERWEIGHT

line. The load is locked in place with a simple concentric lever mounted on a rail. Pushing the lever in one direction wedges it against the rope, and locks it in place. Pulling it back in the other direction releases the tension so the rope can move freely.

COUNTERWEIGHT VS ROPE—The counterweight system, though more expensive, has many advantages over the rope flying system and should by all means be installed in new theatres or in theatres that are being remodelled. The counterweight system is built to carry heavier weights; the lines are permanently trimmed so that counterbalanced scenery units are not sagging at one end, off the floor in the center and trim on the other end; one

8

floor to the grid. This system has advantages and disadvantages over the conventional system that will make it useful as a part of the equipment on some stages. The individual units are more complex, hence more expensive, and it takes twice as much weight to counterbalance an object so the number of available weights must be doubled. However, since the pin rail is mounted halfway to the grid the wall beneath may be cleared of mechanical contrivances so that more wall stacking space is available for scenery and properties.

WINCHES—Another device for lifting scenery is the winch, which consists of a drum upon which the rope or cable is wound, a crank and a gear system. Turning the crank meshes the gears and winds the rope onto the drum or unwinds it off the drum. When properly geared tremendous weights can be lifted by one man with a winch. However, the drum is usually small in diameter and the gear system makes it necessary to turn the handle many times in order to lift the weight. Speed is sacrificed for mechanical advantage.

MOTORIZED COUNTERWEIGHTS AND WINCHES—Electric motors may be installed to operate both counterweight and winch systems. They save a great deal of human energy, but at the same time are so expensive that very few theatres can afford them.

Scene Shifting Devices

Some of the permanent equipment of the stage has been mentioned. There are other scene shifting devices frequently used on the stage, and often considered to be a part of the stage house equipment, which may be stored away from the stage and brought in when needed. These devices fall into four categories: rolling, rotating, sliding and flying mechanisms.

Rolling Mechanisms

The rolling type devices consist of such equipment as wagons, outriggers and tip jacks.

WAGONS—Stage wagons are platforms mounted on casters so that they may be easily rolled around on the stage. The frame work

of the wagon can be made of angle iron, wood or heavy extruded aluminum. Wooden frames are probably the least expensive and easiest to build, though they are not always the strongest or the most durable. Angle iron has many advantages even though it is more expensive. An angle iron frame, with welded joints, will outwear many sets of tops. It may be slightly heavier, but actually a wooden frame with adequate cross braces is also heavy. Aluminum would be ideal if it were not so expensive.

WAGON FRAMEWORK—The size and weight to be carried by the wagon will determine to a great extent the material that should be used for the wagon frame. For a normal sized stage 4' x 8' platforms may be built with 2" x 4" lumber for the frame. After the outside of the frame has been built, additional 2" x 4" pieces should be put in across the wagon and spaced not more than 2' apart. A top of ⅝" or ¾" sheathing plywood may then be fastened on with 1½" flathead wood screws or 6d coated box nails. The 4' x 8' size is convenient because it uses a full sheet of plywood. It is also about the largest platform that can be easily handled by two men. One strong man can juggle a platform of this size but it taxes his strength.

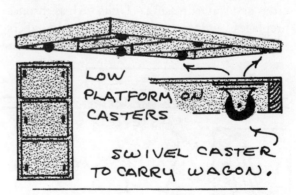

LOW PLATFORM ON CASTERS

SWIVEL CASTER TO CARRY WAGON.

CASTERS—At least 6 casters, 2 on each end and 2 halfway between these, should be mounted on each wagon. The casters should have at least 3" rubber tired wheels. The larger casters make the wagon easier to roll. Unless the wagon is to be moved in straight lines only, it is advisable to use casters with ball bearing swivel bases. Casters should be kept well greased at all times.

The casters should be mounted so they lift the wagon off the floor by about ¾″. Then there will be less danger of small obstacles on the floor wedging beneath the edge of the wagon.

MOVING WAGONS—It is usually difficult to start a wagon rolling. Stagehands find it easier to push on the scenery mounted atop the wagon than to stoop down and push on the edge of the wagon. Naturally, this loosens or even breaks the flats so it is necessary to rig up some kind of device that can be grasped easily in order to pull or twist the wagon unit. Ceiling plates (rings mounted on steel plates), large screw eyes or eye bolts should be mounted on the sides or tops of the wagons. Loops of rope can be tied on permanently or removable ropes can be snapped on at the time the platform is to be moved.

The stage wagon is a convenient scene shifting device if there is adequate offstage space in which to maneuver and store all of the units needed for a given production. Either partial or entire settings may be mounted atop one or more wagons and shifted complete with properties and stage dressing. Units such as thrones, fireplaces, judges' stands, podiums, speakers' stands, stairways, platforms, etc. may be han-

dled easily if mounted on wagons. Hinges, iron straps, wooden cleats or plumbers' strap may be used to fasten wagons together.

JACKKNIFE STAGES—Large wagon units are sometimes rigged so that they operate like blades on each end of a jackknife. The downstage off right corner of one wagon is fastened to a pivot and the downstage off left corner of the other wagon is also fastened to a pivot. Depth of the stage and offstage space must be checked to be certain that there is adequate storage for one wagon while the other is in use.

OUTRIGGERS—The outrigger, or outrigger wagon, is another caster device that can be used to help carry a good deal of the weight of heavy scenic units when they are shifted. Frequently heavy units need to be moved, but it is inconvenient to design a step or level into the setting so that the scenery can be mounted on a wagon. In this situation a wagon or an outrigger (which is a castered frame similar to a wagon frame but designed to fit into specific positions behind the setting) can be mounted to the back of the scenery. Before being mounted the wall section is lifted off the floor slightly so that the outrigger will carry it. This device makes it possible to roll heavy units on and off stage.

TIP JACKS—There are times when an outrigger is not practical. If the weight of the scenic unit tends to pull backwards slightly or straight down, the outrigger will work very well. However, if the weight tends to pull the scenery forward, a tip jack should be used. A tip jack is a right triangular shaped frame with one arm elongated almost to the height of the scenery and with a relatively short arm on the other right angle side of the triangle. The diagonal board connecting these two arms should be about the height of the flat when the frame is completed. Casters are mounted under the short arm and the diagonal is secured to the flat with nails, or loose pin hinges or is fastened in some other way.

Ordinarily, tip jacks are used in pairs. One is mounted near each end of the wall section

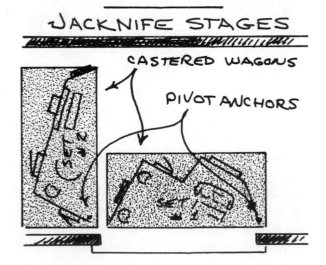

JACKNIFE STAGES

CASTERED WAGONS

PIVOT ANCHORS

10

and the two are then securely cross braced to one another and to the wall section. If they

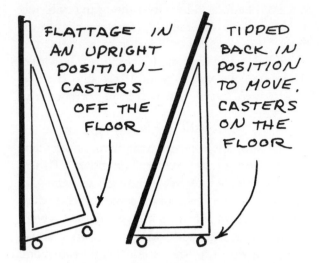

FLATTAGE IN AN UPRIGHT POSITION — CASTERS OFF THE FLOOR

TIPPED BACK IN POSITION TO MOVE, CASTERS ON THE FLOOR

are mounted while the scenery is in place in the setting the front caster of the right triangle corner barely touches the floor. The other, because of the shape of the triangle, is then off the floor by several inches. When it is time to move the scenery the wall section is unfastened at each end and leaned back until both casters are on the floor. The construction of the jack causes the scenery to be lifted off the floor and the entire unit can be easily rolled into the wings. By means of tip jacks one man can move a unit that would require three or four if the unit were being dragged or carried.

Tip jack units can be turned around and mounted with the right angle side against the flat so that both casters are on the floor when the scenery is in position. The units then work in much the same manner as outrigger wagons.

Rotating Devices

The revolving discs, previously mentioned, are installed in the floor as part of the regular equipment of very few theatres. It is possible to build units to fit on top of the stage floor that will revolve and serve basically the same purpose as the built-in device.

PERIAKTOI—Simple rotating scenic units can be built even without platforms under them

that operate in somewhat the same manner as the disc. Three wide flats, or three sections each made up from two or more flats hinged together and stiffened, may be fastened together at the corners to make an oversized prism, similar to the periaktoi thought to have been used in the classical Greek theatre many centuries ago. Casters or large furniture gliders may be mounted under these units so that they may be rotated easily. The unit can then be turned to present any of its three faces to the audience. And of course it isn't necessary to be limited to three sides. Four or even more flats could be fastened together in this way.

ROTATING WAGON UNITS—Wagon units can be used singly or fastened together to form units that may be covered on all sides and then rotated to present their various sides to the audience.

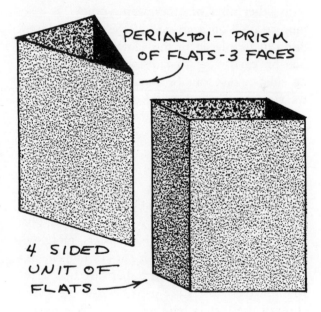

PERIAKTOI— PRISM OF FLATS - 3 FACES

4 SIDED UNIT OF FLATS

TEMPORARY REVOLVING STAGE — Stage wagons may be fastened together to form a square form and then curved sections added on each of the sides to make a disc. Three dimensional scenery units mounted on top may then be moved into the desired position by rotating the mechanism. Of course there is no reason why this device needs to be round except that the curved edge of a disc can be placed near the curtain and then the device rotated without the corners pushing into the curtain.

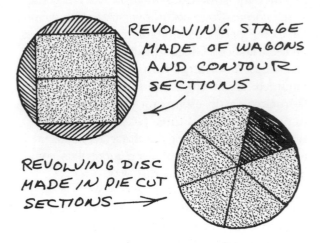

REVOLVING STAGE MADE OF WAGONS AND CONTOUR SECTIONS

REVOLVING DISC MADE IN PIE CUT SECTIONS →

Discs can be used singly or in combination with other discs or other scenic units. A disc may be used on each side of the stage; a large disc can be placed in the center and a smaller one on each side; two discs can be used side by side; a disc can be mounted on a wagon, the wagon moved up and down and across stage and the disc revolved while it is stationary or moving. These are all variations that have been tried at various times.

Revolving discs may be made in wagon sections as indicated or they may be made in halves, quarters or pie sections. Usually they operate better if few sections and a minimum of casters are used. Non-swivel casters, mounted so they are in line with their path of movement, make it easier to move in either direction than when swivel casters are used because the swiveling of the casters requires a slight side movement of the wagon. Swivel casters are all right once they are set in motion in one direction, but it is difficult to change the direction.

A center pivot may or may not be used. If the unit is completely supported by the casters the pivot merely holds the disc in place so that it cannot shift its position on the stage. If a support is needed in the center the mounting of a swivel caster, with the wheel removed,

can be used as a rotor. A specially designed free wheeling, ball bearing device, might work out even better. The wheel mounting and hub section of an automobile wheel work beautifully. Of course it is possible to manufacture a special pivot that will operate even better. This might be worth while if the disc is to be a permanent device that will be used frequently.

Sliding Scenery

The simplest method of moving stage scenery is to drag it across the stage floor. This is usually referred to as "running" scenery. If the floor is fairly smooth some of the units may have large furniture gliders mounted under them so that they will slide more easily. However, gliders lift the scenery off the floor slightly and there might be light leak problems when they are in position for use. It shouldn't be difficult to remedy this, however, and certainly the advantage of easier sliding is well worth the small problem that arises because of it.

TRACKS FOR SHUTTER SCENERY—There are times when the designer might find it advisable to go back to his theatrical forebears and employ sliding scenery that operates in shutter fashion. Strips may be fastened to the floor and slider tracks mounted above so that

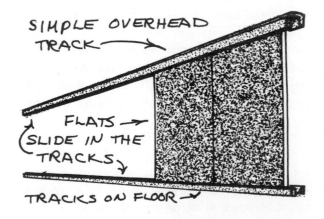

SIMPLE OVERHEAD TRACK →

FLATS → SLIDE IN THE TRACKS

TRACKS ON FLOOR →

scenery can be slid on and off stage. If more elaborate rigging is necessary it is possible to devise a frame to provide tracks both above

12

and below that are completely self sufficient. A truss may be built above and strips mounted to plywood below. Shutters can be pushed in from one or both sides to provide a solid straight wall across all or a portion of the stage. The track above should have just enough clearance so that the flats will move easily and readily. A smooth bottom track with a little grease, wax or tallow rubbed on it will allow the flats to slide smoothly. The tracks needn't be bothersome to the actors since they need not be high nor need the slots be very wide. The sides of the tracks can be made of strips of 1″ board and the slide space need be only about an inch wide.

When this sort of system is used it is necessary to have offstage space in which to push the shutters when they are open. If the flats are built new and of fairly light construction it is possible to hinge flats together and make wide sections that may be easily operated.

Flying Scenery

If there is a flywell available it is probable that a portion of the scenery in the theatre is moved by means of the flying system. Flats, wall sections, ceilings, screens, cycloramas, actors, properties, backdrops and draperies can be moved up into and down from the flywell. With elaborate flying equipment it is possible to fly entire stage settings completely equipped with a ceiling on top. However, most theatres have fewer sets of lines and smaller available clear sections in the flywell than would be needed for this so the stagehands must be content to fly only portions of settings and other smaller units of scenery.

Units that are to be flown must have a support to which rope (or wires, chains or cables) may be attached. Ceiling plates or hanger irons are commonly used for this purpose. There are straps of iron with rings securely mounted to them. The straps are drilled for screws or bolts and are fastened to the flat, ceiling, wall section or drop that is to be flown. Ropes are then tied onto the rings. Sometimes

it is advisable to have a ring at the top of the unit through which the rope passes and a fastener that hooks under the bottom of the unit to which the rope is fastened. Some hanger irons are designed with a foot that hooks under

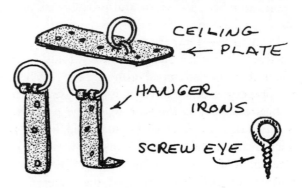

CEILING PLATE
HANGER IRONS
SCREW EYE

the batten. The rope then helps hold the unit upright by means of the upper support that it passes through and the strain is transferred to the bottom batten. This is a safer rigging method on heavy units of scenery. If necessary the rope can actually be tied at both places in order to release the strain on one part even more.

Stage Draperies

The flying system is probably used more for suspending, lifting and lowering stage draperies than for any other purpose.

There are few stages without at least one enclosure type set of draperies and many of them have two or more. The term "enclosure draperies" refers to a set of draperies that surround the acting area to mask off the remainder of the stagehouse from the audience view. They may be used as scenery by themselves or in conjunction with other stage units.

Besides enclosure draperies the conventional stage has drapery units for its front curtain, grand drape, teasers, borders and travellers. These may be made of any one of a number of different fabric weaves and textures, but basically they are put together in the same way.

Drapery material is available in varying widths, depending partly upon the weave and partly upon the size of the panels desired. Ordinarily tall panels are sewn together with the seams running up and down while short ones, such as borders, may be sewn either up and down or lengthwise, depending a good deal upon the fabric, its width and probably its pattern if it has one.

FULLNESS—Draperies are much more attractive when they hang in heavy folds than when they are stretched almost taut. When the drapery is ordered (if it is purchased from a theatre supply outlet) or when the material is purchased (if it is to be made up locally) this must be taken into consideration. For pleasant folds 100% fullness should be added. Fullness of 100% means that the material is two times as wide as the space it is to cover. When the draperies are made the fullness may be gathered and sewn in permanently or the drapery may be sewn flat and the gathering done when the drapery is hung. Act curtains are almost always operated on a track and used specifically for one purpose so the fullness may be sewn in. Other sections may be used variously and it is usually a good idea to leave them flat so that their coverage, and consequently their percentage of fullness, may be varied. If a wide space is to be covered the fullness can be decreased and if the space is narrow more fullness can be allowed. This makes the draperies more flexible and practical for use on the ordinary stage.

CHAIN POCKET—Ordinarily the panels of material are sewed together with a simple flat seam. The bottoms of the sections have a 2″ or wider hem into which a chain is often slipped and stretched across the drapery. Each end of the chain should be fastened so that it cannot slip in the pocket. The chain provides enough weight to stretch the material down slightly when it is hung on a batten. This pulls out many of the wrinkles.

WEBBING—The top of the drapery is almost always reinforced with a strip of canvas or burlap webbing 2″ or more in width. It is securely sewed near both of its edges. If the material of the drapery is gathered into permanent folds it is gathered and stitched, then the webbing is sewn across to hold the folds securely in place. If the draperies are relatively light in weight and fairly short a substitute for webbing may be made from roll type window shades. This material is fairly tough and can be cut into strips that may be sewn onto the top of the drapery.

GROMMETS—The top of the drapery may have grommets inserted at intervals of from 1′ to 2′. Grommets may be described as hole reinforcers. They are metallic and consist of two parts: a washer and a washer with a short inner sleeve. The sleeve is slipped through a hole cut in the drapery material and webbing (in the center of the webbing). The washer slips over the sleeve and a special crimping device, called a grommet die, rolls the sleeve down tightly against the washer. When tie lines are put through these holes and the drapery tied to a batten the strain is transferred over a larger area of the material than it would be if the material were merely slit and the lines passed through.

TIE LINES—Although there are some special fasteners for draperies the usual practice is to loop pieces of shade cord or cotton tape through the grommets and tie the drapery onto the batten with these. The lines should be about

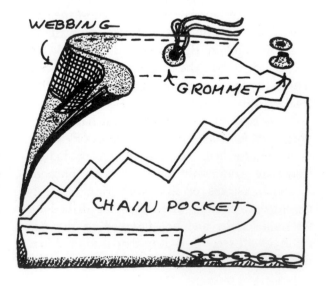

14

18″ long, and when they are tied a bow knot should always be used so they may be loosened easily and rapidly.

Drapery Rigging

Various types of hanging and operating devices are used for stage draperies.

TAB, TABLEAU OR GUILLOTINE CURTAIN —Draperies may be tied onto pipe or wooden battens suspended from the flying system. They may then be raised or lowered from the pin rail as needed. The front curtain, when handled in this way, is called a tab or guillotine curtain. Actually most of the draperies on the stage are suspended in this way, but some of them have auxiliary devices so they may be operated differently on occasion.

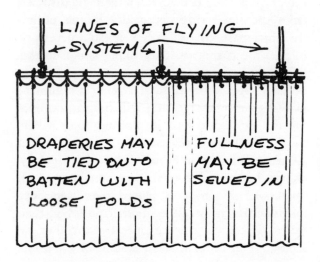

TRAVELLER—A traveller curtain is rigged in two sections that overlap in the center. In operation the sections part in the center and move off to the sides of the stage. Variations from this procedure may be devised so that sections of the drapery move in one direction or so that they move together into the center of the stage.

TRACKS—The drapery may be fastened at the top to rings that slide on wire or to sliders, balls, blocks or small wheel carriages that move in a track made of wood, steel or aluminum.

DRAPERY CENTER OVERLAP — Basically,

traveller sections are operated in somewhat the same way. If wire is used there are two wires stretched as taut as possible across the space. Eye bolts may be used to fasten the ends and a turn buckle placed at one end may be turned to tighten the wires. Two wires are needed so the draperies may overlap one another at the center of the stage; otherwise, they will gap open. If a track is used it is built in two sections that overlap in the center. The overlap will vary but should be at least 18″.

DRAPE SIDE OVERLAP—The drapery sections should be made with sufficient extra width for the center overlap and for an overlap of at least 18″ behind the proscenium arch on the outside end of the drapery. This may have to be even more, so that members of the audience cannot see unmasked space between the proscenium and the drapery. The wires or tracks should be long enough to accommodate this extra length.

HANGING AND OPERATING A TRAVELLER —When the drapery sections are tied or hooked

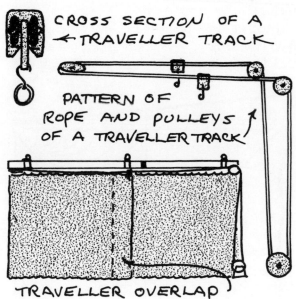

onto the rings on the wire or the carriers of the track, it is time to rig them for operation. The offstage ends are anchored to the wall or

15

to the end of the track so they cannot slide onto the stage. The onstage ends are then tied to the operating ropes.

OPERATING LINE—On the floor, where the operator who opens and closes the curtains stands, a pulley is fastened. A rope is threaded through the pulley and the two ends are taken up to the end of the track above where each is led through a pulley. From there one end of the rope goes to the overlapping center end of each of the draperies and is securely tied after the rope has been cut. This is done so that when tied the draperies remain in their closed positions and the rope is snug around the pulleys. Another rope is then fastened to the tie position of one end of the rope just installed. The new rope extends from there to the far end of the track where it passes around another pulley and comes back to the other knot position of the first rope, where it is pulled snug and tied.

After this has been done it should be possible for the operator to pull one of the lines to open the draperies and the other to close them.

BUTTERFLY—Sometimes for variety it is desirable to drape the curtains open rather than travel or fly them. For this operation a line is

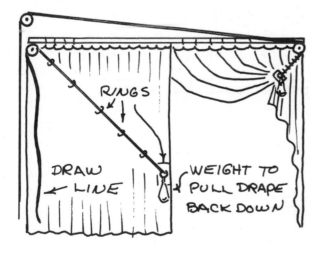

fastened to a ring securely fastened to a heavy reinforcing patch sewed down low near the

onstage edge of one of the curtains. Other rings, approximately the same size, are fastened to patches sewed on in a direct line diagonally up to the outer corner of the drapery section. The rings should be spaced so they come at least on every seam and probably even closer. Others can be added after the original rigging is complete if needed to improve the appearance. The rope, after being tied to the lower ring, is passed up through the other rings, over a pulley mounted in line with the row of rings and then down to the floor. When the rope is pulled down it lifts the drapery diagonally and as each ring is reached by the one below the material is pulled into gathered folds.

For the butterfly to operate correctly, the distance from the lowest ring to the top of the drapery should be greater than the distance from the same ring diagonally to the pulley the rope passes over, unless it isn't necessary to pull the corner up that high. Chain in the bottom of the hem of the drapery (chain pocket) and a small sand bag or weight attached to the onstage ring will help in pulling the drapery back into its normal folds when the lifting rope is released.

A rope may be attached to the other drapery section in the same way. For convenience of operation, this rope is passed over a pulley, taken across the stage to another pulley so that the two sections can be operated together or separately in order that all or half of the stage may be opened.

CONTOUR—The contour, or scalloped opening curtain, is made in one large panel. Its rigging is similar to that of the butterfly. The ring rope is fastened near the bottom of the drapery. A series of rings is attached in a straight vertical line. The manipulating rope runs straight up through the rings and then over to one side of the stage. The rope runs through pulleys wherever it changes directions. Another set of rings and ropes attached and rigged in a similar manner is needed for the position of indentation of each scallop, including one for each end. The individual ropes may be led to the same place of operation where they may be operated together or individually. By operating them individually it is possible to secure a number of patterns in the opening, depending upon the height of the scallops. Here, as with the butterfly, it may be necessary to have chain in the hem and small weights on the bottom ring to pull the curtain all of the way down.

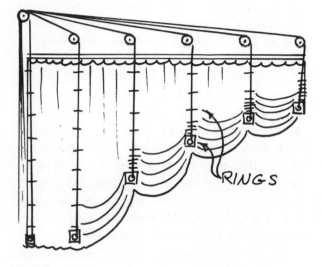

These various types of operation may be used for front curtain or for any other drapery that extends across the stage. They may also be used in false prosceniums and adapted for use with window draperies.

GRAND DRAPE — Frequently the grand drape is not tall enough. It should be possible to lower it and cut the stage down to the minimum height that may be desired for any production and still have it mask the top of the proscenium arch. It is also desirable to lift it up to clear almost the entire height of the proscenium. The grand drape is not only a device for altering the height of the proscenium, but also a masking for the traveller track, light bridge and any other scenic devices that need to be flown in downstage positions.

TEASERS — As in the case of the grand drape, teasers are frequently not long enough. Actually if they are tall fewer are needed to mask since it is necessary to mask the top of the one

behind with the bottom of the one in front of it. Even on relatively small stages 6' or more in height may be desirable. Teasers should have enough fullness so that they may be stretched to carry offstage a few feet.

TORMENTORS — Tormentors, or side maskings, can be fastened onto short pipes and suspended directly from the grid or they can be fastened to pipe battens and suspended from the flying system. They may be mounted on special 180° swivel arms so that they may be turned to extend across the stage or up and down stage. At times double faced draperies are used this way so that they can be reversed with the swivel. The swivel arms can also be mounted on a traveller track so that the legs (tormentors) can be moved on or offstage as well as turned.

Still another method of mounting tormentors is to mount them on traveller tracks so they can be pulled onstage a few feet or pulled offstage into a snug pack.

All of the methods of handling tormentors have advantages and disadvantages. The individual situation and budget will determine which method is desirable.

Drapery Installations With No Grid

There are many stages being built with no grid space; consequently scenic units cannot be flown on these stages. In this type of situation it is possible to either fasten battens to the ceiling and tie the draperies onto them or to install tracks made of steel or extruded aluminum to travel the drapery sections. Some of these are equipped with elaborate switching devices so that the draperies may be switched from one track to another. This type of arrangement is sometimes designed with additional switches and track making it possible to pull all of the sections into a storage cabinet in one corner of the stage.

Enclosure Draperies

Most stages are provided with enclosure draperies for general purpose use. They may be used for meetings, concerts, lectures, assemblies and plays. For these draperies to be flexible enough so they can be practical for all purposes, several factors should be borne in mind.

SIZE OF PANELS—The size of the drapery panels is important. In some installations the stage is surrounded by three large panels of material: one on each side and one across the back. With this design there are four entrances: down right and down left between the act curtain and the front edge of the side panels and up right and up left where the side panels and the rear panel meet. Although this may be excellent for some types of programs, it restricts the director too much when used for plays.

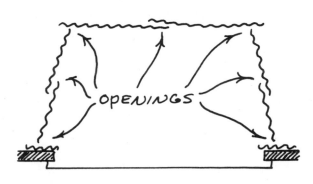

If possible, the sides and back should be broken into two or more sections, in order to add three or more entrances besides the four already mentioned. Each of the panels should overlap the one next to it to prevent gaps, so it is necessary to allow more material in width than would be required for single wide panels.

EXTRA NARROW SECTIONS—The addition of some narrow panels to fit above doors and windows, when they are inserted in openings provided by the parting and the retying of the regular drapery sections, will make simple staging much easier and more effective. These narrow sections can be full length and rolled

or fastened up to allow the insertion of the door or window or they can be shorter panels that extend down only to the top of a normal door.

RIGGING OF DRAPERIES—There are various ways to hang and manipulate an enclosure type set of draperies. The rear panel can be hung on a traveller track so that it may be opened all or part way, or closed. The side panels can be on swivel arms or hung in from the grid. Or the entire set of draperies can be tied onto a large "U" shaped frame that is mounted permanently or flown.

DRAPERY HEIGHT—It is advisable to have the draperies as tall as possible to cut down the number of teasers needed to a minimum. Where there is a grid it might be advisable to have them no more than half the height of the grid so that they can be flown up out of sight lines. But height adds to the physical appearance of the stage. Low hanging teasers seem to give a feeling of claustrophobia whereas tall ones give a feeling of freedom and airiness.

Of course, here again, the budget will probably enter into the picture and many corners will have to be cut before the specifications can be set. Basically the idea of numerous openings and a few narrow panels to fit above openings is sound and should not be sacrificed.

DRAPERY FABRICS—Draperies may be made from materials that are both attractive and durable. Conventionally the materials used are in plain colors.

Front curtains are ordinarily made of velour or plush, both of which are pile fabrics. These materials have a beautiful surface and are fairly opaque, both desirable qualities for the front curtain.

The color of the front curtain is usually consistent with the decorating scheme in the auditorium.

Occasionally textured fabrics, nubby weaves, metallic weaves, textured patterns and colored patterns are chosen.

LINING THE ACT CURTAIN—Ordinarily it is advisable to sew a lining or backing to the rear of the act curtain to improve the opacity and to increase the wearing qualities of the fabric.

All of the other draperies may be made of the same rich quality materials as the front curtain, but usually less costly fabrics are used. One of the most durable of the other materials is cotton Repp. Repp may be obtained in a wide range of colors and with either a plain or patterned weave.

Almost any material could be used. Actually, there is no limit to the possibilities. However, the material should be chosen for durability as much as for any other quality since stage draperies do take somewhat of a beating. It may be well to bear in mind that the curtains are more attractive if the material is soft enough to hang in easy folds.

* * * * *

In the pages to follow there will be descriptions of some of the units of stage scenery, properties and lights that are used on the stage in conjunction with the stage machinery and draperies mentioned here.

RENAISSANCE FESTOON

2 Building Supplies

Throughout the discussion of flat type scenery, the supplies, equipment and tools needed in construction will be referred to with great frequency. This section is placed here so that it can be referred to easily when any of the materials mentioned are unfamiliar. Lumber, including plywood, fabrics used for flat type scenery, glue, tools, hardware and the various wood joints used in the construction of scenery are briefly discussed.

Lumber

LUMBER FOR THE FLAT FRAME—1″ x 3″ white pine (abbreviated W. P.) is the size and type of lumber ordinarily used for the frame of the flat. White pine is plentiful, rather light in weight and relatively soft with slight difference in texture and hardness between the soft and harder portions of the grain (summer and winter growth). The better, or finish grades of lumber are ordinarily used since they have more of the necessary qualities for use when ripped into relatively narrow boards. These qualities include straightness, freedom from knots and checks, and relatively slight cup and warp.

GRADES OF LUMBER—White pine is usually graded as either "finish" or "common." The finish grades are preferred for use in building frames for flats. "B" and better is the top grade, but expensive. "C" is probably the best grade to use for flat frames and should have no knots of any significance. "D" grade will have a few knots, but they will be small and solid. No. 1 common will have a few more knots. No. 2 common will have more and larger knots and some of them may even be loose. As the grade number increases so also does the frequency and looseness of knots. Beyond No. 2 common the boards will even have knot holes sans knots.

There is a use for some of the common grades of lumber in the scene shop. Platforms, steps, doors, door thicknesses and some contours can be made from No. 1 or No. 2 common.

COMPUTING THE COST OF LUMBER—Lumber usually will be priced at the lumber yard at a specified amount per thousand board feet. A board foot of lumber is a piece of wood 1″ thick, 1 foot long and 1 foot wide. At least this was the measurement when the lumber was first cut into boards, but the process of smoothing and drying causes the board to shrink and lose some of its ample proportions. Actually, lumber listed as one inch in thickness is only about ¾ of an inch thick. The width of a board is about ⅜ to ½ inch narrower than its specified width. For example, 1″ x 3″ is about ¾″ x 2½″; 1″ x 4″ is ¾″ x 3½″; 1″ x 6″ is ¾″ x 5½″; 1″ x 12″ is ¾″ x 11½″ and lumber listed as 2″ thick is about 1⅝″.

The lumber dealer may quote "D" finish white pine at $350.00 per thousand board feet (abbreviated $350/1000 bd ft). Since a thousand board feet are $350.00, one board

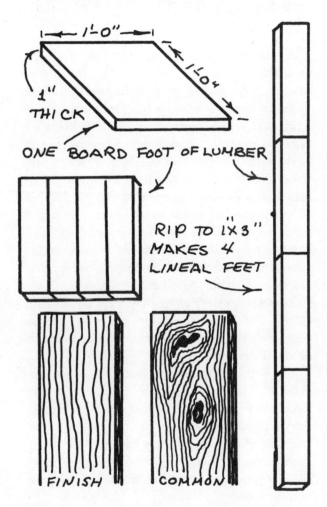

ONE BOARD FOOT OF LUMBER

RIP TO 1X3″ MAKES 4 LINEAL FEET

FINISH   COMMON

foot is 35¢. To divide by 1,000 merely move the decimal point to the left three places.

COST OF 1″ X 3″ LUMBER—A board foot as previously described is 12″ wide. Since a

1″ x 3″ board is only 3″ wide it takes four pieces of 1″ x 3″ laid side by side to make the equivalent width of a board foot. These four pieces laid end to end make a piece of 1″ x 3″ four feet long. So it takes four lineal, or running feet of 1″ x 3″ to make one board foot of lumber; and conversely, one board foot will make four lineal feet of 1″ x 3″. Therefore, in computing the cost of 1″ x 3″ lumber it is necessary to divide the number of lineal feet by 4 and multiply by the cost per board foot.

PROBLEM—A flat requires 4 pieces of 1″ x 3″ that are 6′ in length and 2 pieces of 1″ x 3″ that are 10′ in length. Four multiplied by 6 is 24. Two times 10 is 20. Twenty-four plus 20 is 44. So the total lineal feet of 1″ x 3″ is 44. To convert this to board feet, divide by 4. Forty-four divided by 4 equals 11. If "D" finish W. P. is listed at $350/1000 bd. ft. it is 35¢ per foot. Eleven times 35¢ is $3.85.

OTHER LUMBER—Although white pine is probably the easiest wood to work, there are other types that can be used. Here are a few of them and some of their characteristics.

Ponderosa Pine—Heavier than white pine, more resin content and splits more easily.

Yellow Pine—Heavier and harder than white pine and splits more easily.

Spruce—Many knots, may be firm, tends to twist and warp more than white pine.

Redwood—Excellent except that it is brittle and splinters rather easily.

Cedar—A little too brittle, splinters easily.

White Wood—Excellent, but expensive.

Balsa—Excellent, but expensive; extremely light in weight.

Sugar Pine—Good, soft, but has high resin content.

Fir—Heavier than white pine, strong, tough, coarse grained. Excellent for weight bearing structures and large platforms.

LUMBER SIZES USED IN THE SCENE SHOP—The size lumber used more than any other in the scene shop is 1″ x 3″ white pine as already indicated, but other sizes are required from time to time. Following is a list of the more important widths and thicknesses that are used most often.

White Pine, Finish "C" or "D"

1" x 2" —for small frames and diagonal braces in flats.

1" x 3" —for flat frames.

1" x 4" —for large frames, battens for drops, framing for ceilings, for doors and door frames.

1" x 6" —for doors, frames, thicknesses, platforms.

1" x 6" —1" x 3" may be made by ripping 1" x 6" down the center.

White Pine, Common No. 1 or No. 2

1" x 4" —for stiffeners.

1" x 6" —for thicknesses.

1" x 12" —for steps, platforms, contours, thicknesses, beams and arches.

White Pine, Shop

1¼" —random widths for double covered frames and stage properties.

1½" —random widths primarily for stage properties. Could be used for thicker units, such as frames for door shutters, double covered flat frames.

Fir

2" x 4" —used for units bearing weight; has considerable strength for size, but is splintery. Good for legs for platforms and frames for platforms.

2" x 6")
2" x 8" } —for long span platforms where considerable strength is
2" x 10") needed.

Plywood

Plywood is another lumber yard material used in constructing the flat. It has many uses in the shop since its structure provides maximum strength combined with minimum weight and thickness.

STRUCTURE OF PLYWOOD—Plywood is fabricated by gluing thin layers of wood together. When glued the layers are placed together so that the grains of alternate layers run at right angles to one another. In this way maximum strength with minimum thickness is obtained.

LAYERS OF PLYWOOD

Three layers or plies of wood are usually used to make ⅛", ¼", ⁵⁄₁₆" and ⅜" thick plywoods. Plywood of greater thickness is made by using five or more layers. Ordinarily, there is an odd number of layers in a thickness of plywood so the grain in both exposed faces runs in the same direction. On a large sheet of plywood this grain runs the long direction. The bend test will easily show that the plywood is strongest parallel to the exposed grain, so when small pieces are cut to make corner blocks and keystones they are designed so that the grain runs across the joints of the pieces of wood that are to be fastened together.

THICKNESS OF PLYWOOD—Plywood as thin as ⅛" may be used for irregular profile edges on flats or for covering curved surfaces of small diameter.

The ¼" and ⁵⁄₁₆" plywoods are used for making corner blocks and keystones. These thicknesses may also be used for constructing profile edges on flats.

Plywood ⅜" thick may be used for oversized corner blocks or for surfaces needing slightly more strength than that obtained with thinner wood.

Plywood ½", ⅝" and ¾" thick may be used for making large contour cutouts of irregular form and for making platforms, parallels, and platform and parallel tops. The thicker the plywood the greater the strength is an axiom that may be used in working with this material.

GRADES OF PLYWOOD—*Sheathing plywood* is the most economical grade to use for most stage purposes. This grade is slightly rough on both sides, but not uneven enough to cause any concern or difficulty.

Good One Side is the next grade. This plywood has been patched wherever there were knots or knot holes on one surface and has been sanded.

Good Both Sides is the top grade plywood. It has been patched and sanded on both sides so there are no knots or holes and the surface is smooth on both sides.

Boat Panel is a special type of plywood that is bonded with waterproof glue and manufactured especially for the boat industry. It is available in pieces up to 16′ or 18′ in length. It is much more expensive than the other types of plywood, but might be needed for some special scenic units.

TYPES OF WOOD—The economical grades of plywood are made from the plentiful woods, fir and pine. Special surfaces of other woods may be obtained, but these will have little use around the scene shop.

PRICE OF PLYWOOD—Plywood is usually priced by the square foot or by the hundred square feet. A full sheet or piece of plywood is 4′ wide and 8′ long; thus it has a surface area of 32 square feet (4 x 8 = 32). If the price is 15¢ sq. ft. a sheet of plywood will cost $4.80 (.15 x 32 = 4.80).

CORNER BLOCKS—Corner blocks are right triangular shaped pieces of ¼″ or 5/16″ plywood approximately 10″ on each of the right angle sides. If the flat frame is made with butt joints at the corners, that is, the boards after being cut off square are placed together so that the end of the one is butted up against the side of the other adjacent to its end, then the corner blocks are cut from the plywood so that the exposed grain runs parallel to one of the right angle sides. If mitre joints are used, that is, the end of each board cut with a 45° angle

and the two pieces placed at right angles to one another so that the corner fits like the corner of an ordinary picture frame, then the exposed grain of the corner block should run parallel to the long side of the isosceles triangle shaped corner block. Since each corner block is half of a square with 10″ sides making an area of 100 square inches, each corner block has an area of 50 square inches.

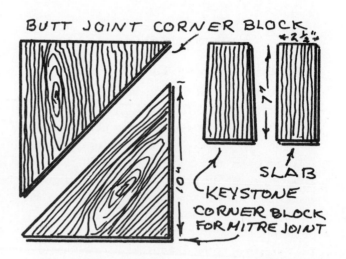

BUTT JOINT CORNER BLOCK

SLAB

KEYSTONE CORNER BLOCK FOR MITRE JOINT

KEYSTONES OR SLABS—Keystones are used to secure joints other than the joints at the corner of the flat. If the keystone shape is employed the pieces of plywood are cut about 8″ long and tapered in width so that they are about 2½″ at one end and 3½″ at the other end. The exposed grain should run the long direction. If the slab shaped pieces are used they are cut so that they are about 8″ long and 2½″ wide with the grain running lengthwise. These may be cut from ¼″ or 5/16″ plywood. It is obvious that the slabs are easier to cut than the keystones and they will hold the joint about as securely. It will take 2½″ x 8″ or 20 square inches of plywood to make one slab.

Flameproofing Compound

Flameproofing of everything flammable that is used on the stage is required in some places and should be standard procedure everywhere.

As soon as a wooden frame is built it should be coated either by spraying or brushing with a solution of one of the following or a regular standard mixture of flameproofing compound.

Mix No. 1:

2 pounds Ammonium Phosphate
4 pounds Ammonium Chloride
3 gallons water

Mix No. 2:

4 pounds Borax
4 pounds Ammonium Chloride
3 gallons water

Fabric Covering For Flat Frames

A number of fabrics can be used for covering flat frames, such as muslin, pocket drill, scene duck and linen scene cloth. For the sake of economy, a good grade of muslin may be used to cover the frame. Type 128 is quite good moderately priced muslin. Muslin is sometimes known under other names such as sheeting, factory cloth and tobacco cloth.

FABRIC SPECIFICATIONS—Fabrics or textiles are frequently designated by their thread count (the number of threads per square inch woven in each direction) or by their weight per square yard. Fabrics are available in many widths. Some of the most common ones are 30″, 36″, 48″, 60″, 72″ and 81″. On special order it is possible to get material as wide as 30′ without seams. This material is excellent for large backdrops. Since most flats are not more than 6′ in width the most convenient widths for the scene shop are 72″ or 81″. For the sake of computing yardage it may be noted that running yards of the following widths are as indicated:

1 lineal yard of 30″ material is $\frac{5}{6}$ or .833 sq. yds.

1 lineal yard of 36″ material is 1 sq. yd.

1 lineal yard of 48″ material is $1\frac{1}{3}$ or 1.333 sq. yds.

1 lineal yard of 60″ material is $1\frac{2}{3}$ or 1.666 sq. yds.

1 lineal yard of 72″ material is 2 sq. yds.

1 lineal yard of 81″ material is $2\frac{1}{4}$ or 2.25 sq. yds.

PROBLEM—A flat is 10′-0″ high and 6′-0″ wide. 6 x 10 = 60. The area of the surface is 60 square feet. There are 9 square feet in a square yard so the surface is 60 divided by 9, which is $6\frac{2}{3}$ square yards. If the material is 36″ wide it will take $6\frac{2}{3}$ lineal yards to cover the flat. If the material is 72″ wide it will take only half as many lineal yards since each lineal yard is two square yards. This means $2\frac{1}{3}$ lineal yards of 72″ muslin will do the job.

Glue

Fabric is secured to the flat frame by means of glue, glue and tacks or glue and staples. Either cold water type carpenters glue, or "dope", which is a combination of melted animal glue and whiting, may be used. *Casein glues* are convenient and easy to use and their use obviates the necessity for a hot plate and double boiler. Casco and Elmer's Glue, both manufactured by the Borden Company, Le Pages casein type glue and Swift and Co.'s Liquid adhesive Glue Bond are obtainable almost anywhere and can be used satisfactorily. Other similar cold water glues may also be used.

DOPE—Dope requires the preparation of flake or gelatine glue which is soaked overnight in enough water to cover and then melted in a

VARIOUS WIDTHS OF MUSLIN AND SQ. YDS PER LINEAL YD.

double boiler. The glue is then mixed with other ingredients as follows:

1 part glue
1 part whiting
2 parts wheat paste

This solution should be kept warm while being used and if it is to be held over for any length of time a little carbolic acid or formaldehyde should be added as a preservative.

Hardware

A number of items that might be classed as hardware are needed when building flat type scenery.

Clout nails and wood screws are used to fasten flat frames together and are probably first in importance.

CLOUT NAILS—There are two or more varieties of clout nails. Clout nails are made of relatively soft iron either tapered rectangular in shape with a round head or round in cross section with a round head and an elongated pinched or chisel shaped point. When driven into a piece of wood so that the point extends through the underside and strikes a steel clinch plate placed beneath the wood the point of the nail easily bends over, or "clinches." For regular flat construction 1¼" blued clout nails are used.

Clout nails may be difficult to find, but their convenience makes searching worth while. There are at least two, probably more, companies that manufacture them. These companies are The Atlas Tack Company and Colorado Fuel and Iron Corporation. Clout nails are sold by the pound and are less expensive per pound when bought in 100 pound kegs.

WOOD SCREWS—First a discussion of the wood screws used for fastening flat frames together and then a general listing of other screws needed in the shop will be helpful.

Wood screws are more expensive to use than clout nails but they can be removed easily and then both the screws and plywood can be reused. When screws are used they should be long enough to extend almost through both

pieces that are being fastened together. Since the wood is ¾" thick and the plywood is ¼" thick, the screws can be 1" in length. When ordering designate the diameter (# 9 will do for hardware also), the length (1" in this case) and type (flat head bright wood screws). So the total designation is 1" #9 flat head bright wood screws. Screws come packed a gross to the box usually and there are 144 screws in a gross. (A gross is 12 dozen.)

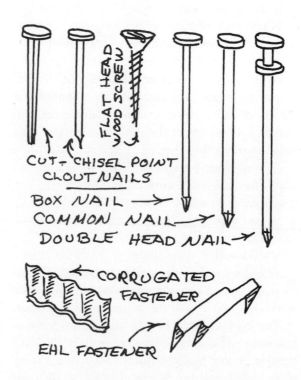

FLAT HEAD WOOD SCREW

CUT-CHISEL POINT CLOUT NAILS

BOX NAIL →

COMMON NAIL →

DOUBLE HEAD NAIL →

← CORRUGATED FASTENER

EHL FASTENER

The 1" #9 wood screws mentioned may be used for most stage hardware. However, there are times when longer screws are needed. Almost all hardware is drilled to receive #9 so it will be just as well to use that diameter. It will also be wise to keep only one type, the flat head, since they will screw down flat on any hardware that has countersunk holes. (A countersunk hole is a hole drilled partially with a larger drill after the original hole has been completed. This allows the heads to pull part way into the hole.) Screws 1½" long will

25

work very well for splicing two thicknesses of 1″ board together.

For most stage uses the stock of screws need include only:

1″ #9 Flat Head Bright Wood Screws

1½″ #9 Flat Head Bright Wood Screws

FASTENERS—Corrugated fasteners and Ehl fasteners are sometimes used to secure or help secure butt and mitre joints. They are elongated metal holders that are driven in across a butt or mitre joint and into both pieces of wood that make the joint.

NAILS—A number of varieties and sizes of nails may be used around the shop from time to time.

Nail lengths are referred to in the United States in terms of "penny", the symbol for which is "d". Here are the penny sizes and length equivalents of the nails that will be used most often in the shop.

4d (four penny) nail is 1½″ long

6d nail is 2″ long

8d nail is 2½″ long

10d nail is 3″ long

12d nail is 3¼″ long

16d nail is 3¾″ long

The thickness of the nail is indicated as common or box. The slender box nail splits the wood less and is a little better for scenery use.

The type of head is still another nail classification. The box and common nails have regular round heads. Finish nails and casing nails have small heads just slightly larger than the nail. The double head, scaffolding, duplex or whatever other name they are known by, nails have two heads, one spaced beneath the other.

The surface of the nail is another classification. Regular nails are made of steel wire with no coating. Resin coated and zinc coated nails resist rust — and resist removal so should be used for somewhat permanent construction.

The nails used most often in the scene shop are:

Clout nails—1¼″

6d box nails (resin coated optional)

· 8d box nails (resin coated optional)

16d box nails

8d double head nails

16d double head nails

Small lath and Celotex nails (not previously mentioned)

The importance of double head nails might be mentioned before moving on to other hardware. The double head nail has many and varied uses. Since it can be driven in to the first head so that it holds securely, yet can be pulled out easily because the neck and top head stick above the surface, it is useful for fastening flats together in a stage set. It can be used in place of lash cleats, and can be used to fasten stiffeners in place. The 8d size will be used most frequently. The 16d size can be used for fastening temporary platforms together.

BACK FLAP HINGES—The most usable hinge is the back flap hinge. This hinge in either the 1½″ or 2″ size (the measurement indicates the size of each half of the hinge) is used to hinge flats together and to hinge doors into frames and for many other purposes. It is obtainable in loose pin (the pin may be pulled out and the hinge halves pulled apart) and tight pin. The pins may easily be removed from the tight pin variety by grinding or cutting the head from one end of the pin.

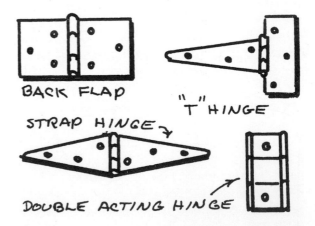

STRAP HINGES AND "T" HINGES—Strap hinges, each half of which is an elongated

26

triangle, and "T" hinges, which are shaped something like the letter "T" with the joint between the top and leg of the "T", have limited use. They are used where larger or at least longer hinges are needed. Strap hinges are used on hinge-lock removable doors and windows.

DOUBLE ACTING SCREEN HINGES—When folding screens are built it is necessary to use hinges that will fold in both directions if the screens are to be completely flexible. The double acting screen hinge is used for this reason.

SPRING SCREEN DOOR HINGES — Stage doors may sometimes be kept closed by using screen door hinges that have a built in spring closer.

DOOR LOCKS, DOOR LATCHES, MAGNETIC DOOR HOLDERS AND FRICTION DOOR HOLD-ERS—There are many items of this nature that may be used for stage doors. The simpler varieties of regular door knob and latch sets really work the best for stage doors and since the doors are used quite frequently they may be the most satisfactory in the long run. There are many varieties. The ones that require the least work to install are the best to use.

TIE LINES—Two types of cotton tie lines are used a good deal on flats and drops.

¼" woven sash cord, which is a soft cotton cord, is used for lash line.

⅛" shade cord, which is also soft woven cotton cord, is used to make tie lines for back drops.

STRAP IRON—Strap iron is used for making sill irons and various pieces of rigging hardware. Strap iron may also be used for decoration on stage settings. It can be bent, twisted, curved and can be used to simulate wrought iron work on furniture, stair rails, and window grills. It is sold by the pound and is available in hardware stores and lumber yards. Width, length, and thickness should be specified when it is ordered. For most stage use the width can

vary from ¾" to 1¼" and the thickness from ³⁄₁₆" to ¼".

ALUMINUM TUBING AND THIN WALL STEEL TUBING—Aluminum tubing and thin walled steel tubing commonly used for electrical conduit can be used for decorative and abstract scenery forms. Tubing can be bent into interesting shapes with a simple "bender" tool that is regular equipment in most electrical shops. Tubing can also be bent around wooden templates. Connectors may be used to fasten sections of tubing together end to end.

WIRE—Various types of wire will be needed from time to time in the scene shop. Here are a few of the varieties that will be used most often.

Stove Pipe Wire and Baling Wire—Soft iron wire such as stove pipe wire or baling wire has many uses around the shop and on the stage. They are in the main utility wires and should not be used where great strength is desired.

Piano Wire—Piano, or music wire has great strength. A thin wire will support a weight of several hundred pounds. It may be used for flying actors or scenery. In a play such as *Peter Pan*, piano wire is hooked onto a harness worn by the actor and extends from there up just beyond the upper sight lines behind an overhead border where it is tied onto a line of the flying system. It is used in a similar manner to suspend scenery from the stage flying system.

Aluminum Wire—Large gauge aluminum wire, ³⁄₁₆" or ¼" frequently used for clothes lines, is malleable and easy to work into intricate shapes for decorative and abstract forms. It may be used in conjunction with tubing, on furniture, or around screen frames to produce additional "lines" and forms.

CARPET TACKS—Carpet tacks are sold by the box or by the pound. The #6 size tacks are ½" in length.

BOLTS—Three types of bolts are commonly used on the stage. They are as follows:

Stove Bolts—Stove bolts have a round or flat screw type head. They are specified by thickness, length and length of threaded space.

Flat head #9 bolts may be used in most stage hardware.

Carriage Bolts—Carriage bolts have a round head and a square throat or shank. They are often used in wood because the square shank sinks into the wood preventing the bolt from turning when in place.

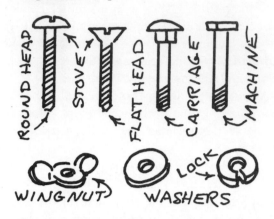

Machine Bolts—Machine bolts have a square or hexagon shaped head and are used primarily in metal work.

WASHERS—Various sizes of washers are used to enlarge the support area of a bolt head or nut. When washers are used under the nut it is easier to tighten the nut.

LOCK WASHERS AND SPLIT STEEL WASHERS—Lock and Split Steel Washers are designed so that they press against the nut when it is tightened. The tension of the washer against the nut prevents it from loosening.

WING NUTS—The broad flattened wings make it possible to turn the nut with the fingers. They are useful where nuts have to be put on and removed frequently and rapidly since no wrench is needed.

Tools

A knowledge of the tools employed in the scene building process is important. Much time and effort may be saved if the correct tool is used and if tools are kept in good working condition. It is important to keep tools clean, sharp and in good mechanical condition. Cutting tools should be sharpened often; mechanical tools should be cleaned and oiled occasionally, and all tools should be stored in some kind of tool box or cabinet.

Tools may be roughly divided into two categories: manual and power. Manual tools depend upon the muscles of the operator while power tools have not only the muscles of the operator but also the power of another motive force such as an electric motor to make the job easier and faster. Many scene shops depend entirely upon the muscles of the building crew for their operation while the more elaborate ones have one or more pieces of power equipment. The hand tools are the most important and should be discussed first.

Cutting Tools

There are a number of different types of cutting tools. The saw family is of primary importance in the scene building trade.

CROSS CUT SAW—The cross cut saw is used for sawing across the grain of the wood. Each triangular tooth is a double-edged blade. Two specifications are needed when ordering a saw: the length of the blade and the number of teeth per inch. Carpenters usually use saws 26″ long. Shorter ones may be used, but a longer blade makes possible a longer stroke and more rapid cutting. For rough cutting 8 point (8 teeth per inch) saws are used. For finer work 10 or even 12 point saws may be needed. Rarely would one need to do finer work than can be done with a 10 point saw.

RIP SAWS—Occasionally it is necessary to split boards and to cut with the grain. This is referred to as ripping a board. The rip saw used for this purpose has teeth that are filed straight across and designed to chip out wood. An 8 point rip saw would be the most useful and fastest cutting.

KEYHOLE SAWS—It is frequently necessary to cut curves and irregular forms. The keyhole saw is designed for this purpose. It has a slender blade sharpened on the end. The blade of the saw may be inserted into a small hole and the cut started in that way, or the cut may be started on the edge of the board. The narrowness of the blade makes it possible to cut where sharp turns are desired. Some keyhole saws are supplied with several blades, which increases the versatility of the saw.

SCROLL SAWS—Scroll saws have rather delicate blades and are used for irregular cuts in small work. They must be used with care or the blades break easily and readily.

HACK SAWS—The hack saw is a metal cutting saw with detachable blades. It is used for cutting strap iron, nails, bolts and other metal objects.

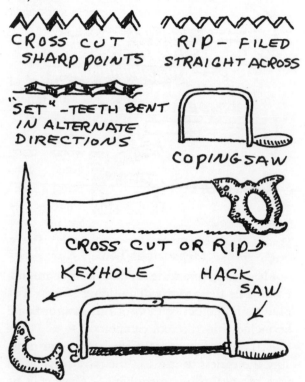

WOOD CHISELS—Wood chisels come in varying widths. Most practical around the scene shop are the ¼″, ½″ and 1″ chisels. Actually the chisel has infrequent use for rough construction, but it comes in handy quite often. Chisels should *never* be used as a substitute for screw drivers.

COLD CHISELS—The cold chisel is a round piece of steel 4″ or longer with a double taper on one end. It is used to cut metal objects.

WOOD PLANES—There are times when it is

necessary to smooth the edge of a board, to trim off a door that fits too snugly, or to round a

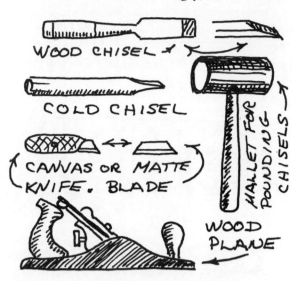

sharp edge. The wood plane is the correct tool to use for these jobs. It is a shaving tool. It cuts like a chisel, but the block in which the blade is mounted makes it easier to operate than a chisel. If one is to do a lot of straightening of long boards a plane with a long frame is the best. If the plane is to be used for small and short boards then a short one will do. The longer the plane the more expensive it is.

KNIVES—Once in a while a paring knife is useful in the shop. A canvas knife is a necessity. It is used to trim away the extra muslin when flat frames are covered. Many types of knives are available. Knives that are made for trimming wall board or cutting picture mattes are usable as are the various razor blade knife holders. Wall board and matte knives are superior since they use a heavier and more durable blade.

DRAW KNIVES—There are times when the draw knife is useful. If many props, such as guns, chair legs, rough poles, are built in the shop the draw knife is almost indispensable. A carpenter or shop man should be consulted about the proper way to handle this instrument. It is a dangerous implement!

SCISSORS — Muslin and paper frequently

need to be cut and for this oversize scissors are all but indispensable.

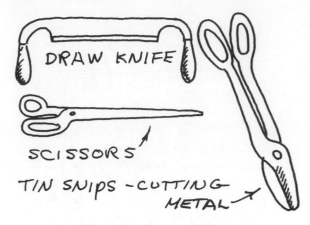

TIN SNIPS—Tin snips and circle cutter snips are made for cutting thin metal like aluminum, tin, sheet metal and sheet copper.

Pounding Tools

There are several pounding or driving tools used in the scene shop. The most important of these are as follows:

CLAW HAMMERS—The claw hammer has a set of curved claws. This is the correct hammer to use for pulling out as well as driving nails. Hammers with wooden handles are more often broken than steel hammers. The hammer should be chosen for weight and balance. A large, strong individual can handle a heavy hammer; others should use lighter hammers.

RIP HAMMERS — The rip hammer has straight claws and although also used for driving nails it is not as good as the claw hammer for removing them because of the shape of the claws. This hammer is useful for ripping things apart; for instance, for ripping off corner blocks and keystones.

TACK HAMMERS — There are occasions when a smaller hammer is desired for driving in small nails or tacks. Tack hammers are designed for this purpose. Some tack hammers have magnetized heads and the tack will be held by the magnet until started in the wood.

MALLETS—Wooden or plastic headed hammers are made to use for pounding chisels. Chisels, especially those with wooden handles, should not be pounded with other types of hammers.

STAPLE GUNS—The staple gun is an invaluable tool for the scenery shop. Actually staples may be used wherever tacks are normally used. The staple gun is easier to operate than the tack hammer. A substantial gun with a steel frame probably will hold up better than one made of aluminum.

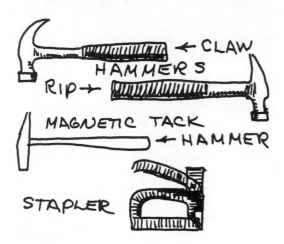

Measuring Tools

Measuring, marking and squaring are important in the process of building scenery. A minimum number of tools of this nature should be included in the tool cabinet.

RULERS—Self encased steel tapes are probably the easiest to use and the most convenient type of measuring instrument. They may be obtained in many lengths: 6′, 8′, 10′, 12′, 25′, 50′ and 100′. The 10′ and 12′ tapes are probably the most convenient lengths for measuring boards for scenery. It will pay to buy tapes of better quality rather than inexpensive ones. They are not so easily broken and when broken it is possible to replace the tape portion.

YARDSTICKS—Yardsticks are usable, but the steel tape makes them somewhat unessential. Free yardsticks may usually be obtained from paint and hardware stores. Heavy yardsticks with metallic edges are preferred to plain wooden ones.

TRY SQUARES—The try square is a small right angle tool used as a guide for marking 90° angles across boards preparatory to sawing them.

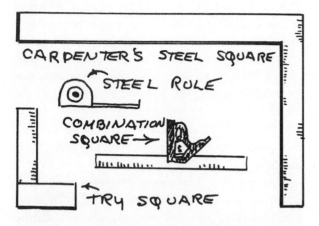

STEEL SQUARE OR CARPENTER'S SQUARE OR FRAMING SQUARE—The framing square is an indispensable tool. It is used for checking the squareness of corners on all types of scenery and for computing angles that are needed for steps and tops of angular flats. This square is "L" shaped with the short arm of the "L" measuring 16″ and the long arm measuring 24″.

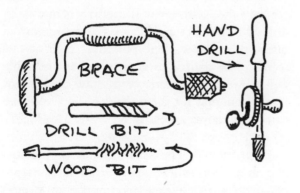

Drilling Tools

Several tools are needed for drilling purposes.

BRACE—The brace is an instrument to hold bits or drills. The brace fitted with a bit is used to drill holes in wood or metal.

BITS AND DRILLS—Bits and drills are round spiral cutting devices which, when fitted into a brace or power press, are used to cut holes in wood or metal. Metal bits can be used on wood, but wood bits should *never* be used on metal.

Miscellaneous Manual Tools

Additional tools used in the scene shop and operated by hand include the following items.

CLINCH PLATE—The clinch plate is a steel plate about 10″ square and ¼″ or less in thickness. Actually larger or smaller pieces may be used, but the 10″ square is a good size. The only requirement for the clinch plate is that it

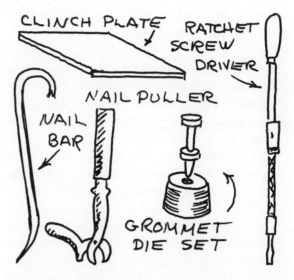

be flat and hard enough that nails will clinch as they are driven through a board and onto its steel surface.

SCREW DRIVERS—The straight screw driver, or rigid screw driver, is used in electrical work and quite frequently on scenery.

MECHANICAL SCREW DRIVER—The mechanical, ratchet or automatic screw driver is a time saver when many screws must be driven; for instance, it is a great help when several flats are being hinged together. This type screw driver may be obtained in several lengths. The

31

longer models are more expensive and more difficult to manipulate. However, screws can be driven more rapidly with them.

PLIERS—There are a number of varieties of pliers and each variety has its use. The ordinary pliers are used for miscellaneous grasping and holding jobs and for tightening nuts. Pointed nose pliers are used for bending a loop in the end of an electrical wire, for reaching into small holes to grasp and for many other jobs. This variety of pliers can also be purchased with a cutting blade far back in the jaws. Side cutter and diagonal or "dike" cutters are useful in electrical work.

CRESCENT WRENCHES—Crescent wrenches are often useful in the shop. There are a number of lengths. If relatively small bolts are to be used an 8″ wrench is probably large enough. (The size indicates the over-all length of the wrench.)

PIPE WRENCHES—If pipe battens are in the theatre and the pipe has connectors of one type or another and if pipe-type light stands are used, it may be wise to have a pipe wrench — 10″ or 12″ or even larger.

ALLEN WRENCHES — Various types of equipment require special wrenches such as the hexagonal "Allen" wrenches that are used a great deal on set screws.

GROMMET DIE — If many backdrops or sets of draperies are to be made in the scene shop, it will be a good idea to get a grommet die set. The grommet die must fit the grommets so sizes should be checked carefully.

FILES—Metal files are used to smooth and to hone off sharp edges of metal.

WOOD RASPS—Wood rasps are really wood files. They are used for cutting down and smoothing wood. The wood rasp is an extremely useful tool around the property making department.

NAIL PULLERS—The nail puller is a special tool used for pulling nails out after they have been driven completely in.

OIL STONES—Oil stones are used for sharpening many tools, including chisels and knives.

An oil stone is indispensable to keep the fabric cutting knife sharp when covering flats.

Power Tools

The operators of the scene shop that builds considerable scenery, that has adequate available space and that has money on hand will find it convenient to add some power equipment from time to time. It is a little difficult to decide which piece of equipment should be purchased first, but there are two items that are extremely useful, the power circle saw and the band saw.

POWER CIRCLE SAW—Either one of two basic varieties is available in the power circle saw.

Table Saw—This saw is designed with either a tilting arbor (motor and saw mount move but the table remains stationary) or a tilting table (only the table tilts). The tilting arbor variety is the most convenient to use.

Pull Over Saw—With this variety of saw, the motor has the blade mounted directly to it. This unit is mounted on an overhead arm. The saw is easily maneuverable for complex sawing. For cross cut sawing it is safer to use than the table saw. Since the saw is pulled over the work there is less danger of getting the hands into the blade.

The power circle saw is useful where a great deal of ripping, straight cut-off and angular cut off work is done. The pull over type of saw seems to be a little safer to use than the table type. An 8″ (diameter of the saw blade) saw is large enough for the moderate shop. Where extremely large amounts of work are done a 9″ or 10″ saw will work better.

BAND SAW—The band saw is so convenient in a shop where many irregular cuts are made on such items as contours and sweeps that it could be considered to be the most important piece of power equipment. The band saw has a single narrow continuous band blade 7′-0″ or more in length that runs around two large wheels spaced a foot or more apart. The blade is covered except for a small space where the cutting is done. It is important to get a band saw that will cut wide material. (This means the wheels the blade runs on must be large — the diameter of the wheel determines the spread of the blade in the machine.)

JIG SAW—The jig saw is an alternate for the band saw. The jig saw has narrow, short blades that may be either fastened at one or both ends. When the blade is fastened only at one end it is possible to start sawing from a small hole and make an inside cut. This cannot be done with the band saw since it has one continuous looping blade. The jig saw does not cut as rapidly as the band saw, but it has many practical uses. It is used for lighter cutting work than the band saw.

PORTABLE JIG SAW—There are a number of small portable jig saws on the market. They use a motor similar to the motor of a pistol drill and are small enough to operate by maneuvering while being held in the hand. It is possible to obtain table mountings for portable jig saws so that they may also be operated as a bench type jig saw. They are convenient for light contour sawing.

POWER DRILL—Power drills, though not as important as the various saws, still are extremely usable around the shop. Hand type "pistol" drills are available that can be used in many ways. They can be used as a hand held drill or can be mounted on special stands and used as "Press" type drills. It is easier to drill through metal for sill irons, straps, etc. with the drill press than the hand drill since pressure may be exerted mechanically. The hand drill is probably more practical than the drill press in a small shop. A large shop may be equipped with both varieties.

The drill press can easily be rigged to operate as a paint and glue mixer by making a special mixing jig.

SEWING MACHINE—A sewing machine is a handy piece of equipment to have in a scene shop. It may be a treadle or a small power machine. Even the treadle machine is easy enough to operate for the amount of sewing

that is done. Back drops and the coverings for large flats require seamed pieces of muslin.

Other power tools, such as wood turning lathes, power screw drivers and wood planers or jointers, have use only in large shops and shops where finished pieces of furniture are manufactured for the stage.

Wood Joints

Woodworkers have developed many methods of fastening pieces of wood together. In special circumstances one type of fastening is more convenient, easier to make or provides a stronger bond. A basic knowledge of some of the joints that are usable in building scenery is essential.

BUTT JOINT—The most commonly used wood joint is the butt joint. When two pieces of wood are placed together so that the end of one is snugly fitted at right angles against the side of the other, or the end of the other, they are "butted" up against one another. This type of joint may be fastened by placing a piece of wood over the top of the joint and by fastening it to both pieces; or by driving nails in on an angle so that they enter both pieces of wood (toe-nailing). Or it may be fastened by using special fasteners — corrugated fasteners or Ehl fasteners — which are driven in such a way that they cross the joint. Or it may be fastened by using metal splicing plates that are placed over the joint and fastened to both pieces of wood.

MITRE JOINT—For a mitre joint the ends

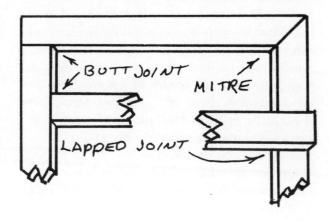

33

of both pieces of board are cut on a 45° angle and the boards fitted together to form a right angle. The joint is fastened in a manner similar to the butt joint.

LAP JOINT—This is one of the easiest ways to fasten two boards together. The two boards are simply overlapped either running together in the same direction or running at right angles and then nails or screws are driven through both boards.

LAPPED SPLICE—When a board isn't long enough it may be lengthened by placing another board beyond its end and then placing a shorter piece over the top of the two and nailing the top one into the other two.

THE SCARF SPLICE—A more complicated, but at the same time satisfactory, method of splicing boards end to end is called the scarf

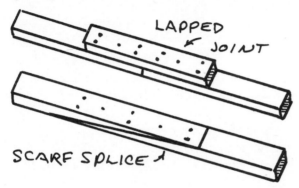

splice. The ends of the two boards to be spliced are cut with long tapers flat wise and then the pieces over lapped until they have the same thickness along the lap as along the board. The joint may be both glued and nailed. Clout nails will work very well on regular ¾" boards.

THE HALVED JOINT—If it is desirable to build frames without corner blocks so that they can easily be covered on both sides, the halved joint should be used. Half of the thickness of each board and the length of the width of the other board is sliced off. The two boards are then fitted together and the joint secured by gluing and nailing through the two.

THE NOTCHED JOINT—The notched joint is similar to the halved joint except that it takes place somewhere along each board rather than

at the end of the boards.

THE MORTISE AND TENON JOINT—Mortise and tenon joints are used by professional scenic shops and by carpenters and cabinet

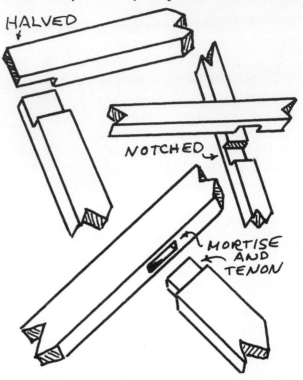

makers, but making these joints is somewhat difficult and time consuming for most theatre jobs. The mortise is a slot cut in one board and the tenon is a tongue cut on the other. The tongue fits into the slot to make the joint.

* * * * *

The small scenery shop will have only a few of the tools and supplies discussed, while the large, completely equipped shop will have all of them and probably many more. Some of the items will be used infrequently while others will be almost in constant use. By adding an item at a time, and carefully husbanding that item after it has been acquired, a good stock may eventually be built up whether on a large or small scale. As indicated previously, the project can be more easily and rapidly built if the correct equipment is available. But at the same time, some shortages stimulate one to try new ideas and procedures.

34

The Flat and Flat Scenery

## 3

Practically every stage setting is made up primarily of flat surface units of scenery. Walls of rooms, surfaces of buildings, landscapes, tree forms, mountain forms, and even skies are made up of painted fabric, either free hanging and suspended from battens in the flying system or stretched across wooden frames. This chapter is devoted to a discussion of this important part of stage scenery.

The Flat

The basic unit of framed scenery is the flat. This is a simple, light weight, rigid, wooden frame covered with fabric. Although it may be almost any size and shape there is a tendency in most theatre plants to use units that are small enough in size to be conveniently manipulated on the stage and stored away when not in use. The majority of a theatre's flats will be rectangular in shape, and have standard proportions for use on a specific stage. They will be built so that they can be fastened together in almost any conceivable combination to produce stage settings of great variety.

CONSTRUCTION OF A FLAT—Assume that a 6'-0" x 10'-0" flat is needed. The first step in its construction is the selection, measuring, squaring, and cutting of the various boards needed for the frame. Select 1" x 3" boards that are straight; then measure two pieces 6'-0" in length. Square across them with a try square at the 6'-0" mark and then saw them off at this point. It is essential to saw carefully so that the ends will be true when cut.

Place these two boards side by side and then take another board that is at least 10'-0" long. Place this board at right angles to the other boards and butt it tightly up against them. Now measure across the width of the two 6'-0" boards and down the longer board to the 10'-0" point. Square across the board and cut it off. Another board is cut the same length. If the boards are measured in this way it is possible to automatically deduct the width of the two 6'-0" boards from the 10' board. The illustration of the flat frame will show that the 6'-0" boards are for the top and bottom members of the frame which are called rails. The 10'-0" boards, minus the width of the two 1″ x 3″ pieces, are for the side members or stiles of the flat.

Two more boards are needed for the cross pieces or toggle rails of the flat. In order to

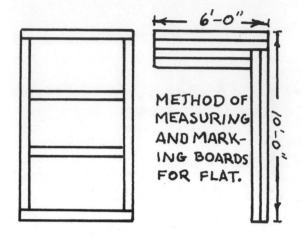

METHOD OF MEASURING AND MARKING BOARDS FOR FLAT.

measure these correctly, place the two longer boards side by side and place one of the 6′-0″ boards atop and even with the outside board. Next measure the new board from a position adjacent to the inside of the longer boards to the end of the 6′-0″ board. In this way the width of the stiles is automatically deducted. It is important to measure and mark the toggle rails at this time so that they are the exact length needed.

The diagram will clarify the entire process.

Cut four corner blocks and four slabs (or keystones). This flat is to have butt joints so the grain of the corner blocks should run parallel to one of the right angle sides.

Butt one of the stiles against one of the rails so that the side of the stile is flush with the end

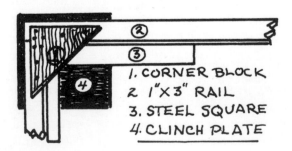

1. CORNER BLOCK
2. 1″X 3″ RAIL
3. STEEL SQUARE
4. CLINCH PLATE

of the rail. · The two boards should now be in the position of an elongated "L" or right angle. Place the clinch plate under the boards at the corner. Next place a corner block over the joint made by the ends of the stile and rail. Be certain that the exposed grain of the corner block runs across the joint so that maximum strength will be achieved. Move the corner block so that it is spaced in from the outside edge ¾″. This may be easily spaced by using a short scrap of 1″ x 3″ and placing it on edge next to the corner block.

A minimum number of nails should be used in securing the corner. A pattern with one

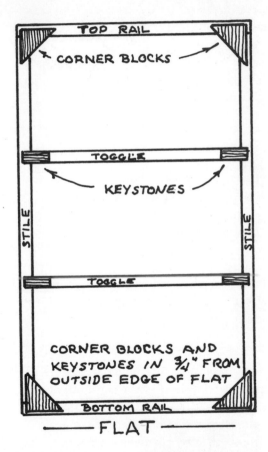

TOP RAIL

CORNER BLOCKS

TOGGLE

KEYSTONES

STILE · STILE

TOGGLE

CORNER BLOCKS AND KEYSTONES IN ¾″ FROM OUTSIDE EDGE OF FLAT

BOTTOM RAIL

— FLAT —

nail in each corner, two on either side of the joint and one on each side halfway between the acute angles and the right angle is basic. If this pattern is followed nine nails will be used.

Nailing the corner with clout nails may be

done easily and efficiently as follows. Lay the boards in their approximate positions. Fasten the corner block to the rail using all five nails. Next drive one of the nails in the stile next to the joint. After this has been done the stile can still be easily twisted to the right or left to square the joint.

Place a steel square in the corner and adjust the boards so that the corner is square or true and drive a nail that has not been nailed as yet. The corner will now be held in place and the other nails can easily be driven in. The nails will be driven through onto the clinch plate and automatically bent over or clinched. It is important to note that clout nails, especially the tapered ones, will not hold unless clinched.

This process is repeated for the other three corners of the flat. A final check on the squareness and trueness of the flat may be made by measuring diagonally across the flat. If the two diagonal measurements are the same the corners are in their true positions.

When the corners have been secured and the frame checked for squareness, it is time to nail in the toggle rails.

Toggle rails should be spaced not more than 4'-0" apart. The toggles are essential if the flat is not to be pulled out of shape by the shrinkage of the muslin when the surface is painted.

Special toggles are sometimes put in to support heavy wall hangings, such as pictures, mantels, animal heads, shadow boxes, wall phones, bracket lamps and other stage dressing units.

A minimum of nails may be used to fasten

the toggles. Six or eight nails may be used in the keystones, depending upon the pattern. Two on each side of the joint are essential, but either one or two may be placed on each end of the slab or keystone. It is essential that the joint be close fitting or the flat may be sprung out, making it untrue. It is also important that the keystones be held in 3/4" from the outside edge of the flat.

The flat frame may be strengthened further by the addition of one or two diagonal braces. If braces are used they should be placed in the

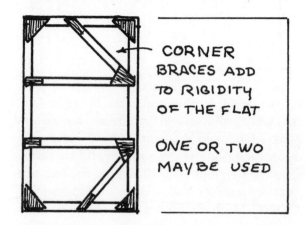

CORNER BRACES ADD TO RIGIDITY OF THE FLAT

ONE OR TWO MAYBE USED

upper and lower right hand corners as seen from the rear. It is important that this procedure be standardized, especially if many flats are to be fastened together with lash line.

COVERING THE FLAT—After the frame has been completed, it is time to cover it with muslin or some other type of fabric. Turn the frame over so that the corner blocks and keystones are underneath. Take a piece of fabric that is slightly larger than the frame (half inch to an inch all around). If 36" material is being used for a frame that is 36" wide or 72" material for a 72" wide frame the material can be used but the covering must be done carefully so that the material covers adequately.

Spread the material over the frame. Temporary tacks or staples may be placed in the corners to hold the material in place but these are not needed if the covering is done carefully.

Fold one side of the material back just far

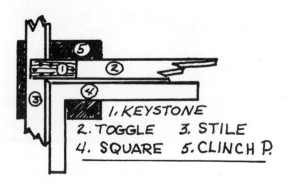

1. KEYSTONE
2. TOGGLE 3. STILE
4. SQUARE 5. CLINCH P.

enough to expose the wood of the stile. With a paddle or brush carefully spread glue on this

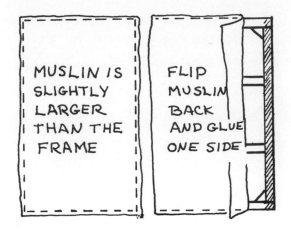

board. Work rapidly and use plenty of glue so that it will not soak into the board or "set-up" before the muslin has been pressed into place adjacent to the edge. Work the muslin down carefully and then rub it briskly. Next glue the opposite side. Then do one end and finally the other end. After the muslin has been glued all around it is a good idea to check and see that there are no loose places. The process completed, the muslin will be glued to the boards all the way around the outside edge of the flat. Do *not* glue to the toggle bars.

After the fabric has been glued to the frame,

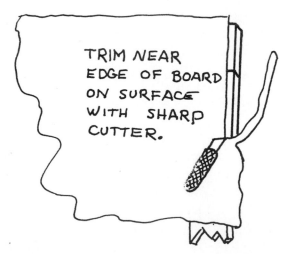

the edges should be trimmed. A sharp knife or cutter should be used for this purpose. In order to prevent the muslin from fraying around the edge of the flat, it should be trimmed in ⅛″ to ¼″ on the boards. After the knife has been run along cutting near the edge and the surplus material has been removed, the edge of the muslin should be carefully rubbed down. This edge will be sealed by paint so that it cannot be seen even upon close inspection.

NOTES ON CONSTRUCTION OF A FLAT—Corner blocks and keystones should always be held back ¾″ from the outside of the flat frame all of the way around. It is also advisable to hold the plywood pieces back ¾″ from the edges of openings in special flats. This facilitates in getting close joints when flats are put together to make corners in settings and when thicknesses are fitted behind openings in flats. This will be discussed more completely farther on in the chapter.

Check the corners carefully for squareness and trueness so that flats will fit together correctly to make stage walls.

Whenever possible use straight boards. There are times when boards that are slightly bowed must be used for stiles. If so, put them together in the frame so that one compensates for the other — so that both boards bow out or in — and then the toggle bars are put in to help straighten the boards and to force them into the correct position.

Cut all of the boards for the flat before assembling them and measure and cut them as indicated so that there is a relationship among them. If this isn't done the toggle bars especially may be cut too long or too short and the flat will bow in or out in the center.

Tighten the muslin only so that it is reasonably snug and wrinkle free and glue it only around the outside edges and/or around openings. Be certain to use unshrunk muslin, which is usually listed as brown or unbleached. The muslin must shrink during the sizing and painting process or it will not have a taut, smooth surface.

After the muslin has been glued onto the

frame, it should become thoroughly dry before any paint is applied. The glue must be set up until it is hard or the muslin may slip loose.

If mistakes have been made or if a flat is to be altered it is possible to remove clout nails rather easily with a carpenter's nail puller.

If no tacks or staples are used when covering the flat the process of removing muslin and re-covering a frame is simplified a great deal. After all, a well built flat frame will probably outlive several coverings of muslin.

There are about 400 clout nails in a pound and the average flat takes about 70 clout nails.

Most materials are less expensive if bought in quantity and, of course, if ordered in standard packaged amounts. Casein glue is less expensive if purchased in 25 or 50 pound cartons than when purchased in the convenient one pound package. Of course, when buying quantity it is foolish to buy a quantity of material that will deteriorate before it can be used up. The life of the material should be checked rather thoroughly if it is perishable.

SUBSTITUTE MATERIALS — There are a number of substitute materials that can be used in place of materials listed in the process of building a flat. There are times and places where some types of materials are not easily obtainable and substitutions must be made.

Some other kind of lumber can be used. Certain requirements should be met if the lumber is to be entirely practical. The wood used should be relatively straight grained. Wood should be straight and free from cup or warp, light in weight, soft and easily workable and relatively inexpensive. Woods that can be used rather easily are: redwood, sugar pine, spruce, cedar and some soft native lumbers. White pine is probably superior to any of the others and should be used if possible.

There are some substitutes that can be used for plywood in making corner blocks and keystones, but plywood is probably the easiest and best to use. Prestwood, Masonite and other tempered hardboards can be used, but they get brittle with age. Tin corner blocks have been somewhat successful. Corner blocks and keystones made from heavy sheet aluminum would probably be excellent but expensive. The professional scene building shops use mortise and tenon joints and then make corner blocks and keystones from slabs of thin wood covered on both sides with cloth which is glued onto the wood.

Muslin is by no means the only material that can be used to cover flats, but it is probably the least expensive material that is durable enough to stand a moderate amount of abuse. Pocket drill, ticking, scene duck, linen denim, burlap, velour and almost any other textile could be used. Special textures and surfaces might be used for special flats to achieve results other than that achieved by the ordinary flat surface.

STOCK OF FLATS—Building up a stock of scenery is a cumulative process that takes place over the years. Flats can be reused many times if they are built with a view toward standardization. One or two heights should be decided upon and then all of the regular flats built to conform. Many different widths can be used, but there is convenience in some unity in this respect, too.

HEIGHT—The standard flat height differs from theatre to theatre. This may be determined by the physical facilities of the stage and the scene storage space. Ceiling height, sight line height, proscenium height and shop space may be factors worth considering carefully before deciding that the scenery should be 24'-0" or 8'-0" in height. It is more practical to start with the minimum height than the maximum. It is possible to fasten extensions onto flats and then to return them to their normal size later, but tall flats will have to be cut off in order to make them shorter. In all probability flats of two standardized heights will allow the designer a certain amount of flexibility in his design and yet make it possible to work with a limited number of flats. Practical heights are 10'-0" and 12'-0", especially for modern productions.

WIDTH—The maximum width of the flats

used on a stage may be determined by the doors through which the flats must pass on the way from the building area to the stage and from the stage to the storage docks. Usually 6'-0" (commercially this is reduced to 5'-9") is considered to be the maximum and is the widest flat that can be easily handled by one person. If, however, there are large spaces to fill it is possible to use few flats if they are wider. Sometimes 7'-0" and even 8'-0" flats have a definite place in the stockpile.

Many different widths are practical. However, anything narrower than a foot is a little impractical since a board can be used to fill such a narrow space. 1'-0", 2'-0", 3'-0", 4'-0", 5'-0" and 6'-0" widths are all needed at times. Occasionally beyond the 1'-0" width it is desirable to progress at only 6" intervals. The amount of storage space available may again determine at least in part the number of widths that are stocked.

STORAGE FOR FLATS — Storage space is needed for scenery. Less floor space is required and the flats are easier to store and remove from storage if they are stored on end rather than on their sides. Either of these positions, however, is better than stacking them flat like pancakes. Partitioning the scene dock into stalls that hold not more than 15 or 20 flats will make it easier to find the desirable pieces when needed and will keep them in better condition. The storage room should be dry. And if there is enough space there should be some orderliness to the stacking of the various widths and heights.

Variations on the Flat

DOOR FLAT—The door flat unit is framed with an opening that may be used in one of three ways. A door may be hinged into it directly. A door unit may be fastened to the back of it. Or a door unit may be slipped into it from the front and be held in place by strap hinges that bind against the flat. These units will be described later.

The size of the opening in the door flat will depend on which of the three types of doors is used. The opening for the first two will be the regular door measurement while the one for

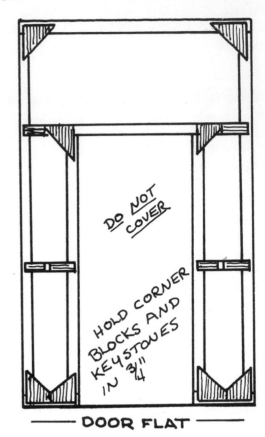

— DOOR FLAT —

the door that is slipped into the opening will be 2" narrower and 1" shorter than the door shutter.

The ordinary door in a home is 2'-0", 2'-6", 2'-8" or 3'-0" in width and either 6'-6" or 6'-8" in height. For convenience, on the stage either 3'-0" x 7'-0" or 2'-6" x 6'-6" doors may be used. Here again it is a good idea to set one standard size so that the units can be used interchangeably. Standardization shouldn't deter one from using other sizes for special effects, but in the main it is better to have one basic size. The door opening can be built into any flat that is wide and high enough to accommodate it. Although the opening need not be centered in the flat, actually for normal use this might be set up as regular procedure. If the door flat is to receive a 3'-0" x 7'-0" door a toggle bar should be placed so that the bottom of it measures 7'-0" from the bottom of the flat. Stiles for the sides of the opening are cut 7'-0" long minus the width of the bottom rail of the flat. These stiles are nailed in place so that the opening is correctly placed in relation to the sides of the frame. All of the joints should be checked for squareness as they are fastened. A set of short toggle bars is fastened in on either side at a height of 3'-6" between the door stile and the outside stile of the flat.

To gain additional strength and rigidity, corner blocks may be used for the door stile fastenings at the top and bottom. Here again it is important to hold all of the corner blocks and keystone ¾" from the outside edge of the flat and from the inside edge of the opening so that the thickness will fit into place without extra trimming.

To make it easier to square the corners, the bottom rail can be put in just as in an ordinary flat and then after the whole thing is assembled the section across the door opening can be cut out and a sill iron fastened to the bottom of the flat to keep the narrow legs on the sides of the opening in their correct positions and to make the flat more rigid.

SILL IRONS—Sill irons are made from strap iron that is anywhere from ⅛" to ¼" thick and from ¾" to 1" wide. Sill irons may be made in a number of ways. They may extend just beyond each side of the door about 6" or 8"; they may consist of a piece of strap iron that is in the shape of a broad "U" with the short upright arms placed so that they fit within the opening of the flat; they may extend across the bottom and turn up about 6" on the outside edges of the flat; or they may have extra pieces riveted or welded on so that they extend across the bottom, up on each side of the opening and up on each outside edge of the flat.

Sill irons are usually drilled for #9 wood screws. The holes may be drilled with a ³/₁₆" or ¼" drill and then the sides where the screw heads will be should be countersunk (drilled

in part way with a countersink or a large drill) so that the heads of the screws will pull up flush with the iron. They should be drilled so that at least two 1½" or longer #9 flat-

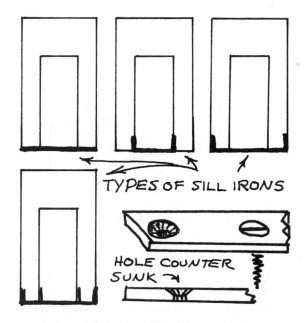

TYPES OF SILL IRONS

HOLE COUNTER SUNK →

head bright wood screws can be placed in the section on each side of the opening. Before the sill iron is put on, file off any sharp edges that might cut into the floor as the flats are run across it.

WINDOW FLAT—The opening in a flat for a window may take many sizes and shapes. An ordinary window in a flat will probably be from 2'-0" to 3'-0" in width, from 3'-0" to 6'-0" in height and be placed from 1'-0" to 3'-0" above the floor. The outside of the window flat is exactly the same as that of a regular flat. The toggle bars are spaced so that the underside of the top one is the height of the top of the window and the upperside of the bottom one is the height of the bottom of the window. Extra stiles are then placed appropriately for the sides of the window and at the halfway point in the spaces at each side of the window short toggle bars are placed.

JOGS—Narrow flats, those of less than 2'-0" width, are usually referred to as jogs.

PLUGS—Small flats are usually referred to

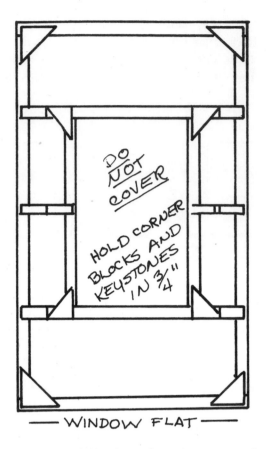

— WINDOW FLAT —

is a strip of muslin bonded to the surface of the flat with paint.

UNCOVERED FLAT SCENERY—Unusual scenic effects may be achieved by using combinations of uncovered flat frames which may be built in the regular manner. In some instances it may be desirable to use keystones in place of corner blocks in order that they will not be visible from the front.

Wall Sections

It may be that no wall sections in a stage setting consist of more than one flat. This would be an exceptional setting. Usually two or more flats are combined to get the desired width for a single wall. When this is done it is almost always desirable to have the flats fastened together so that they may be folded for easier moving and stacking. Ordinarily, back-flap hinges are used for this purpose. Either 1½" or 2" hinges may be used. Each half of the back-flap hinge is the size of the measurement used to designate it.

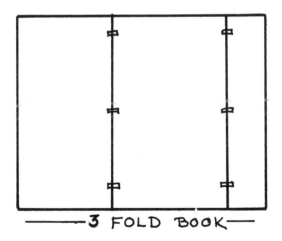

— 3 FOLD BOOK —

as plugs, especially those flats that are used to fill up, or plug up, openings in flats.

CONVERTING DOOR FLATS TO WINDOW FLATS—Sometimes it is easier to hinge or batten a plug into the bottom part of a door flat than to make a new window flat or cut into a regular flat to make an opening for a window. The hinges may be placed on the back and the cracks dutchmaned on the front. A dutchman

HINGING FLATS TOGETHER—Flats are hinged together on the face so that the joint may be covered with a piece of fabric, called a dutchman, giving the appearance of a single solid wall section when painted. Unless the flats are quite short, at least three hinges should be used. Hinges should be placed not more than 4′ or 5′ apart. Hinges are placed on the

ADD PLUG TO BOTTOM OF DOOR OPENING TO CONVERT IT INTO A WINDOW.

42

flat with the thickened roll up and directly in line with and centered over the crack between the flats.

BOOKS—Books are wall sections consisting of two or more flats hinged together. A two flat section is referred to as a twofold, three flats as a threefold and so on.

TUMBLERS—Two flats of any width may be hinged together and they will present no problem in folding. As soon as three or more are hinged there may be some difficulty in folding unless tumblers are put in. A tumbler is a board, usually a 1″ x 3″ the height of the flats, that is hinged between two flats. If three flats

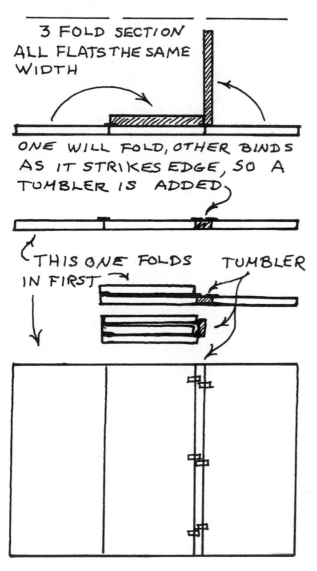

of the same width are hinged together two of them will fold together but the third will bend only up past the halfway mark before it begins to bind against the one that has been folded in from the other side. With a board hinged into this position the board reaches the binding stage but since it is hinged on both of its edges the hinges on the edge opposite the binding edge lift the other flat over far enough so that it will fold down against the other flats. The tumbler isn't needed on all threefold flats. If the center flat is wide and the two side ones narrow the unit will fold without a tumbler. If two of the flats are the same width and one is considerably narrower the narrow one can be folded in first and the wide one last and it will fold. But as soon as the flats approach the same width the tumbler is a necessity if the unit is to fold into a flat pack.

When more than three flats are hinged together two or more tumblers are frequently required.

WALL SECTIONS MADE UP OF FLATS—To keep the weight down to a minimum, it is wise to make a wall section out of as few flats as possible. Actually, there is no limit to the number of flats that can be hinged together to make a section, but there is a physical limit to the amount of weight that can be moved around the stage, from the shop to the stage and packed into a truck if the scenery has to be moved very far. Usually the widest flats practical should be used and the flats hinged together with appropriate tumblers hinged into place so the entire section will fold into a convenient pack.

ALTERNATE METHOD FOR MAKING DOOR AND WINDOW OPENINGS—Door and window openings may be created by using plugs to form the block above a door and the blocks above and below a window. When this method is employed it is possible to use regular flats throughout the structure and no window or door flats need be built. Units put together in this way are heavier and sometimes more awkward to handle than regular door or window flats, but the convenience of having flats with-

43

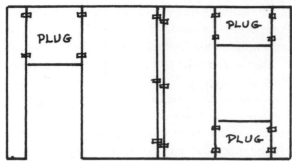

DOOR AND WINDOW OPENING
MADE WITH PLUGS

out openings cut in them may be a compensating factor worth considering.

ALTERING THE SHAPE OF DOOR AND WINDOW OPENINGS — Archways, doorways and windows are not always rectangular in shape. In fact, they frequently have tops that are

RECTANGULAR OPENING
TEMPORARILY ALTERED

curved, horseshoe shaped, scalloped, tapered or any of a dozen other shapes. Many times their shape is used as one of the major factors in suggesting the period or the locale of the setting to the audience.

Archways — Sweeps

SWEEPS — Frequently regular doors, windows and archways can be reshaped by the additions of shaping corners or sweeps. Sweeps may be cut from plywood or inexpensive #2 or #3 common white pine lumber and then fastened into place with slabs of plywood and nails. After the scenery has been used and disassembled these may be removed and the flat returned to its normal shape.

Often half circle tops are desired. To lay these out it is necessary to have an oversize

compass device of some kind. The most common device is the string and piece of chalk compass. The string is held at the center of radius and then the other end, equipped with chalk or pencil, is swept around to draw the curve. Frequently the results are not true since the string stretches rather readily on a large circle. A better method is to take a strip of board (thin and narrow) of about the cor-

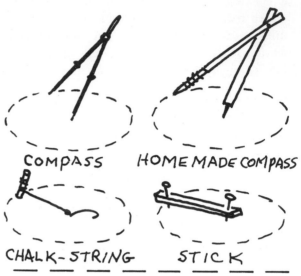

COMPASS   HOME MADE COMPASS

CHALK-STRING   STICK

rect length and nail one end to the point which is the center of the circle to be inscribed. Then locate the position along the board that represents the outside of the circle (distance from center to outside is the radius) and either hold a pencil against it and sweep it around, or cut a notch to hold the pencil, or drill a hole in it, or if a piece of wood is to be marked drive a nail through and use it to scratch the line on the surface of the board.

Irregular curves may be either marked out free hand or by the aid of a simple jig that can be easily made from a scrap of lumber. A thin

THIN BOARD BENT TO CONTOUR

Egyptian motif with canted archway in a setting for *Antony and Cleopatra*.

strip of lumber, not more than ¼" thick, may be used. If the curve is small and tight an even thinner strip may be required. The strip is then simply bent to conform to the desired contour and while being held in that position a line is drawn along side of it with a pencil or piece of chalk.

NOTES ON MARKING AND CUTTING SWEEPS—To get a pleasing edge for the contoured opening it is necessary to mark and cut the sweeps carefully. Where a primitive feeling is desired a rough free hand quality is all right, but if any degree of sophistication is necessary the lines should be true and the curves gradual and regular in their contour.

Long gentle curves may actually be cut with a regular hand saw (rip or cross cut depending upon whether the cut is with or across the grain; usually the rip saw will do very well).

Relatively sharp contours should be cut with a keyhole saw, power band saw, stand type jig saw or a portable jig saw.

Usually the curve of the sweep where it departs from the straight line surface should seem to grow out or spring out of the surface. When completed it shouldn't have a tacked on look.

A paper template or pattern can be cut first and then the paper laid onto the wood in such a way that waste wood will be reduced to a minimum. This is essential when many pieces are to be cut.

ARCHWAY SHAPES—The imagination of the

45

Archways used in setting for *The Madwoman of Chaillot* (above) and
Le Bourgeoisie Gentilhomme (below).

46

designer is the only limit to the shape, size and proportions of archways, windows and doorways. Some of the shapes are based upon architectural characteristics, some on structural materials, some on historical structures and some on the whim of the designer.

WIDE ARCHWAYS—In the alternate method for making door openings it was suggested that door units could be made by taking two

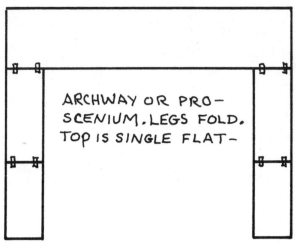

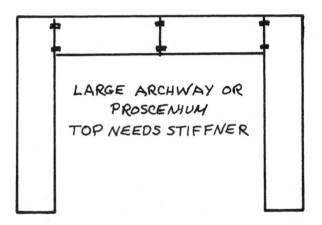

jogs and hinging a plug in between them to make the door flat. Wide archways may be made in the same way. If the opening is more than 6'-0" or 7'-0" in width two flats hinged together may be used for the overhead piece, or header as it is sometimes called. If constructed this way the unit will consist of four flats with three hinged joints. The widths of the flats should be checked carefully for folding and if a tumbler is needed it should be placed in the center. If the over-all width of the opening is critical, the extra width provided by the tumbler will have to be compensated for in the width of the flats. Building the archway and hinging it this way allows it to be folded into a compact book.

WIDE ARCHWAYS, ALTERNATE CONSTRUCTION—There are times when it is more convenient to have a long rigid spread across the top of the archway. In this case a single flat may be used for the header and legs hinged so that they extend down from one edge. Measurements should be checked carefully to be certain that when folded the unit will not exceed

the measurement of doors between the place where it is constructed and where it is to be used. If necessary the legs might even be made with a joint in them in order to facilitate folding the unit.

False Proseniums

The false prosenium is basically an archway. It may be wider and higher than most other arches used on the stage, but it is still constructed in the same way. The unit may be so large that it is inconvenient to fold it into a single book. In this case it should be built and put together with loose pin hinges, bolts and wing nuts, or some other device that will allow it to be rapidly assembled and disassembled.

The false prosenium may not have thickness, but in all probability it will have an indication of depth, either painted or three dimensional. If the thickness is real and no more than 12", lumber will be the best material to use; but if it is deeper, flats will be more convenient and lighter in weight. The thickness can be planned so that it serves as a stiffener for the archway. To do this the thickness should extend across the full width if the width is cut into segments and hinged, or the side pieces should run the full height if the legs are hinged on below the header.

If curtains or drops are to be rigged behind the prosenium it is best to plan a support that will carry the weight and strain of these. This support may be fastened to the archway, but if the stress and strain of pulling the curtains is thrown onto the flats the muslin covering them will probably show wrinkles.

SUPPORT FOR CURTAINS, DRAPES OR DROPS—A relatively narrow, elongated box made of 1″ x 6″ lumber with sturdy legs will

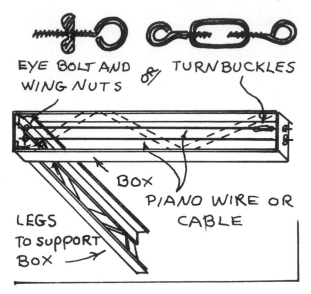

EYE BOLT AND WING NUTS *or* TURNBUCKLES

BOX

PIANO WIRE OR CABLE

LEGS TO SUPPORT BOX

support any of the materials that are likely to be used with the false proscenium. The box should be designed specifically for the individual situation.

Roll drops will require a means of anchoring the top batten, pulleys for the operating lines to pass through (a single pulley above one end of the drop and a double pulley above the other end), and tie-off cleats to fasten the lines to when the drop is in the open position.

Traveller type drops or curtains that can be opened and closed like draw draperies will require a regular traveller track or parallel wires stretched across separated from one another by 3″ or so, depending upon the bulk of the material from which the curtains are made. If lightly painted or dyed muslin is used 3″ will probably be plenty of clearance. Two wires are needed so that the curtains when pulled together can overlap far enough to mask in the center. Some type of draw cord may be needed

on this track to open and close the curtains, unless that can be done simply by pulling the ends of the material.

FULL SIZED SINGLE DROPS—It is possible to make full sized drops, drops large enough for a series of scenes to be painted in one continuous strip, or almost any other arrangement of drop combinations. One wire can be stretched across and if the wire and frame on which it is mounted extend offstage far enough, the muslin drop can be stored just behind one of the legs of the proscenium before it is used, pulled across the stage and stored behind the other proscenium leg after it has been used. If one long continuous strip scene is used the storage space on each side may have to be as much as 4′ or even more. Several wires can be rigged in the frame above the proscenium and individual drops rigged on each, or one stored behind each proscenium leg to be pulled on and off as needed. With the continuous strip method it is sometimes difficult to find the correct section in a hurry. If the other system is used any one may be easily found and pulled on. It is also possible with this system to have individual curtains behind one another so that the

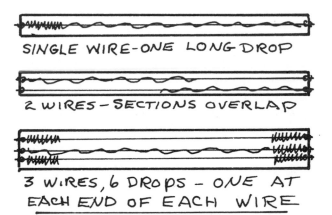

SINGLE WIRE—ONE LONG DROP

2 WIRES—SECTIONS OVERLAP

3 WIRES, 6 DROPS — ONE AT EACH END OF EACH WIRE

one in front can be pulled to reveal the one behind. Any number of other arrangements could be devised for this type of staging and the structure changed to fit the requirements.

Curved Walls

Curved walls or curved corner sections pre-

48

sent somewhat of a special problem on the stage. A curved effect can be achieved by hinging a series of straight flats together and setting them up so they deviate from the

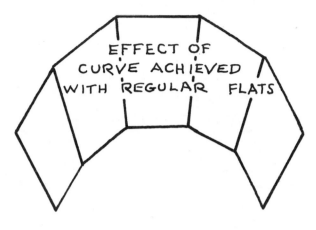

EFFECT OF CURVE ACHIEVED WITH REGULAR FLATS

straight line enough to conform to approximately the curve desired. If a smooth curve is desired, special sweep sections must be built.

Curved surfaces should usually be covered with some type of firm surface material. Fabric on a curve will tend to shrink to a flat surface, which is usually undesirable. The ordinary wall board materials come in pieces that are 4' x 8'. If the surface is designed to make use of this size, in as few pieces as possible, the surface will be more satisfactory since better sweep effects are achieved with large unbroken pieces. Plywood (with the grain running at right angles to the curve if possible), pulp boards, paper boards, sheet aluminum, plastic and cor-

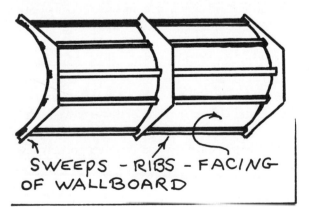

SWEEPS - RIBS - FACING OF WALLBOARD

rugated box board are some of the materials that can be used.

To build the curved section cut the desired contour shape from one or more boards. For this individual pieces of 1" x 6" or wider lumber that are cleated together, or single pieces of thick plywood (¾" sheathing plywood) may be used. The plywood sections, although stronger, have a laminated edge. Wall board nailed into this edge isn't as firmly attached as when nailed into the edge of a solid board. The height of the section, as well as the type of covering material used, will determine how many sweep sections will be needed to hold the form together. It may be possible to make a section out of a single piece of wall board with one sweep at the top, one sweep at the bottom and one 1" x 3" stringer on each edge. The section can be strengthened by adding sweeps and other stringers. The stringer mentioned is an upright piece used to space the sweeps and fasten them together to make the basic form. When enlarging the sweep section in height or width it is necessary to increase the size and number of sweeps and uprights. The framework should be planned so that there are solid supports wherever two pieces of wall board are matched together.

Ceilings

Stage settings are frequently covered, either completely or partially, with ceilings. A ceiling is an oversized flat section either made in one piece or in several pieces which are hinged together. The ceiling may be flown when not in use or built so that it can be taken apart and rolled up like a backdrop.

ONE PIECE CEILINGS—The one piece ceiling is built like a large flat. Since its size in at least one direction exceeds the length of normal lumber, scarf spliced pieces are used.

To achieve greater strength, the size of the corner blocks and keystones can be increased.

The ceiling should be wide enough to cover the width of any setting likely to be used on the stage. Under most circumstances it is not desir-

49

able to have the ceiling extend down as far as the curtain line since it then becomes much more difficult to light down under and inside the setting. How far upstage the ceiling is placed will depend upon the individual theatre, but it should probably be placed at least 4' from the curtain line. To facilitate the overhead masking a flipper is usually hinged to the ceiling. A flipper is a narrow flat, as long as the ceiling, that is hinged to the ceiling so that it forms a facing and stiffener for the front or leading edge of the ceiling when it is in place on top of a setting. The flying lines for the

ceiling uses three sets of flying lines: one set across the front, one set across the center, and one set across the back. The center set is used to fly the ceiling so that it can fly folded and be lifted up higher into the fly well. The other

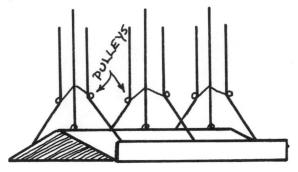

BOOK CEILING LINES
CONCENTRATED-PERMANENT

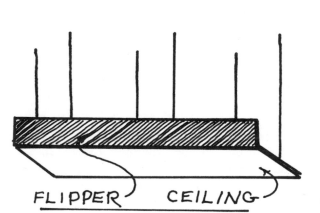

FLIPPER   CEILING

ceiling usually pass through rings attached to the top edge of the flipper and are tied to ceiling plates which are firmly attached with screws and bolts to the front batten of the ceiling. The ceiling is usually provided with two sets of lines, one in front and one upstage, so that it may be swung into position above the setting more easily.

BOOK CEILINGS—A two piece ceiling is used where a single flat will be too large to handle. The two piece ceiling consists of two flats long enough for the width of the setting and half as wide as the depth. They are hinged together with backflap or strap hinges spaced not more than 3' apart. A flipper is hinged to the leading edge as on the one piece ceiling and a stiffener is securely fastened to the edge of one of the flats at the hinged joint. This type of

BOOK CEILING, LINES ABOVE
FRONT, CENTER AND BACK

two sets may be removed when not in use or a complex system using three sets of lines closely spaced can be used to handle the ceiling and can be left on when it is in use and in storage.

ROLL CEILINGS—The roll ceiling is made with only the two long battens securely fastened to the fabric. The other battens, the ends, and all of the toggles are temporarily fastened in place with small steel plates (ceiling plates) that may be easily removed. The fabric is temporarily tacked to the end battens, or the battens are slipped through pockets sewn on for that purpose. When the ceiling is not in use it may be disassembled, the fabric rolled on the rails, the toggles tied up in a pack, and

50

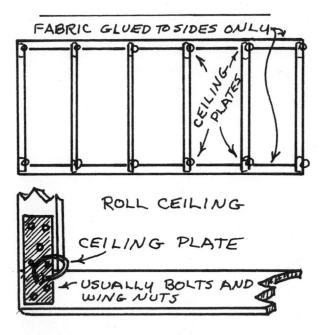

FABRIC GLUED TO SIDES ONLY

CEILING PLATES

ROLL CEILING

CEILING PLATE

USUALLY BOLTS AND WING NUTS

the whole thing stored on a rack or transported to the next stop.

Screens

Double faced screen type scenery has many uses. The screens are much the same as decorative screens often used in the home, except that they are usually, though not always, a little larger. Since a smooth surface is desired on

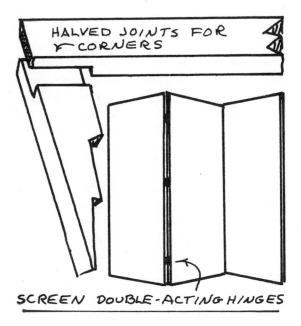

HALVED JOINTS FOR CORNERS

SCREEN DOUBLE-ACTING HINGES

both sides of the screen frame, corner blocks and keystones are a little awkward to use for securing the joints. If they are used it is necessary to put strips around the back of the flat near the outer edge in order to make the entire flat the thickness of the 1″ x 3″ plus the plywood. Strips of plywood or thin, narrow strips of wood can be used for this purpose. It is really better to employ wood joints that will give a smooth surface on both sides. If the flats are made commercially the corners will probably be fastened with mortise and tenon joints. Unless there is special shop equipment available it is a complicated process to put the frames together this way. An easier and simpler type of joint is the halved joint. Although 1″ lumber can be used for screens, something a little heavier, like 1¼″ or even 2″ lumber, is better.

After the frames have been constructed they are covered on both sides. The covering material may be muslin that is painted after it is put on the frame or it may be dyed or patterned print material. The covering can be glued on the frame or sewed to form a tube and then slipped over the frame like a pillow slip is put on a pillow. If a tube is made the material will require gluing or tacking only along the top and bottom.

After the flats have been covered they can be hinged together. Two-way (double acting) screen hinges are used for this purpose. They are a little difficult to find, but most hardware stores of any size should have them somewhere in their stock. The hinges are placed on the edge of the flat rather than on the face or the back, and they are designed so that they will fold readily in either direction. In fact the flats will fold snugly together in either direction if the hinges are at least as thick as the wood of the frame.

String

String may be used on uncovered frames to achieve interesting effects. "L" shaped frames, "U" shaped frames or complete rectangular

51

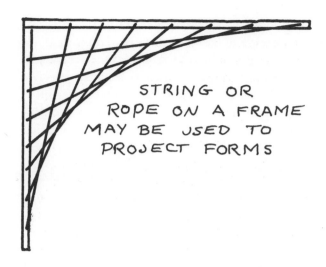

STRING OR ROPE ON A FRAME MAY BE USED TO PROJECT FORMS

frames lend themselves to this treatment. Various patterns may be tried.

Fireplaces

There are literally thousands of different types of fireplaces. The fireplace of each home differs in some respect from fireplaces in every other home. Basically they all have a place for the fuel and most of them have a mantel, but the shape and arrangement of both of these differ greatly.

UNIT FIREPLACE — The conventionalized stage fireplace unit that fits in front of the flats is complete in and of itself. It consists of a

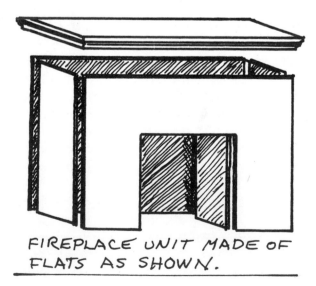

FIREPLACE UNIT MADE OF FLATS AS SHOWN.

front and back, thickness on both ends, thickness around the fire box opening and mantel to cover the top. The entire unit, with the exception of the top, can be made of individual flats that are covered and then fastened together. The top should be of some type of firm material such as boards or plywood. The top can be put on so that it is flush all of the way around and then various moldings can be applied afterward to provide the conventional overhang on the front and ends.

FLAT AND MANTEL FIREPLACES—An alternate type of fireplace uses a flat with a hole cut in it for the firebox and a mantel that is designed to be hung on the flat above the fire-

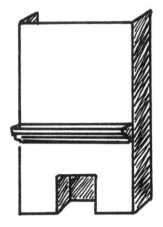

FIREPLACE MADE OF A FLAT WITH CHIMNEY THICKNESS FLATS-MANTLE AND HOLE FOR FIREBOX

box opening in a desirable position. This type of fireplace requires less storage space than the other and the flats are all available for other uses later. With this type of construction it is possible to use a flat the desirable width for the front of the fireplace, and fasten a jog on either side to provide depth for the chimney.

These two types of fireplaces have somewhat different appearances and it is very possible that both may be used at times. There may be other times when other designs will be needed. The setting for *Papa Is All* should be equipped with all of the paraphernalia of a fireplace in which the family cooking is done. The old fireplace in *Ladies In Retirement* must be large enough for a body to be stuffed in through the door. The fireplace in *Shop At Sly Corner* must be rigged so that it can be opened to allow the shopkeeper to enter his secret kiln room. Other fireplaces have secret compartments, are large enough to hide inside, etc.

Usually it will be advisable to look at pictures until the correct type of fireplace is found and then build accordingly.

Thickness

Walls of buildings are more substantial than the flat structures used on a stage. In order to project a third dimensional feeling of solidity it is necessary to suggest that walls have thickness. This is done around the openings in the walls such as doors and windows.

TEMPORARY THICKNESSES—Sometimes boards nailed at right angles around behind the edge of openings can be left in place for the duration of the production. This is possible on a one set show. It is also possible when the units are small enough to be handled without folding or when the thicknesses do not interfere with the folding. When permanent thicknesses are used it is also possible to allow some of them to extend across the entire wall section and serve as stiffeners. The header thickness above a door or window can be extended out this way. Boards used for thicknesses of this type may be nailed or screwed into place. Double head nails can be used to advantage as

STIFFNER AND DOOR HEADER

long as they are not in a position where they will catch on costumes.

CURVED THICKNESSES—One quarter inch

or thinner plywood cut so the grain runs across the thickness direction can be nailed in place around contours to produce contour thickness. Small nails should be used so that the plywood

PLYWOOD THICKNESS FOR SWEEP GRAIN RUNS ACROSS →

can be easily removed and kept for reuse.

PERMANENT THICKNESSES — The permanent thickness is carefully built to the theatre's own standard size and kept as part of the regular stock of equipment.

BEHIND THE FLAT TYPE THICKNESS — There is one type of thickness that fits on the back of the flat and its opening is the same size as the opening in the flat. Since this type of thickness is designed to be used many times it is desirable to set up size standards before the construction begins. For the present purpose assume that the doors are to be 3'-0" x 7'-0". It can also be assumed that the walls are about 6" thick. (Most inside walls in homes are just about 6" by the time they are plastered or covered with wall board.)

There are two basic methods of building this type of unit. The first style requires a little less time for labor and less lumber. However, the finished unit isn't as sturdy and will not stand as much abuse as the second type.

METHOD NO. 1—The opening in the flat is 3'-0" x 7'-0" so the finished door jamb, or thickness, should measure 3'-0" on the inside from side to side and 7'-0" from the outside of the bottom to the inside of the top. When in

53

place the bottom rests on the floor and the underside of the top board will be flush with the top of the flat opening. This thickness resembles a low topless and bottomless box when completed.

The following lumber will be needed:

    2 — 1″ x 6″ — 3′-0″ long (for top and bottom)

    2 — 1″ x 6″ — 7′-¾″ long (for sides)

These boards are nailed together with the sides running through. 8d box coated nails, or 1½″ or 2″ #9 flat head wood screws should be used for fastening the frame together. The

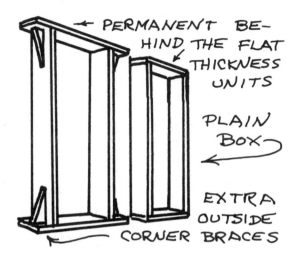

← PERMANENT BE-
HIND THE FLAT
THICKNESS
UNITS

PLAIN
BOX

EXTRA
OUTSIDE
CORNER BRACES

fasteners go through the sides and into the top and bottom. The nails or screws may gradually work loose and if they are put in from the sides they cannot cut into the floor.

METHOD No. 2—If the top and bottom members are cut to run through and are extended at least 6″ beyond the side members of the jamb on each side, it is possible to nail a short diagonal brace into place to stiffen the unit and help it retain its shape when in use and storage. A right triangular shaped piece of 2″ x 4″ may be cut for the brace. The braces are placed just beyond each corner of the frame on the sides where they fit into the corner made by the extended top and bottom and the sides.

WINDOW THICKNESSES — Window thickness units may be built similar to the door thick-

nesses just described. For normal use this thickness will work all right. If the window sill has to support considerable weight it should have supports running to the floor so that the strain isn't thrown onto the flat.

WINDOW FAKING—In many instances the window thickness does not show after the stage dressing has been completed. Window curtains, glass curtains, lace curtains, venetian blinds and other dressing make it unnecessary to have thickness. So unless there is window business or unless there are no trappings to cover the sides, the window thickness may be ignored.

FASTENING BEHIND-THE-FLAT THICKNESSES IN PLACE—Double head nails, 1½″ or longer wood screws and loose pin hinges are the major fastening devices that can be easily used to fasten behind-the-flat thicknesses in place. The double head nails are especially easy and convenient to use.

Behind-the-flat thicknesses are inconvenient to remove during scene changes unless loose pin hinges are used. But of course it is possible to design in terms of using this type unit so that the thickness and wall may be moved all in one piece. However, there is a type of removable door and window unit that may be used advantageously. This unit will be called the Hinge Locking Unit.

THE HINGE LOCKING DOOR UNIT—The jamb of the hinge locking door unit slides into the flat from the front so it is necessary to construct the unit with its outside measurements at least an inch narrower and an inch shorter than the opening in the flat. When this thickness unit is built the trim or casing is nailed or screwed onto the face of the jamb across the top and both sides. The trim forms a stop so that the unit can be pushed snugly into place from the front of the flat. A strap hinge is mounted on the unit about half way up the jamb. It is mounted on an angle with the thin end of one strap toward the bottom of the jamb and about a quarter of an inch from the edge the trim is fastened onto. The center of the hinge is then positioned so that it is about 1″

or slightly more from the same trim edge. This half of the hinge is secured to the jamb with 1″ #9 screws. The other half of the hinge remains free. Two hinges placed along the side of the jamb will allow for even more secure mounting in the flat but one on each side will do well enough in most instances.

This unit is mounted into the flat by pulling the unfastened hinge halves up and holding them in that position while the door is slipped

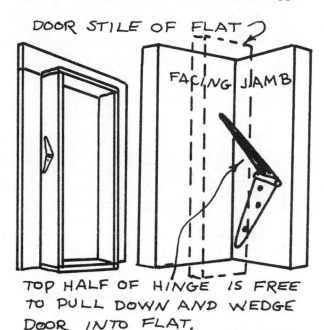

DOOR STILE OF FLAT

FACING JAMB

TOP HALF OF HINGE IS FREE TO PULL DOWN AND WEDGE DOOR INTO FLAT.

into place in the flat. The loose hinge halves are then forced down and wedged against the stiles of the flat, and the unit is locked into place.

HINGE LOCKING WINDOW UNIT — Window units can be made in the same way as the door unit described above. The window unit will have trim all of the way around it and may also have a sill strip mounted to the bottom member of the jamb projecting out in front an inch or so. This is to resemble the sill on an ordinary window. The locking hinges are mounted on the sides of this unit just as on the door unit.

Contour thicknesses to fit behind contour openings should conform to the shape of the

opening. A contour piece may be attached flush with both edges of the thickness in the appropriate places. The space between may

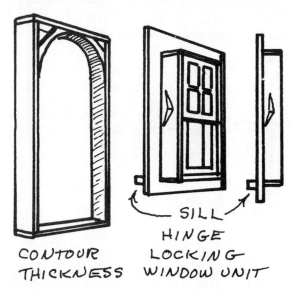

CONTOUR THICKNESS

SILL

HINGE LOCKING WINDOW UNIT

be covered with muslin if the curves are complex; plywood or wall board may be used if the curves are simple.

Other methods of making and mounting door and window units might be devised that are easier to install and more convenient to shift and store.

Door Shutters

A simple stage door, or shutter, may be made like a flat. It should be a quarter of an inch narrower and an inch shorter than the opening to allow for clearance and to prevent the door from binding when it is opened and closed. Muslin, canvas, or more substantial material may be used for covering the door. Heavy paper-type wall boards, wood pulp type material such as Masonite and Prestwood, $\frac{1}{8}$″ or $\frac{1}{4}$″ plywood or any other firm material will do for a harder surface.

Although the harder surface materials will stand more wear and abuse than fabrics for the door covering yet at the same time they will increase the weight of the unit.

At times it is convenient to plan the hard

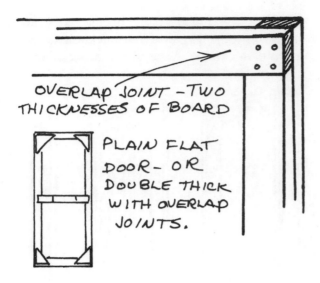

OVERLAP JOINT — TWO THICKNESSES OF BOARD

PLAIN FLAT DOOR — OR DOUBLE THICK WITH OVERLAP JOINTS.

panelling and changed easily and readily each time it is used.

DOOR HARDWARE—Regular door hardware, including bolts, locks, latches, mortised sets, rim lock sets and other types of catches, can be used. Other hardware that might be used includes spring type screen door hinges, hydraulic

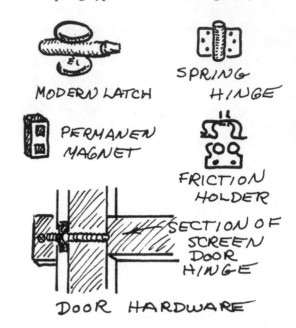

MODERN LATCH

SPRING HINGE

PERMANEN MAGNET

FRICTION HOLDER

SECTION OF SCREEN DOOR HINGE

DOOR HARDWARE

ware for the door at the time the frame is constructed so that door latches, locks or catches can be provided with toggle bars where needed.

DOORS TO OPEN ONSTAGE—Even though most doors are planned so that they will open offstage there are times when the stage business makes it necessary to have one open onstage. This necessitates covering both sides of the frame since the audience can see the one side when the door is closed and the other when the door is open. Usually it is better to build the frame with more thickness so that the door seems to be more substantial.

A rectangular door may be mounted behind an irregular or curved top door opening. The portions above and beyond the opening may be painted black so that the door seems to conform to the shape of the opening.

USE OF REGULAR HOUSE DOORS—Regular house doors may be used onstage but frequently they are heavier in weight than doors built specifically for the stage.

SURFACE FINISH ON DOORS—All of the detail on doors can be painted or applied to the surface. Moldings can be fastened onto the surface to simulate panelling or the doors can be built with actual recessed panelling. A plane surface door can be convincingly painted with

door closers, cabinet door closers, magnetic door holders and spring screen door closers.

DOOR STOP—If no thickness is being used a door stop may be easily made from a lash cleat, hinge half, piece of plumber's strap or a piece of wood. This may be placed on the back of the door extending out far enough on the swinging edge so that it will strike the rear of the flat when the door is closed.

When a door has a thickness the stop consists of a strip of wood not more than 1″ thick and not more than about 1½″ wide. With the door in its closed position the strip is permanently nailed around next to the shutter at the top and on the sides. This not only serves to stop the door but it also prevents light leaks.

It is possible to make double faced universal doors with the knob placed in the center near one edge. These doors may be placed behind the unit so they will swing offstage in either direction by turning them so that either end is the top or bottom, and turned around they will swing onstage in either direction.

Window Sash

Window sash are needed occasionally. If they are plain sash that are never moved they may be built and nailed permanently onto the back of, or into, the thickness piece.

Standard home window sash show about 2" of frame around the glass on the top and sides and about 3" on the bottom. Double hung windows, with sash that can be raised and

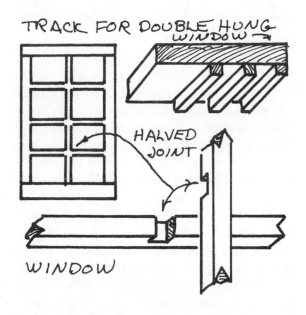

lowered, have a break across the center where the two sections overlap that is slightly narrower than the other framing members. These boards measure about 1½" in width. Sash may be built with halved joints or butt joints with narrow strips of plywood to secure the corners. Cross bars (mullions) may be fastened together with notched joints where they cross one another and may be fastened with strips of plywood where they attach to the outer boards of the sash.

French doors and windows can be built in the same way. French doors will have slightly wider boards for their frame. 1" x 4" for the

top and sides and 1" x 8" for the bottom will do very well and 1¼" strips for the mullions that break the space into small panes.

Double French windows and doors are easier to handle if one side need not be practical. It can then be nailed permanently into place and the keeper for the latch of the other door can be mounted in it. A regular door latch or lock can be used to hold the practical side closed.

Double hung windows are easier to rig for operation if only the bottom sash need be opened. The top may then be fastened permanently in place in the thickness unit. The top sash is outside and the bottom sash inside in relation to one another.

Simple guides for the sash that move up and down are made by fastening strips of ½" x ½" lumber on the sides of the jamb so that the window can be slid up and down. A snug fitting sash will stay in place when lifted open.

Glass

Glass is the poorest substitute for glass on the stage. There is too much danger of breakage. Frequently it is necessary to use nothing in the panes. But if it is necessary to simulate glass, a number of substitute materials may be used. If the glass is to be transparent try sheet plastic, aluminum or plastic screening, cheese cloth or marquisettes that have been dyed a light gray or blue gray. If translucent glass is desired muslin dyed gray or blue gray may be used. If fastened to the frame immediately after being dyed the muslin will tighten up as it dries and provide a smooth, taut surface.

DIAMOND SHAPED GLASS PATTERNS — When small diamond shaped panes are desired in a window unit, friction tape can be stretched diagonally across the back of the sash frame in both directions. Pressing the point of crossing of the tape will help fasten one strip to another.

Miscellaneous Doors

There are times when doors of a slightly unconventional character are desired. Sliding

57

doors and Dutch or half doors fall into such categories.

SLIDING DOORS—Sliding doors are rather easy to make and handle. As a matter of fact, the "pull" on the flattage isn't as great as it is for a regular hinged door. The jamb is built in such a way that the top and bottom members extend out beyond the side on which the door is to disappear far enough to provide a track in which to "store" the door when it is behind the setting. Narrow strips of wood may be used to make the sides of the track in which the door slides. A little heavy floor wax or paraffin (old candle) rubbed on the bottom member of the jamb where the door is to slide

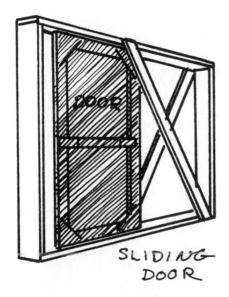

SLIDING
DOOR

will help make the door easier to open. Be careful not to allow too much vertical clearance or the door will twist and stick.

DUTCH DOORS—Dutch doors should be kept light in weight if possible and of course be securely hinged. This type of door usually swings onstage which necessitates double covering and added thickness. Usually additional bracing is needed on the door flat—or careful designing so that the wall section is narrow and braced by adjacent flats which are placed almost at right angles to the door flat.

ABUSED DOORS—Doors that receive great

abuse—that is, doors that are slammed hard and slammed a great many times in a play—are always a problem since the hard slamming

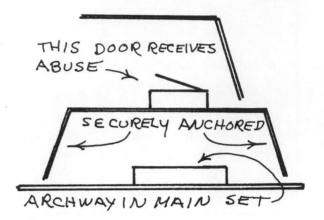

causes the entire setting to quake and quiver. The hallway door in *Junior Miss* is an example of this kind of door. If this type of door can be designed so that it is behind an archway, in an alcove or entry position, it is possible to separate the door's flattage from the rest of the setting. Through the archway only a small portion of the area around the door will show and the apparent shaking of the setting will be diminished a good deal.

SWINGING AND REVOLVING DOORS—Two other types of doors may be needed occasionally. These are the swinging door and the revolving door. Hardware for a swinging door is somewhat expensive and at times difficult to find. A simple substitute that works fairly well is a section of heavy screen door spring mounted to the jamb and then to the door. If the spring is mounted in such a way that the spring tends to straighten back into its normal position when the door is in the neutral position it will work quite well. However, it may be necessary to do a little trial and error work. A piece of spring mounted the same way on each side of the door will also work. Double acting screen hinges will work along with a spring also.

In order to build a revolving door that will work easily it is necessary to have a bottom swivel that operates easily and smoothly. The pin at the top merely keeps the door in position and is not as important. A good swivel may

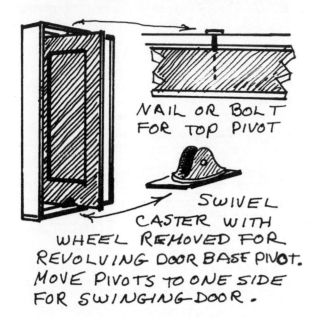

NAIL OR BOLT FOR TOP PIVOT

SWIVEL CASTER WITH WHEEL REMOVED FOR REVOLVING DOOR BASE PIVOT. MOVE PIVOTS TO ONE SIDE FOR SWINGING DOOR.

be made by removing the tire or wheel from a caster. A caster with ball bearing type swivel will probably operate easier than the simpler variety. Grease the swivel well before using. The top of the door may be held in place by driving a nail down through the jamb into the top of the door or by drilling a hole and dropping a pin, bolt or nail into it. It is important that the fittings be carefully positioned so that the door will swing true.

Ground Rows

Ground rows are usually low, relatively long, flat structures with contoured sides and top. They serve several purposes. They conceal the base of the cyclorama, mask base lights that are used to illuminate the lower portions of the cyclorama, and serve as a perspective device. When contrasted with relatively large foreground units and actors playing downstage the lowness of the ground row gives a feeling of greater distance than actually exists between forestage and backstage. Sometimes ground rows are placed in depth, one behind the other, to achieve still greater distance. And some-

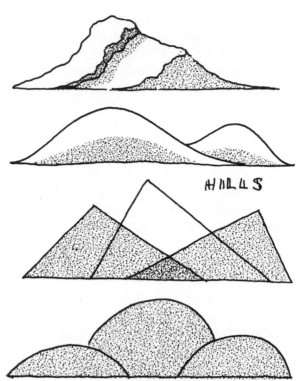

HILLS

times, also to achieve depth, they are spattered with the cyclorama or sky color, so that they will fade into the background. At other times they are set in bold relief when the sky is lighted behind them.

Mountains, hills, bushes, trees, buildings, fences, flowers, city sky lines, rows of buildings,

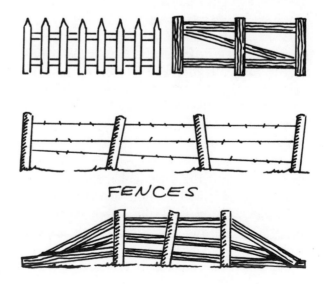

FENCES

ships, seas and almost any other form desired may be represented by such cut out ground row forms. These may be made out of flat frames covered with fabric or may be made of solid surface materials cut to conform to the desired shape. They might be made out of cardboard, corrugated box board, plywood, Prestwood, Masonite or any of a number of different varieties of wall board. They might be built up out of functional three dimensional forms such as steps and platforms and shaped with chicken wire and papier-mache. Usually they should be designed so that they are self supporting if possible.

CONSTRUCTION OF GROUND ROWS — Ground rows made from substantial materials may need no frames, or at most a strip of wood here and there to stiffen and straighten the surface. They may require a jack or some other contrivance to help them stand up. A jack is a triangular shaped wooden frame. The angle between the board resting on the floor and the one extending up the back of the unit is usually just slightly less than a right angle so that the unit will lean slightly backward against the jack. In this position there is less danger of the unit falling forward. Usually there is a diagonal board connecting the upright and the board on the floor. Sometimes space is left on the foot (board on the floor) of the jack to place a weight or sandbag and make the ground row even more substantial.

If the ground row is small it is possible to merely fasten a board to the back either flat or on edge and use that as a supporting foot for the unit.

FLAT TYPE GROUND ROW CONSTRUCTION —If there is a stock of small flats in the shop it may be possible to start with one or more of these and then proceed to construct contours upon them until the desired shape is obtained. At other times it will be more desirable to start by building a framework that approximates the shape and then add contours to complete the structure.

Contours may be made in a number of ways.

Plywood of ⅛", ¼" or ⁵⁄₁₆" can be cut and nailed to the frame. Plywood can be rabbeted into the frame (frame rabbetted or planed

FLAT FRAME - CONTOUR OF PLYWOOD, WALL BOARD OR 1" WHITE PINE

1" LUMBER CONTOURS MAY BE PARTIALLY CUT OUT TO REDUCE WEIGHT.

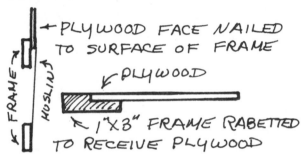

←PLYWOOD FACE NAILED TO SURFACE OF FRAME

←FRAME   MUSLIN   ←PLYWOOD

←1"X 3" FRAME RABETTED TO RECEIVE PLYWOOD

away enough so that the plywood fits into a sort of slot and is flush with the remainder of the frame). 1" boards of # 2 or #3 common white pine can be used and cut to conform to the shape desired and then nailed onto the edge of the framework; or forms may be cut from thicker plywood and fastened onto the edge of the frame.

The use of thicker plywood (½", ⅝" or ¾") enables one to build more elaborate forms that still have a great deal of strength. In fact, if the forms aren't too large it is possible to build an entire ground row from one piece of wood. The plywood can be cut to conform to the outside shape and then in order to reduce the weight, and also to save wood, the inside can be cut out leaving an. outline or frame of wood about 3" wide. To provide more rigidity in the finished product toggle bar shapes can

60

be left in, wherever desired. The front is then covered with muslin and for all intents and purposes a flat has been built using one piece

GROUND ROW SKELETON FRAME CUT FROM 1/2" OR 5/8" SHEATHING PLYWOOD

of wood. The maximum size that can be made in this way with standard sheets of plywood is 4' x 8'. For this purpose sheathing plywood can be used. This is the lowest priced grade of plywood. If 1/2" plywood is joined to 1" lumber (which is actually only 3/4" thick) keystone or corner block fasteners will need 1/4" plywood pads between them and the 1/2" plywood. This makes the connection the same thickness as the 1" board and provides a smooth joint on the face of the flat.

Trees

Trees of small dimension can be cut out of single pieces of firm surface material such as cardboards or wall boards. Medium sized trees can be made as flats. Large trees can be built with separate trunks and foliage so that the trunk rests on the floor and the foliage is flown or supported from overhead.

FLAT TYPE TREES—If the trees aren't too large the flat may be made in one piece. Of course, doors should be checked for size or it may not be possible to get the tree from the shop to the stage. The simplest way to lay out a form of this nature is to chalk it upon the

floor and then cut boards to fit the contour as closely as possible. Some regard for solidity should be considered when cutting and assembling the frame. The outline should be made of as few boards as possible. If the frame is small 1" x 2" lumber will probably be heavy enough. If possible a fairly wide base should be built on the trunk so that the tree will have a firm foot to stand upon. After the frame has been completed the contour may be added. This contour may be made of thin plywood or wall board attached to the front or, if the contours are not too complex, pieces of 1" board

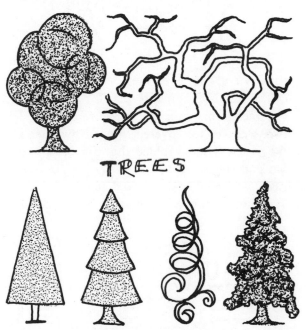

TREES

that are nailed to the edge of the frame boards. When this method is used some of the surplus board can be cut away so that the piece is only about 3" wide following the contour, but with a substantial edge where it is fastened to the frame.

To support this tree it will probably be necessary to have a jack to rest on the floor or hardware so that wire can be used as support from above — either connected to fly lines or to the ceiling above the stage.

Self supporting trees can be built if they are correctly designed to begin with. In general it is necessary to have a slightly enlarged base. This may represent rocks and earth, an enlarged

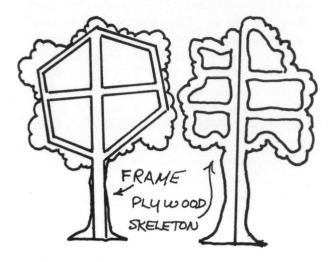

FRAME
PLYWOOD
SKELETON

trunk or a clump of bushes. The remainder of the tree is designed so that it can be built in two pieces that split the center vertically. The two sections are covered, hinged together and the tree will stand folded slightly, like a screen. Since this tree needs no anchoring it can be easily and readily set up and struck.

Either of the types of trees discussed previ-

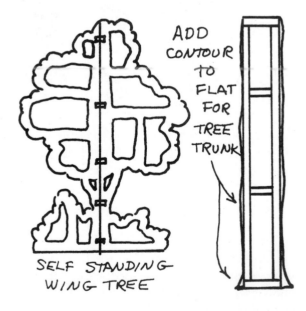

SELF STANDING
WING TREE

ADD CONTOUR TO FLAT FOR TREE TRUNK

ously can be made using the heavier plywood one piece method described for smaller trees.

One piece of plywood may not be enough to cut the entire foliage section so two or more sections will need to be fastened together. If a book or screen type tree is being made it is necessary to split the foliage section anyway so this can be done with two pieces of plywood. This method has much to recommend it. The cost may be slightly more, but the amount of work is no more and the rigidity of the finished product is probably greater and the weight less.

FOLIAGE-TREE-TRUNK TREE—The foliage-tree-trunk variety of tree is satisfactory and probably easier to handle where there is a flying system than the other types of trees. Tree trunks are made by taking jogs (narrow flats)

TREE TRUNKS OF FLATS

of the appropriate width and tacking contour strips along the edges to achieve the slight irregularities that a tree trunk might have. These can be cut on a band saw from scrap strips of lumber 1″ or 2″ in width. A piece of wood may be added to each side of the bottom of the flat to suggest the beginning of the root structure and with that the trunk is completed, unless a limb or two is desired, in which case a board cut to the correct conformation is attached so that it projects out and up toward the top of the flat. The foliage is then made in the form of a border which is suspended from the ceiling or fly loft. The foliage may be painted first and then attached to a long board or batten or attached to the batten first and then painted. While being painted it should be temporarily tacked to the floor or some other surface so that it will tighten flat and not shrink in an irregular fashion. The foliage may be designed in depth so that smaller sections are dropped down in front of and behind the tree trunk. The foliage must be planned so that it extends down far enough to mask the top of the tree trunk when this method is used.

Tree forms can be built in still another way which will be discussed with backdrops.

Miscellaneous Standing Units

Other standing units may be built flat with contours to provide the silhouette shape and

HOUSES

then detail painted on to project their three dimensional form. Objects like houses, barns, sheds, columns, posts, and statues can be handled in this way. Sketch them first to determine their outline form and then build a unit to conform to that shape.

Railings for stairways, patios, theatre boxes and balustrades can be built to conform to the

size and shape required. The face of posts and the balusters or spindles can be cut from flat

CLOUDS

material such as plywood, fastened into place and painted to appear three dimensional. Thicknesses may need to be added to posts and rail-

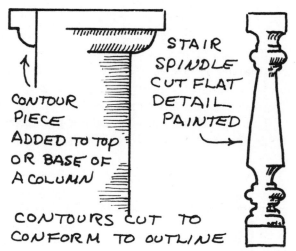

CONTOUR PIECE ADDED TO TOP OR BASE OF A COLUMN

STAIR SPINDLE CUT FLAT DETAIL PAINTED

CONTOURS CUT TO CONFORM TO OUTLINE

ings later to complete the unit, but the basic form can be built as a flat.

Three dimensional buildings can be built of separate flat sections for the walls and roof which are fastened together later with loose pin hinges, lash line, hooks and eyes or other types of fastening devices.

Backdrops

The backdrop is a large sheet of muslin or other fabric. It may be permanently secured to a batten at the top, at the top and bottom, or it may be equipped with tie lines along the top so that it can be tied to the pipe or wooden battens of the theatre's flying system. If the top or top and bottom are fastened to battens permanently the drop is rolled up for transportation and storage. If the drop is equipped with tie lines it may be folded and packed in a box or trunk. Conventionally the drop is placed in a position on the stage where its top and sides can be masked by other scenery. However, drops can be designed and built with finished edges all of the way around so that they are complete units in themselves. There are several varieties of drops and they will be discussed individually.

ORDINARY BACKDROP—The ordinary backdrop consists of a large flat surface upon which a picture is painted that may represent a specific locale. The drop is usually suspended above the stage in such a way that it may be raised and lowered. There are times when a drop is permanently rigged in one position, usually as far upstage as possible, where it serves as the universal scene for use when outdoor settings are called for in any production.

This type of drop may be fastened to a batten by means of tie lines. If so, then the top of the

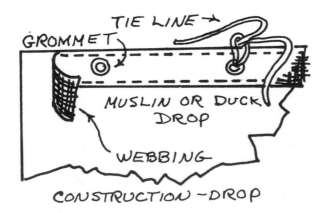

drop probably has a 2″ hem which may be reinforced with a strip of canvas or burlap webbing. Grommets are put through the drop and webbing and spaced about 1′-6″ apart. The lines, of shade cord, or ½″ heavy cotton tape, are tied through the grommets and used to fasten the drop to the batten of the flying system. If this construction is used the bottom of the drop may hang free or may have a pipe pocket sewn into it. The pipe pocket is a hem open at the ends and large enough to slide a pipe into. The pipe pulls the drop downward, tightening and stretching it.

The method just described would be used if the drop were to be moved frequently. A permanent drop will more likely be fastened securely and permanently along the top to a

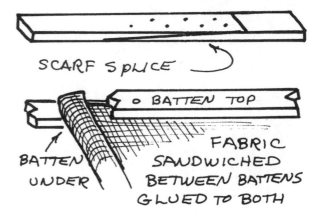

wooden batten. This batten is made of 1″ x 4″ white pine lumber. The boards can be extended to the full width of the drop by means of scarf splices. The batten will be stronger if it is doubled with the drop sandwiched in between the two layers of wood. Before fastening it together the top of the drop will be glued to one board and then glue will be applied to the muslin so that the other batten will also be glued in place. 6d box nails, which will go through two thicknesses of 1″ board far enough to clinch, or 1½″ wood screws will be used to fasten the two thicknesses of wood together. This batten may have holes drilled through it to pass rope or wire through to use for fastening it to the flying system or it may have screw eyes, ceiling plates, eye bolts, drop holders or other similar fastening devices for the same purpose. The bottom of the drop may have a batten, single or double, to which it is permanently secured or the batten may hang free.

FRAMED DROPS—A drop similar to the one just mentioned may be used with some type of stretchers on the sides. These are usually temporary and may be boards that are fastened

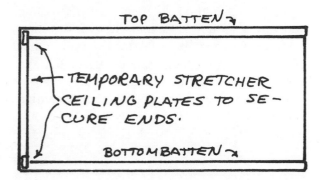

TOP BATTEN

TEMPORARY STRETCHER CEILING PLATES TO SE-CURE ENDS.

BOTTOM BATTEN

to both the top and bottom battens, probably with bolts and wing nuts, and then the sides of the drop may be temporarily stretched and secured with tacks or staples.

A completely different variety of drop has grommets on all sides and is laced into place on a framework. The framework is portable

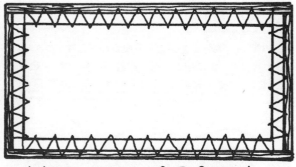

LACED DROP OR SCREEN

and fastened together with bolts and wing nuts. The laces fasten to pegs or screw hooks that are appropriately placed around the frame. Motion picture screens and rear view projection screens of the translucent variety are rigged up in this

fashion so that they can be stretched taut on the framework.

TWO FACED BACKDROP—A backdrop can be painted on both sides and then rigged so that an extra set of lines can be snapped into eyes on the bottom batten and the drop reversed by pulling up the bottom and lowering the top. The lines should be fitted with snap hooks so that they can be hooked and unhooked rapidly. In preparing this style drop the artist paints his designs so that one is upside down in relation to the other.

TRIPPING A DROP—The process used on the drop just described indicates a method of storing a backdrop where there is a relatively low grid. Attach a set of lines to both the top and bottom of the drop. The bottom lines can extend behind the drop and be in place all of

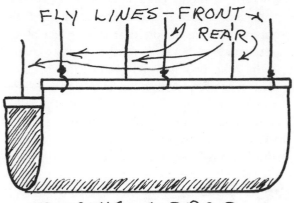

FLY LINES—FRONT

REA'R

TRIPPING A DROP

the time. The drop is then raised as high as possible with the lines attached to the top and then the bottom is raised or "tripped" up far enough to take it out of sight lines.

TRANSLUCENT DROP — The design on a drop may be applied with thin paint or dye. When lighted from the rear this drop will have a pleasant glow that cannot be reproduced by front lighting, especially if the drop is painted with harsh opaque paint. It is also possible to vary this procedure and obtain effects that will alter as the light is changed from the front to the back of the drop. The face of the drop is painted with dyes and the rear of the drop is painted with heavy opaque colors so that sections will allow no light to pass through. The effect when the back lighting is used will be a combination of glowing sky and dark areas of mountains or trees or buildings in silhouette.

SCRIM OR TRANSPARENT DROP—Scrim is an open weave fabric like cheese cloth, marquisette, theatrical gauze, sharktooth gauze, camouflage netting or screening. It is possible to see through this material in the direction of the heaviest concentration of light. This operates like the lace curtains on windows in a home. During the day time when it is lighter outside than inside it is possible to easily see out, but no one can look into the house. At night it is possible to see in when the inside is lighted, but impossible to see out into the darkness. Sheets of material of this open weave nature used on the stage make it possible to conceal actors and objects behind the drop until the light is brought up on that side. The object can be made to fade out again by simply changing the concentration of light to the other side.

ROLL DROP—A regular drop rigged so that it can be rolled up like a window blind is called a roll drop. The top of the drop is securely anchored to an overhead support. The bottom of the drop is fastened to a round or cylindrical

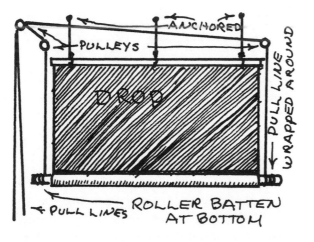

shaped batten. This batten might be made of heavy dowel, cardboard rug or linoleum rolls fastened together, a pole, a downspout from a roof drainage system or any other tubular shaped

material that the drop can be glued or stapled onto. The bottom batten should extend out beyond each side of the drop from 1'-0" to 1'-6" depending upon the height of the drop. A rope is wound around this extension of the cylindrical batten enough times to use up a length equal to the height of the drop. This rope then extends up along the side of the drop at least as high as the top of it, is passed over a pulley and then allowed to drop back down to the floor. Another rope is fastened onto and wound around the batten on the other end in the same way — and wound around in the same direction — front under to back. After the same number of turns have been put on the roller the rope goes up and over a pulley at the top, extends across to a position beside the other rope and is brought down to the floor. Either another pulley can be placed beside the one for

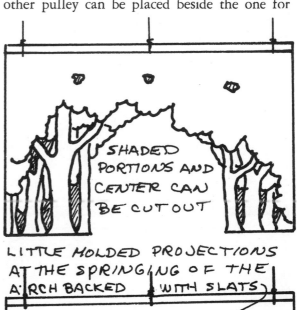

66

the first rope or a double one for both of them to come through. When the ends of the ropes are pulled downward the ropes begin to unwind from the batten and as they unwind the drop rolls up. It will be necessary to have some kind of anchor to fasten the ends of the lines to when the drop is rolled up or a long suffering curtain puller will have to stand and serve as ballast until the curtain is closed.

CUT DROP—The cut drop has sections cut out to represent openings in foliage, doors, windows, archways, cave entrances, spaces between trees or any other kind of opening imaginable. The holes are usually cut out after the drop has been painted so that the material is somewhat stiffened and stretched. Sometimes after the drop has been cut it is found advisable to turn it face down and glue netting across some of the openings to keep the cut edges from curling. If there are small projections extending out in such a way that they are likely to sag a thin strip of wood may be glued so that it extends horizontally across the drop and out into the opening far enough to support the projection.

CONTOUR DROP—The contour drop adds a new variation to the old drop. This type of drop can be suspended in space with all of its sides showing since it is designed with a finished edge on the top, sides and bottom. In place of a plain top batten this unit has a flat of the appropriate contour attached to it. The drop is then glued onto the bottom batten of this flat section and allowed to hang down from there. It may be a plain surface or a cut drop. When flying this unit it is advisable to use wire (piano wire will take the strain easily) for the support extending from the top of the drop up behind the overhead masking where it is attached to the flying lines or counterweight batten.

FABRIC FOR BACKDROP—Muslin, linen and scene duck are materials commonly used for backdrops. For convenience wide material is used. It may be that more than one width is needed for the height of the drop; if so, it may be sewed together with a plain flat seam. It is ordinarily advisable to sew the material so that the seams on the finished drop are horizontal rather than vertical.

CONTOUR DROPS —

Cyclorama

One of the standard background pieces for the stage is the sky cyclorama. It has many uses as a sky, as a neutral background for scenery, as a screen for projected scenery, and as just a plain background for action.

The cyclorama is composed of a large sheet of fabric. The ideal cyclorama will be high enough and wide enough to mask the entire stage area with a minimum of assistance from borders or teasers above and from tormentors

67

or other scenic units on the sides. It is physically impossible to mount a cyclorama on most stages that will accomplish this so usually something less is accepted. The ideal cyclorama begins from a position offstage and upstage from the

CYCLORAMA

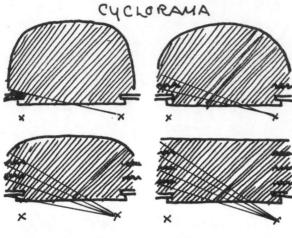

VARIOUS AMOUNTS OF SIDE MASKING NEEDED

proscenium a few feet, moves toward the back of the stage, sweeps around the back of the stage and then moves forward to a position just behind and offstage from the proscenium on the other side of the stage. When this type of cyclorama is installed only a small amount of masking is needed on the sides for the extreme front corner seats; and a minor amount of masking is required above for the extreme front seats. If it isn't possible to have a cyclorama that provides this coverage then as much of the shape and proportions of the ideal cyclorama as possible should be kept. In order to determine the size and shape of the cyclorama gradually move back until the practical proportions for the stage are reached. In the extreme situation the cyclorama will consist of a sheet of muslin stretched straight across the back of the stage. This type of cyclorama should be as wide and high as possible.

Cycloramas may be purchased from theatrical supply houses or manufactured in the theatre. Material of maximum width should

be used and the seams planned to run horizontally. The top should be reinforced with 3" or 4" canvas or burlap webbing and should be provided with grommets placed about every 1'-6". The sides should be hemmed but need not be reinforced with webbing. A few grommets placed along the sides, maybe every 3' or 4', will be helpful if the material needs to be pulled taut when in place. The bottom may have a chain or pipe pocket hem or it may be reinforced and grommetted like the top. The bottom is treated this way to hold it down with weights or tie lines in order to get a wrinkle free sky.

Various fabrics can be used. The ideal material is pale blue or aqua colored velour since velour has such pleasant texture. However, this is also the most expensive material to use and for that reason impractical in many theatres. Material similar to light blue denim can be used. It should be checked carefully under lights to be certain that there is no dye variation within the width of a piece or from bolt to bolt. At best there will be slight variations that will cause the seams to be visible. Muslin, linen or scene duck may be used. These should be painted with dye after they have been sewn and stretched out. If possible they should be in place where they are to be used before any dying or painting is done. If dye is impractical the surface may be painted with scene paint. Although it may be possible to get a smoother paint job by using a spray gun yet at the same time the tiny spray that flies off into the air will probably be found all over the building upon completion of the job. At any rate some method should be used that will produce a smooth, even, blue surface.

There is probably no other single unit of scenery that will be used as much or be as pleasant with which to work as a smooth, beautifully painted cyclorama. On the other hand, nothing is quite so disheartening as to have to work with one that is dirty, stained and torn.

* * * * *

With a basic knowledge of the construction

of various types of flat and drop scenery it is possible for the theatre technician to plan and build other units that are similar. There should be no hard and fast set of rules concerning construction procedure or materials that can be used for constructing stage scenery. The scene builders of the past used many techniques that were sound and practical but their procedures need not be accepted as today's end standard. The easiest, fastest and most efficient method should be accepted as long as the end product will stand the abuse of stage handling.

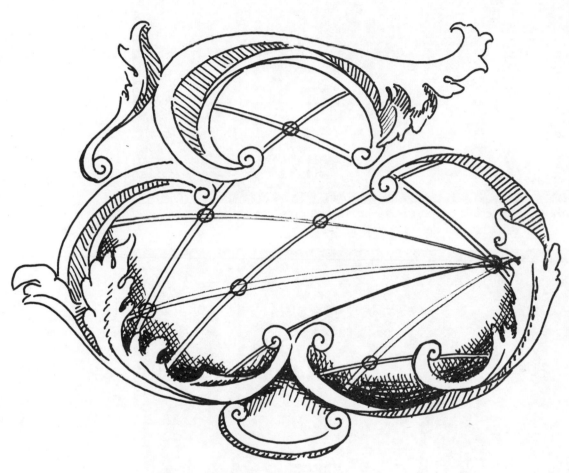

ROCOCO DESIGN

The Ghost of Mr. Penny.   Setting consists of two rooms side by side.

The Petrified Forest.   Numerous properties are needed to dress the setting for this Arizona desert eating joint.

Another Part of the Forest.   Heavy cardboard forms are here used for columns.

## 4

Three Dimensional Forms

Three dimensional and molded forms are used in conjunction with flat scenery in the theatre. Some of these forms are platforms, steps, built up rocks, columns, ramps, built up ground sections and mache units of various kinds.

If the theatre has a stock of stage wagons it is easy to convert them into platforms by equipping them with legs. The legs may be fastened on temporarily for a single production or may be made up in reusable sections that are bolted into place. Leg sections can be removed and stored away for future use. A 4'-0" x 8'-0" wagon should have 6 legs under

it to make a substantial platform. If leg sections are used each section may consist of two legs tied and braced together and bolted onto the wagon. Then, on each side, a stringer is bolted across to space and fasten the sections to one another and at least one diagonal brace is fastened on to stabilize the unit. When this is done the wagon becomes an elevated platform. If it is desirable to cover the sides of the platform this may be done with flats, wall board, plywood or muslin. If muslin is used it will be necessary to fasten furring strips to the legs and braces to make them flush with the side of the wagon so that the face of the frame (which will be covered with muslin) will be smooth.

In case the platform is to be 1'-6" or less in height it is possible to fabricate each leg from two pieces of 1" x 6" nailed edge to edge. This type of leg may be fastened in place on the wagon; thus without using ties or braces a fairly substantial platform is created. Bolts and wing nuts or double head nails can be used to make removal of the legs easier.

Short legs may also be made from pieces of heavy plywood which have been tapered so that they are wider at the top than the bottom. Two pieces of plywood should be fastened together edge to edge to form corner legs just as with the two pieces of 1″ x 6″. It may be advisable to nail both pieces to a corner strip of 2″ x 2″ in order to have a more secure corner since the

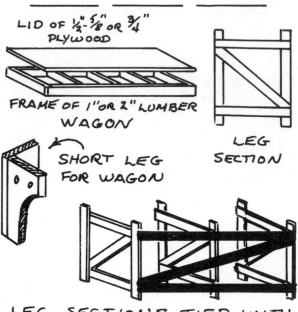

LID OF ½″-⅝″ OR ¾″ PLYWOOD

FRAME OF 1″ OR 2″ LUMBER

WAGON

SHORT LEG FOR WAGON

LEG SECTION

LEG SECTIONS TIED WITH STRINGERS AND BRACES TO MAKE PLATFORM OUT OF WAGON

edge of plywood does not hold nails satisfactorily.

Parallels

Ordinarily stage platforms are made up in the form of parallels. The parallel is a collapsible platform consisting of a removable top and folding support. This type of unit can be stored away more conveniently than the stage wagon.

LIDS — Parallel tops may be made from single pieces of plywood ½″ to ¾″ thick and up to 4′-0″ x 8′-0″ in size. Sheathing plywood will work very well for this purpose and is much less expensive than any of the other grades. It may be necessary to fasten small stop blocks underneath near the corners so that the lids will fit snugly onto the frame, but this can be done very easily. The lid should then be covered with padding of some kind and muslin or

canvas. Canvas is better than muslin because it will withstand much more abuse. The covering should extend over the top and around the edges and then it should be fastened underneath with glue and tacks or staples.

Parallel lids may also be made from square edged boards 1″ x 12″ or narrower or from tongue and groove flooring boards. If boards are used it will be necessary to cleat them together with 1″ x 4″ boards on the underneath sides. The cleats can be spaced to hold the top snugly in place on the frame. This type of lid should also be padded and covered in order to soften the sound of footsteps when the platform is used on the stage.

FRAMES—The support, or parallel, is made of frame sections that are similar to the frames for flats. A 4′-0″ x 8′-0″ parallel will be made of two sections the full length of the platform and the desired height minus the thickness of the lid. There should be two ends and at least

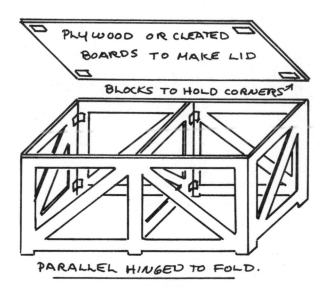

PLYWOOD OR CLEATED BOARDS TO MAKE LID

BLOCKS TO HOLD CORNERS

PARALLEL HINGED TO FOLD.

two other cross frames the width of the platform (minus the thickness of the sides where they are fitted in place) and the height of the platform (minus the thickness of the lid). It may be desirable to design the frames so that the legs extend down to the floor, but the bottom rail should be placed so that it is lifted off the floor by at least half an inch. This will insure a more stable support. There will be less chance of the platform rocking than if the rails are flat on the floor providing a support all of the way around the frame. All of these frames should be provided with diagonal braces to make the platform rigid in all directions.

An alternate method of building the parallel frame makes use of single pieces of plywood for each end, side and cross section. ½" to ¾" sheathing plywood may be used. The framework may then be cut out of the piece of plywood so that it has legs, braces and supports similar to the regular framework but made out of one piece of wood. This method works quite well especially on smaller parallels. It would be impractical to make this type of support for platforms that exceeded in any one direction the size of a regular 4'-0" x 8'-0" sheet of plywood.

HINGING—Hinging the parallel together is a tricky process. The position of the sections should be located rather carefully and then the

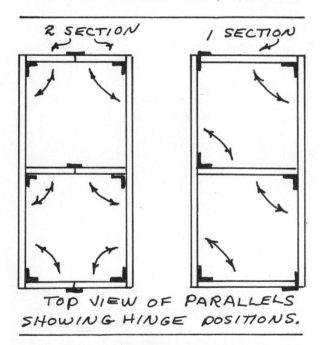

TOP VIEW OF PARALLELS SHOWING HINGE POSITIONS.

hinges placed so that they are lined up with the joint. If the end sections are spaced in about three inches it is possible to place the

hinges on one side of the parallel so that they are on the right side of the ends and cross sections and on the opposite side of the frames on the other side of the parallel. If the ends are spaced flush it will be necessary to place one pair of the hinges so they are half inside the frame and half outside on each end of the framework.

Parallels such as the one just described fold into a pack that is equal to the length of the side plus the length of one end. A 4'-0" x 8'-0" parallel will be 12'-0" long when folded and a 3'-0" x 6'-0" parallel will be 9'-0" long. Cross members of parallels may also be folded in the center; then the folded length will be the same as the open length of the parallel. This type of parallel makes a better stack when stored but requires more time and material for its construction. The hinges should be placed so that the centers of all of the cross sections fold inward.

GENERAL FACTS — Parallels need not be 4'-0" x 8'-0". For a large stage it may be advisable to make them even larger and for small stages it may be advisable to make them smaller. Here as with most of the stage equipment it is a good idea to set up some standard sizes. If more than one size is decided upon it might also be advisable to choose proportions that will work with the other stage equipment. Usually it is necessary to have more parallels than lids since it is possible to use a lid with varying heights of parallels.

When the parallels are completed it may be practical to fasten gliders on the bottom of the legs so that they can be easily moved about the stage. Of course there are times when this can be a disadvantage. If the platform moves too easily it might scoot away when it is supposed to remain planted in one spot.

Parallel sections may be built so that they can be stacked on top of one another to make higher levels. It is also possible to heighten parallels by having extension legs that can be bolted into place when the parallel is assembled.

Frequently it is advisable to fasten the lid to

the parallel so that it will not be noisy when walked upon. Hooks and eyes, loose pin hinges, wood screws or nails may be used for this purpose.

Ramps

Ramps, platforms of more than one elevation, work benches, stage risers for seating and other similar weight supporting stage levels may be built in the form of parallels. The unit may be in any parallelogram form and it may be hinged to fold. Odd forms with one raked

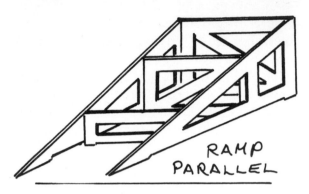

RAMP PARALLEL

end may be rigged so that one corner is fitted with loose pin hinges. After the pins have been removed the rest of the support frame will fold into a compact unit.

To facilitate the handling of parallels, it is a good idea to fasten a tie line permanently onto the parallel so that it is always available to tie up the unit for transportation and storage.

Boxes

Low rectangular boxes of varying sizes are extremely usable on the stage. These may be built one step high (6″ to 8″) and used in many combinations. They may be stacked and used as stairs, covered and used as rocks, or used together to make irregular platform units. ½″ plywood nailed on a 1″ x 6″ frame will make a box 6″ high and ½″ plywood on a 1″ x 8″ frame will make a box 8″ high. Square, triangular, round, ½ round, ¼ round and oblong boxes may all be useful on the stage.

A round, partially round or curved box may

be made by cleating 1″ boards (1″ x 12″ # 2 Common W.P.) together after they have been cut to the desired shape. For a solid box the

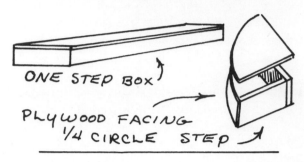

ONE STEP BOX

PLYWOOD FACING
¼ CIRCLE STEP

top and bottom forms should both be provided, although the bottom need only be the contour shape without being a solid support form. ¼″ or ⁵⁄₁₆″ plywood facing, cut so that the grain runs across the narrow direction, can then be nailed around the contour to cover the riser. If the platform or box isn't too large, say not more than 3′-0″ in diameter, it is unnecessary to use inner support other than the plywood facing. If the curves are sharp it may be necessary to either use thinner plywood or paper-type wall board for the riser. Another method of facing curves is to use strips of board between the top and bottom contours for support and then cover the edge with muslin or canvas. If this is done a strip of muslin 4″ to 6″ wider than the thickness of the box is cut and placed so that the material can be glued to both the top and bottom of the box as it is applied.

Step Units

As previously indicated it is possible to make step units by stacking several boxes together. Usually it is more convenient to build step units that can be added to the regular stock of scenery and be reused when needed.

The individual step has three measurements that must be considered when it is constructed. The part of the stair that supports weight is the tread. The tread has width, depth and height. The height is referred to as the "rise" of the step.

The proportions of a set of steps is determined

by the space in which it must fit. Ordinarily there is a landing that must be reached within

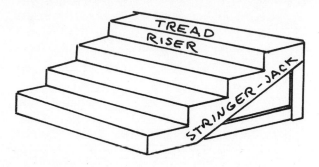

specific confines of width and length. The depth of the tread, height of rise and width of each step will be computed from this spacing.

Stage step units will differ in some details from the stairs in public and private buildings. On the stage the stairway is a device to be used for the actor. It is in a sense a functional acting area consisting of a series of levels one above the other and each tread should be large enough for easy, comfortable and graceful stage movement.

The tread of the step may be almost any width but it is rarely advisable on the stage to have less than 12″ depth to the tread.

The rise of the step unit should be determined partly in terms of other scenic units in stock. In order to work with parallels or platforms it might be advisable to choose a rise that will in multiples be 1′-0″, 1′-6″, 2′-0″, 2′-6″, 3′-0″, 4′-0″, 5′-0″ and 6′-0″ in height. 6″ rise steps are used in most public buildings. In homes rises of 7″ may be found. For the stage multiples of 6″ and multiples of 8″ will work out very well. An 8″ rise is actually rather high for comfortable day in and day out climbing but on the stage it has the advantage of working out with various levels and is a means of gaining height rapidly. A 6″ rise can be used on many stair units and this rise will also work with many platform levels. In general it might be said that 8″ rise steps should be used on large stages for visual proportions and where it is necessary to gain height rapidly and that 6″

steps should be used for graceful appearance and minimum elevation gain.

CONSTRUCTION OF STEPS—Several ways to build step units will be discussed.

The first method uses stringers or jacks for the side contour pieces. The stringer is marked off on a piece of 1″ x 12″ white pine lumber. This piece of lumber should be fairly clear of large knots in order to keep it as strong as possible — any finish grade or carefully selected #1 common grade lumber may be used. The carpenter's square is used for computing the various angles needed for the tread and riser positions. Turn the square on a diagonal across and near one end of the board. Maneuver it so that the 11¾″ mark of the long arm of the square is about 6″ from the end of the board and the 6″ mark on the other arm of the square is at the edge of the board. Mark along both edges of the square. When this is done a right

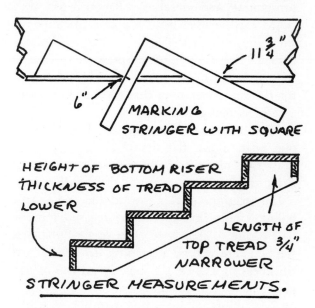

triangle is outlined on the board with the edge of the board serving as the hypotenuse of the triangle. The measurements suggested presuppose that the rise of the step is 6″ and the tread 11¾″ and those measurements on the triangle just drawn represent the positions of those elements on the stringer being marked off on the board. The square is now moved along the board and the process is repeated so that a series of triangles are drawn with their points just touching along the edge of the board. The number of triangles drawn represents the number of steps on the final unit. If two are drawn it will be a two step unit and consequently 12" high; three will make it 1'-6"; four will make it 2'-0" and so on. If 8" risers are desired the measurements used on the square for marking out each step will be 8" on the short arm and 11¾" on the long arm. 11¾" is used for the tread measurement in place of 12" because the width of a 1" x 12" board will be about 11½" to 11¾" and these boards will be the most convenient to use for treads.

Before proceeding with the stringer it is necessary to determine what type of material is to be used for the risers. The unit may be made without facing for the risers, but the facing stiffens the step and makes the entire unit more substantial and durable. Plywood or wall board can be used but 1" boards are superior since they stiffen the leading edge of the step better. For the present purpose the discussion will be based upon the use of 1" x 6" boards for the risers assuming that a set of steps with 6" rise is being built.

Now take the square again. Place it with one edge along the first 12" line that was drawn. This will be the first or bottom step. From the beginning point of the 12" line draw a line at right angles toward the end of the board. This line should be measured to be 5¼" long. This is for the riser of the first step. There will be a tread of ¾" (the actual thickness of a 1" x 12" board) on top of this piece; hence the measurement of 5¼" in place of 6". Now draw a line parallel with the 11¾" line diagonally across to the other side of the board. This will be the under side of the stringer and may be referred to as the bottom of the board. The line just drawn is the foot of the first step. This portion will rest on the floor.

The square is next placed on the 11¾" line representing the top step of the unit. Since the riser is to be a 1" x 6" board and is to fit under the top tread, the support for the top need be only 11" across. So with the square in position in line with the top tread measure 11" on the long arm of the right triangle and at right angles in the opposite direction toward the bottom of the stringer mark across the rest of the board.

The board is now completely marked and the jack or stringer is ready to be cut. Carefully saw along all of the lines.

If this is to be a step unit with permanent legs a side frame may be completed by using 1" x 4" boards to extend back from the foot and down from the back of the stringer to complete a triangle. The finished side stringer section will then look like a right triangle with saw teeth on its hypotenuse side. The boards may be fastened together with slabs of plywood and clout nails. The full height of the side should be equal to the sum of the height of the risers and the length of the side should be equal to the sum of the tread depths.

If the step unit is to be narrow, say from 2'-0" to 2'-6" or even in some cases 3'-0", a single riser on each side of the unit may make it strong enough. If, however, it is to be wider or if it is to carry considerable weight other stringers should be placed underneath and spaced not more than 2'-0" apart.

Next it is necessary to determine the width of the completed step unit. The risers and treads are then carefully measured to that length, squared and cut. A riser and tread will be cut for each individual step. The only piece that will vary in width is the bottom riser which should be ripped so that it is ¾" narrower than the height of the rise. When the tread is nailed on top of the riser the step will be the full planned height.

The risers should be nailed in place first. For a permanent unit it is wise to use screws or coated nails. 1½" flat head screws or 8d box nails are good sizes to use. Nail all of the risers so they are flush on top of the triangle cuts and so their ends are even with the outside of the stringers. After the risers have been nailed in place it is time to fasten the treads onto the stringers and risers. The treads should be placed so they are flush with the front of the risers, and the stringers should be lined up to coincide with the end cut of the tread. If this is carefully done as the unit is being assembled the entire unit should be square and true as far as the steps themselves are concerned. The treads should be nailed into the top edge of the riser and into the stringer at each end. The step should be turned over and the bottom edge of each riser nailed into the side of the tread it is adjacent to.

In order to stabilize the rear edge of the top tread a 1″ x 4″ should be nailed across under this edge. The 1″ x 4″ can be notched into all of the stringers or it can be nailed between the end ones and notched into any others.

The entire unit is further strengthened by nailing a 1″ x 4″ across the back near the bottom to tie the right angle corners of the two side pieces together. A diagonal 1″ x 3″ brace is also advisable.

The step is completed as soon as the treads are padded and then the steps, risers and sides are covered with muslin or light weight canvas.

This type of unit can be built without permanent triangle sections below the stringer. These may be added when the step is being readied for a stage setting. Support sections may also be designed with hinges so that they will fold flat under the steps. Or, the step may be used without legs and supported on the legs of the platform or parallel. When this is done a cleat is nailed across the platform at the right height so that the supporting board under the top step will slide on top of it when at the correct height. Brace cleats or strap iron pieces may be screwed to the board on the step unit so they project down an inch or more. When the step is placed in position, the back of it is lifted enough to allow the cleats to slip over the board on the platform. This simple device will help hold the step in position.

Stringers can be made up in other ways. A straight piece of 1″ x 4″ or 1″ x 6″ can be fitted with triangular pieces fastened onto one edge to form stringers that are the same shape as the ones cut from a single piece of board. These pieces may be cut from scraps of 1″ x 6″. Actually the triangles cut out of the 1″ x 12″ when the regular stringer is made are just the right size. So these individual pieces are

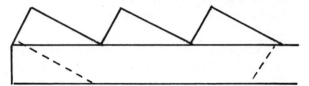

TRIANGULAR BLOCKS FASTENED TO EDGE TO MAKE STRINGER.

STRINGER BUILT FROM SHORT PIECES OF BOARD.

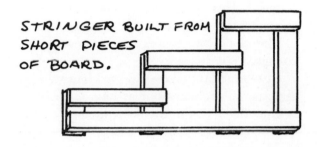

marked out in the same way using the carpenter's square. The simplest way to do this is to mark and cut one carefully and then use it as a pattern when marking out the others. These small triangles are then fastened to one edge of the stringer with slabs of plywood and clout nails. Be careful to get the angles all in the same direction.

Side frames for the step unit can be marked on a piece of plywood and cut out in one piece. It is more difficult to nail the risers and treads securely in place since they must be nailed into the edge of plywood and nails tend to split the plies apart.

The stringers may be solid pieces, marked as for the first type of stringer discussed. Instead of cutting the stringer it is possible to nail strips of 1″ x 2″ or 1″ x 3″ where the treads are to be placed and then nail the treads on top of these. Added strength is then gained by nailing into the tread from the outside of the stringer. Risers may be nailed in without extra strips since they will not carry as much weight as the treads. Risers may be eliminated in this type of step unit but actually they stiffen the treads and add stability to the entire unit. A step unit of this nature without risers may be used as an off stage return from a platform. If the space is restricted in which to reach the floor the steps may be steeper. When the riser is eliminated there is toe space to make climbing easier.

Still another type of stair side may be made as if it were to be a flat frame. Although this type of side support may take longer to build it uses many short pieces of lumber and may be more economical as far as supplies are concerned. This type needs to be carefully designed so that the strain of the treads is carried to the floor; otherwise, the framework will collapse.

CURVED STAIRWAYS—Curved stairways present special problems but as long as each step is supported down to the floor the problems are not too difficult. However, it will take considerable time and material to build one several steps in height.

The curve should first be laid out very carefully on paper and then chalked out on the floor. The floor plan of the curve is laid out and since it shows the treads as they need to be it is possible to easily cut out the pieces for them. Treads may be made of pieces of heavy plywood or pieces of 1″ lumber cleated together.

The major form supports may be built as riser sections that extend from the floor for each step. Except for the first riser these will probably be built in the same way as flat frames with corner blocks and keystones. The first one may be a piece of board the correct height minus the thickness of the tread. If the rise is to be 6″ this will be a 5¼″ wide board — that is, providing the tread is ¾″ thick, which it will be if regular lumber is used.

The front of the tread will be nailed onto the top of this board and the back of it, as well as

the front of the second tread, will be supported by a board 11¼″ high or a frame that high with a strip of 1″ x 4″ spaced 5¼″ to its top fastened to the front of it. The third riser will be 17¼″ in height with a strip of 1″ x 4″ on its face 11¼″ above the floor to support the

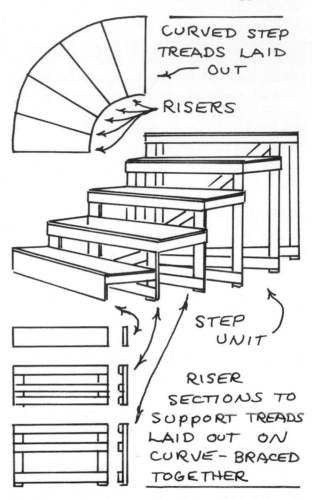

treads of the second and third steps. This process is continued until the top is reached. All the way along in the process the correct width must be maintained for both the risers and the treads. After all of the risers and treads have been made it will be necessary to nail the sections together with 1″ x 4″ strips to tie the riser sections together and to support the ends of the treads. Additional bracing should then be placed where needed.

Firm surface material, such as plywood or

78

wall board, makes the best covering for the sides of the unit. Muslin is not satisfactory for this purpose since it tends to pull in too much in shrinking and flattens the surface.

Curved stair units can also be made from individual step or box units. Each step may be provided with legs the proper height to elevate it into position and then the legs may be tied together with plumber's strap, strap iron or short pieces of wood to make a single stair of the various steps. After the step unit has been used the boxes can be salvaged and used for other purposes. These boxes need not be the exact shape of the desired treads. They may be oblong and overlapped to fit the curved contour shape.

Tubular Forms

Another type of three dimensional form that is frequently needed for stage construction is the tubular form. When and where possible it will be easier to find tubular units that have been manufactured for some commercial purpose and then adapt these forms for use on the stage.

Mailing tubes, heavy cardboard tubes around which rugs, linoleum, plastic and yard goods are wrapped, tubes used in the manufacture of oatmeal boxes, cardboard casings for concrete column forms, cardboard barrels and packing cases — these and many other inexpensive tubular forms may be found in many communities. Round hollow wooden porch columns, dowel, closet poles, aluminum tubing, electrical conduit, iron pipe, asbestos chimney flue liners, aluminum and sheet iron stove pipe are some of the other tubular materials that may be adapted to stage use on occasion.

Smooth, regular, small diameter tubular forms are difficult to make since there are very few inexpensive materials that can be easily and readily bent to conform to the desired curve. A few of the materials that can be curved are: thin wall boards such as EZ Curve Upsom board, ⅛" plywood cut so the exposed grain runs up and down rather than around the

diameter of the curve, corrugated box board with the corrugations running up and down, corrugated paper with only one side faced, building papers such as Sisalcraft, roll roofing, cardboards of various kinds, sheet aluminum and sheet iron.

When building a tubular form it may be possible to use a simple process and simply wind tape or wire diagonally around the form to help it hold its shape. A strip of wood can be used to fasten the two edges at the seam. Tacks or staples can be driven through the material and into the wood.

It may be necessary to build a simple basic frame consisting of circles of the correct diameter and wooden strips to serve as spacers or ties to hold the circles in position and to fasten

BASIC FRAME FOR TUBE FORM

the seam edges of the material. If firm material such as plywood is used it will tend to spring back into its normal flat position so it must be fastened securely. If the surface of the material will stand to be soaked with water and can be softened slightly in this way it will sometimes facilitate the bending process and the material will maintain its new shape better.

In order to use muslin as a covering material for such shapes it is necessary to have a fairly substantial base. Any of the materials mentioned can be covered with muslin after they have been fabricated into the desired shape. A column can be made by nailing closely spaced narrow slats onto end and medial discs. The covered column will have vertical lines where the edges of the strips are located. Before covering the column some of these edges can be sliced down with a draw knife, shaved with a plane or sandpapered with a hand or electric sander in order to produce a smoother surface.

It is also possible to build up columns by laminating layers of wood together and then carving them with a draw knife, wood rasp and plane to produce the desired curve. This is a lengthy process and the resulting column is heavy, but it is certainly sturdy and will stand a great deal of abuse.

Another type of core may be made from one of the various types of wire mesh. Ordinary screen wire can be used if there is to be no strain on the surface. Chicken wire or hardware cloth can also be used. Hardware cloth of ¼", ½" or 1" square weave will make the most substantial base of any of these materials. The wire from which it is manufactured is stiff, which makes it difficult to handle but it can be bent into shape and fastened with stove pipe wire. Chicken wire will also do, but the wire from which it is made is of lighter gauge usually so the form is less solid when completed.

The core, after it has been shaped, can be covered with papier-mache, muslin or possibly both.

Although fluting can be convincingly painted on a columnar surface there are times when it is desirable to have three dimensional columns with indented fluting. First build a core consisting of discs of the correct diameter and wooden slats. The slats should be fairly narrow and spaced an inch or more apart. The size of the slats and spaces will determine the width of the flutes and the space between them. The strips will represent the surface and the spaces the flutes. This is now ready to cover. Glue the muslin to each strip but allow enough material between the strips so that it will sag fairly deeply into the spaces between. If muslin that has been painted once is used there will be less shrinkage when the column is painted and better flutes will be produced than with new muslin.

Miscellaneous Forms

Tubular or column shapes are not the only three dimensional forms that can be made with the wire core and mache. Stumps, logs, log walls, rocks, stone fireplaces and other pieces may be made with these materials.

PAPIER-MÂCHÉ — Basically the acceptable papier-mâché process uses a core or basic form that may be built solid and remain under the covering as a weight bearing portion of the scenic unit. It may be a screen wire, chicken wire or hardware cloth form that will remain permanently or be removed after the paper has hardened; or it may be a modelled or molded form into which the paper is cast and from which the paper is removed after it has hardened.

Weight bearing structures such as the tree and tree house in *The Grass Harp*, Peter's cave in *Peter Pan*, the river bank in *Ah Wilderness*, the rock levels of *High Tor* and other units of this nature should first be built in terms of support areas. These areas should have solid platform structures under them and substantial decks on top. They can be made from paral-

Step forms constructed with a wooden frame which has been covered with hardware cloth and newspapers.

lels, boxes, old chairs, benches, stools or from new material designed to have roughly the basic form needed. Chicken wire or hardware cloth can then be shaped to the correct contour for the finished form. The entire surface is then covered with papier-mâché and for additional strength a finish coating of cloth mâché is applied.

The paper is cut into strips, wide ones for flat surfaces and narrower ones for sharp contours. The strips are pasted in three or four layers over the wire. Any one of various binders may be used. Paper hanger's paste,

Toadstool with removable top. The stem has a disc top and bottom. The top is of hardware cloth bent to shape and covered with paper and cloth mâché.

wheat paste, flour and water (plain or cooked), a weak solution of glue — any of these will work all right. The paper may be dipped into the solution, the paste may be brushed onto it, or, after the first layer has been applied, the

paste may be brushed onto the surface and the dry pieces of paper applied to the pasted surface.

The paper will tend to check and crack as it dries. It is a good idea to allow a layer to dry completely and then apply another. This will make a much more substantial surface. And in order to produce an even more durable covering strips of muslin may be applied over the paper. These may be pasted on or painted on like dutchmen. A mâché surface treated in this way with a coating of cloth over the paper will be much smoother and will withstand more shock than one merely covered with paper.

If the mâché is to be applied inside a cast or over a molded form and then removed when dry the first layer should be wet only with water rather than with paste so that it will not stick in the cast. Succeeding layers may be pasted on top of this. Additional precautions may be taken. If the form that is to be cast over is plain plaster of paris a thin coating of green soap (or any other soap) may be used first to fill the pores and seal the surface of the plaster. If the mâché work is done right after this has dried it should be easily removed. Aluminum foil is an excellent parting agent.

Many types of paper can be used for the mache work. Newsprint is all right but soft when wet. Wrapping paper may be used to produce a tough surface. Paper towels work well since they can be stretched a little and even toilet tissue can be used for comparatively fine finish work.

Sometimes mache surfaces are too fragile and harder finishes are desired. For this any one of a number of materials may be used. These materials are more expensive, but for some uses their permanence may make them more economical in the long run. Some of these materials are Celastic, fibre glass, plastic wood and medical plaster impregnated cast tape.

Plaster of paris or casting plaster and cloth such as net, burlap or cheesecloth may be used. The cloth is dipped into mixed plaster and then placed over the form of chicken wire or whatever it happens to be. Additional cloth and plaster may be added to build the surface to its desired form. The fabric supports the plaster and keeps it from cracking. If additional layers are added after the first have "set" the surface should be wet to reduce the suction and porosity; otherwise, the new layer may not bond firmly.

Three dimensional surface patterns for brick and stone may be made from blocks of wood of the required size glued or stapled to the flat. Thick, pulpy wall board, Styrofoam, foam rubber, rubber castings, cast asbestos pulp and cast mâché forms may also be glued, nailed or stapled onto the surface. Some precast forms of this nature may be purchased from window display shops.

* * * * *

Many three dimensional forms other than those described in this chapter are needed for stage settings. Each play requires its own particular structures, objects and gadgets. Only a clairvoyant could foresee all of these needs. It is to be hoped that the discussion of some of the basic materials, structural problems and building procedures that are described here will aid the stage carpenter in contriving and manufacturing other three dimensional items that are needed for any one particular stage setting.

WROUGHT IRON PATTERNS

## 5

Painting Equipment

A scene painting department can be set up with a minimum of equipment. And then, as the shop continues to operate, other items may be added from time to time. Many of these items need not be purchased, but can be made in the scene shop.

Paint and brushes are the most essential elements in the shop and should be discussed first.

Paint

TYPES OF PAINT — There are four basic types of paint commonly used for painting stage scenery. These four, all water mix paints, are:

1. Dry pigment-size water paint.
2. Resin base paint.
3. Rubber base paint.
4. Casein base paint.

A brief discussion may acquaint the novice with the paints that are available and help him decide which to use.

DRY PIGMENT-SIZE WATER PAINT—Size water, a mixture of glue and water, is used as the liquid carrier for water soluble dry pigments. Size water is made this way: Soak white flake or gelatine glue overnight in just enough water to cover it completely. After it has been soaked, heat the glue in a *double boiler* until it is completely melted. Mix one part of glue to 16 parts of water (1 cup of glue to 1 gallon of water). If the size water is to stand for any length of time, it is advisable to add a preservative to prevent spoiling. A teaspoonful of formaldehyde or carbolic acid added to each gallon of size water is sufficient. If this precaution isn't taken the glue may decompose and give off an extremely unpleasant odor.

Size water may be checked for its adhering power by dipping the fingers into the solution and then allowing the liquid to partially dry. Press the fingers together and they should stick to one another slightly. A little experience helps in judging the correct consistency.

Pigment is added to the size water while it is being stirred. The paint may be tested by dipping a clean stick into it. When the paint covers the stick rather easily, without piling up, or running off and leaving streaks on the clear area of the stick, it is about the right consistency to use. By brushing some of the paint on a flat surface, the consistency can be determined more definitely. If the paint doesn't spread easily it is too thick; if it runs and leaves unpainted rivulet lines it is too thin. Obviously, if it is too thin more pigment is added and if it is too thick more size water is added.

Glue size paint has some definite advantages. There is a wide range of dry colors available; it is relatively inexpensive (especially in the less intense pigment mixes); it is easily cleaned from brushes and other equipment, and it may be scrubbed off surfaces (including flats), if necessary.

On the other hand, glue size paint has some disadvantages. Melting and mixing the glue takes time and is somewhat of a nuisance since a hot plate of some kind must be used. The odor of burning and spoiling glue is most unpleasant. Unless exactly the correct size water and glue mix is used the paint will rub off. Many colors will bleed through from below when new paint is applied over them. The mixed paints disintegrate with age. And the dry powder is a nuisance to store.

It may be added that some theatre supply houses and theatre paint supply companies carry ready made size water in stock.

RESIN BASE PAINT—Resin base type inside house paints have many features that make them good for painting scenery. They are available in a thick paste form. A gallon of paste will, when mixed with water, produce up to a gallon and a half or two gallons of paint. The color range is fair but not as good as that in the dry pigments. The surface finish is flat. And the colors intermix easily and readily and the mix is somewhat predictable.

However, the resins in this type of paint tend to be somewhat "gummy" and accumulate in the brush as the paint is being applied. Brushes must be washed frequently and carefully when this paint is being used. The resins of some of the colors defy almost all cleaning agents.

RUBBER BASE PAINT (*Water Type*)—There are both water and oil type rubber base paints. For the stage the water type should be used. Rubber base paint has one feature that is com-

mendable and absent in all of the other types: the colors remain in suspension so that at any time it is possible to repaint without the newly painted areas showing up as a different color. The rubber base paint comes mixed ready to use and very little water should be added to it. The range of colors changes from brand to brand, but is only fair. It is readily available in almost any paint store.

Rubber base paint dries with a hard, slightly lustrous finish. Where hinges fold, pressing the muslin firmly together, the surfaces tend to stick together so that when the flats are unfolded a small patch of paint will be missing from one side or the other. Rubber paints have an interesting live lustre that none of the other types of paints possess. The lustre isn't great enough to give a shine to the surface, but is just enough to reflect more light than the flat surface of the other paints. However, the surface is almost too hard, especially for backdrops. Rubber paint dries to such a hard finish that a backdrop, when rolled or folded has a stiffness almost like paper.

CASEIN BASE PAINT—Casein base paint has many things in its favor. Its major disadvantage is its cost.

Casein base paint is available in some areas in both powder and heavy paste form, but most stores carry only the paste. Casein is a milk product and has high adhesive qualities. Paint purchased in the paste form will, when mixed, be equal to one and a half to two times its unmixed volume, so the cost isn't as great as it seems when priced by the gallon.

Casein paint comes in a fair range of colors and mixes easily with water. The colors intermix, producing expected results. Even fairly thin solutions of the paint seem to have very good adhesive qualities so they can be used for washes as well as for heavier mixes. There is very little bleeding when new coats of paint are applied over old ones. Although casein paint cannot be washed off after it has hardened completely, it does not crack or peel off as readily as glue size paint. Coat after coat can be applied before there is need for recovering the flats (which is the solution to having to wash off glue size paint.)

The cost is reduced if dry pigment colors, mixed with water to produce a thick paste, are added to white or pastel casein paint to produce the desired color mix. Analine dye and water-mix tube colors may also be used to color casein paint.

Miscellaneous Supplies

A number of other paint products are used in the scene shop from time to time and a slight knowledge of them may be helpful to the scene painter.

METALLIC PAINT — Gold, silver, copper, brass and aluminum paints are needed occasionally for painting stage properties and details on scenery. Finely ground metallic colors are available not only in the metal tones indicated above but also in some colors such as red, green and blue. Gold is available in several values: bright, dull and normal. Most of the metallic paints may be mixed either with glue, bronzing liquid or any other adhesive.

When brushes are used with glue they should be washed with warm water. When they are used with bronzing liquid they can be washed with lacquer thinner and then with soap and water.

METALLIC, GLASS AND PLASTIC CHIPS— Glistening chips of metal, glass and plastic, variously known as flitter and glitter, may be used for special effects. They may be sprinkled onto a surface that has been freshly painted with any good adhesive, such as glue, bronzing liquid or varnish. They should be used sparingly on flexible surfaces since the bending of the surface will cause them to flake off.

FLUORESCENT PAINT—A few minerals will glow when activated by the rays of ultra-violet light while all other substances remain substantially unlighted. It is possible to produce startling effects with this type of paint. The paint is available upon special order from many paint stores.

LUMINOUS PAINT—Sometimes it is conven-ient to paint "spike" marks to locate positions of scenery and properties on the stage floor so that these positions can be located on the dark-ened stage. Luminous paint has a faculty for storing energy while it is being illuminated by the house lights or stage lights. After the lights have been "blacked out" the paint continues to glow.

SHELLAC—Shellac is available in orange or white varieties. Orange shellac colors the surface with an amber glaze while white affects the color very little. Shellac may be used to produce a slight gloss on a surface that has been coated with flat finish paint. It may also be used to cover resin spots on boards that persist in showing through scene paint. Shellac may be used over washes to produce a transparency that will give the appearance of stained glass. Brushes used in shellac should be cleaned with alcohol.

FLOOR WAX—Floor wax may be applied over flat scene paint to produce a slight sheen on a surface.

OIL PAINT—Regular oil paints are not often used around the scene shop (partly because they are flammable), but if they must be used, the equipment can be cleaned with turpentine, paint thinner, gasoline or kerosene. These materials should be kept in the shop only when absolutely necessary.

CLEANER FOR SCENE PAINT—All four of the types of scene paint listed may be cleaned out of brushes by using warm water and mild soap. All brushes should be cleaned immediately after they have been used.

Paint Brushes

Although it is desirable to have a large collection of paint brushes it is better to have a few good ones than a rack full of poor ones. There is one general way to judge the quality of a paint brush: by the length and quality of the bristles. A good paint brush has long flexible bristles that hold their shape until they are practically worn down to the handle. Paying a larger price for a good brush is worth while because the brush will last longer and give better results.

BASING BRUSHES—Brushes that are used for painting large areas should be relatively large and long bristled. It is obvious that sur-

BRUSH FOR "LAYING IN" LARGE AREAS

faces can be painted more rapidly and efficiently with a large brush, than with a small brush. Excellent for this purpose are 7″ or 8″ brushes, frequently referred to as Dutch Primer or Calcimine brushes. The best brushes contain pure bristle but the new flagged-end-nylon are excellent and only about half the cost of the pure bristle brushes. Large brushes cost a good deal, so a small shop is not likely to have more than one or two. Although smaller brushes can be used, it is not advisable to use anything narrower than 4″ for basing in sizable areas.

DETAIL AND LINING BRUSHES — Brushes ranging in size from 1½″ down to ½″ in width with long pure bristles are used for striping and detail work. Brushes known to house painters as "sash tools" are excellent for most work. The 1½″ and 1″ sash tools may be used for almost all work except the finest details which require smaller brushes. Brushes in this category should have long bristles that are care-

CHISEL EDGE

LINING BRUSH SHOULD HAVE CHISEL EDGE

fully "set" in the brush so that a chisel edge is obtained.

Miscellaneous Supplies

There are a number of other supplies that should be added to the paint department's collection. A short description of some of these items follows.

SPONGES — Both a n i m a l and cellulose sponges have a use in the paint department. For most texture processes an animal sponge

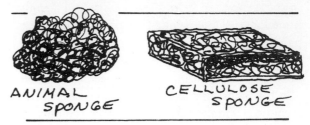

ANIMAL SPONGE   CELLULOSE SPONGE

is superior to the cellulose since it has an irregular rather than a regular patterned surface.

CHALK LINE BOX—Frequently it is necessary to chalk a straight line of some length. A

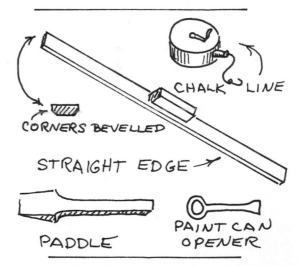

CORNERS BEVELLED

CHALK LINE

STRAIGHT EDGE

PADDLE   PAINT CAN OPENER

chalk line is excellent for this purpose and small boxes containing chalk, reel and string are available.

STRAIGHT EDGES — Straight edges can be made in the shop. The straight edge is a thin, narrow, straight piece of board with a small block in the center of one side for a handle and with the edges of the other side planed on a

86

taper so that the paint will not run under and smudge as the brush is being drawn along the edge to paint a line.

PADDLES — Simple board paddles may be made in the shop. Usually the paint dealer will provide them free on request.

PAINT CAN OPENERS — The paint can opener is a small screw driver type instrument that can be obtained from the paint dealer on request.

PAINT BUCKETS AND CONTAINERS — Almost any type of container can be used to hold paint, including 2½ gallon pails, 5 gallon paint pails, gallon food cans, and large fruit juice cans.

LARGE COMPASSES—Compasses and dividers of large size are difficult to find and expensive to buy when found. Compass devices can be made in a number of ways. Chalk or a pencil tied to the end of a piece of string and then the string held on the center of the radius of the circle and the string or chalk end swept around is one of the simplest. If the string is very long there is danger of stretching and slackening. A strip of wood of the correct length held at the radius center by a nail and the chalk or pencil held in the correct position on the other end and swept around works very well.

TOOL FOR LONG GENTLE CURVES — A long thin strip of wood can be bent around to achieve a desired long gentle curve and while this is held in place a line can be drawn along its side.

STENCIL PAPER—A supply of stencil paper should be available so that stencils can be cut out when they are required.

HOMEMADE STENCIL PAPER — If regular stencil paper is not available a substitute can be made from almost any kind of paper, although heavy wrapping paper or butcher paper will probably hold up better than newsprint or other lightweight paper. Heat the paper with an electric iron and then while it is hot rub the surface with canning paraffin. The paraffin will melt into the paper giving it a waterproof surface that will make acceptable stencils.

MARKING SUPPLIES—Chalk, charcoal and large soft lead pencils can be used for marking out painting details.

PASTELS—Pastels can be used for coloring small areas and for drawing property pictures.

JIGS—Various crutches, aids or jigs should be made as needed and then kept for future use. Special devices for making forms such as curves, eggs and darts, dentils, molding ends, undulating lines, circles, etc., should be designed

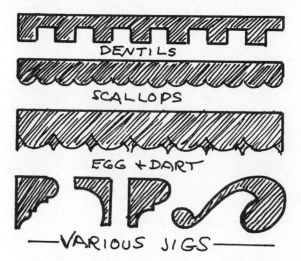

—VARIOUS JIGS—

when repeat forms are needed. Spacing sticks, measuring sticks for standard spacings on a set of flats and many other types of devices will be contrived from time to time and should be retained for future use.

Some of the equipment already suggested as needed in the scene shop (such as steel tapes, carpenter's squares, hammers, staple guns, screw drivers and the various cutting equipment) is necessary, but may be assumed to be available in the normal shop.

* * * *

Although the above list is not complete, it at least includes the important items needed for painting. It is possible to start painting with a brush and a bucket of paint, but as more and more settings are painted many of the above items will be accumulated. Still other items are suggested in the discussion of *Scene Painting*.

Cyrano de Bergerac. Areas of the setting have been blacked out with paint to achieve the effect of a contour edge.

## 6

Color

Since much of the mood and appeal of a stage setting comes from color, the designer needs to be aware of principles that govern its proper use and make it such a versatile element of set decoration. He should have a basic knowledge of the nature of color and the effect of colored light on colored pigment. Moreover, he must know something of the psychology of color.

Colored Pigment

COLOR THEORY—There are a number of color theories, some simple and some relatively complex. For scenic purposes a fairly simple yet practical theory of colored pigments is advisable. The one described here will help the designer mix paints and help him determine how to get the color effects he wants.

COLOR VARIABLES—There are three variable factors in color:
1. Hue
2. Value
3. Chroma

The name usually associated with a color is its *hue.* For example, red, yellow, blue and green are all names of color hues. The *value*

of a color is its apparent lightness or darkness or, in other words, its light reflective quotient. *Chroma* refers to the intensity of a color. A color of high chroma is brilliant or pure.

COLOR FORM—To show these qualities of color and their relationships to each other a three dimensional form is used. This form is

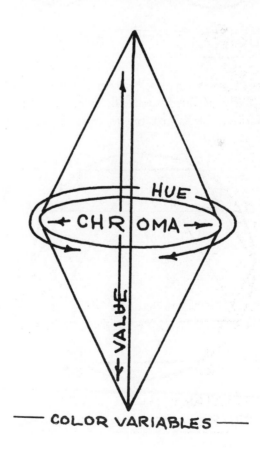

— COLOR VARIABLES —

shaped like a double cone with the bases of the cones together and the points at opposite ends. The qualities of color are distributed on the form as follows: the hues of color are located around the circumference of the widened center; the values are located on an axis running from point to point through the form; chroma is the relative position of the color within the solid form extending inward or across the circular form toward the central axis.

HUE—Infinite variations of color are possible. Around the circumference of the center

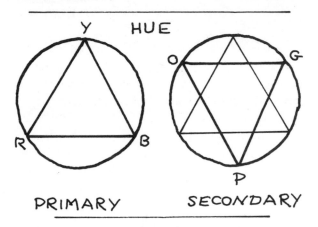

PRIMARY   SECONDARY

of the color form the hues of the rainbow are gradually blended with all of their countless variations. It is possible to start anywhere on

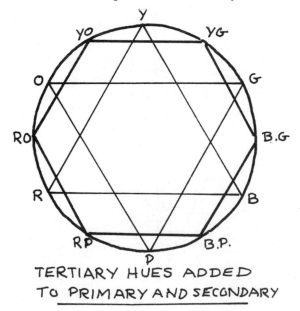

TERTIARY HUES ADDED TO PRIMARY AND SECONDARY

90

the circle and pass around in almost any number of steps. The usual process is to begin with the primary triad of red, blue and yellow. The secondary triad, produced in pigments by mixing pairs of primaries, is composed of purple, green and orange. The tertiaries are produced by mixing adjacent primary and secondary hues: red purple, blue purple, blue green, yellow green, yellow orange, red orange. This process can continue endlessly until it is impossible to differentiate between one hue and its neighbor.

CHROMA—The intensity of a color, or its chroma, is altered by adding other hues. If the hue directly across the wheel is gradually added, there is a systematic graying until finally the center of the circle, or the neutral gray position, is reached. Adding one hue to an-

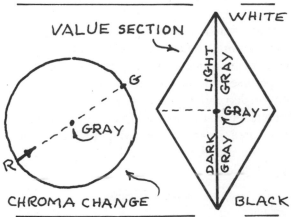

VALUE SECTION

CHROMA CHANGE

other tends to move the final mixture into a position somewhere within the circle and away from the circumference. In other words, the color loses its brilliance and is reduced in chroma.

VALUE—The axis of the double cone represents the value or white-to-black scale. This is frequently referred to as the achromatic scale. If the axis is shown by itself it appears to be a pole, white at the top, progressively darkening to a neutral gray in the center and darkening to black at the bottom. Colors are changed in value by adding white or black. Adding white to a color produces a *tint*, which has a

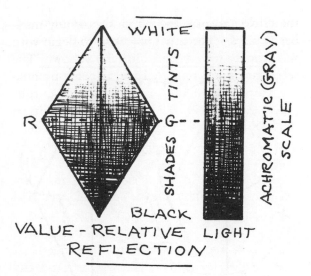

VALUE - RELATIVE LIGHT
REFLECTION

hazy and the mountains seem covered with a sky-colored glaze that makes them almost fade away. They seem distant, indefinite and mystical. Actually, this type of situation completely defies the idea of light value moving forward and deep value receding. The haze covered mountains are light in value but seem distant

CONTRAST - SHARP CONTOUR

HAZE - CLOSE IN VALUE

high light-reflective surface. Shades, which have low light-reflective surfaces, are produced by adding black to a color.

This theory, although brief, contains the basic information needed to mix and use colored pigments. However, the following additional facts about the color form and its use will help the designer in his work.

ACHROMATIC SCALE—An achromatic scale is one without color, composed completely of grays. Black and white photography, black and white printing, and black and white television all make use of this scale. The scale ranges all the way from pure white down to the deepest black. White reflects all of the light that falls upon it and black absorbs all of the light that strikes its surface.

In general light values tend to move forward and dark values tend to recede. In actual practice the opposite may appear true sometimes because of other factors. On the stage and in nature objects which tend to fade into the background appear to move away. In this type of situation the contrasting object gains dominance over the ones that fade into one another. Anyone who has lived in the mountains realizes the truth of this statement. When the sky is clear the mountains seem so near that one could reach out and touch them. They seem sharp, stark and rugged. At other times the sky is

because there is little color contrast between them and the sky. In the other situation there is a high contrast between the deeper values of the mountains and the soft blue of the sky.

Another demonstration that substantiates the theory of dominance and recessiveness may be graphically shown by painting patterns with tint colors on a flat black background. The patterns seem to be suspended in space because they pick up and reflect light, while the background of black absorbs light and seems to have infinite depth.

CHROMATIC SCALE—A chromatic scale of color is a scale of hues as they appear around the circumference of the widest part of the

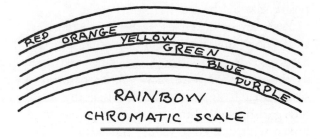

RAINBOW
CHROMATIC SCALE

double cone form. The rainbow is a chromatic scale of color. In fact, the hues appear in what is considered to be their true order in the rainbow form.

MONOCHROMATIC SCALE—In a monochromatic scale of colors one hue and all its variations are used. If one hue is cut out of the color form its monochromatic scale will be in the

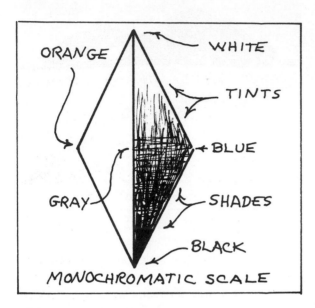

MONOCHROMATIC SCALE

form of a flat isosceles triangle. Infinite variations are possible. The pure color, its complement, black and white are used to get all of these variations. Any amount of white or black—even to and including the pure pigment with none of the hue present—can be used. Only enough of the complement to achieve neutral gray when the two are mixed, which may be an equal volume, can be used. If more than an equal amount of the complement is used the resultant mixture moves to the opposite side of the axis.

Red can be taken as a specific example to show how this works out in actual practice. Saturated or high chroma red is decided upon as the color for a surface. After painting a small area it appears that this is going to be too garish, so a little of the complement is mixed with the red to reduce the chroma. The

color directly across the wheel, the complement, is green. So green is used to gray the red.

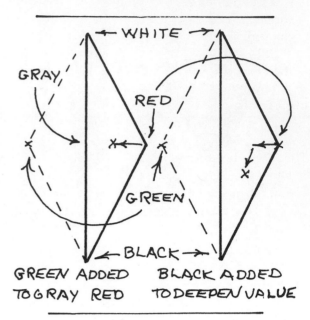

GREEN ADDED TO GRAY RED   BLACK ADDED TO DEEPEN VALUE

If the red happens to be too high in value and reflects too much light some black can be added. After the correct light reflective value is reached it might still be too red so a little green can be added to move it toward the gray scale.

Pink can be mixed in a similar manner. First, white is added to the red to get the correct value. The result might be a sickening pink,

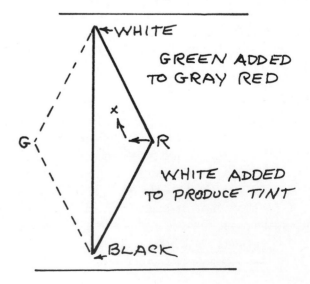

GREEN ADDED TO GRAY RED

WHITE ADDED TO PRODUCE TINT

92

so next a little green is added to cut the effect of the red by reducing the chroma.

The addition of the complement will affect the light reflective value very little but will cut the brilliance or chroma of the color.

All of the red variants described are within the monochromatic scale of red—the lightest of pinks, the darkest of blackened red, the grayest of red and the most brilliant red. Any or all of them can be used with one another—at least in theory.

The above process can be used with any hue—blue, green, orange, purple, red purple or any other—with basically the same results.

COLOR RELATIONSHIPS—There are certain suggestions about using colors together that might be helpful to anyone who has worked very little in this realm. Actually the determination of color combinations that have appeal is a matter of individual feeling, but there are certain general facts to keep in mind.

Any single hue may be used with black, gray or white in almost any quantity.

Any monochromatic combination can be used effectively. A hue, its shades, its tints and its grayed chromas are attractive in combination.

Analagous colors—those immediately adjacent to one another on the wheel—may be used together. Many of them can be used effectively as long as they are not too far apart on the circumference of the wheel. And of course they may be used in varying values.

Analagous color combinations sometimes can be improved by the addition of a small area of the color that is complementary to the dominant one of the group.

Complementary colors of equal dominance and intensity should be avoided. When used together in this way, each tends to accent the other to the point of conflict of interest. So if complements are used together one must be dominant. The dominant one may be of a lower intensity and then the addition of a small area of the other will tend to accent each of them. Yet to say that complementary colors can never be used together would be denying nature some of its best shows. Is there anything as gorgeous as a red rose set off by its brilliant green foliage? In the fall we glory in the sight of leaves turned orange against the purple background of the mountains.

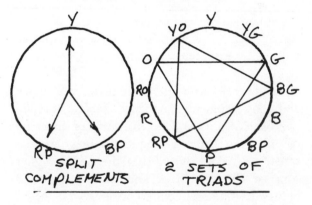

SPLIT COMPLEMENTS   2 SETS OF TRIADS

Split complements are frequently used. One hue is combined not with its complement but with the hues adjacent to the complement.

Triads—colors that are located at the points of an equilateral triangle placed upon the color wheel—may be used together.

COLOR DOMINANCE—In general when any color scheme is employed one hue is dominant over the rest. It is dominant in area, in intensity, in value or in all three. And in a scheme of this nature an important item of

ANALAGOUS COLORS

93

stage business such as a small property, a lamp, a box, a vase, a single flower, an item of wearing apparel or a picture on the wall may have a contrary color, an "accent" that either calls attention to itself deliberately or adds that "touch" which completes the picture.

COLOR FACTS—Unity and coherence can be achieved by using color carefully. If the stage is literally divided with one-half painted one hue and the other half another hue, the two sides seem not to belong to one another. By simply carrying a little of each color over to

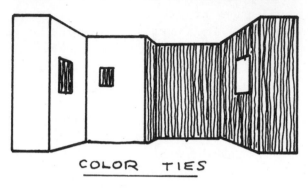

COLOR TIES

the other side of the room the sides will be at least loosely tied together. It is almost like tying the two sides together with pieces of string.

In general warm colors are better with black and cool colors with white. Warm colors appear to have higher reflective surfaces than cool colors, even though frequently they are the same. So it is logical that there is a higher contrast between black and warm colors and between white and cool colors.

Certain colors are associated with warmness while others are associated with coolness. In nature the sunlight seems to be associated with yellows and fire is associated with reds and yellows; these have become known as the warm colors. Coolness is associated with night and the blue of the sky is deeper at night. Foliage has a cooling effect so green is associated with coolness. Blues and greens are considered to be the cool colors. There are probably many other reasons why these associations have been

made, but even this brief explanation may be sufficient to warrant the classification.

Other generalities regarding the use of color can be made, and although these needn't be observed, they are nonetheless true. Comedy usually has a feeling of warmth and a glow that is satisfied with the use of warm hues and tint values. The sombreness of tragedy frequently suggests cool colors and shade values. Mystery plays often carry an aura of shade values. And fantasy has an airiness that is interpreted best by colors that move at least somewhat into the tint area.

Too many tints tend to give an anemic feeling to a setting and too many shades will give a gray, musty feeling. And neither of these feelings can be overcome by the use of lights since the white of tints will reflect too much light and the black of shades will absorb too much and reflect too little light.

Colored Light

Colored pigment cannot be discussed strictly by itself since in the theatre it is always illuminated and light can, and usually does, change the character of the color.

COLORED LIGHT—There are numerous colored light theories just as there are numerous theories about pigments. For the purpose of this study the theory that employs red, green and blue as the primaries will be used. This differs from the pigment color theory which employs red, yellow and blue as the primary colors.

In nature we receive direct and reflected light from the sun. The direct rays are obvious. What isn't so obvious is the fact that everything the sun shines upon reflects light and that there is an intermingling of all these sources of light. If this were not true our surroundings would take on a completely different character. We would live in a world with more blacks since every shadow receiving no reflected light would be perfectly black.

If a beam of white light from the sun is directed through a glass prism it is broken down

94

into a wide range of colored rays of light varying all the way from red on one side of the

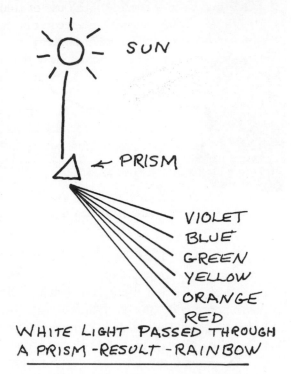

WHITE LIGHT PASSED THROUGH A PRISM -RESULT -RAINBOW

spectrum to purple on the other. When a rainbow appears in the sky basically the same thing occurs that happens when the beam of light is passed through the prism. In one case the light rays are bent as they pass through the glass, and in the other case they are bent as they pass through rain drops and moisture in the atmosphere. Hues fall into the natural order that we accept because they are bent progressively more until purple is reached. Ultra violet, used for special theatrical effects, appears below purple; and infra red, used in secret photography, appears above the red. However, neither ultra violet nor infra red are visible to the eye.

The foregoing discussion is designed to show that white light is a composite of the various individual colors. Experimentally it can be shown that not only is white light composed of many individual colors but that conversely white light may be produced by mixing the beams of various colors. Red, blue and green beams accomplish this effect and consequently

can be accepted as workable primary colors for stage lighting purposes.

All objects have the ability to reflect or absorb certain wave lengths of light. The apparent color of an object is determined by a combination of the wave lengths of light ab-

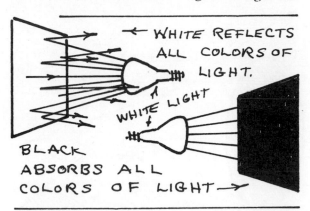

sorbed and those reflected by its surface. A white object reflects all wave lengths, hence it is white. A black object on the other hand absorbs all of the wave lengths and theoretically has no color at all. An object is red because it reflects red wave lengths and absorbs all of the others. A pink object reflects some of all colors but reflects more red than others and so becomes a light value of red or pink. A green surface reflects green, a blue surface reflects

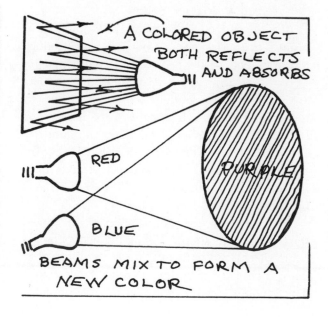

blue, a blue green surface reflects blue and green, a yellow surface reflects red and green, and a purple surface reflects red and blue.

PRIMARY COLORS OF LIGHT—The primary colors of light, as previously listed, are red, blue and green. By mixing additively, that is, by mixing beams of any two primary colors of light, a secondary color is produced. The sec-

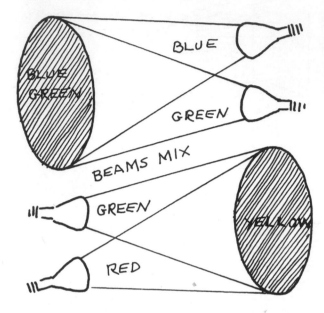

ondaries are produced with these combinations:

    Red + Blue = Purple
    Blue + Green = Blue Green
    Green + Red = Yellow

Mixing can continue from this point combining primaries and secondaries to produce tertiaries and so on just as with pigments.

Now, return to the basic fact that objects are colored because they have the ability to reflect and to absorb certain wave lengths of light. This fact should be borne in mind by everyone who is working with colored light on colored pigment. Many startling things happen in the theatre lighting world that are traced back to this basic idea.

To point out the importance of this idea, start with a question. What happens when a beam of colored light falls upon an object that does not have the ability to reflect that color? The obvious answer, considering the previous

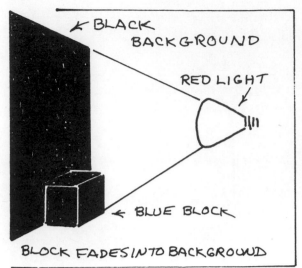

discussion, is that all of the light is absorbed and the object becomes black or at least extremely dark. A red light, for instance, is beamed upon a blue block. If the block is on a black background it will fade completely into that background. If the blue block is on a green background the background and block will both turn almost black. If the blue block is against a red background the block will appear to be black against red since red will reflect red.

To show another effect that operates in bas-

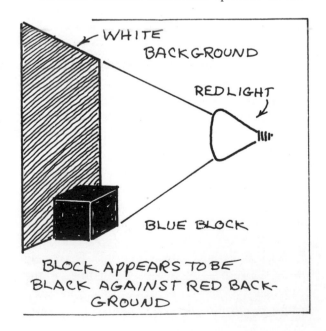

ically the same way, a colored light can be placed so that it shines on a white background. Since a white surface reflects all colors the background will assume the color of the light. If the light is red the surface will appear to be red. Now place a blue block on the surface. The blue block absorbs the light and appears to be black, while the surface reflects the light and appears to be red. Next, place a green block on the surface and the same thing happens — black against red. Finally, put a red block on the surface. The red block fades into the back-

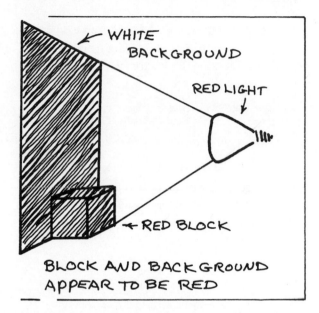

BLOCK AND BACKGROUND APPEAR TO BE RED

ground and cannot be seen at all because both the white and red surfaces have the ability to reflect red rays of light.

By using pure colored beams of light it is possible to make objects seem to appear and disappear. In actual practice on the stage exactly the same thing happens unintentionally at times. For example, a red color medium is placed on a spotlight and that light is used to illuminate actors. Immediately the makeup seems to disappear from the actors' faces. This is logical since the pink of the face and the red of rouge and lipstick all have the ability to reflect red light. They all turn red and the actors have completely red faces. Costumes in this

RED BEAM WASHES OUT ROUGE AND LIPSTICK

BLUE LIGHT TURNS RED LIPSTICK AND ROUGE DARK

case might be made of blue and green materials, which under a red light appear to be black.

In another situation a midnight blue effect is desired. The lights are turned on and the makeup now changes in a different way. The skin takes on a sickening blue color except for the rouge and lipstick areas which become black holes in the actors' heads.

COLOR MEDIA—Mixing the beams of light from various sources is referred to as additive mixing of light. There is also a subtractive method which is used when color media are employed to obtain colored beams. The color media filter out some wave lengths and allow others to pass through. Hence the light is "colored." The probable resulting color can be determined by looking through the color media. Various materials are used for color media, including gelatine, glass, cellophane and other plastics.

To demonstrate the subtractive color method,

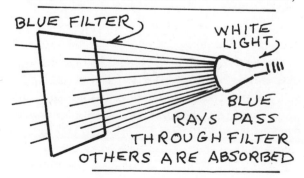

BLUE FILTER

WHITE LIGHT

BLUE RAYS PASS THROUGH FILTER OTHERS ARE ABSORBED

provide a spotlight with a blue color media. All of the beams except blue are absorbed or filtered out and only the blue rays pass through. Then place a green media in front of the blue media. For all intents and purposes all of the

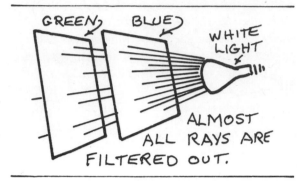

light is now cut out because the green will allow only green rays to pass through and there are no green rays passing through the blue. However, because of the impurity of the media a few rays will probably still come through. To cut these

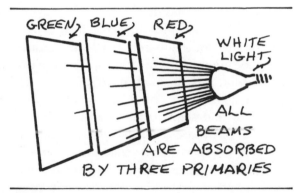

last rays out place a red filter in front of the blue and green. This should absorb all of the other rays.

Colored Light on Colored Pigment

To discover which wave lengths of light will pass through any given filter it is necessary to analyze the color of the filter. Ordinarily in stage lighting pure color media are rarely used except for special effects. Usually tint colors—colors that allow a good deal of white to pass through—are used. They have some filtering

effect and that effect is determined by the amount and colors of the dye in the media.

Here is a random list of colors of gelatine and an analysis of the colors that are likely to pass through.

Light Blue	= White + Blue
Pink	= White + Red
Straw	= White + Red + Green
Lavender	= White + Red + Blue
Light Blue Green	= White + Blue + Green
Chocolate	= White + Dominance of Red + Blue + Green

If two media are placed together in front of a light the resultant color can be approximated. If they are tint colors a good deal of white will pass through. If there are common colors in the dye mix of the color media they will be dominant. So one looks for the common denominators. Here are some likely results:

Light Blue	= White + Blue
Straw	= White + Red + Green

White is the only common denominator and much of it will be filtered out by the three primary colors.

Light Blue	= White + Blue
Lavender	= White + Blue + Red

Blue is a common denominator along with the white so there will be a dominance of blue.

Light Blue Green	= White + Blue + Green
Straw	= White + Green + Red

The green will likely be dominant.

A filter tends to lower the intensity of the beam since as the name implies it cuts out or filters out a portion of the light's rays.

To find the effect of colored light on colored pigment it is necessary to analyze the pigment colors in the mixes used. Here are just a few.

Pink	= White + Red
Blue	= Blue
Orange	= Red + Yellow
Green	= Blue + Yellow
Lavender	= White + Blue + Red
Blue Green	= Blue + Green

The only color that might prove to be confusing as regards its light reflective qualities is yellow. In colored light yellow is made up of red and green wave lengths, so the pigment yellow will reflect both red and green providing both are falling upon it. Yellow will also reflect either red or green alone and take on that color.

COLORED LIGHT AND PIGMENT COMBINATIONS—Here are some combinations of colored lights (L) shining on colored pigments (P) and the probable results. Of course there will be deviations because of color mixes and because of the varied gelatines available so that in actual practice some of the results will not be exactly as analyzed here. In general, though, here are the results.

L. Light Blue Green = White + Blue + Green
P. Lavender = White + Blue + Red

> Since the blue will reflect from the blue surface and the red will tend to turn dark in blue or green light there probably will be a blueness and a darkening of the surface caused by this light.

L. Straw = White + Red + Green
P. Orange = Red + Green + Red (Yellow-Red)

> Straw is basically yellow, although at times it has a touch more of red. This is dominantly yellow on yellow with maybe a slight dominance of red. (Pigment orange is a mixture of yellow and red; and since red and green produce yellow light the combination above is arrived at.)

L. Pink = White + Red
P. Green = Blue + Yellow (Red and Green will reflect from Yellow)

> White light will show the true color of the green while the red portion of the light will tend to gray the green. Undoubtedly a little ruddiness will come through since some red will be reflected by the yellow in the green.

L. Light Blue = White + Blue
P. Orange = Red + Yellow

> The white portion of the light will cause some of the orange to come through, but the blue will tend to neutralize it so the total effect will be a dusty grayed orange.

Although the probable effects can be predetermined when colored light shines on colored pigment, it is always a good idea to make tests under actual stage conditions before deciding definitely about the effect of light on pigment.

Certain light media produce skin tone effects that are flattering. These colors will likely be used. Fortunately, they are tint colors that allow a good deal of white light to pass through. Their general tone is in the pink range. Straws and light blues and lavenders are also frequently used. However, during the ordinary production there are light intensity and color changes not only from scene to scene but even within a scene. These changes tend to enhance the pigment color effects rather than destroy them. Interest is added through the changes in the color and intensity of the light.

Psychology of Color

Certain psychological factors should be considered in any discussion of color. It has been proved experimentally in numerous tests that most people react to color in a similar manner. It is true that some are hypersensitive while others react only in a dull fashion to color. Ideas or experiences associated with specific colors in the past may warp the feelings of scattered individuals, but in general the reactions to particular colors are similar from person to person.

A few of the more important colors and their general feelings and meanings will be discussed. Since these are the basic colors and the colors used most often, a little knowledge about them may be helpful.

YELLOW—Bright, clear, cheerful yellow is associated with sunlight and is sacred to the Chinese and to the European Christian religions. Yellow was used freely in the 1890 period.

The darker yellows, neutralized or grayed yellows and the greenish yellows are frequently associated with sickness and disease; with indecency, cowardice and jealousy; and with deceit and treachery.

Yellow is sixth in a list of popular colors.

RED—Red is one of the most exciting of all

colors and universally the most popular. Defiance and violence are associated with red. The red cape of the bullfighter and the red flag of anarchism are symbols that reflect this spirit. The basic passions of rage, danger, courage, sex and strife are symbolized by red.

It should be noted that red used in large quantities is fatiguing.

GREEN—Green is relatively neutral in its emotional effect. It is the fourth most popular color. Green symbolizes youth and growth. It is restful and associated with faith and immortality.

PURPLE—Purple was one of the rare dyes of the Roman Empire and partly because of its rarity and great cost it was used to dye the Emperor's robes. It symbolizes nobility and also death and sadness and spirituality.

BLUE—Blue projects a feeling of cool serenity. Fidelity and aristocracy are associated with blue. Distance, boundlessness, nothingness are symbolized by blue.

BLACK — Black carries the sombreness of death and the depression of gloom. Yet sharp smartness is achieved by combining white and black.

WHITE — In China white is the color of mourning. In the Western World it is the color for the bride, symbolizing truth, chastity, innocence and purity.

NEUTRAL GRAY—Humility and passive resignation are symbolized by gray, as are sedateness and old age.

There are a few other general facts worth enumerating. In general the warm colors of yellow, orange and red are positive, aggressive and stimulating. The cool colors of blue, green and blue violet are retiring and serene. In general women prefer red and men blue.

There are certain preferred color combinations. Pure colors are preferred to shades and tints in small areas, while in large areas, logically enough, shades and tints are preferred. Contrasted color schemes are more popular than analagous or monochromatic schemes.

* * * *

Knowledge of many other factors concerning color would be of value to the theatre worker. This smattering of information about the nature of color, the effect of colored light on colored pigment and psychological factors concerning color may stimulate the investigation of books devoted to these subjects. There are many excellent books available, a few of which are listed in the bibliography.

GOTHIC ORNAMENT

Painting and Texturing

## 7

When it's time to paint everybody wants to get into the act. And everybody can to a certain point.

Painting is an extremely important step in the preparation of scenery for the stage. Literally everybody can paint—under careful supervision. Painting must be carefully and painstakingly done if it is to be effective. Effectiveness does not depend wholly upon beauty or glamour but it does depend upon the desired effect being achieved. And to achieve effects it is necessary to know some of the basic painting techniques.

Preparation of Surface

PATCHING FLATS — The first step in the painting process is preparation of the surface. If there are any holes in any of the flats they should be patched. Patches may be applied on the surface of the flats or on the back of them. Usually the patch shows no more on the surface than on the back if it is applied before any

of the painting is done. Patches should be made from the same weave material as that used to cover the flats. Cut a piece of material large enough to cover the hole. (Patches should never be smaller than 5" or 6" square.) Apply paint to one side of the patch and to the surface to be patched. Place the patch over the hole, paint side down, and smooth it in place with the fingers and the paint brush. Be certain that the edges are carefully rubbed and smoothed down.

DUTCHMEN—After all of the patches have been put on it is time to apply "dutchmen." Dutchmen are strips of material—the same type material as that used to cover the flats—that are applied over the joints between the flats to cover the hinges and the crack. For a regular hinged joint a dutchman should be about 5" wide, although it can be slightly wider or narrower. For a joint with a tumbler the dutchman should be cut 8" in width.

When applying a dutchman, a coat of paint is put on one side of the dutchman and on the surface it is to cover. While both are wet the dutchman is carefully applied, paint side down, to the joint of the flat. With the fingers and the paint brush, carefully rub the edges outward on both sides in order to secure and stretch

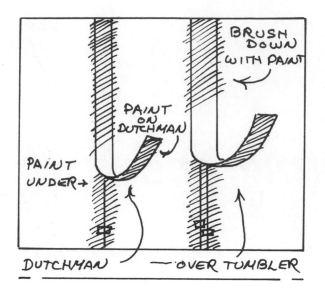

the dutchman so that it will not sink into the crack and so that any loose threads will be imbedded in the paint.

CUT PATCHES AND DUTCHMEN — Both dutchmen and patches are easier to smooth down if the edges are cut rather than torn. Torn edges tend to curl and if a strip of muslin is torn on both edges the chances are that the threads on one edge will curl up and the ones on the other edge will curl down. This makes one edge easy to paint down while the threads on the other edge turn under and produce a thickened edge that cannot be rubbed down and flattened without tediously straightening out the thread ends.

GLUING DUTCHMEN — Dutchmen and patches may also be secured with glue or "dope." Sometimes the glue tends to bleed through and produce a differing color and texture after the flat has been painted.

ADVANTAGE OF PAINTED DUTCHMEN — Dutchmen that are secured with paint fade into the rest of the surface without much difficulty since they are completely coated with the same paint that is used for the surface. So the paint method is recommended over the glue or "dope" process.

When applying dutchmen it is a good idea to stand or lay the flats in a position where they may remain undisturbed until the dutchmen have dried. Otherwise, the dutchmen may pull loose.

Base Painting

BASE COAT—More often than not a stage setting is put together with a conglomeration of flats that were previously used in a variety of productions. Consequently, their surfaces are of many colors and many patterns. To get a good final paint finish it is necessary to bring all these flats to somewhat the same color before starting any of the finish paint process. A base coat, which may consist of almost any neutral color, is therefore applied.

In general if the finish paint is to be a tint, the base should be relatively high in value; and conversely, if the finish coat is to be in a low key, the base should be low in value. If the shop is continuously active it may be standard procedure to mix all of the left overs from the previous production and use that mixture as the basis for the undercoat of paint.

PAINTING TECHNIQUE — When paint is evenly applied to a large surface, it may be referred to as a flat coat. When applying a flat coat use the largest brush that can be handled easily or that is available, and then use a rapid criss-cross or every-whichway stroke. This type of stroke leaves little or no distinguishable pattern. The surface may be painted while laid out flat on the floor, while leaned up against a wall or while secured to a paint frame.

RUNS, PUDDLES AND HOLIDAYS — If the flats are in an upright position the paint should be brushed out carefully and rapidly so there are no streaks or "runs" from the running of surplus paint. If the flats are on the floor the paint should be brushed out so that there are no "puddles" that cause dark and light patterns where superfluous paint was allowed to gather in pools. The puddles take on a different color than the rest of the surface when dry because of the longer drying time they require. The varying density of the pigments causes some to settle to the bottom while others rise to the top. In puddles there is no longer an even mixture of pigment as there is on the surface that dries more rapidly. Blank, unpainted spaces, or "holidays", should also be avoided.

Ground Coat Mix

While the undercoat is drying, paint may be mixed for the ground coat and for the textures that are to be applied with it or over it. The ground coat should be basically the hue, value and chroma desired for the completed surface. The textures will tend to move the color in several directions from this, but the overall effect will return to the ground coat coloration.

Texture Mixes

It is usually desirable to break the paint surface by using various texturing techniques. These are accomplished by employing variations of the ground coat color. Sometimes the textures do not work out as desired colorwise. Frequently they do not work out because the various paint mixes used are too far from the ground color in one direction or another. To correct this fault it is good procedure to begin with some of the ground paint and then move out in various directions by adding other colors to it. For instance, warm texture paint may be produced by taking a container of ground color and adding a little red to it; another container of ground color may have some yellow added to it. Cool textures may be produced by adding blue to one container of ground color

and green to another. Lighter values are produced by adding white to some of the ground color and deeper values by adding black to some of the ground color. Any number of texture colors may be used and each time they are produced by adding a new color to a portion of the ground color. The closer the textures and ground color are in hue, value and chroma the more subtle the finished surface;

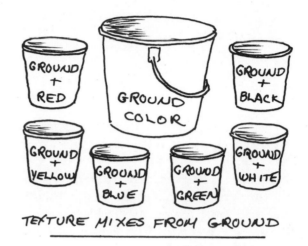

TEXTURE MIXES FROM GROUND

and conversely, the further they are apart the coarser the finished surface.

Texturing

An almost endless variety of texture effects may be achieved through painting. But regardless of what effect is desired or of what devices are used to get the effect, the quality of the finished surface will depend in the main on how carefully and skilfully the undercoat and textures are applied.

Some textures are applied simultaneously with the ground coat while others are applied after it has dried. A few of the processes and how to achieve them are described below.

SCUMBLING—Scumbling is the process of applying texture mixes simultaneously with the ground coat. A brush is used for each color and the colors are alternately applied and partially blended together. The effect is lost with too much brushing since the colors are then completely mixed. This technique is used a

Flats for a large stage production of *Aida* spread on the ground for spattering.

good deal when there is a definite desire to move from one hue, value or chroma to another.

SPATTER—The process of spattering is literally throwing paint out of the brush. A large brush with long, somewhat flexible bristles is best for this process. The brush is swung downward or outward, depending on whether the flats are on the floor or standing up, and stopped when the forearm and brush are parallel with the surface being spattered. The brush may be stopped by snapping the wrist of the brush hand or by swinging the brush and striking it against the free hand. The wrist snapping technique wears out one hand and arm while the striking process wears out both hands and arms. Considerable practice is required before one becomes accomplished at spattering, but it is a process that is used more than any other both by itself and in conjunction with other processes. The spatterer will get better results if he keeps twisting and moving so that the swing is in constantly changing directions. The spatter will be applied in tiny dots if the brush is lightly charged with paint and the brush swung with great vigor. Large dots are made by loading the brush more heavily and swinging with less effort. The first swing, after dipping the brush, should always be an easy one to determine how heavy the spread is going

to be. Then succeeding swings can be regulated accordingly.

When spatter is applied the dots can vary from the size of a pin head to the size of a nail head. They should be evenly distributed unless deliberately planned otherwise. And usually medium sized rather than large or small dots are desirable.

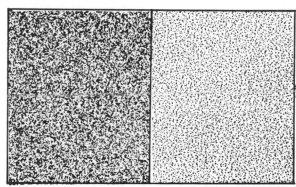

SPATTER WITH A GARDEN SPRAY—Most air pressure tank-type garden disinfectant sprays work well for applying a fine spatter. If used, they should be tried out first on something other than the finished paint surface. It is advisable to turn the valve on while the gun is pointed to a surface off the flats and then sweep into position for the spatter. And it is advisable to finish the run in the same way by sweeping

104

off the surface as the valve is closed. As the valve is turned on and off there are likely to be spurts of paint coming out of the gun. Continuous movement in varying directions while spraying is necessary for successful use of this type of contrivance. It is an excellent device for final toning spatters.

SPATTER BLEND—Rapidly apply a section of ground coat and, while it is wet, spatter texture mixes heavily onto the surface so that there is a blending of the colors. This process works better, of course, with the flats on the floor than with them upright. The results are sometimes extremely satisfying. This process is also known as puddling.

DRY BRUSH—The dry brush technique is another that has varied uses and is one that should be mastered. After the ground coat has been applied, a streak type texture may be put on by pulling a partially charged brush lightly across the surface. The process is much easier if plenty of paint is used in the brush than if the brush is almost dry. The operator must then use a light touch, but he can spread paint for long distances and does not have to press so hard against the surface. This texture may be applied while the ground coat is wet or dry.

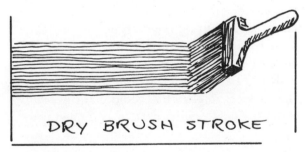

DRY BRUSH STROKE

Usually when it is wet there is a great deal of blending, while on the dry surface definite streaks appear. This is a good texture for simulated wood grain, straw, thatch and many other effects.

CROSS HATCH — Cross hatching is a dry brush technique in which the brush is operated in a criss-cross fashion to streak the surface.

SWIRL STROKE — Another dry brush technique entails the use of a swirl stroke with the

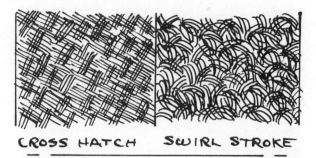

CROSS HATCH   SWIRL STROKE

brush rather than a type of criss-cross stroke. This gives somewhat the effect of roughly trowelled plaster walls.

WET BRUSH CROSS HATCH OR SWIRL — The cross hatch or swirl stroke may be used on a wet base as well as a dry base. With the wet base the stroke should be rather light or too much of the paint will be blended with the ground coat.

LONG STROKE DRY BRUSH—If it is desirable to get long, unbroken dry brush strokes a well loaded paint brush or a narrow push broom may be used. The broom must be handled carefully, but it does an amazingly good job. The broom enables a painter to cover large surfaces rapidly.

WET BRUSH BLEND—Definite movement from one color to another can be accomplished by gradually brushing from one color into another and blending between the two. If the blend isn't as smooth as desired it is possible to spatter the blend area with both of the colors to finish the process.

SPONGE TEXTURE—Texture colors may be applied over the ground coat with the aid of a sponge. The natural or animal sponge is usually better for this purpose than the artificial cellulose sponge since it has a less regular surface. The sponge is partially charged with paint, lightly squeezed and then the paint is applied by lightly pressing the sponge against the flat surface. The patterns should be close together and in order to avoid too much regularity of pattern the sponge is twisted slightly when raised in the air between applications.

Alternate sponge textures might be developed by twisting the sponge on the surface, by stroking it across the surface or by rolling it across the surface.

The sponge is a good paint applicator to use when stencilling a surface. The paint can be applied more lightly and with a less definite edge by means of a sponge than with a brush.

The ends of the bristles of the brush are used to produce the texture.

STIPPLING—The process of stomping paint onto the surface with the ends of the paint brush bristles is called stippling. The term "stomp" should be interpreted lightly.

SLAP STROKE—Textures may be achieved by using the side of the brush and lightly slapping it onto the surface, leaving rectangular patterns. This stroke may be used effectively when painting foliage.

BURLAP STOMP—A texturing tool can be made by taking a piece of burlap about 6" wide and 3' long. Pull threads from one side lengthwise until about 2" of the 6" are without cross threads. Roll the burlap into a tight pack and tie a wire or cord around it. Dip the loose

A push broom being used as a texturing tool.

ends into texture paint and lightly press them against the flat surface.

WASHES—Thin solutions of color, referred to as glazes or washes, may be applied over a painted surface to cut the sharpness or brilliance of the pattern. Washes may be lightly stroked across or spattered onto the surface.

MISCELLANEOUS TEXTURES—Various other devices might be developed for applying textures. Flails, feather dusters, crumpled newspaper, wall texture rollers, rough textured pads, wrinkled burlap on a block, bunched up rags— all of these can be used. There are no rules regarding the tools that must be used to produce paint textures.

However, in spite of the fact that there are no rules, there are some general suggestions about textures that are helpful to the applier.

Use several colors. Do not be satisfied until the surface has a finished look.

To get a more interesting surface, "spot areas" of more intense color may be applied

The flat surface of a set piece for *The Madwoman of Chaillot* with shadows painted on to achieve a three dimensional effect.

here and there on the surface first, using the texture technique that will be used for the rest of the surface. The texture is then applied over the top and when it has been evenly applied the under colors will project slight alterations in the surface here and there.

When the overall texture has been completed the surface should be complex enough and the applications dense enough that the total effect from a short distance is one of a blend of color. It should be difficult to distinguish between the ground coat and the textures.

If the effect is too broad when the textures have been completed, the entire surface may be spattered with the ground coat to bring it back toward the original mix. The texture mixes may also be used as spatters for softening effects.

Spatters may be used over a texture to high light or to shadow or to soften the total effect.

If there is considerable doubt about the color of the light to be used for a setting, or if it is certain that the light color will change from time to time, it is good practice to use textures

of many hues to insure pleasant and varied light reflective surfaces under all conditions.

Specific Procedures

AERIAL PERSPECTIVE—If distance is to be achieved on objects, ground rows or backdrops and there is a sky effect in the background, aerial perspective may be used. To accomplish this the objects are spattered with the color of the background. The nearer they are to the background, the heavier they should be spattered. As they approach the color of the background they fade into it more and more. Near objects, or objects designed to appear to be in the foreground, should be painted in contrasting colors. Heavier textures, more intense colors or heavier values will all help to achieve this effect.

If the background is black, objects in the foreground will stand out more if painted in light values. And to achieve the effect of fading into the background, one uses dark spatters on surfaces. Other colors work in basically the

107

same way. Dominance is gained by contrast and recession by similarity in color.

PROJECTING FORM WITH PAINT — With these painting techniques in mind it is easier to explain how specific effects can be achieved. It is frequently easier to paint a flat surface to give the impression of roundness than it is to build three dimensional forms. Tree trunks, columns, cannon barrels, posts and logs can all be simulated on a flat surface. The basic process of revealing the form is the same regardless of what the object happens to be. In this case it can truly be said that "It's a question of values."

Basically, it is possible to give any painted surface three dimensional form by the use of varying values of a color. To repeat a statement already made, light values tend to make a surface advance and deep values make it recede. The form of an object is revealed to the eye through the ability of the surfaces to reflect or to absorb light. Simple forms are made up of a series of simple planes; usually each plane has a different value depending upon its position in relation to the source of light. If one plane faces the light directly it has a high value. A receding surface might be less bright and have a slightly lower value since the light strikes it on an angle. A third area receives only reflected light and has a deeper value. Still another surface has hardly any light falling on it

and appears to be the darkest value of all. In reproducing the form, the painter will use four values of paint to reproduce the ability of the four areas to reflect light. If he were using an achromatic scale the paints might be white, high value gray, low value gray and black. These four would give high contrast.

THE CURVED FORM—Now to return to the column form. This can be reproduced by employing three values of color. A ground color may be chosen. From one portion of this a high light value is made by mixing in some white. Another portion of the ground color can be mixed with black to make a shadow paint.

The form can be painted by using any of several texture processes. Assume that a 1'-6" x

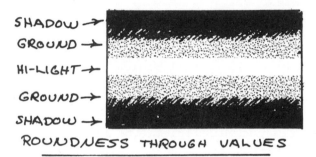

SHADOW →
GROUND →
HI-LIGHT →
GROUND →
SHADOW →

ROUNDNESS THROUGH VALUES

10'-0" jog is to represent a column. Start at one end and paint the center 12" the full length of the flat. With another brush rapidly brush some of the deep value along each side of the flat extending over to the 12" strip of ground color. Then, where the ground color and deep value meet brush them into one another, blending as smoothly as possible. It may be necessary to use both brushes and work both colors together just a little. Be careful not to blend too far in either direction or all of the surface will become a mixture of the two colors. After this has been done, take a small brush and paint a streak of the light value down the center of the flat. Work this just a little, blending it slightly into the ground color. As the final step in the process, paint the remaining portions of the edge with the deep value. If there are areas that need just a little more blending,

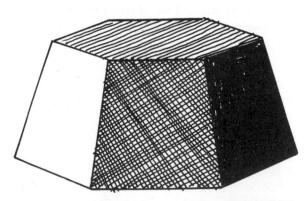

VALUES OF COLOR TO INDICATE VARIATIONS IN LIGHT REFLECTION

take a brush and some plain water and brush carefully over the surface. The water will tend to soften the paint and allow it to run together a little more. The water should be used only where and when necessary and used sparingly.

Now stand the flat up and move back a few steps and look at it. The first trial may be a bit ragged since this is a difficult process, but the form will begin to reveal itself. With practice, working more rapidly and carefully and painting relatively small areas at a time, more skill in this process can be achieved. The surface may be spattered to finish and soften the effect. It may be spattered with one or with all of the paints used.

The other methods of painting to achieve somewhat this same effect permit the complete painting of the surface with the ground color. After this has been done and the paint has been allowed to dry, it is possible to proceed in one of various ways.

If all of the surface except 2″ of the center is masked with boards, old flats or paper, it is possible to spatter a light value strip down the center. After this has been done, remove the masking and place a 10″ or 12″ board or strip of paper down the center so that only about 4″ of each side of the flat is exposed. These two side strips can now be spattered with the dark value. Remove the center masking. If there is too much contrast between the strips or if the result seems harsh, it is possible to spatter the entire surface with one or all of the colors. After one has become adept at spattering he can spatter a surface like this almost without using any masking. The maskings do provide a sharp edged demarcation between value areas that sometimes is needed to help sharpen the form.

The high light and shadows may be applied by using the dry brush technique or by using a sponge or by using a shadow wash of a little black in a lot of water and a high light wash of a little white in a lot of water. Whichever method is used, the basic plan is the same— darken the edges and lighten the center.

It is possible to move the apparent light source over to one side by painting the shadow area on one side wider than on the other side of the flat. The high light should then be moved in the same direction so that it will have the correct relationship with the shadows.

LIGHT SOURCE—When painting three dimensional forms on flat surfaces, the apparent light source must be considered in order to get the high lights and shadows in their correct relationship to one another and to the light. In general, where no definite light source such as a window, lamp or fire is indicated, it may be assumed that a natural direction and angle is motivated.

Sunlight shines down on an angle during a great portion of the day and forms reveal themselves best during those hours of the morning and afternoon when the angle is from 30 to 45 degrees. Usually the painting is not so exact that it requires precise angles for the light source, but general direction is a definite aid in determining the location of high lights and shadows.

MOLDINGS—Almost all moldings—wood, metal, plaster or plastic—are modeled from a few basic forms. These consist of the square, the oblong, the triangle, the circle and the oval.

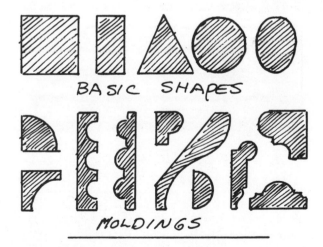

BASIC SHAPES

MOLDINGS

The inside or outside shape of the form and simple distortions may be used either alone or in combinations.

Moldings may be analyzed in a simple man-

109

ner to determine how and where to use high light and shadows to give an impression of the form on a flat surface. In general, breaks in direction of the surface will show as sharp lines and may be painted that way. If one side of the break is especially sharp it may catch a glint of light. The light is indicated with a narrow stripe of high light paint. If the other side of the break recedes it casts a shadow so it will have a shadow value painted next to it.

Undercuts, straight or curved, will tend to be in shadow while overcuts, straight or curved, will pick up high light. Complex moldings are made up of many of these individual shapes placed one above the other and can be analyzed in terms of the individual shapes. It may be that the position of an undercut under a heavy downward curve will cast a shadow across the whole form. The painting should take such things into account, although at times it may

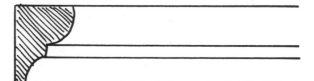

LINES REPRESENT CHANGES IN DIRECTION OF THE SURFACE

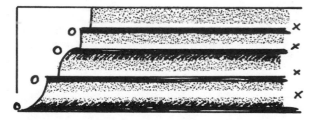

x = HIGH LIGHT
o = SHADOW

be necessary to take some license to project the shape more clearly.

SHADOW WASHES—Shadow washes, mentioned before, are convenient to use on moldings and many other shapes since it is possible to lower the value of any color by using the same wash. The wash should be mixed carefully, adding just enough black to a container of water to get a wash that will lower the value of the surface it covers by one or two steps. It should be tested carefully before being used on a surface that is almost finished. The wash should be applied with careful, continuous, unbroken strokes of the brush.

Moldings may have complex carvings within their surface. Dentils (blocks), egg and dart forms, leaf forms and other forms may appear on a quarter circle curve or on a flat surface.

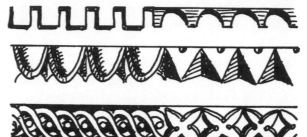

MOLDING PATTERNS DRAWN ON SURFACE—HIGH LIGHT AND SHADOW ADDED TO GIVE DIMENSION

These should be treated just like the rest of the molding. Outline the shape, use high light where the light strikes and use shadow wash where there are undercuts or where no light strikes the surface.

WOOD GRAINING—Wood grain effects are achieved by means of the dry brush process. But before the dry brushing begins it is necessary to decide upon the desired general coloration so that the ground coat can be prepared accordingly. Finished wood surfaces range all the way from the honey color of pine to the black of ebony. After the ground coat has been mixed, use the texture mixing process and prepare three or four—or even more—colors from the ground coat.

After the ground coat has been applied, prepare for the dry brushing by drawing the board outlines with chalk or charcoal. Before the graining can start it is necessary to decide the

110

directions in which the various boards run. Ordinarily, to gain strength, the grain of the boards will run in the longest direction of the

DRY BRUSH WOOD GRAIN IN DESIRED DIRECTION.

measured space. This is especially true in panelled rooms where some wood runs in all directions. The frame runs around a panel and so does the wood grain. Look at wood. See how it fits together, how the grain looks, what the malformations, grain patterns and texture look like. It is rarely necessary to be so exacting on the stage that specific kinds of wood have to be suggested, but the general effects are used frequently.

If pleasant color variations are desired in the wood area—especially if the area is large—dry brush a few areas of more intense texture mixes here and there at random. Be careful that it isn't too spotty. Make the strokes rather long but not too evenly distributed.

Now dry brush the other paints onto the surface in the correct directions with long, uninterrupted, but light strokes. Be certain that paint flows from the brush, but do not allow so much to flow that each brushing covers the ones underneath. When the project is finished it should be possible to see the strokes of all of the mixes even though, in general, there is a slight blending from one to the other.

Begin strokes carefully where a board ends, brush as far as possible and end with a light up-sweep to produce a "feather-edge" rather than a hard edge. If it is necessary to start again and continue from the point where the brush was stopped in a feather-edge stroke, either sweep in lightly continuing in the same direction, or begin from the other end and finish by brushing into the feather-edge with another feather-edge. Heavy or hard edges should occur only at the ends of boards or at joints between two boards.

If the effect is too broad, or has moved too far from the original color, it is possible to dry brush some of the ground color over the top of all the other dry brush colors.

A room may have an entire wall panelled in wood, may have panel areas on each wall, or may have trim consisting of base board, casing around doors and windows, ceiling molding, picture molding, chair rail molding, or special wood areas. Whatever the wood areas they may be treated as indicated above. If it is wood, surface grain will be likely to show through even if it has been coated with paint.

GRAINING WITHOUT SPECIAL GROUND— In order to short circuit the painting process it is sometimes possible and practical to grain over the regular ground coat used for the walls of the set. If graining is carefully done with several mixes the results are perfectly satisfactory, especially if it is desirable to have the trim on the wood appear to be almost the same color, texture, and value as the walls.

LINING—After the graining has been completed the board edges are striped with lining color. The lining color may be black or a deep value of the ground color. Black has advantages in that it can be used as a standard outlining paint for all colors. However, it provides a high contrast against a light value color and should be checked for appearance. The painter will have to be the final judge as to which— dark value or black—should be used. While the striping is being done it is necessary to determine where edges will show and draw two lines to represent the thickness of the board. And where there are moldings, lines should be painted for all of the direction breaks in the surface.

DRAWING LINES—A brush about the size of a 1″ sash tool (window sash brush) can be used for painting lines. After dipping the brush in paint the bristles are carefully shaped on the edge of the paint container to get a trim chisel edge. A brush that shapes to a fine edge is important when painting lines. Place the straight edge in position where the line is to be drawn. Hold the brush at right angles to the surface so that the bristle tips all of the way across the brush touch the surface. Stroke the brush lightly along beside the straight edge, hardly bending the bristles, and an even, narrow line can be drawn. The pressure on the

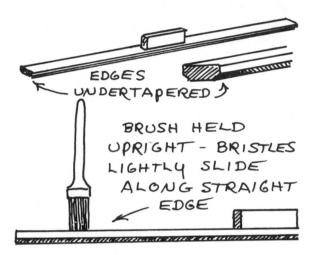

EDGES UNDERTAPERED

BRUSH HELD UPRIGHT - BRISTLES LIGHTLY SLIDE ALONG STRAIGHT EDGE

brush and on the straight edge should be so light that the straight edge need hardly be held in place. Wider lines may be drawn by placing slightly more pressure on the brush. By turning the brush sideways it is possible to get lines that are a full inch in width, and by applying pressure even wider lines can be painted. Use a larger brush and even the light touch lines are wider.

SHADOWS—Locate a light direction and determine the shape of the wood to find where shadows will be placed. A little freedom may be taken. If a strip of molding projects out from the wall a light shadow may be drawn above it on the wall and a wider one below it on the wall. The molding itself will require shadows for undercuts to reveal its shape. The side of a door casing will cast a slight shadow if it is away from the light. Here again a light

shadow can be painted on the wall all of the way around to make the wood seem to project out from the wall.

SHADOW ON WALL NEXT TO HOLDING TO INCREASE PROJECTION

MOLDING PAINTED ON FLAT SURFACE TO REPRESENT 3 DIMENSIONAL FORM AT LEFT

To reveal three dimensional form, shadows are generally painted under projecting surfaces and next to the side away from the light source.

HIGHLIGHTS—Highlights usually consist of narrow lines of light value or light wash paint. High light placed adjacent to a shadow will heighten the effect of the shadow. All sharp edges will usually catch high light.

To reveal three dimensional form, high lights should be placed on the surface edges of projecting forms and on the light source side.

PANELLING—Ordinarily panels are recessed areas with molding to contour the break from the edge of the framing board down into the panel. There are times when panels are built in reverse with the panel projecting above the framing members, but this is exceptional.

Draw the molding line breaks and the board edges with narrow lines of shadow value or black. If the panel is recessed there will be a shadow at the top where the molding cuts down to the panel and there will also be a shadow on the light direction side. High lights can be drawn between each pair of lines on the bottom and on the side away from the light. A high light may also be drawn next to the out-

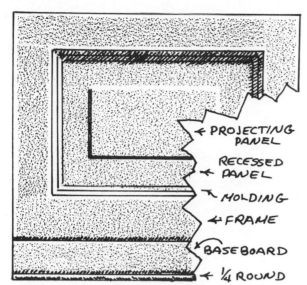

← PROJECTING PANEL

RECESSED
← PANEL

↖ MOLDING

←FRAME

← BASEBOARD

← ¼ ROUND

USE OF HIGH LIGHT AND SHADOW IN PAINTING PANELS.

side black line all of the way around. This high light accents the sharp edge of the framing board.

On a projecting panel the area pattern will be reversed.

ROUGH BOARDS — Boards are not always smooth. Sheds, barns, fences, shacks, piers and frontier houses may be built of rough timber. The texture is coarse, so the dry brushing should be broad and probably have some contrast. Boards do not fit together perfectly so there should be some double lines where the sides try to meet one another. The boards are random cut in width and probably have some knots and even knot holes in them. Knots may be made by painting rough circles of shadow wash

ROUGH BOARD FENCE

with grain lines that form concentric patterns moving around and out from them in a haphazard fashion. The boards may have checks and splits in their ends. And they may be fastened with oversized nails or pegs which may be indicated by drawing small circles or partial circles with the upper half light in value and the lower half dark in value. The upper half may even be drawn with chalk.

FLUTED COLUMNS — Various methods of painting to make a flat surface seem curved have already been described. Frequently when columns are painted in this way it is desirable to indicate fluting (indented half round carving) or reeding (half round applied to the surface). A round column appears to have flutes that diminish in width as they approach the sides. It may be difficult to draw the flutes free hand and get the correct proportional narrowing. Here is a mechanical method of computing the proportionate positions of the flutes.

Draw a horizontal cross section (through the column) having a diameter equal to the width of the column being painted. Determine the width and depth of the flutes and draw them in position on the circular cross section. Next

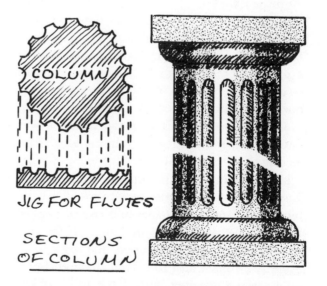

COLUMN

JIG FOR FLUTES

SECTIONS OF COLUMN

draw a line across the circle through the center of the radius. Then drop lines down at right angles to this from both edges of each flute on the half of the column below the line. This will provide the painter with the relationship between the flutes. A jig may be easily made from this by drawing the positions of these lines on a strip of board. The jig will be even more useful if the curves for the tops and bottoms of the flutes are cut into the edge of the strip of board. The center curve is a half circle. The rest of the curves will be gradually squashed in.

Use the jig to locate the positions for the vertical lines on the flute and draw them in place with chalk. The light source direction was determined when the surface was given its roundness treatment, so this direction should be used in drawing the flutes. Each flute has two lines to represent its edges. The one toward the light side will be striped with dark value or shadow paint. A little more than half the circle above will also be painted since it will have a shadow cast under it. Now the other line and most of the bottom will be painted with the high light and the flute is completed. Repeat the process for the other flutes, gradually diminishing the high light until none is used where the shadows will be the heaviest on the sides.

Although this isn't an exact duplication of the appearance of the column, it will project the shape. Under real conditions there will be a place where the high light and shadow will change from one side of the flute to the other, but that is for easel artists to paint.

CAPITALS—Capitals that top columns will have shapes that conform to the style of architecture used for the column. Some capitals are relatively simple while others are complex. The simple ones frequently consist of a combination of molding shapes and can be painted in much the same way as molding. If the capital moldings extend around the column it might be a good idea to extend the high lights only across the center half of the width of the flat to project the feeling of the light being less intense on the sides of the column.

If a more complex form, like the Corinthian

capital, is to be painted it will be wise to cut a pattern out of paper first. Draw all of the detail lines on this. Then cut off a section and use the pattern to draw the line of the cut on the flat. Cut off another and trace the new con-

DRAW ENTIRE CAPITAL PATTERN—CUT TO PIECES—TRANSFER ONTO FLAT.

tour. This process may be continued until all of the pattern has been transferred to the flat. The lines may be drawn with a pencil, with chalk or with a brush and paint. If several columns are being made each set of lines should be put on all of the columns before another section of the pattern is cut.

After all of the lines have been striped in place determine the high light and shadow positions and paint them in. The process is really easier than it seems and the results are amazing.

STONE—Stonework has tremendous variation. There are coarse textured stones in rough and smooth finish, in regular cut stone shapes and field stone shapes. And there are smooth textured stones in broken and cut shapes with broken and smoothly eroded edges. It is necessary to determine the general color desired and the general feeling to be projected by the

A FEW VARIETIES OF STONES

stone before one can attempt to draw and paint it.

If a feeling of overpowering weight is desired huge blocks of rough textured granite in grays might be used for a wall. Heavy sponging textures with blues and greens and perhaps

STONES OF HEAVY TEX- TURE AND VALUE

some purple for warmth might be used as under textures. An over all texture of deep value gray sponged over the top might give the desired coarse texture. The outlines could be painted free hand with general rectangular form of slightly irregular lines. The high lights and shadows could be sponged carefully—

sponged to keep the same rough feeling used on the rest of the surface.

If a setting using a paint texture like the stones just mentioned is fairly tall and enclosed or masked with black drapes, the upper portion of the flats can be heavily spattered with black, the spatter blending out as it comes downward and fading out by the time head height is reached. This treatment will give a feeling of great height, since the top cannot be seen, and at the same time a feeling of great oppression, since the weight of the black seems to pull downward. The large stones will give a feeling of vastness and strength.

Smooth, sharply defined stone might be used for the wall around the home of a well-to-do Victorian. The stones would probably require subtle texturing. The color might change slightly from stone to stone by either varying the texture colors used or varying the order in which they are applied. The stone will usually take on a little more of the hue of the last texture color applied. An over all spatter or a stone by stone sponging could be used. If the spatter texture is used, the change will be general with the areas of spatter varying, while with the sponging individual stones can be sponged. Of course a rather tedious process of masking all but one stone and spattering stone by stone could be used to change the spatter on individual stones. The outlines of these stones would be sharply drawn and the high light and shadow areas carefully defined. The edges of the stones might be tapered or flat; might have

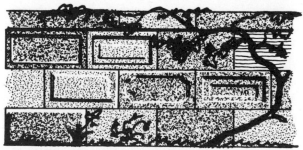

A FEW TREATMENTS FOR SMOOTH CUT STONE EFFECTS.

a raised center panel or a recessed panel. These are but a few of the variations possible.

A fireplace in a cabin may be made of a variety of broken slab type field stones. The individual stones might have relatively smooth surfaces since they can be broken easily. They

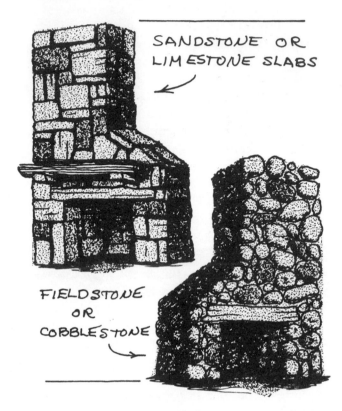

SANDSTONE OR LIMESTONE SLABS

FIELDSTONE OR COBBLESTONE

do not fit together too well, so irregular mortar joints fill the spaces between them. The smooth surfaces might be treated with subtle dry brushing, spatter or sponging. The textures will be near in value and color and evenly distributed to give a feeling of a relatively smooth surface.

The stones in the cabin may be rounded forms. They will be fairly smooth, but not all the same shape or texture. All may have a sponging texture, some smooth, some rough. There will be color variations. High lights and shadows should be carefully sponged in place to project the correct shape.

Stones are frequently used to top walls as sort of a cap. The stones may have rough texture, but are usually smoothed so the texture

will be quite regular and the high light and shadow will be smoothly applied.

Some general facts about stones are worth considering. The textures of stones vary so the type of stone used should fit the general texture feeling of the play — rough, smooth, sharp, glazed. For rough texture stones use heavy sponging, heavy uneven spatter, stippling or the burlap stomp. For refined stone surfaces use light, evenly distributed spatter, sponge or stipple texturing. The outlining of the stone should project the same basic feeling as the texture of the stone unless there is a definite reason for anachronism. In general, straight even lines are used for refinement and uneven lines for coarseness. Uncut stones neither fit perfectly nor have even mortar joints. Usually mortar is used to fill the spaces between stones.

In walls there are times when it is advisable not to show all of the stones. Partially plastered areas with a few well placed stones show-

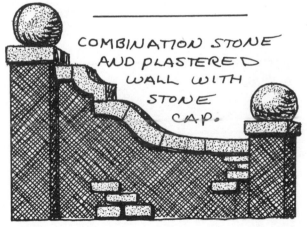

COMBINATION STONE AND PLASTERED WALL WITH STONE CAP.

ing here and there make a pleasant surface. This treatment, of course, must fit the feeling of the play if it is used. The stones provide color to break up the wall section without there being so many stone forms that the recurring pattern projects a feeling of busyness.

Small set pieces, or cut-outs made to resemble stones and placed on the stage, depend a good deal on values to reveal their various surfaces. Flat painting of areas, somewhat softened by over all spattering, works out fairly well in projecting the shape from a flat surface. The

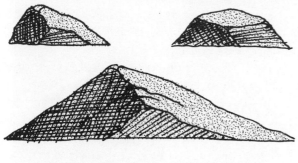

ROCK SET PIECES—VALUE CREATES FORM.

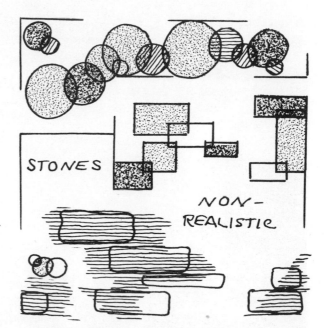

STONES

NON-REALISTIC

spattering can be done in all of the texture values used for the various facets. In applying them it is necessary to use some care and judgment or the surface will lose its three dimensional values.

Three dimensional built up stones (made of wood, chicken wire and paper or cloth mache) may need various values painted on the surfaces to help project their shape to the audience. An over all spatter on something like this is also helpful.

All of the discussion of stones so far has been based on how to achieve a somewhat naturalistic reproduction of stones. Stones need not be so real—as long as the feeling of the play does not preclude naturalism and as long as the rest of the design is consistent with the stones.

Stylistic stones could be simplified forms. Curved forms such as circles, ovals or distortions of these two are often used. Or the stones could be rectilinear forms—squares, triangles, hexagons. A monochromatic scale could be used; for instance, a tan surface with forms outlined in deeper brown. The areas could be patches of many colors with a solid color to fill each stone form. Color areas could be painted on with dry brush streaks having no definite form but placement to get the color where desired. And then stone outline forms

could be painted over them with no attempt at focusing the color patch and the stone outline.

But regardless of whether the stones are to be realistic or impressionistic, the best way to discover their forms is to go out and find real ones where they are scattered about the ground, where they are piled together by nature in hills and mountains or where they are piled together by man in walls, fireplaces and buildings. Observe their size, shape, texture and color and then try to either duplicate the effect exactly or draw an impression of the form and color.

BRICK—Brick surfaces are basically in the red and analagous color range—yellow, orange, red, red violet, purple. Solid colors or variations are possible on the surfaces of individual bricks. Although we usually think of one brick as being just like any other brick, there are many varieties. In texture bricks vary from old, soft, round edged sand brick to sharp, smooth edged, glazed brick to rough textured tapestry brick. Soft spatter, heavy spatter, dry brushing or sponging may be used to get the surface feeling for various types of brick. The mortar joints may be white or colored; may be flush with the surface, weeping or indented.

Bricks are about 2″ thick, 4″ wide and 8″

Simple painted brick around the openings in a setting for *Romeo and Juliet*.

long. Actually there are larger and smaller ones, but the standard conforms to this measurement. On the stage a little license may be taken and the size varied. Small brick could be used to give a busy effect. Large brick could be used to make an area seem smaller.

An entire wall with all of the brick carefully

BRICK AND MORTAR —

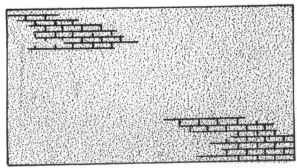

AREA LESS "BUSY" WITH ONLY A
FEW BRICKS OUTLINED

painted frequently becomes too busy with all of its lines and regularity. Simplification of the brick wall will help allay this feeling and can be achieved by using a few areas of brick here and there and impressions of the texture on the remainder of the surface.

In small brick areas it is sometimes easy to paint individual brick on a mortar colored background by stroking individual bricks in place with a 2″ brush and brick colored paint.

This will work quite well for rough, irregular bricks. Various mixes can be used and the individual brick colored as painted.

Painting the surface brick color, texturing and then striping in the mortar joints is the usual process. Remember that brick courses overlap one another by half a brick when laid in the ordinary brick wall.

A little more form is given to the brick if it

HIGH LIGHT AND SHADOW ON BRICK — SHADOW ON MORTAR

is outlined and if it has narrow lines of high light on the top and one end and narrow lines of shadow on the bottom and the other end to accent the edges. If the mortar joints are raked or indented the brick will cast a narrow shadow onto the mortar on the side and end away from the light.

To get more information about brick look at brick walls, fireplaces, chimneys and buildings.

MARBLE—Although rough cut marble may have a relatively sandy textured surface it is usually smoothed and frequently polished to a glistening, shiny surface. There is a wide color range in the background and in the streaks. There are white, cream, pink, deep red, black, brown, green, gray and sienna marbles. The general color, texture and streak pattern should

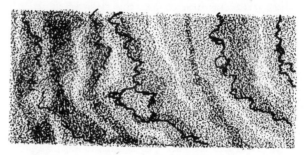

be decided upon before the reproduction begins. The streaks in some are thin-lined and sharp; in others the patterns formed make the surface look as if it were struck with a heavy hammer (shatter crack-like streaks run in all directions, intersecting one another and breaking the surface up into many fairly small patterns). And of course there are marble surfaces that seem to have hardly any pattern at all.

Here is a general process for reproducing marble. Employ the wet brush process. Apply the ground color and while it is wet streak in jagged, but somewhat parallel, lines of texture colors. The streaks can vary between high contrast and subtle variations in color and pattern. The surface will probably be broken into blocks or panels of marble and the streak patterns may vary from block to block. Some may run across, some on an angle, some straight up

119

and down, but always the direction should be kept pretty much the same within a block. The streaks can begin thin, then widen out and then thin down again. Apply enough streaks—with enough variation — to make the surface seem complete, but be careful not to get it too busy and broken.

If the streaks have too much contrast after they have been applied, prepare a wash from the ground color paint. This is done by thinning the paint considerably. The wash when applied and dry should act as a glaze or screen placed over the surface, softening but not obliterating the streaks.

If marble columns are being painted, the wash process for creating the curve should be used. A light shadow wash should be employed. If necessary a second coat may be applied over the first to get the desired depth of shadow.

If the marble has a glossy finish, well placed dry brushed streaks of high light and a few high light windows may reveal the shiny surface. Here again a wash should be used rather than a solid coating of high light so that the base colors will show through.

Marble must be seen to be duplicated. There are so many colors and so many patterns that it defies description.

FOLIAGE—Bushes, trees and plants of every variety are called for in scenic design. Almost any texture device may be employed to produce desired surface effects. Except in the case of large leafed plants where individual leaves can be drawn easily and painted almost flat, after which veins can be painted in, it is usually advisable to attempt to project general impressions of foliage rather than to realistically duplicate individual leaves. Painting individual leaves is an endless job if the painted area is large and the leaf forms lose their identity in the extra busy surface.

FOLIAGE: SOLID COLOR PATTERNS — The foliage area can be broken up into basically rectilinear forms or curved forms. It can be broken so that there is a series of definite areas

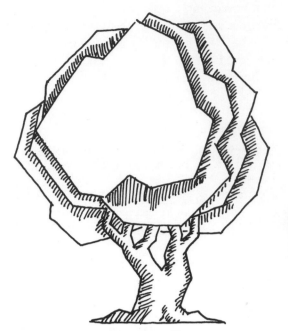

RECTILINEAR TREE – LINING AND SHADING TO GIVE FORM.

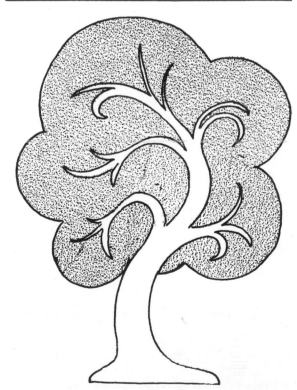

STYLIZED CURVILINEAR TREE PAINTED FLAT – LINE AND PLANE

120

and then the areas painted with various green mixes. The outlines can be left as they are or sharpened with black lines or with lines drawn using the mixes of the areas, but using them in positions where they have the most contrast. A yellow green line might be used to separate a blue green from a gray green; a blue green might be used to separate a yellow green area from a gray green.

FOLIAGE: SOLID COLOR PLUS TEXTURE— The interest value of the forms mentioned above might be increased by sponge texturing for variation within each area — or by using some other texture device or pattern.

FOLIAGE: COMPLEX PATTERN—Paint the entire foliage area using the scumble technique brushing various greens into the surface. If foliage pattern areas can be determined as the paint is being applied it will be possible to put in general high light areas by brushing in a

FOLIAGE PATTERNS

dominance of light texture colors. Shadow areas may be indicated by deeper texture values.

After the scumbled surface has dried, texture patterns to indicate leaf forms may be applied. A sponge, slapping paint on with the side of a brush, a burlap stomp, flogging with a feather

duster or some other device might be used. Patterns are rapidly applied with a painting instrument that will produce patches of color. While applying these patterns it is possible to indicate areas where leaves are behind by using deep values; where they are in the foreground by dabbing on intense values of green; where they catch the sunlight by applying patterns of yellow green. Branch forms can be shown here and there passing through the foliage, but remember the structure of the tree so that the position and size of the branches are logical.

FLOWERS—The foliage patterns along the ground level that represent grass, bushes and hedges become somewhat monotonous. A few flowers here and there will add color and break the regularity of the surface. Simple flowers can be painted easily and quickly with little brush dab combinations.

TREE TRUNKS—The method of painting in the round has already been discussed. Tree trunks may have rough bark, like walnut, oak or maple, or they may have relatively smooth bark like quaking aspen, birch, apple, cherry. The bark may be light in color like aspen or birch; deep red brown like many fruit trees; or deep blackish brown like walnut, maple and oak. Determine the general feeling and then proceed. If the general coloration is used in painting to get the roundness of the trunk and

TREE TRUNKS

branches, then painting the surface structure of the bark is the main problem.

Smooth bark trees frequently have dark streaks in them that tend to go around the trees. On aspen they are not too close together, while on fruit trees they are spaced only a short distance apart. Rough-bark trees have patterns made up of a myriad of interlocking ridges. These may be painted by using deep value paint in the brush and drawing wavy diagonal lines in either direction across the surface. The angle of the diagonals should approach the vertical rather than the horizontal so that the shapes are squeezed diamonds rather than true ones. If the surface begins to lose its roundness, lighter values may be used in the center and deeper ones on the edges. Or a dark wash can be brushed over the side areas after the bark has been drawn.

SMALL TRUNKS—Simple small trunks and branches can be painted using one of the rounding processes—brown for the whole surface, dry brush deep value or wash along the edges and a streak of light value up the center.

These processes for painting trees are suggestions. Others might be developed that will work out even better. Here again it is advisable to observe, draw and paint sketches of trees. Become aware of their structure, form and color.

MIRRORS AND GLASS—Real glass cannot be used successfully on stage because of the danger of breakage and because of the ability of glass to reflect images of objects on, around and above the stage that should not be seen by the audience. A simulated glass surface can be painted with a middle gray background and then streaks of other gray values can be applied judiciously to the surface. Experiment to determine whether the streaks should be applied straight up and down or diagonally across the surface. A streak or two of high light in the same direction as the gray dry brushing will help project the feeling of a reflecting surface. A window here and there may also help. A window on a surface like this is a small rectangular form with square

or distorted angles that represent the light coming from a real window, striking the surface and being reflected from it into the eyes of the observer. The window is painted with a high light value.

BOOKS ON SHELVES—The face outline of the bookcase (with lines for the shelves) should be painted first if a shelf of books is to be painted on a flat surface—and this is certainly the easiest way to provide the books for a bookcase. Various book cover colors are then mixed —red, blue, green, black, brown, tan. Recall

how books look in a bookcase. Remember the thickness, height and general shape of the bound end of the book. Here and there are shelves not quite filled so the books are slightly tilted. The arrangement of book colors may be carefully composed or mixed at random depending upon the desired impression to be conveyed to the audience concerning the owner.

Paint vertical, or nearly vertical, strips for the individual books. The bottoms of the books rest on the shelves, the tops are uneven; so paint the strips accordingly. Vary the heights and widths with here and there a set of several books the same size and color. The binding has a slight roundness at the edges so a subtle high light on one side and a shadow on the other or shadows on both sides (depending on the direction of the light) should be used. Tiny

A Traveller curtain for *Antony and Cleopatra* consisting of two large panels
of camouflage netting, painted with a spray gun.

scribble lines drawn with a brush or a big soft
lead pencil to represent the titles may be applied to a few of the books. The space above
the books can be coated with shadow wash to
give the bookcase depth.

WALLPAPER AND STENCILS — Patterned
wall surfaces used to be more common than
they are today. The patterns were—and still
are—achieved with wallpaper or paint stencils.
On a stage setting, unless real wallpaper is used,
wallpaper and stencil patterns are applied with
a stencil, by free hand brushing or by using cut
patterns. Real wallpaper that is pasted on is
almost impossible to remove from the flats.

CUT PATTERN—Interesting effects may be
achieved by cutting out many pattern forms—
the same or different—and laying them on the
flat to form the wall pattern design. Each cut-
out may need a pin pushed through it to hold
it in place. Then the surface is spattered. The
cutouts prevent the spatter from striking the
surface under them, so when they are removed
the pattern appears. A spray gun can be used
over them to produce somewhat the same effect.

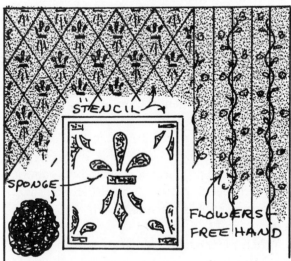

If this process is used the cutouts should be
placed on the flats after the undercoat has been
painted and before the texturing has been applied.

STENCILLING—It may be possible to buy
some stencils from paint companies, but most
of these will be small and inconvenient for

123

most stage use. Usually it will be necessary to make them yourself. They may be cut from commercial stencil paper or home made stencil paper.

The pattern should be planned so that there are plenty of reinforcing strips between the cut-out portions of the pattern. Otherwise the stencil will become easily torn and corners will tend to curl up. In designing the stencil pattern it is also a good idea to have the beginning of a repeat of the pattern all of the way around so that matching is made easier. For instance, at the top of the sheet are two tiny cutouts that are placed in a position similar to two at the bottom of the stencil pattern; on the left edge are two that can be matched by two on the right of the stencil, and so on all of the way around. In this way the patterns can be lined up with one another as they are applied.

In some instances it may be necessary to square the surface off with chalk lines in order to space the stencil correctly each time.

A natural sponge works very well for applying paint through the stencil. It may be handled carefully so the stencil sections are not readily torn. When the sponge is used the pattern is less definite since the sponge surface's irregularities produce a combination open and solid pattern. Usually this is good on a stencil since it produces a more subtle pattern. Too often stencil patterns on wall are too sharp and attract undue attention with their harshness.

When planned the stencil pattern should be neither too simple nor too complex. It should give the impression of filling the space without clutter.

When the stencil is cut it is good practice to cut more than one or at least to transfer the pattern to another piece of paper. This may be done by simply stencilling it onto another sheet of stencil paper.

Surface areas may be panelled and a stencil used in the panel area. Picture mo!ding may be spaced down from the ceiling and chair rails up from the bottom to restrict the area to be stencilled. Or the entire wall area may be stencilled. Stencil patterns may be used by themselves or in conjunction with vertical stripes. They may be placed in patterns set up by painting diagonal stripes in both directions forming diamond shapes. Or they may be used in any other conceivable manner either by themselves or in combination with other forms.

Straw — Straw in bales, straw stacks or straw on roofs may be painted by using the dry brush technique. Use various values of yellows and browns, and underneath use a little

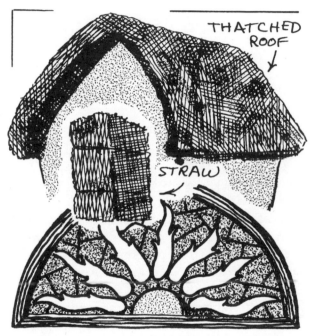

LEADED-STAINED GLASS

red and green to add interest and variety to the finished surface.

Stained Glass—Thin muslin may be used as the base for stained glass effects. Paint the color areas with thin washes, with dyes, with food coloring or with colored inks. The leading between the panes should then be painted on heavily with dark gray or black opaque paint. Regular scene paint will do. After the painting has been completed, coat the surface with shellac or varnish to soften the colors of the paint and to make the surface more translucent.

Celo glass, plastic glass, sheet plastic and rolled plastic can be painted with special translucent plastic paints. The materials are available in hardware and housegoods stores. The paint may be obtained from hobby shops. This is excellent for glass effects but might be somewhat expensive. Black adhesive tape can be applied for the leading.

Colored cellophane and sheet gelatine can be fastened to a transparent or partially transparent surface and used to simulate stained glass. The colors of these materials are excellent and more intense than painted muslin. Gelatine is water soluble and by moistening pieces slightly they may be softened enough to adhere to one another. An entire panel may be made of pieces stuck together in this way. Cellophane pieces can be glued to get a similar effect. Panels might be sandwiched between pieces of screen wire or hardware cloth. Black tape can be applied to represent the lead between the pieces of cellophane or gelatine in the simulated stained glass window.

Translucent glass effects can be obtained by dipping a piece of muslin in a wash and then stretching it onto the back of the window frame and fastening it before it dries. If a smooth effect is desired the dipping should be done carefully so that the wash soaks into the muslin evenly. If an uneven effect is desired the muslin can be thrown in casually and wrung out in the same manner. As a result the coloring will be uneven and the dried surface will be mottled. Any color may be chosen depending upon the desired results.

Backdrops

In painting a backdrop it is possible to use all of the painting textures and all of the painting techniques one has learned and often it is even necessary to develop a few new processes.

The backdrop is mounted on a paint frame if one is available or on the floor if there is no frame. All of the edges should be securely fastened so that the surface will not shrink out of shape as it dries after being painted. (Information about construction of the backdrop may be found in the section on flat scenery.)

The process of painting, the desired end results and whether or not the drop has been previously painted will determine if the surface requires a ground coat of paint.

Interesting results can be obtained on new muslin by a simple process of dry brushing and outlining. This presents a finished product with much the character of pastel drawings. Areas of unpainted muslin remain so the entire surface has a light value and a pleasant translucent quality. A small amount of backlighting on a drop of this nature produces interesting results.

If new muslin is used and a ground coat is desired in order to obtain large solid color areas, the over-all painting process can successfully be done with a power spray gun. Spraying is more successful than brush painting on a new surface for several reasons: a thinner coat of paint is applied, less paint soaks through the muslin (consequently the muslin does not stick if it is painted on the floor), and the drop can be painted more rapidly. The spray process does raise a slight nap on the surface and unless a regular shop is used there is the problem of the spray that floats through the air and settles on everything in the room. Of course, if no spray gun is available the method of painting is easily decided without going into the other details.

If a previously painted drop is to be used, a ground coat is almost obligatory. It may be applied with a spray gun or a brush.

After the drop has been prepared for the painting of the scene it is time to refer to the design plate. This painting should be marked off in one foot squares in order to enable one to transfer and enlarge the design more easily. As a matter of fact, designs can be painted on squared paper so that the squares are already visible. The resulting picture isn't as nice as a piece of easel art, but it is far more practical

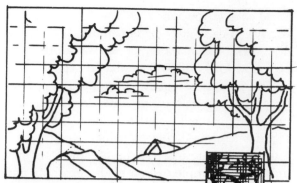

ENLARGE AND TRANSFER SQUARE
BY SQUARE. FROM DESIGN

from the standpoint of the painter of the back-drop.

The design plate may be covered with a piece of refrigerator plastic or Saran wrap to keep dirty fingers and spattered paint from ruining it.

To transfer the design to the backdrop the drop is prepared by marking it off in squares to correspond to the grid plan on the design. This may be done with a chalk line.

With lines drawn vertically and horizontally across the drop corresponding to the ones on the design it is possible to transfer the design square by square, enlarging it to scale as it is drawn.

Chalk, charcoal, a heavy soft lead pencil or a brush may be used to do the drawing on the muslin. If a paint frame is being used it is relatively easy to do the drawing. If, however, the drop is flat on the floor the artist must stoop, squat or crawl. A stick attached to the drawing medium makes it possible to stand up. This is not only more comfortable, but makes it possible to see the results more easily. A long handled sketching brush is often used to draw patterns on backdrops for this reason (a handle may be easily wired onto a regular sash brush). If a brush is used, an extremely thin wash should be employed so that the mistakes can be covered as the paint is laid onto the various areas of the drop.

After the design has been enlarged and trans-ferred to the drop, the areas are painted. As nearly as possible try to duplicate the effects indicated on the color plate. Everything including texture patterns should be enlarged. Aerial perspective may be used to push objects back into the distance. Aerial perspective is achieved by using a mix that is ever so slightly away from the background color and mixed from it. Clouds may be painted with a brush or a sponge or sprayed on. If the edges are too harsh, spatter them back out using the ground color of the sky for the spatter. Objects in the foreground should be sharp-edged and sharply defined color wise. Similar objects in the foreground are larger than those in the background and the distance between them determines the amount of difference in their proportions.

Whether painting with the drop on a paint frame or on the floor, be extra careful about spilling and dripping paint.

Occasionally step back and look at the work with half closed eyes to gain distance and perspective. If the drop is on the floor, climb as high as possible on a step ladder and look down on it.

Use high light, middle value and shadow to get dimension into the work.

SCRIM DROPS—Scrim drops are painted in very much the same manner as muslin backdrops except that the surface is much more difficult to work on. There is a tendency for the eyes to focus on and then through the material. If scrim is painted on a frame its resilience makes it difficult to paint. If it is painted on the floor a good deal of the floor surface will be painted, too, unless it has been covered first. Then, of course, there will be the problem of pulling the scrim loose from the material under it.

AGING SURFACES—Occasionally it is desirable to age a nice new shiny paint job. This is satisfactorily and easily done by spattering the surface with a thin black wash. The wash must be thin (very little black in the mix). If necessary two or three coats may be applied. Unless running and streaking are de-

126

Stencilled pattern applied to the walls of a setting for *The Damask Cheek.*

liberately desired this spattering should be done with the flats or drops laid flat on the floor. The spattering may be done with a brush, but an even better result can be obtained by using a tank type garden spray. This spray gives a fine drop spatter and it is possible to cover surfaces rapidly and easily with a minimum of physical effort.

PASTEL DRAWING — There may be times when it is easier to execute small details with pastels or colored chalks rather than with scene paint. Pastels offer an opportunity to work more leisurely when blending colors and it is easier to have a large pallette of colors available. Pastels can be used when it is advisable to paint pictures directly on a wall. The frame can be painted around them with scene paint afterwards. If they are used, the flats must be handled carefully to prevent smudging or the pastels must be sprayed with fixative or a plastic coating upon completion.

General Comments About Painting

A few helpful facts about painting are worth mentioning before concluding this discussion.

If lighting units are to be mounted behind a section of scenery it is a good idea to "back paint" the rear of the flat so that light will not show through the muslin.

Once in a while a flat is bumped and the

127

muslin loosened. It may be tightened again by brushing or spattering water on the rear surface of the flat.

Texture mixes may be thinner than the paint for the ground coat.

A surface may be given a slight gloss by over painting with glue or shellac.

If a flat is damaged and a hole or tear results, place a patch on the back. Fasten it with paint and if possible use the ground color or a similar color of paint.

Remove chalk and charcoal guide lines by dusting with a soft brush, duster or moist sponge.

* * * *

The foregoing discussion of scene painting is by no means complete nor definitive. Each production, each setting, sometimes even each wall section, is a completely new problem and should be treated in that way. When painting scenery there should be more than "only one way to do it." There should be an infinite number of ways of getting desired results. For the individual painter there may be only one way at this particular time on this flat. But even for him there should be another way to do it next time. Painting is one place where creativity and freedom of expression have wonderful latitude. Even if the painter must tie himself down to someone else's designs he has great freedom of execution. If he executes his own designs his chances for expression are even greater.

GREEK ACANTHUS

ACANTHUS SCROLLS

128

8

Rigging and Shifting

Erecting, rigging and shifting the scenery is usually planned, at least in part, when the setting is being designed and built; but the actual process cannot be completed successfully until the setting is on the stage.

ONE-SET PRODUCTION—A production having only one setting can be erected in a manner that differs from that used when two or more settings are required. The one set production can be erected and allowed to remain in place for the duration of the production. Even if it is necessary to remove all or part of it for another program to be held in the hall it is possible to make the change in a leisurely fashion. Consequently it is possible to use fasteners that are of a semi-permanent nature. Corners can be fastened with double head nails; stiffeners can be permanently nailed or screwed onto the wall sections; door units can be securely fastened into the flats with screws or nails (either double head or regular); and the entire setting can be anchored to the floor if necessary.

MULTI-SET PRODUCTIONS—If there are two

or more settings in the particular production it will be necessary to rig all or part of the first setting so that it can be easily and rapidly moved off stage ("struck") so that other scenes can be moved on. If one setting is used more than once during the performance it might be a good idea to plan, where possible, to make portions of that setting permanent and shift the others around it. If all of the settings are about the same size, if some have odd contours, if some require a clear stage for outdoor effects or if others are larger than the recurring scene it will be necessary to make every scene completely "strikable."

If settings are to be erected and struck during the course of the production the rigging should be carefully planned so that all of the sections can be easily and rapidly assembled and disassembled. Shifting should always be accomplished in minimum time. Many theatre plants have special permanent stage devices to facilitate making rapid changes. Wagons, revolving stages, flying systems, jackknife stages and overhead track systems are all plant facilities designed for this purpose.

Assembling the Setting

FLOOR PLAN—The first step in erecting a setting consists of chalking out a simple outline of the floor plan on the stage. This will save time later since there will be less juggling to locate the positions of the various units as they are erected.

STIFFENERS—Before setting up the scenery all of the wall sections consisting of two or more flats hinged together (twofold, threefold, fourfold books) should be provided with stiffeners. If the production has only one setting, or if the wall sections can be run on and off stage unfolded, the stiffeners may be fastened on with double head nails, hinges, bolts and wing nuts, or screws. The stiffeners may be made of almost any width of 1″ boards, but should probably not be less than 3″ wide. Sometimes even 2″ x 4″ lumber or small built up trusses may be needed. Usually minimum rather than maximum requirements will be met. Although it is desirable to have walls stiffened so they will not shake during the performance when a door is slammed or when someone accidentally bumps against a wall, still at the same time, economy of time and effort will usually specify that bracing be held to a minimum.

A board has greater stiffening quality when it is fastened onto the back of the scenery on edge than when it is flat.

If the stiffener is to be fastened on with double head nails the flat is "floated" (allowed to fall flatwise with the air cushioning the fall) to the floor face up, the stiffener is then slipped underneath and nailed in place. If the wall has little or no strain on it when in place the stiffener may be nailed near the upper edge against the top rails of the flats. This is the easiest place to fasten it since it is possible to see and feel where to nail. One stiffener may be sufficient but two, one at the top and the other at the bottom, will make the section more substantial. If there is a door or window in the wall section it may be advisable to place the stiffener immediately above the thickness and nail it down into the thickness as well as into the flat.

Stiffeners may be fastened with screws in a

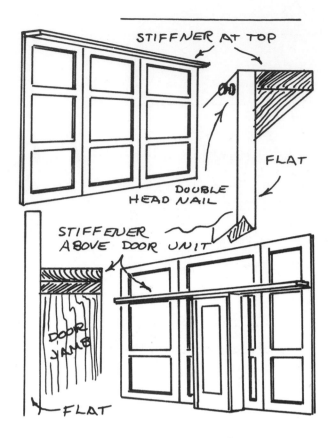

similar manner. Usually it is advisable to drill holes through the flat and then sink 1½″ or 2″ #9 flathead bright wood screws through the flat and into the stiffener.

If bolts and wing nuts are to be used it will probably be easier to work on the flats when they are in an erect position. Ordinarily the stiffener is placed in a flat position when bolts are used. If the board is placed on edge it may be necessary to place blocks where the bolts come through in order to thicken the stiffener in these positions so that the bolts will not weaken the board. This can easily be done.

HINGED STIFFENERS—Hinged stiffeners require slightly more time and effort to install but are sometimes more satisfactory than those that are nailed in place. Loose pin hinges are used when the stiffener is to be removed. The wall section is "floated" face down for this installation. The stiffener is then laid in its desired position and hinges are put on in the proper places. Usually it is advisable to have at least one hinge near each end and one near each hinged joint of the wall. Sometimes even more are put on to make the wall more rigid. Hinges may be placed on either toggles or stiles. In order to keep the stiffner in its correct position against the rear of the flats the hinges are placed on alternate sides of the stiffner. If loose pin hinges are used it may be advisable to fasten the pins with string to either the stiffener or flats so that they will always be available when needed. Pins for this purpose should be slightly smaller than the pin holes of the hinges so that they can be easily put in and taken out.

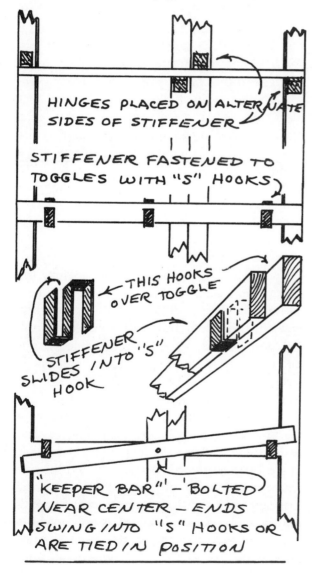

HINGES PLACED ON ALTERNATE SIDES OF STIFFENER

STIFFENER FASTENED TO TOGGLES WITH "S" HOOKS

THIS HOOKS OVER TOGGLE

STIFFENER SLIDES INTO "S" HOOK

"KEEPER BAR" – BOLTED NEAR CENTER – ENDS SWING INTO "S" HOOKS OR ARE TIED IN POSITION

The wire of coat hangers is usually just about the right size for these pins.

S Hooks—The S hook is another device that can be used with stiffeners. An S hook is made from strap iron and bent into a modified angular S shape so that it can be slipped onto a toggle bar and then when it is in place a stiffener can be slipped into the bent up hook. Screw holes may be drilled into the hooks so that they can be fastened either onto the flats or stiffeners. The hooks may also be designed so that the stiffener can be placed in a flat or edge position. If the stiffener is to be placed in the edge position it will probably be advisable to fasten the hooks permanently to the stiffener.

Keeper Bars—Swinging keeper bar stiffeners may be rigged so that they are permanently bolted to the flat (near the center of the stiffener usually). When the flat is being shifted, stored or packed for shipping the stiffener is swung into a position parallel with the stiles of the flat. When the unit is set up on the stage the stiffener is swivelled around so that it crosses the flats and its ends are tied, fastened with hooks and eyes, fastened with bolts and wing nuts, screwed into place, nailed with double heads, or secured with keeper hooks or S hooks.

If more strength is needed in stiffening than can be provided with a 1" board it may be necessary to use a 2" x 4" or even to make a simple truss. These are handled in basically the same manner as other stiffeners. However, if a truss is used, it may be necessary to provide some kind of support so that the weight of this frame extending behind the flats will not sag and pull loose from the wall section.

Assembling Walls—After the walls have been stiffened it is time to fasten the sections together. Provisions for fastening may have been made before the painting was done—this is especially so if all or part of the fasteners are on the face of the flats. If it is a one set show double head nails will work and can be put in and removed rapidly.

Double Head Nails—As few as three 8d

double head nails can be used to fasten two flats or wall sections together at right angles if they do not exceed 10'-0" in height. If there is some strain on the joint caused by swinging doors it may be necessary to add a couple more nails. After the nail is driven in as far as its shoulder there is still enough head to grasp with the jaws of a hammer or crow bar for easy and rapid removal. If the corner made by two flats is on an angle greater than 90° it is easier to nail it at 90° and then twist the flats into position afterwards.

LOOSE PIN HINGES—If loose pin hinges are used to fasten walls together they should be mounted on the flats with the flats in position so the hinge will allow the flats to be placed on the correct angle. Pins can easily be removed from loose pin hinges but sometimes it is difficult to get the hinges aligned and the pins placed in a hurry.

LASHING—Lash lines are used almost exclusively on some stages for fastening wall sections together and they can certainly be used advantageously, especially where the flats form an outside corner at the back of the setting. It is more difficult to get snug joints that will remain tight on inside corners, but even these are perfectly satisfactory when handled correctly and when the flats have stop blocks and cleats to prevent them from slipping.

The lash lines should be uniformly fastened to the upper right corner of each unit as viewed from the rear (except in special cases—there are always exceptions to the rule). Lash cleats are then spaced so the line can be laced back and forth from one side of the joint to the other. A minimum number of cleats requires a pair of tie off cleats from 24" to 30" above the floor on the inside of each of the stiles of the joint and one cleat on the right side of the joint half way between there and the position where the line is tied to the corner of the flat to the left. As additional cleats are added the spacing is changed so that the lacing space is fairly even.

Lashing and tie off cleats may consist of regular commercial cleats, strips of strap iron drilled to receive screws for fastening to the stiles, long screws, double head nails or strips of plywood.

When lashing flats together a little experience will make it possible for the operator to snap the line around the cleats rather easily. If it is desirable to have the rope slip off the cleats easily they should slope slightly upward. If it is desirable to have the rope cling the cleats should slope slightly downward. In general all but the tie off cleats will slope slightly upward; the tie off cleats will slope downward.

LASHLINE KNOT—If the lashline knot is tied correctly it will be possible to untie it by jerking on the end of the line. If it is incorrectly tied much time will be wasted in fumbling with the line. To correctly tie the knot the line passes under one tie off pin, across and under the other one. A loop or bight is made in the line and passed over and behind the line where it goes up toward the lashing pins. The loop is pulled tightly downward without pulling the end through. A loop is now made in the line toward its end and this loop is pulled through the first loop. This loop is pulled until

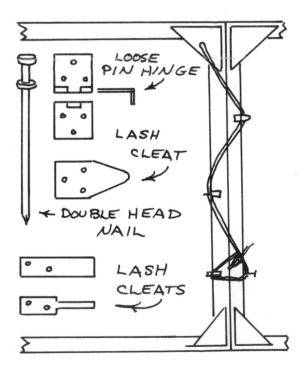

LOOSE PIN HINGE

LASH CLEAT

← DOUBLE HEAD NAIL

LASH CLEATS

132

the other loop tightens down and binds against it. Notice that the end of the line is never passed through either of the loops. To untie

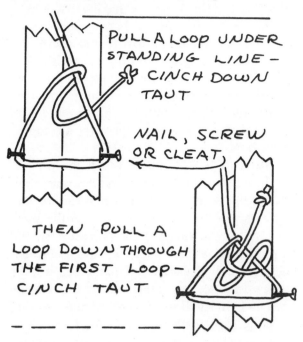

PULL A LOOP UNDER STANDING LINE — CINCH DOWN TAUT

NAIL, SCREW OR CLEAT

THEN PULL A LOOP DOWN THROUGH THE FIRST LOOP — CINCH TAUT

the knot the end of the line is pulled or jerked pulling out both loops and releasing the line.

Other devices might be used for fastening flat sections together. Hooks and eyes, picture hangers, short lengths of rope and screw eyes, ropes and small boat cleats, angle irons and removable bolts, and clamps are all contrivances that might be used.

In some cases where the entire setting is small it may be possible to hinge the setting into a single piece so that it may be moved as one unit. Loose or tight pin hinges can be used.

GLIDERS—If the scenery is being dragged across the floor (or "run") it may be advisable to consider mounting large "gliders" under the flats in places. The wall sections can then be slid across the floor quietly and easily. They also reduce the danger of marring the floor.

Many times it may be possible to leave doors, windows, pictures and all of the dressing on a section of scenery in place while it is being shifted. If this can be done the entire job will

take less time and the process of re-setting the scene will be much easier. If there are many heavy units in and on the wall it would be wise to consider using tip jacks, wagons or outriggers on which the scenery can be mounted. These are all described in the stage machinery section.

Large units such as steps, platforms, fireplaces, oversized doors, and windows should be rigidly braced and provided with casters, gliders or other contrivances to make shifting them as effortless as possible.

BACKINGS—After the main setting is placed in position the backings are placed where they belong. If the backing fits snugly against the flat of a wall or against the side thickness of a door or archway it may be possible to securely fasten it to that unit by lashline, hinges, nails, or other means and use it as a bracing device.

BRACING—If walls, and especially doors, are not rigid enough it will be necessary to use stage braces, jacks or similar contrivances to provide more rigidity. The stage brace is an adjustable length device with a hook type fastener at one end designed for fastening into a brace cleat secured to a flat, and an angled foot iron on the other end provided with a hole through which a stage screw can be fastened by hand into the floor. Hardwood floors should be provided with some other type of fastener at the floor end if stage screws are to be used. Iron plates

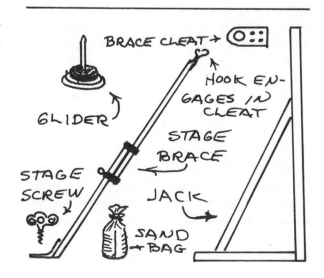

BRACE CLEAT

HOOK ENGAGES IN CLEAT

GLIDER

STAGE BRACE

STAGE SCREW

JACK

SAND BAG

with threaded holes or bolt head holes may be used. If a jack is used in place of a stage brace the jack is fastened to the flat with hinges, nails, screws or bolts and its foot end on the floor is fastened down with a stage screw or weighted with a sand bag counterweight or any other heavy object. In the absence of these devices it is possible to fasten other flats or parallel lids to the rear of the set and also to the floor. If the base of the setting is secured in place it is also possible to lash the setting to the wall of the building with line. Sometimes a combination of a board that is the correct length to make a spacer and reach a nearby wall of the theatre building and a line that can be tied to a pipe or cleat fastened in the wall will provide stiffening support. The board will prevent the flats from moving one direction and the rope will prevent them from moving in the other.

When scenery is used on an outdoor stage lashing to a permanent or semi-permanent framework or to a solid deck is a good solution. The lashing lines in this case might be just short snatch cords rather than regular long lash lines. The outdoor scenery requires extreme precautions in anchoring since even the slightest gust of wind can twist and break a flat.

FLYING—Portions of scenery, back walls, drop sections, property pieces or even entire settings may sometimes be flown into the flies rather than moved on the floor level. When this is done it is necessary to carefully mount some type of hook or eye device to the flats. If the flats are not heavy it may be possible to use large screw eyes. Usually some piece of hardware similar to the commercial ceiling plate or hanger iron is used. These must be rigidly fastened to the flat where the rope or cable is to be tied. The rope may be fastened to the top of the object or passed down through rings or eyes near the top and extended down toward the bottom of the object where the rope is tied to other supports. The ropes should, if possible, be fastened so that the weight is somewhat evenly distributed and so that the weight will also level the scenic unit as it is raised into

the flies; otherwise, it may get "fouled" in other units that are stored in the fly loft.

The flying of scenery can be more successfully handled in a theatre having a counterweight system than in one having only a rope and sand bag system. The permanent levelling of the counterweight is much more satisfactory than the constant struggle with ropes. But even with the rope system it is frequently advisable to lift some things into the flies in order to retain more available floor space for a complex production.

SHIFTING SCHEDULE — When the production being staged is complex and has more than one setting — as well as much furniture and many props — it is necessary to carefully work out a shifting schedule. The procedure should be plotted on a floor plan with the movement and storage of live scenery (that which is to be used), dead scenery (that which has already been used and will not be needed again during the current performance), and the setting that is being played. Storage area, path of movement and individual crew member assignments should all be worked out carefully.

CREW—Except for shifting small items it is advisable to work the crew in pairs. If the same two work together on all shifts they will help one another and one will remember what the other forgets.

Efficiency of packing, movement and storage are necessary. In order to achieve this it is advisable to do paper and trial work first and then have technical "run throughs" for just the crew. The entire effect of a play can be ruined by careless or lengthy manipulation of scenery.

SPIKING—In order to enable exact placement of scenery, furniture and properties it is necessary to "spike" or mark the floor with small dabs of paint for each object for each scene. If the work lights are to be turned on for the shift it is possible to use a different color of paint for each setting. If the setting is to be changed in almost complete darkness, white, light tints or even luminous paint should be used for spike marks. If paint cannot be used

134

on the floor it may be advisable to use white adhesive tape for spike marks.

MARKING EDGES OF STEPS AND PLATFORMS—The actors and stagehands frequently have difficulty seeing the edges of stairsteps and platforms in the dark. A narrow stripe of paint wherever there is a change in elevation will help in alleviating this difficulty. White paint should be used if the stage is bright to dim and luminous paint should be used where it is dim to dark. Marking passageways and positions for actors and scenic units in theatre-in-the-round stages in this way is extremely important if the shifting is to be done in the dark and if the actors are to assume their positions on the stage during a "blackout".

NUMBERING SYSTEM—A numbering system will be helpful if there are more than two scenes. An acceptable system is to use the act number as a prefix and the scene number as a suffix. Thus 11 would indicate Act 1, Scene 1; 12 would be Act 1, Scene 2; 24 would be Act 2, Scene 4; and 33 would be Act 3, Scene 3. If a system of this nature is used consistently there will be little or no confusion about markings and identification.

SHIFTING PLAN — When the shifting and storage plan is worked out it is necessary to work out all of the various elements at the same time. There must be space for storage and movement of: 1. Scenery, 2. Furniture, 3. Properties and 4. Actors. In the case of the actors there must be space for them to move to all of the entrances and to wait at the entrances for their cues. If the production has a large cast this is often the most difficult problem of all.

HAND PROPERTIES — Stage properties carried by the actors and known as hand properties should be available as close to entrances as possible. It is good procedure to have a property table on each side of the stage and to regulate the flow of these items. If the properties are picked up just before the actor makes an entrance and checked back in to the table as soon as he is through using them there will be

less trouble in keeping track of these items — and sometimes there are literally hundreds of them.

FURNITURE—Furniture may be stacked but it is necessary to be careful so that the various pieces do not get scarred or broken. Careful planning of the stacking may make it possible for one crew member to carry a chair and items that can easily be stacked on the chair.

FLOWN UNITS—If a number of backdrops or flown pieces of scenery are being used in a production it is advisable to check their order of appearance. Placing them in the correct sequence may make it possible to have one set behind the other ready to go as soon as the front one is flown away.

Correctly masking the stage should always be considered in the shifting plan. There are times when more space is planned than is available if this isn't taken into consideration. This is especially true when there are outdoor scenes consisting of nothing but a clear stage backed by a cyclorama. All of the scenery for the other scenes must be cleaned completely out of sight lines. When enclosure type settings are used, on the other hand, it may even be possible to have parts of other settings in place behind the one being played.

MANPOWER—The planning process should also take the available manpower into consideration. If units of scenery are flown it will be necessary to have one or more crew members at the pin rail. Frequently, especially if the pin rail is above the floor, the pin rail operator cannot be counted on to climb to the floor and help with the shift and then shinny back up to his perch. The strong should be assigned to move large objects and the weaker to handle the smaller objects. That is an obvious factor but sometimes when under pressure a stage manager fails to remember such simple things.

Miscellaneous Facts

There are a few random facts that should be known by the stage crew. They should know the various methods of handling flats, common knots that are useful on stage and some miscellaneous facts about handling various rigging problems.

The lashline knot, already described, is used wherever joints are laced with rope.

CLOVE HITCH—The clove hitch is used where the rope is to be secured around an object for pulling or lifting where there is danger of the rope sliding. This is the knot usually used in tying a pipe or wooden batten to a set of lines in the flying system. The rope extending down from the grid is referred to as the "standing line." Assume that a line is being tied onto a pipe. The standing line passes down behind the pipe, and the end of the rope is led around the pipe once on one side of the standing line and started around a second time on the other side of the standing line. As soon as it passes just beyond the standing line it is slipped through under the first turn around the pipe. The end of the rope and the standing line are then pulled so that the rope tightens on the pipe. The end of the rope is then looped in two half hitches above the knot.

BOWLINE—If the rope is to be tied into a ring a bowline knot can be tied. A bowline has the advantage of always remaining easy to untie. In order to describe this knot assume again that there is a standing line coming down from the grid. Pass the end of the rope through the ring to be tied. Hold the standing line in the right hand just above the ring. With the left hand place the end of the line across the front of the standing line. Hold the crossing position with the left hand and with the right cast a small loop over the end of the line. With the left hand pass the end of the line around the back of the standing line to the front and down through the loop it just passed up through.

PIN RAIL TIE OFF—If the ropes on a rope flying system are correctly tied off it is possible for one person to release a set of lines and lower a heavy object to the floor. To tie this all of the lines of a set (usually 3 or 5) come down on the far side of the rail and are passed under, then pulled up and around the pin. For ease of handling, the ropes should not cross one another in this operation. The friction of the rope rubbing against the rail is utilized to give it holding power. The rope is then pulled down to the lower end of the pin and wrapped around it. Then a loop is twisted into the line before it is placed on the top pin again with the end of the line (as distinguished from the standing line) passing underneath. This will lock the lines in place. This process may be repeated for added security. If there is surplus line it should be coiled and hung on the pin so that it will not be under foot. If all of the ends are thus coiled after being tied off there will be less danger of lines getting fouled up in one another.

To prevent the end of a line from fraying it can be wound with heavy thread, friction tape

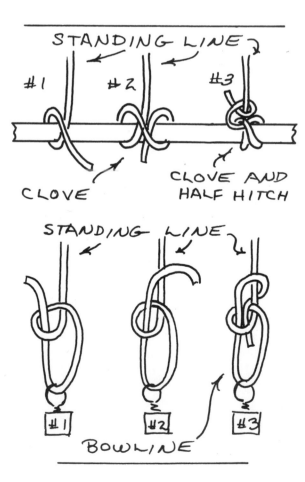

STANDING LINE

#1   #2   #3

CLOVE   CLOVE AND
             HALF HITCH

STANDING LINE

#1   #2   #3

BOWLINE

or braided back upon itself or tied in a simple knot.

BROKEN BATTENS—Accidents are bound to happen on the stage. If a batten is broken—whether it's a stile, rail or flying batten—it can be temporarily patched by fastening a piece of wood along it to make a lapped splice. This splicing board should be long enough to secure the break without danger of the accident happening again right away.

TIGHTENING MUSLIN—Sometimes the fabric will be lightly bumped, loosening it. As long as the material is not broken it will be possible to tighten the area by spattering either the surface or back with plain water. As it dries out the material will usually shrink and tighten up again. Alum added to the water may increase the shrinkage.

PATCHING—If the surface is torn or slit it will be necessary to make a temporary patch.

It may be possible to do this with Scotch tape, by stapling a small board to the back, or by adhering a patch to the rear with paint while holding a flat board against the face. When this is done carefully with paint that comes close to matching the paint coloration of the surface, the patch is almost unnoticeable from the audience. Glue should not be used for patches since it tends to pull the material unevenly and throw wrinkles into the surface.

CREW DEPORTMENT — The stage shifting crew should consider every performance and rehearsal as important. They should be briefed by the stage manager, who is the stage performance "boss", to work efficiently and quietly. The success of the performance depends on the dispatch with which their work is done. Absolutely no carelessness or horse play should be condoned back stage during the performance. There is a time for this after the show is over.

Madame Butterfly.   Research into the architecture of a country and the history of an era often precede the design process.

Stage Properties

## 9

The entire process of decorating the stage is important, but the final touches of the stage property department usually add the flavor that completes the setting and makes it appear to be lived in—whether it's a room, a garden, a patio or a barn. The term "stage property" is a general one that may refer to almost any conceivable object. As a matter of fact, the ordinary property storage room looks like a huge collection of castaway junk—and it usually is just that. Whenever someone wants to get rid of something it can profitably be added to the prop room stock. The stage technician looks upon every bottle, pillow, pin cushion, spear and empty whiskey bottle as an object that some day may be called for on stage. Some of the most impossible objects have been used in plays ranging all of the way from a mummy case in *The Man Who Came to Dinner*, to a horse in *Green Grow the Lilacs*, to a roll top desk large enough to hide an escaped convict in *Front Page*, to trees that grow on stage in a flash in *Sing Out Sweet Land*, to a

pin ball machine that when defeated flashes lights, sends up an American flag and plays *America* in *The Time of Your Life*.

It is physically impossible to collect all of the items that may be used at one time or another in stage plays, but it is possible to gradually accumulate objects, such as dishes, pots, pans, furniture, pictures and vases, that are used most frequently. The number and variety of objects collected will depend a good deal upon the storage facilities available. Properties not available in the stock room may be begged, borrowed, rented or purchased. They may be found in old homes that are being torn down, in furniture stores, at auction sales or may be obtained by letting it be known that they are needed by the theatre. Sometimes the material is junk, but even this can be repaired.

If the properties are borrowed and are to be returned it is advisable to keep a close record of where they were obtained, check them carefully after each rehearsal and performance and return them as promptly as possible after the final performance. A written thank you note should either accompany the object when it is returned or be mailed out immediately thereafter. Actors should always be cautioned about the value of stage properties and urged to handle them carefully.

Since the term "stage properties" in itself refers to a vast conglomeration of objects this discussion will likewise consist of a conglomeration of information. Properties will be discussed in terms of where and how they may be used. Frequently the stage decorator is baffled about the objects that may at times be used on a desk, on a table or in a bar. For his convenience some of the possible objects will be listed. The unusual ones will be described and where objects can be faked or simplified or built this will be suggested and the method briefly described and illustrated. Stage furniture, extremely important in the stage dressing process, will be discussed in a separate chapter.

WALL PROPERTIES — Simple or complex shelf sections may be mounted on the wall. They may be fastened to toggle bars with double head nails, bolts and wing nuts, picture hangers or suspended from the top rail of the flat by wire. The shelves may be used to hold books, knick knacks, statuettes, statues, vases, toy animals, fish, stuffed fowl, planter boxes, dishes, clocks, bottles, medicine, photographs, lamps, lanterns, tools, decorated china or paper plates, pieces of drift wood and maps.

PICTURES — Pictures, including paintings, photographic enlargements, murals, pictures painted directly on the flat surface with moldings, painted or real, framing them, framed pieces of interesting wall paper patterns, beautiful magazine illustrations, cloth patterns or simple line drawing illustrations and cartoons, may be mounted on the walls. These may be mounted directly to toggle bars if they are correctly spaced; extra toggles can be installed or wires may be used to extend from the desired position of the picture up to the nearest toggle or rail of the flat above it. The wires may be concealed by piercing the flat with tiny holes behind the picture, pushing the wires through and extending them up to the nearest cross bar. String may be used in the same way. A picture will retain its balanced position better if two supports are used rather than one. One support will allow it to twist out of position easily, especially if the wall takes the strain of a slammed door or something of that nature.

Water paint or pastels work quite well for painting directly onto the flat surface. If pastels are used they should be lightly sprayed with fixative in order to prevent smearing.

PICTURE TRANSFORMED INTO REAL PERSON—Sometimes it is desirable to have a picture "come to life." To do this the picture is painted on scrim and mounted on the wall. Cut the muslin out behind the picture and locate the actor in back of the portrait. When the real person is to appear illuminate him with high intensity light behind the picture and in place of the picture the actor will be seen.

PLAQUES—Plaques made of plaster of paris, wood, plastic, plastic wood, metal or cloth may be mounted on the wall. The method of casting some of these materials if they are to be created in the shop will be described later. The design on the plaques may be in bas relief or flat and may consist of masks, coats of arms, abstract designs, or figures. Plates, paper or china, trivets, antlers, and clocks are other objects that may be mounted on the wall like plaques.

SIGNS — The religious home may have framed decorative signs.

PLATE RAIL—A plate or dish rail may hang on a wall, especially in a dining room. It may have a china collection — demitasse, plates, cups, bowls — on it.

LAMPS — Lamps of many varieties may be mounted on the wall as decoration, light motivation or both. The lamps may be electric, kerosene, gas or of candelabra variety. They may be mounted on their own bases or on small bracket shelves. Usually for the sake of safety it is advisable to have flame variety lamps electrified.

MIRRORS—Mirrors of all sizes and shapes are used on the stage. Frequently they are mounted on the wall although there are times when free standing full length varieties or small mantel or desk varieties are used. When mirrors are used they should be checked carefully from the audience area to see that they do not reflect images of actors waiting offstage for entrances, images of untidy fly lofts, or images of spotlights. These images can be most annoying to members of the audience. If a mirror is on a sharp angle so the audience sees but little of the surface a false mirror painted with a middle gray base with streaks of tint and shade gray may provide a substitute. Placing net over a real mirror or spraying it with wax, scene paint or grease will diffuse the light from the reflective surface so that it is less annoying.

WINDOWS — Windows allow many and varied treatments. In fact a window effect may be achieved on a flat wall without even having a hole in the flat if the space is completely dressed with window paraphernalia. Pull down shades, Venetian blinds, split or toothpick bamboo blinds, accordion folded paper blinds, glass curtains, drapes, valances and cornices may all be used in decorating the window. The paper blinds are made by folding paper (butcher paper works very well) of the correct width into accordion pleats. This can be mounted to a molding at the top. A strip of wood is stapled to the bottom and the blind is completed. Strings may be run through holes drilled in the paper while the folds are pressed tightly together. These strings will make it possible to raise and lower the blinds.

GLASS CURTAINS—Patterned lace, marquisette, cheese cloth or any net material may be purchased in yardage. The top and bottom may be hemmed or left with the raw cut edge. The edges may be cut with regular or pinking shears. Glass curtains may be suspended in two sections with one section mounted to the top sash and the other to the bottom sash. They may be cut just long enough to extend from the top of the window down to the window sill or may extend all of the way to the floor. They may have fulness or not. They may hang straight to the floor; may be butterflied; or may be a combination of the two. Glass curtains may be used by themselves or in combination with draperies. They may have plain or ruffled edges. Glass curtain material may be obtained

GLASS CURTAINS

in white, ecru, egg shell, dotted swiss and colors.

DRAPERIES — Window draperies may be mounted in a permanent position or may be rigged to open and close. They may open and close by having butterfly tie backs or by operating on a traverse rod or on wires. If they are on a traverse rod the pleats should be sewn in so that fulness will remain in place whether the draperies are opened or closed. Draperies may have a cornice at the top to conceal the rigging; they may have a valance; or they may have nothing at all. The cornice may be made of cardboard, wallboard, or wood and may be

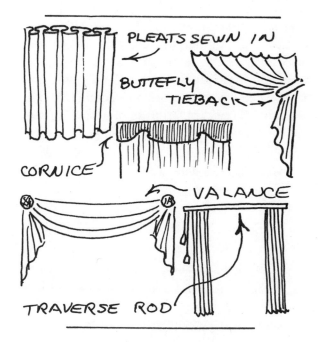

PLEATS SEWN IN

BUTTEFLY TIEBACK

CORNICE

VALANCE

TRAVERSE ROD

141

painted, unpainted or cloth covered. The draperies and valance may have a tassel trim, may have rope worked into the folds or may be plain. The draperies may be made of plain, striped or patterned cloth or may be made out of muslin and designs applied with scene paint and brush, textile paints, silk screen, or linoleum blocks. These processes will be described later. Draperies may be mounted directly to the flat on a rod, pipe or wire or to a board that is then mounted on the flat. If the draperies are to be removed rapidly for a scene change it is possible to mount them on a board and use hangers to hold the board, or rig up a pulley system to pull the board up into place and lower it for shifting.

The search for drapery materials should extend into the paper, synthetic and plastic, as well as cloth sections of the department store since these materials are frequently used to manufacture inexpensive draperies.

WINDOW SILL BOX—The window, inside or out, may have a sill planter box complete with real or synthetic leaves, flowers or both.

FIREPLACES—There are several decorative areas in connection with a fireplace. These are: the space above the mantel, the mantel and the hearth.

Space Above Mantel — The space above the mantel may be flat or recessed; it may be exposed stone or brick; it may be plain or panelled. Regardless what its finish there are times when essential props are required in this position. These may consist of masks, armament, pictures or plaques. At other times objects of the same nature are added to the decor to make the fireplace a more interesting or dominant unit in the total design.

Mantel — The mantel may be loaded with knick knacks or be tastefully decorated with one or two select pieces depending upon the total mood and feeling of the setting. Some of the objects that may be found in this position are: planter boxes, clocks, photographs, mirrors, ash trays, pottery, candelabra, vases, flowers, candy dishes, match boxes, books, figurines, boxes and candle snuffers.

Hearth — The hearth area may have the usual fire screen, andirons and fireplace tools consisting of shovel, poker, broom, tongs and stand to hold them. It may also have a coal scuttle, wood box, crane and iron kettle, cooking facilities, popcorn popper, log unit, logs, bellows and salt holder.

CHAIR DECOR—A chair may have a pillow tossed onto the seat, may have slip covers or robes casually or carefully thrown across them. In an immaculate household they may have antimacassers (a tidy or cover to protect a chair or sofa, usually placed where the arms and head are likely to rest and soil the upholstery finish).

SOFA DECOR—Antimacassars, robes, quilts, slip covers, pillows, dolls, teddy bears and many other objects may be placed on sofas to add color and atmosphere to the room.

BED DECOR — Regular bed linen, quilts, decorative bed spreads, rolled blankets, dolls, extra throw pillows, canopies, bed lamps, book holders are all items that might be used with a bed.

DESK PARAPHERNALIA—Desks have character that is determined by their topside clutter. They range all the way from completely cleared tops to the ones with animal collections, blotter, pen and ink, quill and ink, letter baskets, telephones, intercommunication speakers, typewriter, books, mirror, photographs, lamps, candles, ledgers, receipt books, stationery, figurines, vases, flowers, ash trays and general clutter.

TABLE PARAPHERNALIA — Table cloth (lace, white, checkered, oil cloth, tasseled, patterned), magazines, books, sewing basket, fruit basket or bowl, lamps, figurines, nut dish with nutcracker and picks, telephone, liquor services, decanter, tea set, coffee set, flower arrangement, newspapers, dinner service (plates, cups and saucers, crystal, napkins, silver, service dishes), playing cards, writing equipment and candy boxes are all items that may be found on a table.

A room may have much miscellaneous clutter—pillows on the floor, footstools, waste baskets, screens and grandfather clocks.

DISPLAY CABINET — Open display type shelves or cabinets may have select china (painted paper plates even), crystal or pottery, figurines or books.

BAR — A bar, whether it is a small home variety or a place of business, will have a variety of bottle types (wine, champagne, whiskey, Bourbon, beer, gin); it will have a variety of glasses for the various types of drinks; and it will have a variety of objects such as ice bucket,

tongs, stirring rods, lemon and lime squeezer, seltzer water bottle, decanter, ice pick, corkscrew, jigger, cocktail shaker, beer can opener, lemons, limes, soda water mixes, cherries, olives, onions, pretzels and napkins—and might even have beer kegs.

RESTAURANT—The restaurant setting may have a thousand and one items including: cash register, stools, counter, tables and chairs, piano, coffee maker, vendor (cigarettes, candy), juke box, stove, gum machine, dishes, silver, napkin holders, doughnut and roll jars, signs, cigars, cigarettes, toothpicks, china of all kinds, food,

hat and coat racks (wall hangers or standing tree type).

DRESSING TABLE DECOR — Powder boxes, lamps, mirror, comb and brush set, atomizer, perfumes, powder puff, photographs, miscellaneous boxes and bottles and jewelry are all items that might be found on a dressing table.

MISCELLANEOUS SEATS—An odd collection of items can be used for seating in various places. Stumps, logs, kegs, barrels, boxes, crates, packing cases, stools, chairs, benches and dozens of other objects can all be used.

Manufacturing Stage Properties

The property man with imagination and a modicum of mechanical ability will be able to manufacture many of the property items needed. Basic tools and a few materials can be used to make any number of items.

MÂCHÉ — Mâché, paper or cloth, will be useful for molding objects. This can be used over a wire form, over wadded paper, over matted cloth or almost anything else that can be used to provide a basic shape approaching the desired finish form. Mâché may also be used to alter or build up other forms that already approach the desired shape. It is a process of pasting or gluing strips of paper together to make a solid surface.

POLYSTYRENE—Polystyrene, or Styro-Foam, the feather-weight firm, white, sponge-textured material used a great deal by florists, has countless uses in making stage properties. It can be worked with regular wood working equipment including saws, knives, rasps, and sandpaper. It is carried in stock by some lumber yards and some florists supply houses. It is used as an insulation as well as decorative material. It may be obtained in various thicknesses, comes in fairly long pieces and is purchased by the board foot. Several thicknesses can be glued together or fastened together with wire, string or thread. It can be painted readily. Artificial fruit, cakes, roasts, hams, books, inedible rolls, doughnuts, steaks, mashed potatoes, cut out forms, letters, signs and a host of other

143

things can be made from it. Wherever lightness of weight is desired it is an ideal substance to use.

DOWEL — Dowel is round cross section wood that comes in many sizes. It is obtainable in either soft or hard wood and can be used for making fake candles, gun barrels, stair rails, spears, flag poles, pennant poles, and tent poles. Dowel is obtained from lumber yards, cabinetmaker shops and some hardware stores.

PIPE AND TUBING—Iron pipe, steel pipe, aluminum and steel electrical conduit, aluminum tubing, rubber tubing, plastic and glass tubing can all be used for stage properties. The metallic tubings may be used for most of the same purposes as dowel. Rubber tubing can be used to conduct fluid, smoke or air onto or off the stage and can be used for making objects that need flexible tube structure.

LUMBER—White pine of varying widths and of thickness up to 2″ is useful for carving wooden properties. If more thickness is desired two or more thicknesses may be glued together. White pine may be used for gun stocks, musical instruments, stools, benches, tables, beds, etc. Plywood of varying thicknesses is also useful for table tops, bed tops, cabinet doors, drawer bottoms, base forms for papier-mache and boxes.

SPONGE RUBBER—Sponge rubber is another material that should not be overlooked. Although it is relatively expensive in large quantities, it has many uses and small pieces may be used to good advantage. Scraps of sponge rubber rug padding are useful for many property items. It curls, bends, twists and stretches for forming odd shaped items. Pieces of it can be used to simulate food, flowers, large leaves, etc. Thicker sponge rubber might be used for padding, for pillows, for various irregular objects. Department stores, upholstery shops and rug departments handle sponge rubber.

FELT — Felt, especially the heavy weight varieties, may be used for making some small decorative pieces. Felt may be steamed and worked into almost any shape. After it has been shaped it can be loaded with size, glue or paint to stiffen it and layers can be glued together. It can be used for brooches, for flowers, armour pieces, all kinds of head gear, epaulets and many, many more items. It may be gilded to look like gold and used for some jewelry items.

Breakaways

UNFIRED POTTERY—There are times when it is necessary to have a vase or similar object that can be broken over an actor's head without damage to the head. Unfired pottery, especially if it is a thin "slip" casting in the green state, can be used for this purpose. In fact, it is usually so fragile that it must be handled with great care or it will be broken too soon.

BREAKAWAY FURNITURE — Old pieces of furniture should be used when a piece is to be broken when sat upon, thrown or used to strike an actor. The pieces can be pulled or broken apart and then loosely fastened together in such a way that they will easily crumple when pressure is applied. Scotch tape, loosely fitting dowel, joints that will easily slip apart, joints held together by easily broken thread, pieces cut or sawed through and then fastened with gummed tape or some similar material should be used. Sometimes the parts may be held together with loose pin hinges and the pins pulled at the opportune moment. Properties to be broken may also be made from materials that look substantial but which may be easily broken, such as sections of Styrofoam, hollow papier mâché, or sponge rubber.

Cast Forms

There are many stage properties that can best be made as cast forms. Lightweight reproductions of bulky objects, many reproductions of the same piece, the outer shell of a heavy article, and rigid but durable forms may be made in this way. A master form consisting of the object itself or a clay model of the object may be used to build the negative cast. Puppet heads, bottles, book backs, artificial foods, masks, armour plate, helmets and statues are a few of the props that may be made in this way.

If the surface of the object to be cast is porous it will be necessary to coat it with a sealing material or build a facsimile form from sculptor's plaster or Plasticene (clay ground in oil so that it will not dry out). Since Plasticene has an oil surface it is possible to make shells of some objects over the top of a sculptured form Mâché, cornstarch-cheesecloth, plaster of paris and some other processes will work without further surface processing.

CASTS — Plaster of paris or casting plaster can be used to make the negative cast so that models can be made inside the cast. Formed this way, the object will have a surface conforming to the shape of the object over which the cast is made. If the object to be cast is merely a form raised from a flat surface in bas-relief it is possible to make a one-piece cast but if it is in the round it will be necessary to make the cast of two or more pieces. If the form is modelled in clay undercuts should be avoided so that the cast will pull straight off without hooking on portions of the clay.

A one-piece cast is made somewhat as follows. The object from which the cast is to be made is laid on a flat, nonporous surface such as a slab of glass or marble. If there seems to be danger of the cast sticking to it the surface should be lightly coated with vaseline, liquid

soap, aluminum foil or similar material. Plaster is then mixed by sifting the dry plaster slowly into water until dry plaster begins to build slightly above the water. With the bare hands, or with a spoon or spatula, mix the plaster and water. The less the plaster is mixed the less danger there is of getting bubbles in the cast. Coat the surface with this plaster mixture. The cast should be built so that it is from ½" to 1" in thickness. After the surface of the object has been thoroughly coated the plaster should be allowed to set and dry. During the setting process the plaster will become warm to the touch. The cast should not be removed from the model until it has cooled and is thoroughly hardened. There are stages in the process when the plaster is crumbly and easily broken. It may take a couple of hours for the plaster to harden sufficiently so that the clay or object being cast over can be removed. If possible the cast should be left undisturbed even longer.

CASTS OF TWO OR MORE PIECES—If a three dimensional object is to be cast it will probably be necessary to make a two-piece cast (sometimes three or even more pieces may be needed). The object should be studied to be certain that the cast can be pulled off without destroying the object being cast—especially if more than one copy is desired. If the original form is Plasticene it will be possible to build separating walls from pieces of tin or aluminum. Strips can be sunk into the surface far enough to hold them in place. These will form a collar or fence around one area. Plaster can be poured into this area. After this plaster has set another area can be blocked off. Where plaster is to be poured against plaster notching indentations should be carved into the edge of the dry section and then this edge should be lubricated with soap, vaseline or oil so the new plaster will not stick to the old. This area is then coated with plaster. The process is repeated until all of the form is coated with plaster. After the sections have set they may be pulled apart and away from the original form. It may be that the form from which

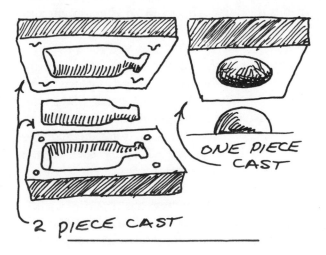

ONE PIECE CAST

2 PIECE CAST

the casting is being made cannot be split into segments with metal strips as indicated above. Perhaps similar "dams" can be fastened on with Scotch tape, string, wire or some other material.

Another method may be used for a two-piece mold. A cardboard or wooden box can be made that is large enough to half submerge the object being cast. Soft plaster is poured into the box and the object half submerged. After this plaster has set the edges can be lubricated and plaster poured on the top half.

After the cast has been removed it may be prepared for any of a number of different kinds of castings. For convenience the processes for some of these are described below.

PLASTIC WOOD—Plastic Wood is somewhat expensive but makes a surface that can be worked rather easily. It can be patched, sawed, carved, sanded and treated very much like wood itself. If Plastic Wood is to be used in a plaster of paris cast the cast should first be soaked in water for about fifteen minutes. The plaster

CAST SOAKED IN WATER BEFORE PUTTING PLASTIC WOOD IN IT.

PLASTIC WOOD SHELL PRESSED INTO CAST

SHELL IN CAST IMMEDIATELY RE-PLACED IN WATER TO SET.

absorbs water which tends to seal the pores and makes it somewhat nonabsorbent. Immediately after the cast is taken from the water the can of Plastic Wood is opened and, working rapidly, the modeller presses wads of it into the cast, being careful to overlap the material

and press it firmly into place. The Plastic Wood should be from $\frac{1}{8}''$ to $\frac{1}{4}''$ in thickness. A thin shell of Plastic Wood when dry is quite strong. In order to keep the Plastic Wood from sticking to the fingers, the fingers should be dipped into water each time before getting a new wad of plastic from the container. Immediately after the wood has been pressed into the mold the cast should be immersed in water again so that the solvent of the Plastic Wood cannot soak into the plaster. Keeping the cast wet all through the process is important. If any of the plaster dries out where the wood is pressed against it the wood will stick. The process is really quite easy, even though from the above description it may seem complicated. The cast is left in the water for about eight hours after the plastic has been pressed into it; even longer will allow it to become harder. When the cast is removed from the water, both cast and Plastic Wood casting may be allowed to dry out. During the drying process the Plastic Wood will shrink and pull away from the cast slightly which will make it easier to remove. If there are no undercuts it will then pull out easily.

If in removing the casting a piece is broken it may be mended by applying a little Plastic Wood to the broken edge and then firmly pressing the two parts together. A string may then be wrapped around to hold the piece in place while the new Plastic Wood sets and mends the joint. If the wood is extremely dry before this patching is done it may be advisable to moisten the broken edges with lacquer thinner or Plastic Wood solvent to keep the dry section from absorbing the solvent from the new wood before the joint adheres. If a two-piece cast is used and there are two pieces to be fastened together this may be done in the same way by using fresh Plastic Wood for the adhering agent. Extra sections may be built onto the casting in the same way.

After the Plastic Wood has dried for awhile it may be further fashioned and smoothed by using woodworking tools such as saws, knives and sandpaper. The surface may then be treated as if it were wood.

PLASTER OF PARIS CAST IN PLASTER OF PARIS—If it is desirable to make a plaster casting in a plaster cast it is necessary to seal the pores of the cast before pouring plaster into it. One of two methods may be tried. The simplest, and possibly least safe, is to use soft soap. Liquid washing soap or tincture of green soap may be used. The surface is carefully coated with this material in thin layers until it feels almost like marble. The plaster should then immediately be poured in. The soap should seal the pores enough to prevent the new plaster from being absorbed. The second method, more complicated, is handled as follows. After the surface of the mold is thoroughly dry coat it with orange shellac. After the first coat of shellac is dry apply a second. When the second coat of shellac is hard coat the surface with stearine. Stearine is made by melting two tablespoons of stearic acid and adding to it eight tablespoons of kerosene. *Great care must be taken to extinguish the flame and add the kerosene where there is no danger of it catching fire.* This solution may then be brushed onto the shellac surface. This second process seals the pores much more completely than the first and the cast is ready to be used any number of times by merely recoating it with stearine. The plaster for the casting is mixed and poured into this form.

It is frequently difficult to remove a cast piece of plaster of paris and the mold must be broken before it can be removed, especially with a one-piece mold.

If it is necessary to patch either the mold or the final casting the pieces may be cemented together with a good grade of glue or plastic cement. If it is necessary to add more plaster of paris after a portion has dried it will bond only if this piece is soaked with water over the area where the new plaster is to be placed. If this isn't done the porous surface will cause the water to be absorbed from the new plaster before it goes through its setting process.

PAPIER-MÂCHÉ—Papier-mâché can be used to make a casting from the plaster form. A coating of liquid soap or vaseline will remove the porousness enough so that the paper will not stick. Three or four layers of paper in narrow overlapping strips should be used. If it is possible to place the whole works near a heat blower the paper will dry more rapidly. If too many layers of paper are put on at one

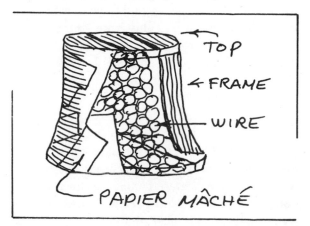

time and the drying process is too slow the mixture will become moldy before it dries. Wheat paste, paper hangers' paste, flour paste or a thin solution of glue may be used for the adhesive. Papier-mâché may also be made into a pulp by shredding the paper, soaking it in the adhesive solution and then pressing the pulp into the cast. For a fine finished surface tissue paper may be applied as a last coat. Brown wrapping paper may be used for sturdy objects.

Mâché may use paper (shredded, in strips or pulp), cheesecloth, muslin, asbestos (paper or pulp) and may be textured by scattering or pressing sawdust, sand, shavings, flock, flitter or similar material onto its surface. If the mache is cast in two or more pieces they may be attached to one another with strips of mache.

CORNSTARCH-CHEESECLOTH—Cheesecloth or other mesh cloth can be moistened to make it flexible enough to press into a mold and then cooked cornstarch about the consistency of thick cream can be brushed onto and into the cloth. Add a second layer and repeat the process. The layering can continue if a heavy "shell" is

147

desired. This can be dried to a hard finish. Masks can be readily made from this material.

PLASTER CAST CLOTH—The cloth, impregnated with plaster, that is used by doctors to wrap broken bone areas for supporting casts is a material that can be easily used for making some items. It comes in a roll and is easily used. It needs only to be dipped in water and it is ready to wrap around or over an object for use. It dries rather rapidly and when dry has a hard surface. This with crepe paper mâché over the top for smoothing makes an excellent surface. The material is available at many drug stores and comes in a variety of widths. Strips of cheesecloth dipped in wet plaster may be used in the same way.

PLASTER OF PARIS AND BURLAP—Burlap impregnated with plaster of paris can be used to build up forms. A basic core of chicken wire or other material may be constructed first. Then pieces of burlap dipped in wet plaster are placed over this. Plaster can be molded over the top to get the desired modelling. It is necessary to work quickly since the plaster will harden rapidly when it begins to "set."

PAPER TAPE—Most dressmakers are familiar with body dress forms that are made from gummed paper tape. This same gummed paper may be used for making some property forms. It will work best if the object has rolling contours rather than sharp turns. However, the paper may be cut or torn into small pieces and used even for sharp curves and turns.

STYROFOAM—Styrofoam is excellent to use as a base for forms that are completed with plaster molded over the surface. This can be used beautifully for such objects as cakes, stones and logs.

RUBBER LATEX—Rubber latex may be used for making either the cast or the casting. It is obtainable in a milky liquid form that is poured into a cast or over a form. The directions that come with it will help in determining how long it takes for it to set. Thin shells of objects can be easily made with this material. Special

paints will be needed to color its surface. The finished form is tough and durable. Prop food forms such as loaves of bread, vegetables, fruits, fowls and roasts may be made in this way.

FIBRE GLASS—Fibre glass imbedded in resin can be used to make tough, durable properties. It requires special agents. Information may be obtained from the dealer who supplies it. Fibre glass may be purchased from some sporting goods stores where boats are sold since it is frequently used for building boats or for coating wooden boats. This is excellent for making permanent units like armour. It is rather expensive, which is its major drawback.

CELASTIC—Celastic is a sheet plastic molding material. It requires special softening and parting agents. The material and information about its use can be obtained from costume houses or from the manufacturers.

PLASTAB—Plastab is a colloid impregnated fabric similar to Celastic and handled as a molding plastic.

PAPER FLOWERS—Paper flowers may be purchased from ten cent stores, from window display houses and from specialty companies or they may be manufactured by the property crew. Since they are rather expensive to buy it is likely that the latter method of obtaining them will be the one most often used. There are some times in exterior settings when they can be painted directly on the scenery or set pieces. Large stylized flowers may be cut from cardboard, wall board or even plywood and painted. Flowers may be made from regular or double weight crepe paper, stiff painted muslin, plastic and cloth materials or combinations of all of these materials. Heavy textile material such as felt can be used beautifully for some flowers. The stems can be made of wire. Soft wire can be used to hold the petal sections together and to fasten leaf sections onto the steam and then the wire can be covered with florists green tape. Rubber flowers were used in the original Broadway production of *Knickerbocker Holiday*. The actors could step or sit on them and when they moved the flowers sprang back up into place.

A little experimenting will help in making flowers. Pamphlets on flower making can be obtained from the crepe paper manufacturers.

GRASS—The easiest thing to do about grass is to forget about it, but if the demands cannot be quieted there are a number of methods of supplying a substitute for grass. A colored section of floor cloth or rug might serve the purpose if it is painted in a grass green and then spattered with various other greens. The simulated grass mats sometimes used by funeral directors are excellent but expensive. Shredded green paper or cellophane can be glued to the surface of the grassy plot. Grass ground rows with painted cut out grass blades can be used and grass blades can be painted on the base of drops and some set pieces. Sometimes the suggestion of grass is better than an attempt at realistic duplication.

PLANTS—When plants are desired it is often easier to borrow or rent them from a greenhouse than to try to simulate them. Palm fronds can be purchased and rigged onto a tree limb which is then spirally covered with shredded strips of burlap and the result is a passable palm tree. Artificial large leafed plants may be purchased from window display houses. And of course it is possible to make stylized cut outs of plants if the technique fits in with the feeling of the rest of the production.

LEAVES—Leaves may be made of muslin, velour, felt, flocked paper, stiff paper, plastic, crepe paper or any of a host of other materials. The material can be stiffened with paint or glue size and after it has dried the leaves can be cut and mounted on wire stems to be fastened to the plant. Real leaves, especially palm varieties, may be purchased from florists.

HEDGES—Potted real hedge bushes may be used for hedges or three dimensional built up flat units may be painted and used or realistic papier-mache on wire units may be shaped, covered and painted. Another effect to try here is to use chicken wire for the basic form and then stuff the holes with green crepe paper

or paper napkin sections the way that parade floats are often decorated.

Grasses, weeds, grain, corn stalks and natural materials of this nature may sometimes be used. They can be sprayed with paint in order to color them and then be mounted on a board base to hold them in place.

VINES—Vines may be painted onto the scenery or simulated by stringing rope where desired. The rope can be painted and artificial leaves of muslin, paper or cloth wired on where needed.

SMALL TREE TRUNKS—Branches of real trees or shrubs will probably make the best tree trunks. At times extremely stylized tree trunks can be cut out of heavy plywood or be formed by twisting heavy wires together. They may be painted, wrapped with cloth or left plain.

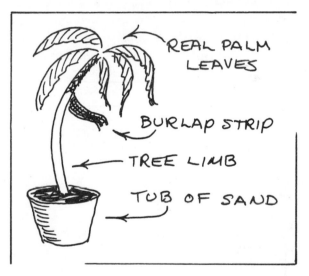

Leaves can be fastened on with wire and made as indicated above or can be completely non-conformist shapes made from twisted wire, pieces of sponge rubber, tufts of cotton or almost anything else.

ARMAMENT—A veritable arsenal of equipment will be used from time to time in plays. When guns are called for it may be possible to get real ones from private owners, the National Guard, police, sheriff or armed forces branches. If extreme naturalism is desired this should be done. They should be handled with great care and kept locked up when not in use. Some miscellaneous arms equipment of recent date may on occasion be purchased from War Surplus or Army and Navy stores. Costume houses also have equipment of this nature.

GUNS—Convincing wooden guns, both revolvers and rifles, can be manufactured if one has the time and material. Gunstocks can be cut out of 2″ shop pine and fashioned with a wood rasp, draw knife, plane and sandpaper. A piece of dowel, pipe, or electrical conduit can be used for the barrel. And the trigger guard can be made from a piece of plumber's strap or thin strap iron. Either the real thing or adequate pictures or illustrations should be used as models. Pictures may be found in a good dictionary or encyclopedia.

DAGGERS — Daggers may be made from wood or metal. Bayonets, often obtainable in surplus stores, can be ground down to dagger size. Obviously they should be dull so that no injuries are invited when they are in use on the stage. Sometimes wooden daggers are more practical for just this reason. Fake rubber daggers are obtainable in "trick" stores so that the dagger may actually be pushed against a person without injuring him.

SWORDS—Some swords can be manufactured of wood or metal but usually this type of equipment should be rented or borrowed. It is advisable to check rather carefully and determine the correct style and variety of weapon for the period and action of the play.

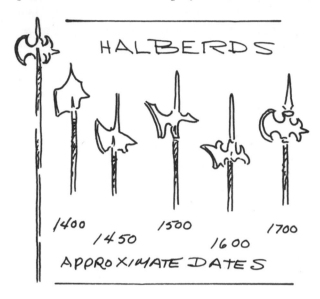

SPEARS — Convincing spears can be made from curtain rod, dowel, or aluminum conduit and a wooden head. Metallic heads could be made but the wooden ones will probably be easier to make and may be more convincing. These can be cut from ½″ or ⅝″ plywood. Here again it is advisable to check rather carefully in order to be certain that the head of the spear, halbred or whatever it is, has the correct shape. Spears may have a bit of cloth tied to them beneath the head to add color—again if it seems to fit the period and style.

HELMETS — The helmet liners used in the second world war are excellent for helmets. If they are not the correct style and shape for the period of the play the correct ones may be made from them by using them as a base

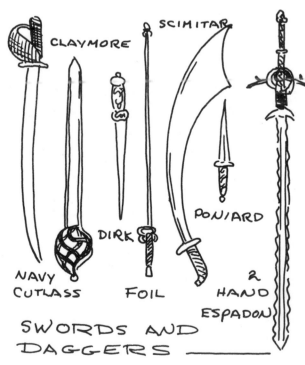

and adding Celastic, wire and mache, or wire and plaster cast bandage.

PENNANTS—Pennants and flags add a good deal of color and smartness to a battle scene. This is especially true in productions of Shakespeare. At times they also help to keep the various factions straight in the minds of the audience. They may be made of muslin, rayon, silk, nylon or almost any material that will hang in nice folds. Correct designs may be applied free hand, silk screened, block printed or stencilled. The pennants can be mounted on poles of wood or metal and a fitting emblem or point mounted at the top of the pole. A bit of rope with tassels can hang down as added decoration. For the rope the twisted soft cotton rope used in upholstery for beading may be used. This can be painted or left white depending upon the color desired for contrast.

FLAGS — If real flags are desired they may usually be obtained from civic and service organizations.

POLICE EQUIPMENT—A policeman's night stick can easily be made from a piece of fat dowel or a straight piece of a tree limb. A badge may be cut from aluminum. It may be possible to borrow all of the equipment needed from the local police station.

MILITARY EQUIPMENT — When conventional and contemporary military equipment is needed it is usually advisable to get on the telephone and contact local or nearby installations of active or inactive military establishments before arranging to make or rent equipment. They are usually most cooperative and helpful in either providing equipment or furnishing information about where it may be obtained.

ARMOR—Armor, such as breast plates and other paraphernalia of that nature, can be rented or made up by the crew. Some sections might be made from aluminum, available in hobby shops and department stores. It may also be possible to mold armor on the body. If it is to be molded to fit the body a number of methods might be used. Obtain some plaster of paris medical cast tape. Use an old "T"

shirt for chest covering, and the knit material that doctors use for leg or arm undercover for a cast; place them on the body and then over the top of these mold the shape desired. Several thicknesses of this material will dry to a hard shell that can be reused many times. Another method of making forms of this nature uses a screen wire base. Cut and shape the screen wire to the correct contour and then coat it with papier-mache, cloth mache, gummed tape or similar material. Still another process uses felt over a plaster of paris cast. In order to shape the felt correctly it is necessary to use steam or moisture. Over a cast the felt can be steamed into shape. A couple of thicknesses can be glued together if necessary and the whole thing heavily sized and painted with gilt or aluminum paint. Celastic, plastab, and fibre glass might also be used for armor.

SHIELDS — Shields can be made from plywood or metal. The plywood will probably be the easiest to use and most satisfactory in the long run. If desirable this may be partially or completely covered with metal for the sound effects. There is no reason for not using any of the other molding materials for the shield. A round, slightly dished shield could rather readily be made by cutting a circle of metal and then after slicing in to the center making the sections overlap slightly and fastening the joint with rivets. Wall board material such as EZ Curve Upsom board might be used in the same way. The EZ Curve shield wouldn't stand as much battle service as the metal one but for short time use might be perfectly satisfactory.

Printing Processes

Patterns and designs may be applied to pennants, banners, draperies, costumes, signs and posters by one of at least four methods: 1. Free hand, 2. Linoleum Block Printing, 3. Stencils and 4. Silk Screen.

FREE HAND—The free hand method of designing and painting patterns is easy and takes less preparation than other methods. If an identical pattern is to be duplicated several times the other methods have certain advantages. Free hand patterns become tedious and boring to duplicate.

LINOLEUM BLOCKS—Heavy battleship linoleum may be used on a block, or without a block for some printing, but it is usually easier to handle when mounted on a board base. The linoleum may be purchased ready mounted or

LINOLEUM BLOCK IS NEGATIVE, UN CUT PORTIONS PRINT,

CUT-OUT PATTERN OF STENCIL— DARK AREAS CUT OUT LEAV— ING LINKS BETWEEN THEM.

may be cemented to a block of wood just before the pattern is cut. The pattern is drawn in reverse on the linoleum after having been planned on paper first. In fact it may be transferred with carbon paper if desirable. Linoleum knives or cutters are the most satisfactory tools to use for carving out the unwanted linoleum. Only the portions of the pattern that are to print are left. These raised portions are then inked and pressed onto the surface to be printed. In order to ink the block evenly a squeegee is used. The ink is placed on a flat surface, such as a piece of glass, and then the squeegee is rolled back and forth to coat the roller evenly. The roller is then pushed across the face of the block carefully to ink the printing surface. Any one of a number of devices may be used as a press. The material to be printed may be placed flat on the floor. The block may be inked, laid in place where it is to print, and then pressure applied to the block with one or both feet. The block may be placed in a regular press and printed on the surface. Or the material may

be placed on top of the block and rubbed by hand to transfer the pattern. The pattern is applied wherever desired.

STENCIL — The stencil pattern may be cut out of the stencil paper with a sharp knife, razor blade, Exacto knife or matte knife. The portion of the paper representing the pattern to be colored is cut out. Great care must be taken to plan the pattern so that connecting links remain so that the paper will not tear out between stencil pattern sections. After the stencil has been cut the paper may be mounted on a wooden frame, similar to a picture frame, in order to make it easier to handle. A sponge, brush or cloth swab may be used to apply the paint. If a sponge is used it is possible to get open rather than solid coverage. Of course the paint may also be applied with a brush, but the sponge makes the process less regular and harsh. Almost any variety of paint can be used with a stencil which is one of its advantages. It is possible to use oil, water or textile paints.

SILK SCREEN — The silk screen requires a a little more equipment than the other processes but the finished products are often more satisfactory and most of the equipment will last for a long time and can be reused time after time. The first requisite is a sturdy wooden frame to fasten special silk onto. Although any tough silk will work it is best to get the silk that is specially prepared for silk screen work. The silk is stretched and tacked or stapled onto the frame. It is important to get the silk surface as taut as possible. After this has been done masking tape is placed over the tacks and edge of the silk extending at least half an inch toward the center of the frame. Next the frame is turned over and masking tape is placed around the inside of the frame to cover the tape on the bottom and extend up on the frame slightly in order to seal the edges where the paint might seep in between the silk and the frame. When this is done the frame is ready to use. A squeegee similar to a window washer's squeegee is used to pull the paint across the silk screen that has just been applied to the

152

frame. A regular silk screen squeegee or a heavy floor squeegee or a heavy window washer's squeegee will do. The squeegee must have

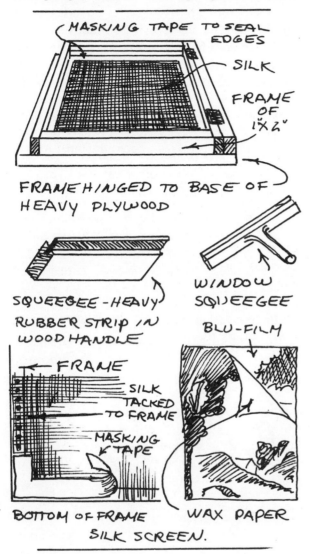

MASKING TAPE TO SEAL EDGES

SILK

FRAME OF 1"X2"

FRAME HINGED TO BASE OF HEAVY PLYWOOD

SQUEEGEE - HEAVY RUBBER STRIP IN WOOD HANDLE

WINDOW SQUEEGEE

BLU-FILM

FRAME

SILK TACKED TO FRAME

MASKING TAPE

BOTTOM OF FRAME SILK SCREEN.

WAX PAPER

fairly heavy rubber or it will not pull the paint across the silk evenly.

Designs for the silk screen may be made in several ways. If the pattern isn't too complex it may be cut from paper. Paper that is not too absorbent will work the best. If a paper pattern is used it is placed under the screen on top of some old newspapers. The pattern is attached to the frame with masking tape. Some silk screen paint is then poured across at one end of the screen. The squeege is then used to pull the paint across the surface. Even pressure should be applied as the paint is pulled across. The paint will be squeezed through the screen transferring the pattern to the old newspapers and causing the paper pattern to adhere to the silk.

Areas of the silk screen can be opaqued (or sealed) with Le Pages liquid glue, with Block Out Lacquer or with Blu Film. Glue and lacquer are applied with a brush. The glue is really much easier to apply and at the same time is less expensive and easier to remove when the screen is cleaned.

Blu Film is a special thin film material mounted on a wax paper base that is manufactured specifically for use with silk screen equipment. It is rather expensive but for small detail work is superior to most of the other materials. With a sharp knife it is possible with extremely light strokes to cut portions of the film and remove them from the paper base. Fine detail can be thus removed. The film is removed wherever it is desirable to have the paint squeeze through the pattern. After the pattern has been completed the Blu Film is placed under the silk and adhered to the silk with a special liquid. This step in the process must be executed carefully but with a little practice and the expenditure of a good deal of energy it can be done successfully. Two soft cloths are used, one to apply the adhering liquid and a second to rub it vigorously to dry it. The liquid is applied rapidly to a small area and then with the dry rag the area is rubbed briskly with pressure. When this has been done inspection will reveal that the film has been pulled in to seal the spaces between the threads. After all of the film has been adhered and is dry the paper back is carefully peeled from the film thus opening the spaces through which the paint is to be squeezed.

All of the block-out substances may be used on the same job. Detail areas can be covered with Blu Film while the rest of the space is covered with paper. Dry brush effects can be

153

accomplished by lightly brushing glue across the surface.

Multi-color silk screen printing is accomplished by repeating the process, cutting out other areas of the pattern and squeezing other colors of paint through the stencil thus created. Sometimes it is wise to hinge the frame onto a base of some sort so that the paper, cloth or material being printed can be kept in register for single or multi-color printing.

All of the paraphernalia will require cleaning. This is usually a messy process. The paper can be pulled off and thrown away. Glue can be washed off with soap and water, but special solvents are required for the lacquer, Blu Film and paint. Acetone will probably work very well for both Blu Film and paint if regular silk screen paint is being used (and this is the paint that is usually recommended).

* * * *

If there is space available it will usually prove advantageous to keep as many stage properties in a "morgue" as possible. When units are built this may be borne in mind. Genuine artificial simulated roasts, hams, Thanksgiving turkeys, fruits and vegetables as well as a myriad of other items will be needed for play after play and if they are available in the property stock room the job of "propping" the show will be made much easier. If the objects are durably made they will last for a long time.

Polonius' words from *Hamlet* may give a cue to the property manager:

"Neither a borrower nor a lender be;
For loan oft loses both itself and friend,
And borrowing dulls the edge of husbandry."

This will prove true if properties are borrowed, mishandled and returned without being carefully checked for damage. Broken, scarred and soiled objects should be repaired, cleaned or replaced. The kindness of the lenders must be respected if a repeat of the kindness is expected in the future.

LEAF PATTERNS

10

Special Effects

It would be impossible to describe all of the special effects that could be encountered even in a dozen plays. However, it is possible to suggest a few of the more common devices and contrivances that might be called for from time to time.

Manual Sound Effects

Many stage sound effects can be created with manual devices that can be manufactured in the shop. Among these are the following:

WIND—The conventional wind machine is composed of a slatted drum mounted so that it can be rotated. This is rigged with a sheet of canvas thrown across the drum. When the drum is turned the canvas drags against the slats and creates a wind-like sound. By placing pressure on the canvas an increase of volume may be obtained.

RAIN—The sound of rain may be manually created in a drum with hardware cloth or window screen sides. Dried peas, small pebbles or similar articles are placed inside. When the drum is rotated the particles roll around and produce a sound similar to that of rain.

THUNDER—The standard thunder sound machine is a large piece of sheet iron. It is usually rigged with a batten on the top and bottom. This should be suspended from above; then it is possible to grasp the bottom batten and give the thunder sheet a sudden shake.

HORSES' HOOVES—Coconut halves or plumber's helpers (plungers) may be used to reproduce the sound of horses' hooves. The coconut halves can be used on different surfaces

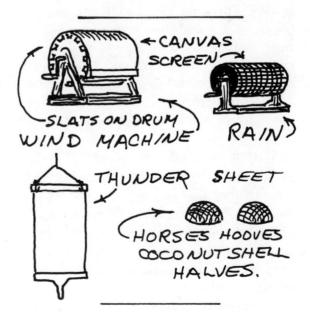

to create the sound of hooves under various conditions. The sound of hooves on soft ground is made by patting the chest with the coconut halves; a box of gravel is used for the gravel road effect and a piece of Masonite for the hard surface effect.

BREAKING GLASS — Pieces of broken glass can be placed in a box. A handful of the pieces dropped into the box create the sound of breaking glass. If a crash is to accompany the breaking sound the box holding the glass may be dropped onto the floor.

GUN SHOT—A blank gun may be used for gun shot sounds. On the stage even a .22 caliber gun may provide a loud enough sound. Shooting the gun into an empty barrel will give a reinforced sound. In an emergency such a simple thing as briskly slapping a stack of newspapers onto a table or holding a piece of board diagonally from the floor and then crashing it to the floor with the foot will provide a resounding bang!

SQUEAKY HINGE OR DOOR — Old rusty hinges may be used for squeaky sounds, but too often they lose their squeak at the crucial moment. Sometimes twisting a moistened cork stopper in a bottle will work if the sound need not be loud. New Year's eve rotating noise makers will work fairly well. Prying apart boards that have been nailed together with rusty nails may work. Effects of this nature are not always predictable and should be tried several times before being used in a production.

CANNON SHOT — The sound of a cannon shot may be simulated by striking a tympani or bass drum.

WHISTLES — Whistle sounds of varying pitch may be made with real whistles or organ pipes or they may be made by blowing across the tops of various sized bottles and jugs.

CHIMES AND GONGS — Real chimes and gongs, symphony chimes, old brake drums, sections of pipe or cymbals may be used for sound effects.

MARCHING SOLDIERS — A device to dupli-

cate the sound of marching feet is easy to make. Short wooden pegs about three or four inches long are drilled near one end and wires strung through them. The wires with the pegs hanging on them are then mounted on a framework. By bouncing this so the pegs strike the desired type of surface the sound of many feet is created. This may be used with or without a microphone.

DOOR SOUNDS — Usually a real latch mounted on a small, heavily built door will provide a substantial door closing sound. However, there is usually a real door on the stage area that can be used for this sound.

Electrically Operated Effects

BELLS, BUZZERS AND CHIMES—The sound effects department will have need for various types of bells, buzzers and chimes. These may all be mounted onto a single board and oper-

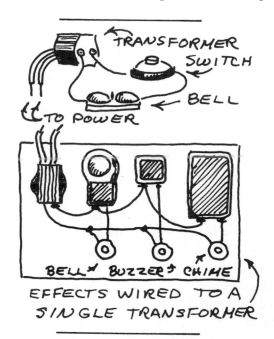

EFFECTS WIRED TO A SINGLE TRANSFORMER

ated off of a single power source. This will be convenient since most of these devices will require a 6 volt source of power and in order to get this power it will be necessary to use a transformer or batteries.

The transformer will have lead-in wires that

156

are to be connected to the ordinary 120 volt power source. These wires extend out from one side of the transformer. On the other side of it are 6-8 volt terminal screws. A simple series circuit is then arranged by extending a wire from one of the transformer contact screws to the bell, buzzers or whatever it is. A wire goes from the other contact on the transformer to a contact screw on the base of a push button. Another wire goes from the other contact on the base of the push button to the second contact on the bell. The circuit is then complete so the power passes from the transformer through the bell to the push button and back to the transformer.

If dry cell batteries are used as the source of power to operate the bell a similar series circuit can be wired. The power contacts in this

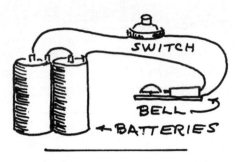

instance are the posts on top of the battery. Each battery is a 1½ volt source of power. If greater voltage is desired two or more batteries are connected in series. This is done by connecting the center contact of one battery to the side contact of the next and so on until they are all connected together.

SOUND AMPLIFYING SYSTEM — A sound amplifying system to be used with a microphone, a record player or a tape recorder is an electronic device of value on a stage where there is need for background music and sound effects. It is possible to record the sounds and then have them played on cue.

TAPE RECORDERS—Although it is possible to use a microphone for some sound effects and to use disc records for others, it is far more practical to record all of the desired effects on

tape and then, using a single tape with all of the effects recorded in correct order, play them back on cue. If the recorder is equipped with a head set it is convenient to set up the cues with the main speakers turned off.

RADIOS AND RECORD PLAYERS — Scenes calling for the operation of record players and radios can best be handled by "faking" onstage and actually operating offstage. Careful rehearsal and cuing is necessary but the results are satisfying. Sounds of this nature can be set up along with other recorded sounds on a tape recorder.

MICROPHONE SOUNDS—If it is desirable to use a live microphone and produce sound effects in front of it or if it is desirable to produce the sounds for reproduction on tape a few of the more frequently desired sounds are created as follows:

Chopping Wood—Drive an ice pick lightly into a soft piece of wood.

Motors — Run a vacuum cleaner near the microphone or hold a piece of paper against the blades of an operating electric fan.

Hail—Drop dry rice onto glass, tin or wood.

Rain—Let free running salt run onto paper or glass; roll cellophane lightly in the hands.

INTERCOMMUNICATIONS SYSTEM—For the convenience of the operational crew of the theatre it is advisable to have some type of intercommunications system. The regular box type combination speaker and microphone will work all right and so will a regular powered telephone system. However, sound powered telephones perfected during the second World War are extremely practical for this type of theatre use. They require no power source except the human voice and maintenance is held to a minimum. One of the only disadvantages is that if a bell system is desired it must be wired in separately. Head sets for the men operating the show are probably more convenient to use during the performance and this minimizes the need for bells. Intercommunication between the stage manager, light control booth, pin rail and special follow spot operator may be all that will be necessary for the ordinary stage.

Fire and Smoke Effects

FIRE—There are frequently occasions on the stage when it is essential to have fire effects. Log units can be rather readily built using pieces of real wood, papier-mache logs or screen wire and plaster logs. Sockets and small wattage lamps are mounted under them. A few pieces of colored gelatine covered over the lamps or placed in the spaces between the logs will make a fairly convincing fire. The whole affair is usually mounted on a board base so that it can be moved around more easily.

MOVING FLAME EFFECTS — In order to make the fire seem more realistic and give the appearance of moving flames, any one of a number of devices can be contrived. Here are a few of them.

1. Project motion pictures of actual flames on the surface where the flames are desired.

2. Allow flame colored beams of light to be broken by some moving object. Something as simple as hands moving through the beam of light will produce this effect. A spoked wheel placed in position can be turned to do the same work.

3. A mechanical device to break up the light pattern can be easily manufactured from an electric fan and a few strips of cloth, ribbon or paper. The strips are tied onto the face frame of an electric fan and the fan placed face up on the floor so that the air current set up by the fan will cause the ribbons to rise and flutter in front of the light source.

4. A color wheel device with irregular patterns of colored gelatine can be rotated in front of the light source to provide a changing light or flame effect. The wheel can be rigged up to an electric motor to facilitate in turning if desired.

5. The device used for fire insurance signs can be used also. This is a plastic tube with variable flames painted around its periphery. This is provided with a vented metal cap. The

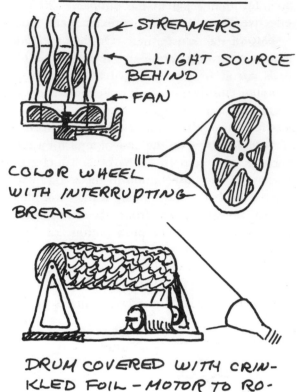

STREAMERS
LIGHT SOURCE BEHIND
FAN

COLOR WHEEL WITH INTERRUPTING BREAKS

DRUM COVERED WITH CRINKLED FOIL - MOTOR TO ROTATE - LIGHT TO REFLECT

whole thing is then rigged to fit above and around a lamp. A needle shaft fastened around the lamp with a wire extends upward and supports the tube affair. The heat from the lamp moving upward sets up air currents that cause the tube to rotate slowly as the warm air passes up through the vents.

6. A rotating drum of crinkled aluminum foil with one or more lights rigged to shine upon it and be reflected from it onto the surface where the visible flames are desired is an extremely effective device. Devices of this nature are to be seen in many of the displays of fireplace equipment shops. Either the foil or source of light may be colored to produce colored flames and the light units may be rigged to be reflected wherever desired. They may be below and shine upward or above and shine downward. This type of unit, and all others,

too, for that matter, will probably be more effective if used in conjunction with a log unit.

SMOKE—A few of the methods of achieving smoke effects on the stage are the following:

1. *Sal Ammoniac*—Sal Ammoniac (or ammonium chloride which is its correct chemical name) will change from a solid to a gas form when heat is applied. Various devices can be used to furnish the heat. A hot plate, a cone shaped heating coil from an electric room heater, or even an incandescent lamp may be used as the heat source. The heater cone works beautifully since it is possible to place the powder on the inside of the cone. Sal ammoniac fumes are somewhat offensive and should not be breathed for any length of time.

2. *Dry Ice*—Dry ice (solid carbon dioxide) will change directly from a solid to a gaseous state when exposed to air. The change will take place more rapidly in water and if the water is hot the change is speeded up even more. Carbon dioxide is heavy and tends to sink rapidly to the floor. A device for getting dry ice "smoke" to rise may be easily contrived by using a sizable container with a narrow neck. If dry ice is placed in hot water within this container the rapidly escaping gas will be forced through the narrow aperture and shot into the air.

3. *Titanium Tetrachloride*—Titanium Tetrachloride should be used only on special occasions and where the fumes will not be breathed since they are extremely dangerous. This is very easy material to use since it changes from a liquid to gaseous state upon exposure to air. It is merely necessary to open the container and white smoke rolls out.

4. *Zinc Dust, Ammonium Nitrate and Ammonium Chloride*—Prepare a mixture of equal parts of zinc dust, ammonium chloride and ammonium nitrate. Squeeze a few drops of water onto this mixture and in a few seconds smoke will be created.

5. *Powder Blown into the Air*—A simple mechanical method of producing a smoke-like effect may be achieved by directing a puff of air onto or into a container of face powder, precipitated chalk or other lightweight material. The air used may be produced by mouth, released from a compressed air tank, emitted from an inflated tire or balloon, or blown from a vacuum cleaner or a compressor and it may be conducted to the container of dust through a small rubber hose or a piece of tubing. The powder material may be in any kind of container, including the air tube itself. A mechanism can be contrived by taking the dust bag from a cylinder type vacuum cleaner. The dust can be fed into one end and allowed to blow out through the hose at the other end.

6. *Steam*—There may be some times and places where it will be more convenient to use steam for a smoke effect than anything else. It will probably be wise to use only low pressure steam for the sake of safety and sound.

FLASH EFFECTS—Sudden flashes of light are frequently needed for spectacular effects. A number of devices can be used. Among them are the following:

1. *Flash Lamps*—The simplest and safest flash effects can be achieved by using photographers' flash lamps. These may be set off in a circuit containing batteries, which may in turn be portable with self contained wiring or may be plugged into a regular AC circuit.

2. *Flash Powder*—Flash powder is more spectacular than flash lamps but it is also more

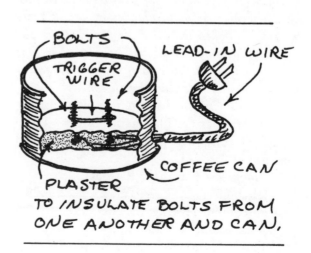

dangerous. The danger may be cut to a minimum if the material is handled carefully and set off in an insulated container. A "flash can" made from a one pound coffee container will do. Lead wires are passed through the side of the can and each is secured to a stove bolt about an inch long. Plaster of paris is then mixed and poured into the container. As the plaster hardens, the bolts are lifted so that they are clear of the bottom of the can and spaced 1½" to 2" apart. The plaster of paris serves as an insulation between the bolts (or contacts) and between the bolts and the bottom of the container. The plaster should be built up about 1½" thick in the bottom of the container.

The trigger for the flash is composed of a piece of magnesium ribbon, two or three strands of wire from rip cord or a small wad of fine steel wool. The wire or steel wool is stretched across so that it forms a contact between the bolts. When the current passes through the strands of wire or steel wool it produces a short. This heats the wire or steel wool to the melting point, which in turn sets off the powder that has been placed on top of the wire.

Powdered magnesium may be used alone to produce a flash. A more rapid explosion may be obtained by using the following formula:

1 part powdered magnesium
1 part potassium perchlorate
1 part sugar

Black gun powder may also be used to produce a flash. *A small quantity of any of these materials should be tried first and then the quantity increased until the correct charge is determined. Not more than ½ teaspoonful of any one should be tried the first time.*

Bennett's *Chemical Formulary* lists the following formulas for Flashlight powder. These should be carefully prepared by a qualified chemist.

1. Smokeless Flashlight Powder.
   Zirconium ....28 g
   Zirconium Hydride .... 7 g
   Magnesium .... 7 g
   Barium Nitrate ....30 g

Barium Oxide ....25 g
Rice Starch .... 5 g

2. Flashlight Powder. (U. S. Patent #2,098,341)
   Powdered Magnesium ....120-140 g
   Powdered Aluminum .... 25- 32 g
   Precipitated Calcium
       Carbonate .... 45- 56 g
   Powdered Silica .... 18- 24 g
   Calcinated Magnesium
       Oxide .... 8- 12 g

The flash may be colored by adding chemicals. To color the flash some of the following may be added:

Table salt for a yellow flash.
Calcium chloride for a yellow red flash.
Potassium chloride for a purple flash.
Copper sulphate for a green flash.
Lithium chloride for a bright red flash.
Strontium chloride for a bright red flash.

Another flashing trigger may be made by using a fuse plug from which the mica window has been removed. The fuse strip when shorted will heat and melt, setting off the powder.

WARNING — Flash devices should all be handled with care. The materials should be

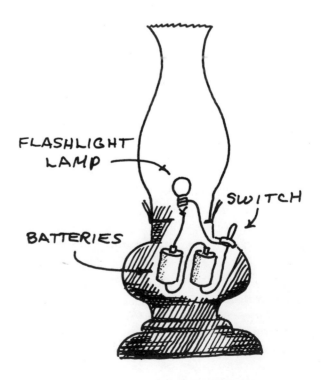

prepared only by reputable chemists or chemical firms. Be careful to have the flash pot disconnected when loading. Be certain to place the flashing device in a position where the flash will not start a fire in scenery or draperies or where it will not burn the actors.

Electrified Lamps

Lamps, fake candles and flash bulb tripping devices are usually wired in series. They are simple to make providing there is space for batteries. Solder a piece of bell wire to the button contact of the lamp base and extend it to the base of the battery where it is soldered. Fasten a wire from the cap of the battery to a small switch or push button terminal. Then connect another wire from the other terminal of the button to the screw base of the lamp. If a socket is used the process starts with one terminal of the socket and ends with the other.

Visual Effects

Many visual effects can be set up and operated rather easily. A few of these are as follows:

WAVES—Cut out waves moved up and down or sideways, using possibly two or three rows of waves in depth, will give an interesting effect. Painted or dyed scrim or cheesecloth stretched across the stage and manipulated from the sides so that air caught underneath causes the material to undulate produces an interesting wave-like effect.

TORCHES — The easiest and safest way to make a torch is to mount a flashlight in the end of a club and then cover the illuminated area with loose cellophane or gelatine.

Large candles can be enclosed in the torch, but the flame will be rather small and it will also probably be blown out.

Alcohol soaked cotton or "canned" heat may be placed in a container on top of or in the end of a torch. *There is danger of the alcohol dripping to the floor unless one is careful.*

Railroad Fusee torches can be used, but they are a fire hazard indoors.

BREEZE EFFECTS—A scrim or cyclorama may be shaken from one or both sides, setting up visual waves that move across the stage. A large fan can be set up on stage to blow lightweight material such as marquisette, silk, nylon or cheesecloth.

SPIRITS MOVING OBJECTS—A tiny hole can be cut through the flat and then wire or string can be threaded through the hole to move or manipulate objects. Vases can be knocked off the fireplace, pictures can be tilted, objects can be moved on a table—all by manipulating the wire or thread. If the object is to be lifted, fine piano wire or, if it is not too heavy, fish line can be used. Even a fishing pole—especially a long fly pole—can be used if there is a place for the operator to stand so that he can manipulate the pole out of sight lines.

PICTURES KNOCKED OFF THE WALL—Pictures may be suspended with thread that extends through the flat and up to a batten. The thread can be broken or released, dropping the picture.

LIGHTNING—Lighning may be simulated by setting off photo flash bulbs, striking a carbon arc or flashing a series of small wattage lamps (large wattage lamps take too long to heat and cool). A series of four 26 volt sealed beam spotlight lamps or signal lights will make beautiful lightning.

PRACTICAL RAIN — Rain effects may be achieved with an overhead pipe, pierced for water to come through, attached to either a hose leading to a tap or to a hose leading to an elevated container of water. A trough should be placed underneath the pipe to catch the water. This works well when the rain area is restricted, but utilizes much water and is messy if the rain area is wide. Designing the rainfall so the audience sees it through a window, across a doorway or across an arched opening is a way to restrict the rain area. A rain effects machine, such as the effects machine referred to in the section on electrical equipment, may work under the correct conditions. Actually, a darkened sky and the sound of rain will project the idea quite well. Audiences do have collective imaginations! It is also possible to "slosh" water over an actor just before he makes an entrance to show that he had sense enough to come in out of the rain.

SNOW—Devise an overhead slotted or punctured cradle of canvas or sheet metal that can be rocked. A sheet of canvas with battens top and bottom and suspended by two sets of lines to form a hammock will work. By juggling either set of lines the snow material used can be controlled so that it will be shaken out of the affair like salt out of a shaker. The snow

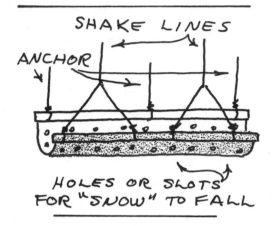

material may be mica flakes, corn flakes (unbaked if possible), Christmas tree snow, paper confetti, Lux Flakes or Styrofoam flakes.

LARGE MOVING OBJECTS—Cut outs can be pulled, pushed or dragged across the stage. Sometimes crew members can be inside or behind such objects.

COLLAPSING COLUMNS—Columns or similar objects can be built in sections and the sections can be bolted together at an overlapping point. The column can be suspended from a line or wire fastened to the top; the bottom of the column can be anchored to the floor. On cue the suspending line can be released or eased down, allowing the sections of the column to collapse. Flat forms will work very well this way. The tumbling columns of the opera *Samson and Delilah* can be made in this way.

"POP UP" OBJECTS—Objects that need to pop up or pop out on cue can have springs

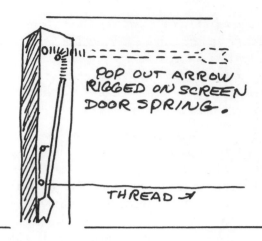

(screen door springs, for instance) rigged onto or within them. These objects can be "cocked" and held with thread or string. Then on cue the thread is broken or cut—and "boing"! The object springs up.

RUNNING WATER—A sink with taps is often needed on a stage setting. When this is desired it may be possible to make an artificial sink although a real one will probably prove more satisfactory in the long run. A hose may be run from the nearest backstage water source to the sink in the stage setting. If this method is used enough water should be run through the drain of the sink and into a bucket or tub below, or through another hose running off to the nearest drain, so that the air will all be removed from the hose. The tap at the source may be left on or the hose may be filled with water and the end raised up into the flies so that the hose itself becomes the water chamber. Another method may prove more satisfactory. A water container is hoisted up on a small platform or on a ladder behind the setting and a hose or tube is run from there to the tap above the sink.

PUMP—For a pump it is usually necessary to have a relatively flat tank of water under the pump platform, which is perfectly logical since that is the way most pumps are set up on farms. The pipe from the pump reaches down into the water in the tank. The pump will draw water out as long as the water level is

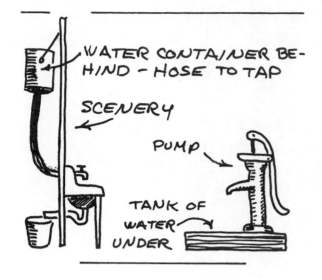

WATER CONTAINER BE-
HIND - HOSE TO TAP

SCENERY

PUMP

TANK OF
WATER
UNDER

above the bottom of the pipe extending down into the tank.

FOUNTAINS — Small electric water pumps are available to pump water from a tank, spray it in the air and allow it to run back into the into the tank.

WATERPROOFING — When water effects such as those suggested above are used, the areas that the water will come in contact with should be coated with spar varnish or water-proof sealer so that all of the scene paint will not be washed off the surface.

* * * *

The effects listed above are the more common ones. A little ingenuity and imagination will help in contriving ways of solving other problems of this nature that may arise.

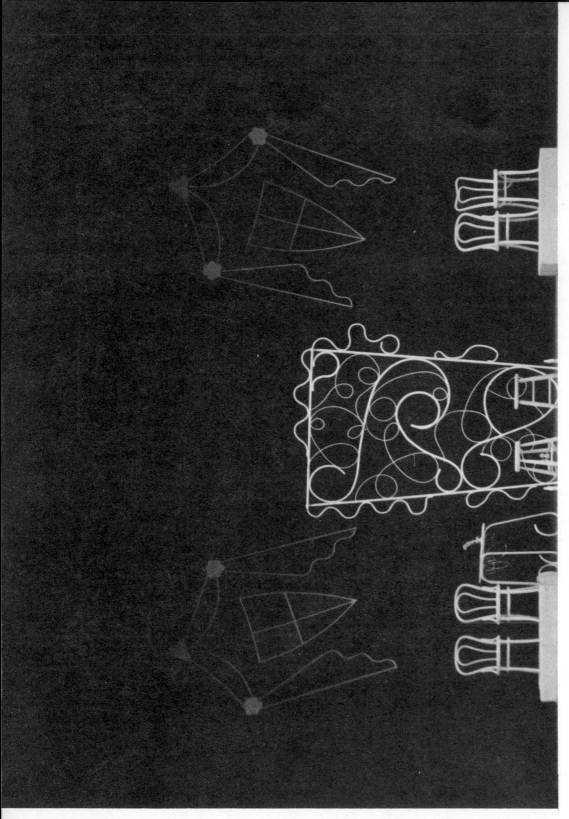

The Marriage of Figaro. Simplicity of setting achieved through the use of chairs, stools, aluminum tubing and wire.

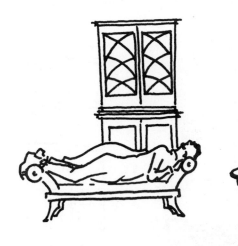

11

Furniture

The furniture and decoration of the stage setting frequently make the difference between a pedestrian and a finished production. Although it is not always possible to get exactly the correct chair or table for a period play it is helpful to know the salient features of the historical era so that an approximation can be made. Frequently it is possible to add color, surface decoration or slip covers to alter a piece of furniture and move it closer to the correct design stylewise.

The purpose of this chapter is to provide brief basic information rather than definitive historical facts about furniture. The text and illustrations are purposely brief and pointed. Included are basic facts about furniture and decorative motif that may be helpful to the stage decorator.

Egyptian 1500 B.C.

The Egyptians used numerous pieces of furniture including chests, sarcophagi, tables, stands, stools, chairs and folding seats.

The folding seat, which persists down to the modern day, probably had its origin in Egypt. This seat had X-crossed legs and a leather seat. The Egyptians had low, rush covered seats, chairs with backs and throne chairs. The tables were plain but attractive. The legs on furniture frequently terminated in animal feet such as bull hooves and lion paws. Chairs were often painted white, while sarcophagi and chests were painted in brilliant colors and had bands of geometric designs. Stylized animal

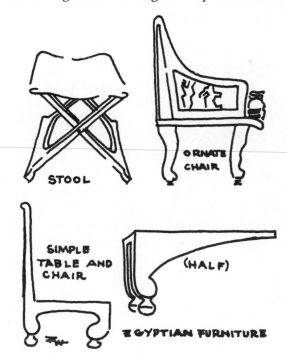

STOOL

ORNATE CHAIR

SIMPLE TABLE AND CHAIR

(HALF)

EGYPTIAN FURNITURE

forms were used frequently in the design motif.

Wood was scarce so was frequently featured in the design. Various types of surface design such as inlaying and veneering were used. Inlays of mother-of-pearl, ivory, metal and semi-precious stones were used.

Color had symbolic meaning to the Egyptians and so was used rather carefully. Plant forms were used stylistically in design motif. These included forms of the lotus, papyrus, acanthus, palm, lily and reed. Geometric forms including the spiral, triangle, square and circle were used on the furniture and in wall decorations.

The throne, a prominent piece of furniture, may be seen in many of the Egyptian drawings. The thrones were wide and had low square backs and arms that curved down from the back on a diagonal to the front edge of the seat where they were held by straight posts. The sides of the thrones sometimes represented the entire figure of a striding lion.

Although some beds were merely piles of quilts on a simple frame others appear to be chairs with stretched out seats.

Furniture of the later Egyptian eras had cushioning and even some upholstery.

Greek 12-300-B.C.

There is great variation between the furniture of the earlier and later periods in the Greek civilization. The early period shows influences from Egypt and other countries of the time. As the Greeks began to excel in architecture they also developed graceful and practical furniture. Well developed beds, chairs and tables appear in vase paintings. The chairs had sweeping curves on the backs and legs. The couches were elongated chairs similar to those of the Egyptians. The tables were low, portable and at times had bronze animal legs and feet. The chests had a pronounced architectural roof shaped top.

The Greeks used olive, cedar, yew and boxwood. The surfaces of the furniture were decorated with inlaying, painting, carving, gilding

and encrustings of precious stones. Purple, scarlet and gold seem to have been popular colors and some of the pieces were upholstered with silken cushions.

The decorative motifs used included the egg and dart, bead and reel, honeysuckle, braid,

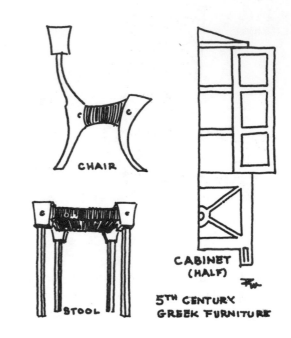

CHAIR

STOOL

CABINET (HALF)

5TH CENTURY GREEK FURNITURE

acanthus leaf, leaf and dart, guilloche and dentils.

The proportions and refinement of the Greek furniture influenced artisans of the eras that followed.

Roman 1000 B.C.-500 A.D.

Rome borrowed heavily from the Greeks but the borrowings never had the gracefulness or beauty of the originals. Roman furniture made of wood or stone was rather heavy and ponderous.

There seemed to be several types of chairs, among which were: the Curule with a square seat and X-shaped legs, the Biseleum which was a double chair or settee made of turned wood and sometimes decorated with carved horses' heads, the Solium which was a throne like chair with a back and the Cathedra chair which was used solely by women. The legs on most of the chairs were turned.

The Roman beds and couches were similar to modern ones. The couch was an important piece of furniture since it was used for sleeping and semi-recumbent dining. For dining purposes it had arm rest cushions. This couch was composed of a platform supported by legs and piled with cushions.

There were chests for the storage of arms.

Many types of tables, tripods, pedestals and stools were used.

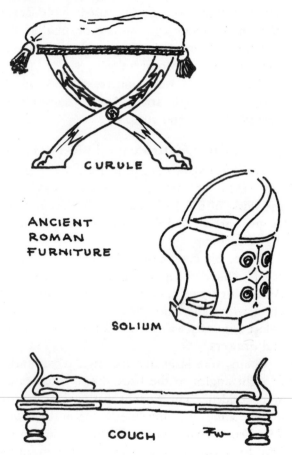

CURULE

ANCIENT ROMAN FURNITURE

SOLIUM

COUCH

Painting, engraving, carving, inlaying, metal applique and varnishing were all used as finishes on the furniture.

Gothic 1160-1530

The strong influence of the Gothic period was the Christian church. This was the era in which the great cathedrals were built. It was also the era of Byzantine showiness and of the barbaric Teutonic people. Furniture is usually heavy with carving that reflects the

OAK CABINET LATE VX CENTURY FRENCH

structure of the Gothic arch and of various religious motifs. Chests were important items. They were portable and used to carry the family valuables. Chairs were often made from chests. They were simply chests with arms. There were a few portable chairs. These frequently had high backs and sometimes canopies. The beds were at first entirely enclosed and then later merely covered by canopies to provide warmth. The fireplace was moved from the center of the room to the side wall. Tables consisted of trestles and planks.

Architectural forms, including skeletal forms of Gothic buildings, linen fold tracery and finally painted designs were used on the furniture. The idea of skeleton framework for buildings was finally carried over into the furniture and the chests became lighter in weight.

With the skeleton construction of furniture came more ornamentation. The carving in oak was usually large in scale and made use of floral

CHAIR
ITALIAN GOTHIC 1450-1500

LATE GOTHIC ALPINE BED
(GERMAN) ABOUT 1500

forms, vines and leaves, grotesque animal and human forms. Cusped arches, trefoil, quatrefoil, ogee curves and deep full moldings were freely used.

The greatest craftsmen built for their God and church. They built altars, screens, chests and great church doors.

Italian 1100-1400

Although the Italian was similar to other Gothic furniture there were influences from the Near and Far East and Africa.

Heavy chests of planks and boards were used. The decoration varied with the provinces. Gothic details, including the pointed arch, pierced tracery carving and landscape patterns,

ITALIAN GOTHIC
ARMCHAIR
14TH CENTURY

were painted, sometimes raised with gesso, sometimes inlaid with mosaic or marble and sometimes there were geometric patterns of bone or ivory in Moorish style.

Enclosed beds were unnecessary because of warmth, so simple frames were covered with Oriental fabrics and rugs.

Italian Quattrocento 1400-1500

The Renaissance began in Italy. The growing wealth of families and cities, trade with the world of the 15th century and development of great art all had their influence on the making of furniture.

Chests and cupboards set on bases were decorated architecturally with pilasters and cornices. A form of settee appeared in the Cassapanca, a chest with sides and back. The credenza developed in Italy was a low sideboard with doors and drawers.

Chairs were large and rectangular with arms at right angles to the back posts. Some seats were padded. The X-chair was evident in variations, some showing the Moorish influence. The Dante chair, with a fabric seat and back, had four curved legs continuing into arms. Sgabelli wooden side chairs either had three legs dowelled into the seat with a flat board back or had two carved slab bases.

The trestle type table was further developed with baluster legs or shaped slabs. Four legged types with box stretchers appeared early.

The ornament was classical with pilasters, flutes, scrolled volutes, moldings enriched with

168

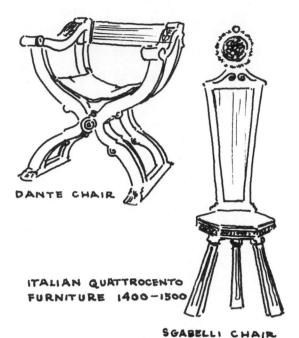

DANTE CHAIR

ITALIAN QUATTROCENTO
FURNITURE 1400-1500

SGABELLI CHAIR

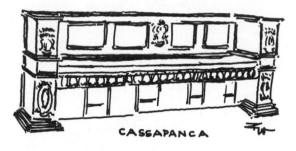

CASSAPANCA

ITALIAN
CINQUECENTO
CHAIR

egg and dart and dentils. Decorated flat areas were painted or gilded.

Italian Cinquecento 1500-1600

Further development in terms of classical motif appeared in the 16th century. Architectural cornices, guilloches, the acanthus leaf, rinceaux, pilasters, molded panels, gargoyles, scrolls and volute animal forms, caryatids, imbrications, gadroonings were used along with the newer forms like cartouches, strapwork, turned rosettes and broken pediments.

More chairs with cushions, more chests, more beds in four poster frames and more sideboards in many shapes appeared during this period.

Italian Baroque 1660-1700

The Baroque in Italy is further development on a lavish scale of the decoration already begun during the earlier periods. The Baroque in general was a masculine, highly decorative style of furniture. The wealth and power of the owner was shown in his furniture. The designers employed broken pediments, deep moldings, huge scrolls and profuse sculpturing.

Furniture of this period was designed in terms of entire rooms so that individual pieces were designed to be units in an architectural whole.

Wall furniture was in evidence everywhere. Included were tall cabinets, console tables and wall seats. Dominating the room was one huge cabinet with a sculptured base and decorated with cherubim, mermaids, lions, eagles and negroes in combination with scrolls, shells and leaves. The top had great broken pediments gracing it while the center doors were richly carved with small veneered panels.

Table legs were elaborately carved and table tops were marble or painted imitations of marble.

Chairs were heavily carved and upholstered with rich silks and velvets. Nail heads were arranged in patterns.

The beds of the early period were light and graceful four posters. Later these, too, became

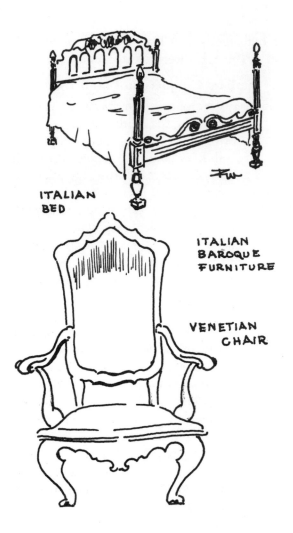

ITALIAN
BED

ITALIAN
ROCOCO

ITALIAN
BAROQUE
FURNITURE

VENETIAN
CHAIR

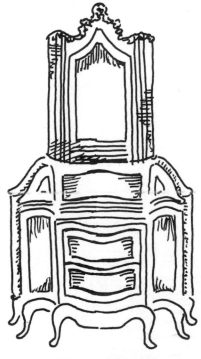

ITALIAN BAROQUE.
CHEST

more ornate and carried large flat areas on which to paint landscapes and floral patterns.

Italian Rococo 1700-1750

The furniture of the Rococo era was smaller and prettier than that of the Baroque period. Asymmetry and the curved line were the rule in Rococo design. The scale was smaller and more feminine. Decoration was lavish with the motif now toward foliage, ribbon, rocks and shell. Rococo did not reach the heights in Italy that it did in France.

Spanish Mudejar 1250-1600

Very little furniture was required by the Moors. Cushions were used for seating and tables were low. The Moorish influence in construction and decoration continued after Spain had once more become a Christian coun-

170

try. Moorish inlaying with ivory, bone, mother-of-pearl, metal and woods remained. The Arabesque designs came from this influence. This consisted of intricate and elaborate geometric interlacings. Ornamental bands using brilliant colors were popular design motif.

Spanish Plateresque 1500-1556

Plateresque refers to the art of the silversmiths whose work became the dominant metal work of the period. Most of the wood craft was rather crude and joinery was poor. Inferior workmanship was frequently covered with polychrome painting. Turned work was flat or repetitious. The Portuguese influence showed in the wrought iron work.

The tables were trestle forms with turned or cut out members. The ties were of wrought iron. The tops were cleated and square cut.

A painted ladderback chair with rush seat appeared. Most of the chairs were rectangular in form with upholstery stretched across. The X-type chair was common, either in the heavy Italian or the light Moorish type.

Beds with iron posts and panels of decorative iron, turned spindles, arches, etc. were evident.

The Vargueno, a fall front desk mounted on a table support, was the major contribution of the period. The base had turned posts and the cabinet was fitted with many small drawers. The door had decorative lines and hasps of iron.

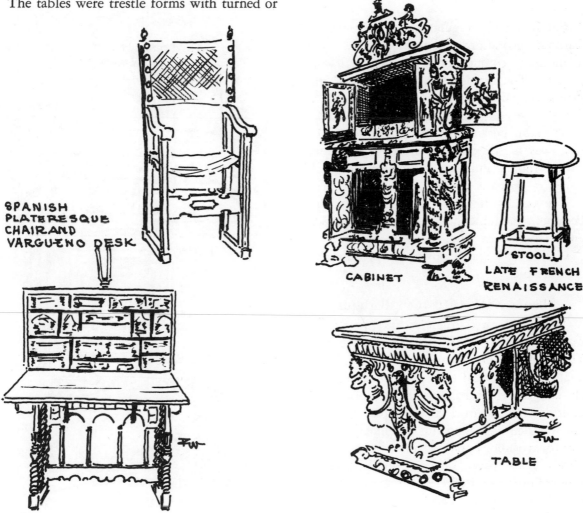

SPANISH PLATERESQUE CHAIR AND VARGUENO DESK

CABINET

STOOL
LATE FRENCH RENAISSANCE

TABLE

Spanish Baroque-Rococo 1600-1700

The Baroque and Rococo influences from France and Italy mixed with the Moorish influence to produce furniture that never reached the decorative extremes of these movements in the other countries.

French Renaissance 1515-1616

The early French Renaissance shows the influence of Italian, Spanish, German and Flemish artisans. Walnut became the most-used wood. Everything was covered with surface carving. The Gothic vegetable carving changed to the olive, laurel, acanthus and endive. Cabinets, tables, chairs and beds were the important elements of furniture during the early period.

Cabinets had irregular, jagged outlines and Baroque decorations. Pilasters were used often as motifs in conjunction with circle or lozenge panels. The diamond shape, stars and other geometric patterns were used as decoration on doors.

The table became an architectural form. The base was highly carved and began to show a strong Italian influence. Smaller tables also began to appear.

The bed with posts, canopy and draperies became a monumental affair with heavy posts and elaborate carving.

Chairs were scaled down and became more comfortable.

Louis XIII 1610-1643 Baroque

The exaggerated Jesuit architecture of Italy was the basis for the French Baroque furniture. The furniture of this period had a masculine quality with straight lines predominating. Panels had curved transitions in the corners and inserted circle or oval curved tops. The carving was rich and abundant. Animal forms of nature, mythology and allegory were employed. Masks, lions' paws, satyrs, sphinxes, dolphins and griffins were used either in entirety or just their heads or feet. Various types of acanthus, water lilies, oak, laurel and olive leaves as well

CONSOLE TABLE

SOFA TYPE BAROQUE

SOFA TYPE LOUIS XIII

FRENCH LOUIS XIII AND BAROQUE SOFA TYPES AND TABLES

TABLE

172

as ribbons, festoons, swags, agricultural implements, weapons and musical instruments were carved in the surface design.

Painting with strong colors such as red and green, inlaying of tortoise shell, ivory, bone, pewter, brass, mother-of-pearl and tin in complex detail was to be found in all kinds of wood. Real gold and silver were used where possible; otherwise, silver and gilding were substituted.

Bookcase cupboards and drawer cupboards with legs curved and ending in a doe's foot (destined to become the cabriole leg later) developed during this period.

Beds became more complex. Some canopies were detached from the frame and fastened to the ceiling. Partial canopies extended out above some beds. The bedstead, detached from the canopy, was also handsomely treated.

Heavy stone topped console tables with elaborate bases were immovable objects and were permanently installed against one wall. The wall side was undecorated. Table legs were turned or flattened balusters. Important tables were gilded. Smaller tables were natural or painted wood. There were coffee tables, candelabra tables, writing stands, toilet tables, night tables and all kinds of specialized game tables.

Seats were designed for protocol purposes.

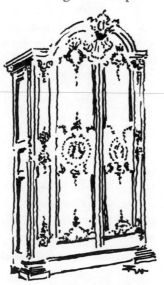

FRENCH REGENCE

In importance these ranged as follows: arm chairs, chairs with backs, joint stools, folding stools, hassocks with gold gimp and hassocks with silk edging. King Louis XIV's throne chair was, of course, the most elaborate in the kingdom. It was solid silver and was draped with crimson velvet. The back was 8' high, draped with full gold embroidery carried by caryatids 15' high.

Arm chairs always had stretchers, first H shaped and later X shaped. The legs were scrolled, flat or turned balusters. The arms were well molded and swung into the back with great curves. Carving in chairs was popular.

The Confessional was the first fully upholstered arm chair.

The sofa was the most important invention of the period. Almost bed in shape it was upholstered.

French Regency 1715-1723

The Regency period is the short transitional span between the masculine Baroque of Louis XIV and the feminine Rococo of Louis XV. Straight lines became curved, ornament became freer, scale diminished and the Chinese influence as well as the rock and shell came in. The cabriole leg became the characteristic shape of legs.

Louis XV Rococo 1700-1760

The Rococo of Louis XV really began to develop before he came to the throne. This feminine style furniture seemed to be constantly avoiding straight lines. It was florid and devoid of symmetry and right angles. One line always seemed to flow into another without any joint showing.

Ornaments were many and varied, including shells, flowers, musical instruments, pastoral objects like shepherd's crooks, and baskets.

Painting and lacquering of furniture became popular. Lacquering processes of great superiority were developed. The brightest reds, yellows and greens were used with black and these

173

were emphasized with fillets of gold. Gilding was popular for console tables, mirrors, chairs and small tables.

Metal appliques were used functionally and decoratively. Carefully designed pieces were

FRENCH LOUIS XV AND ROCOCO FURNITURE

CHAIR WITH GUILDED FRAME

TABLE WITH ROCOCO ORNAMENT

CHAISE LOUNGE

used for locks, handles, escutcheon plates, keys, feet or fillets and covers for weak veneer edges. Many types of wood were used for marquetry, including rosewood, satinwood, amaranth, tulipwood, mahogany, cherry and plum. Marble

of many colors, onyx and alabaster were used for tops of tables large and small. Imitation stone, mirrors and small china plaques were inserted in table tops.

The great variety of tables used in the Louis XIV period was increased considerably.

Chairs and chaise lounges were used in great numbers. They were designed to fit the human form and were fitted with loose cushions. Chair backs and seats were low. Armless chairs were designed for the voluminous costumes women wore.

Bedrooms were smaller and more efficiently heated than formerly. The canopy and draperies supported on four posts were retained but now became decorative. The Angel bed had similar head and foot boards and a half canopy that hung from the ceiling with two loop back draperies at the head. The Polish bed had the head and foot board and a curved dome canopy carried on four posts with four curtains looped up at the corners.

Louis XVI 1774-1793

Renewed interest in the classics combined with weariness of the endless curves and elaborateness of the Rococo caused a movement toward simple forms and straight lines. Legs once more became vertical members jointed at right angles to the aprons. The vertical was emphasized with fluting and grooving and the capital and base were suggested in the moldings and feet. Curves were segments of circles or ellipses. Panels were flat and moldings simple. The ornament of the classics was employed, including laurel, acanthus, egg and dart, oak leaves, palm leaves, fret work, riceaux, ribbons, etc. Fluting was frequently partially filled in with the filling ending in small vase turnings or torch effects. Greco-Roman influence was seen in bound arrows, swans, urns, wreaths, festoons and fanciful animals.

Black and gold lacquer as well as gray and subdued grayish white and gray green paint were used. Geometric marquetry, in the forms of the diamond and lozenge, were employed in rosewood, tulipwood. The dominant wood was mahogany.

Most of the pieces of furniture used in previous periods were retained but the lines changed to conform to the new conservative classicism. Sofas with roll backs, Roman tripods for tables,

smaller beds and the Angel bed were still popular.

Directoire 1795-1799 and Consulate 1799-1804

For the most part furniture was changed but little except that revolutionary symbols were added. These included the Phrygian cap, ar-

BED WITH WALL MOUNTED CANOPY

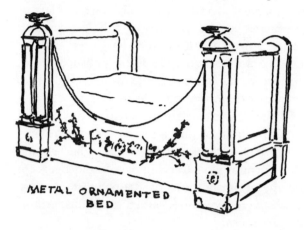

METAL ORNAMENTED BED

SOFA TYPE

FURNITURE OF LOUIS XVI TYPE

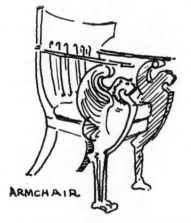

FRENCH EMPIRE FURNITURE

ARMCHAIR

DRESSING AND WRITING TABLE

EMPIRE CHEST

175

rows, pikes, triangles, wreaths, clasped hands, the fasces and lictor of Rome.

Empire 1804-1815

Under Napoleon, furniture became classical. However, the specific needs of the day were ignored. Consequently much of the furniture was clumsy and uncomfortable.

Absolute symmetry, cubic, rectangular or geometric shapes and heavy solid proportions characterized all furniture. Large flat surfaces emphasized the quality of the polished wood. Bronze or flat gilt appliques were tacked on to provide ornamentation. Military symbols such as swords, shields, arrows, wreaths and winged figures were used plus a few of Napoleon's own inventions such as the letter "N", the bee and the Cornucopia. Carving was avoided except on the arms and posts of chairs and table legs. These were sometimes carved into lions, griffins or caryatides.

Fabrics rich in color (mostly reds, greens, yellows and deep browns) all in hard textures with large imperial patterns or diaper patterns with the usual stars were used. Mahogany was the wood most used. Rosewood, ebony and woods stained to simulate them were used often, also. Marble was classic and hence acceptable.

Tripod or pedestal tables with marble tops are typical of the era. Cabinet furniture seems to have been designed as if it were miniature architectural units. Desks with banks of drawers in temple facade form or large cabinets with flat fall fronts were used. The typical Empire bed was the boat style with richly scrolled ends of the same height.

Provincial French

The furniture in the provinces outside Paris was more honestly designed for family life, and its restraint of proportion and style gave it distinct charm.

Furniture of the 17th century was composed of the bare essentials, including a closed bed, straw bottomed stools and a cupboard or hutch.

The buffet and cupboard and the chest were

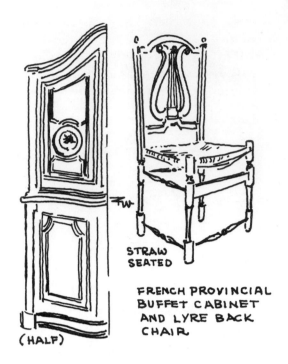

STRAW SEATED

FRENCH PROVINCIAL BUFFET CABINET AND LYRE BACK CHAIR.

(HALF)

forms used everywhere. Beds depended upon the locale and climate. In the south they were open while in the north they were cabinets within a room (or a room within a room).

German Gothic

North German furniture showed the Scandinavian influence and south German furniture showed the Italian influence. The chest was slightly different in Germany, having post and panel construction with the posts extending down to provide short legs. Coffers and cupboards with carved ornament painted red and green were found in south Germany. Turned chairs, trestle tables and beds with square posts, side pieces and a short wooden canopy were developed early.

German Renaissance App. 1575

The Italian and classic influences were used during the German Renaissance. Pilasters appeared. Veneered panels of walnut and ash were to be found on a base of fir or pine. Chairs were four legged board types, folding chairs

176

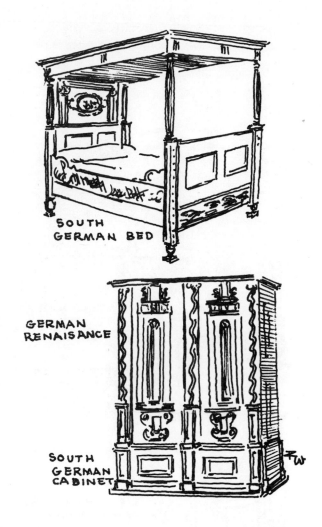

SOUTH
GERMAN BED

GERMAN
RENAISANCE

SOUTH
GERMAN
CABINET

GERMAN BAROQUE
DOUBLE BODIED BUFFET

chair backs with smooth wooden splats were in abundance.

German Rococo 1730

The French influence became more pronounced and with it came consoles, mirrors, commodes, chairs decorated with fruit, flowers, garden tools, musical instruments. These decorations were carved, gilded and painted.

German Classicism 1770

The classic lines of German furniture were more florid than in France. Much of the furniture was light and graceful but devoid of excessive ornament.

and later arm chairs with square legs. Turned legs appeared later.

Beds with carved posts and canopy frames appeared and state chairs were inlaid with ivory and silver. Cabinets were decorated with elaborate carvings and architectural features.

German Baroque App. 1660

Heavy cornices, rich molded panelling, large bun feet with carved enclosed leaf, flower and fruit ornaments characterized the great walnut cupboards.

The cabriole leg gradually replaced the spiral turned leg and styles were borrowed directly from Paris. Bombe commodes and high

BIEDERMEIR SOFA
GOTHIC TRACERY MOTIF

German Biedermeier 1830

The Biedermeier is lightly based on the classic lines with a mixture of the Gothic. It is middle class and comfortable. Curved chairs and sofas were upholstered with horse hair, calico and rep, and were decorated with graceful ornaments of the swan, griffin, cornucopia, domestic flower and fruit variety.

Scandinavian

Evidence of Romanesque, Celtic and even Far East influences are to be found mixed with the Viking system of intricately interlaced ornaments using birds, beasts and vines. Painting

SCANDINAVIAN CUPBOARD WITH ELIZABETHAN INFLUENCE

and carving were used on flat surfaces. The furniture had a simple native feeling that was never completely lost in any of the other styles.

English Renaissance (Elizabethan) 1558-1603

The Gothic style was well established in England and the Italian influence that came with Italian architects manifested itself only in details of ornamentation. Romayne work, scrolls and dolphins were added to the Tudor rose, palmetted band and zigzag that were already in use. The furniture was massive and

large scaled. It was structurally simple with well braced right angle joints. The huge bulbous melon turnings appeared in almost all up-

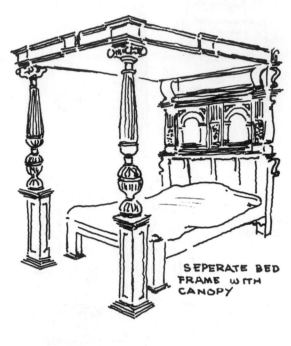

SEPERATE BED FRAME WITH CANOPY

ENGLISH RENAISSANCE ELIZABETHAN

WALL CUPBOARD WITH SEAT

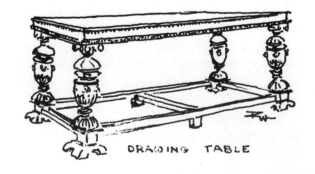

DRAWING TABLE

178

right members; stretchers were square and low.

The principal pieces of furniture used were chests, cupboards, wardrobes, desk-boxes, dressers for tableware, settles, chairs, stools, tables, beds, and cradles.

The wainscot and turned chairs were characteristic of the period. The wainscot had a nearly rectangular seat with turned or column legs, arms that were slightly shaped and a big solid back that frequently had low relief carving or inlay. The turned chairs were heavy in proportion with triangular wooden seats. This chair had heavy arms, back and legs composed of short, thick turnings. The X-shaped seat was in use.

The beds were composed of four heavily carved corner posts, often enriched with bulbous carvings, and an architectural capital that supported a heavy tester or canopy. Pull drapery hangings of rich velvet could be used to enclose this huge bed for warmth and privacy.

The permanent table began to replace the trestle and plank during the 16th century. Large refectory tables, some with extension tops, were built of solid oak. The host and guests sat on one side of the table while the serving was done from the other.

Chests were still popular and were used for storage, as seats and as beds. When used as seats and beds they were cushioned. The chests were richly carved.

Many decorative motifs were used including: Tudor rose, rosette, roundel, medallion, acanthus leaf, arabesque, dolphin, mask, quatrefoil, grotesques, vase, jar, lozenge, guilloche, rope molding, Gothic traceried arch, and coat of arms.

Jacobean 1603-1688

Furniture in modern use dates from the Jacobean period in England, 1603 to 1688. The influence in the Jacobean period came primarily from the Elizabethans.

Jacobean furniture was masculine, vigorous, somber and austere. The wood used was primarily oak. The moldings followed geometric forms. And the strap work hardware had scrolls, acorn leaves and geometric forms carved into it. Slender baluster, Flemish scroll and

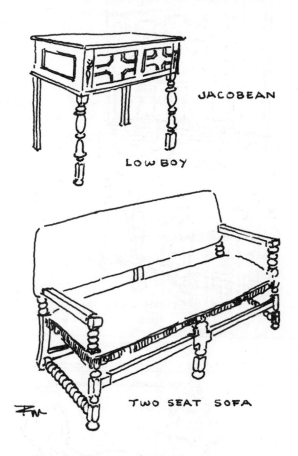

JACOBEAN

LOW BOY

TWO SEAT SOFA

spiral legs appeared. Chairs became more comfortable and sometimes had padded seats and backs. These were upholstered with tapestry material and decorated with fringes. The seats and backs sometimes had caning. The wing back sleeping chair appeared during the reign of Charles II.

Jacobean furniture fits well into the English half timbered houses. It is highly masculine and massive and so will fit into men's apartments, large oak panelled libraries and dignified dining rooms.

William and Mary 1688-1702

William and Mary ruled England from 1689 to 1702. During their rule life was simpler

179

and more leisurely than it had previously been. Many cabinetmakers were brought in from the

HIGHBOY WITH TURNED LEGS

WILLIAM AND MARY

FALL FRONT SECRETARY

Lowlands. Display cupboards decorated with a canopy or hood were designed for porcelain. This same form was carried over to secretaries, chairs and settees. From this cupboard the first highboy was developed.

The table had a curved apron which carried down to the legs.

Chairs became more comfortable and graceful. Legs were cup turned, trumpet or octagonal tapered. A stretcher was used between the legs of the tables, chairs, settees and cupboards. The flattened bun foot was common as was the Spanish scroll and the ball and claw. Veneering and marquetry were used for surface design. Needle point and tapestries were used for upholstery. William and Mary furniture fits the Early English and Colonial architecture.

Queen Anne 1702-1714

During the Queen Anne period, except for the characteristic shell carving, furniture depended upon its lines and the grain of the wood used for its beauty. Finishes included lacquering, marquetry and veneering. Curves were used rather than the straight lines of the William and Mary style and no stretchers were used between the legs. William and Mary and Queen Anne furniture became known as the furniture of the walnut age. Toward the end of Anne's reign mahogany became popular.

Chairs of the Queen Anne period were graceful and usually armless to accommodate the ladies' full skirts. The backs of chairs were slightly curved at shoulder height, and a splat down the center of the back was introduced. The fiddle back and the oval base back were characteristic shapes. Armchairs had continuous arms. The curved or cabriole leg was typical. The knee of the cabriole leg was decorated with shell carving. A club, or ball and claw, foot was used. The settee was a combination of two or more chairs. Needle point and tapestries were used for upholstery.

During the first quarter of the 18th century the Windsor chair appeared. This type of chair,

180

QUEEN ANNE

TEA TABLE

SETTEE

in many variations developed outside of court circles.

A variety of small tables were designed, including drop leaf tables, tilt top tables with plain tops or raised and carved pie crust edges.

Highboys, cabinets and china cupboards had carved, broken curve tops or broken pediments. Washstands, wigstands and tall clocks had characteristics similar to those of other cabinets with graceful drawer pulls and key plates to enhance their beauty. Drawer handles were frequently pear shaped.

Georgian 1720-1810

Beginning with the Georgian period the furniture styles took the name of the designer. In this period from 1720 to 1810 there were four important designers: Chippendale, Adam, Hepplewhite and Sheraton. Chippendale was probably the most important of the four. This was the golden age of furniture and mahogany was the wood most used.

Chippendale 1718-1779

Chippendale (1718 to 1779) understood and used all of the embellishments. He employed veneering, turning, carving, gilding, marquetry, inlay and metal mounting. Four influences are to be seen in Chippendale furniture.

1. *Queen Anne.* In the Queen Anne furniture Chippendale used the cabriole leg and the splat back for chairs. The splat back was pierced and carved.

2. *French influence.* The French influence was shown in the ribbon carving in the splats and in the cupid's bow top rail of the back.

3. *Revival of Gothic architecture.* Some of this, especially that with arched tops, pierced backs and straight squared legs, was good; but others in which he attempted to duplicate stone carving in wood was not successful.

4. *Chinese.* With the Chinese influence the backs of the chairs became nearly square and filled in with Chinese fret or latticework. The legs were square and straight and sometimes

resembled several bamboo rods bound together.

The most popular Chippendale chairs reproduced today are the pierced ladder back chair, the ribbon back chair and the wing back upholstered chairs called the "forty winks" chair. The forty-winks chair is more graceful with

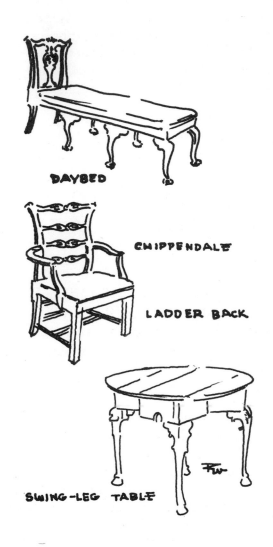

DAYBED

CHIPPENDALE

LADDER BACK

SWING-LEG TABLE

cabriole legs and ball and claw foot than it is with the plain straight leg. All of Chippendale's chairs had broad fronts and narrower backs.

Chippendale sofas and settees were of two styles: the all wood back combining two or three chair backs and the upholstered serpen-

tine back with rolled arms which is popular today. Legs were cabriole or straight. Upholstery materials included fine leather, needle point, tapestry, embroidery and damask.

Chippendale tables were tilt top with a center pedestal and three legs, console or wall types supported by curved and carved supports, drop leaf types and tea and coffee styles. The intricate carving or interesting lacquer made them distinctly Chippendale.

Cupboards, straight or break fronted cabinets and desks had panelled and latticed glass doors with symmetrical swan neck decoration. The doors were usually topped with a carved broken-curve pediment and centered finial urn or eagle. The beautiful brass hardware added a distinctive finish to all of the cabinet pieces. Chippendale mirrors, either severely plain or elaborately carved, and grandfather clocks are among some of the best of his works.

Adam 1762-1794

The Adam period, from 1762 to 1794, is frequently referred to as the neo-classic period. The four Adams brothers were primarily architects. They designed and decorated homes. They employed plaster on wall in place of wood panelling. They used raised plaster designs around ceilings, as borders and as panels. Wedgewood plaques were employed over doorways and fireplaces. Their fireplaces were especially attractive. They used festoons, frets, honeysuckle designs, swags, flat circular disclike ornaments known as paterae, wheat ears, husks, urns, and rosettes. The Adam brothers were influenced by Louis XVI furniture. One of their most important pieces of furniture was the dining room sideboard with a commode at each end. On top of each commode was a large carved knife urn.

Hepplewhite 17....-1786

Hepplewhite's furniture was delicate and beautiful. He designed some furniture for Adam interiors. The Pembroke table, a small four legged table with drop leaves, was one of

THREE PART SIDE BOARD

ADAM FURNITURE

beds with light delicate posts, and wardrobes.

Hepplewhite used mahogany and satinwood. Occasionally he employed artists to decorate his pieces with painting. Frequently the hardware was inconspicuous. He used veneers and inlays. His favorite upholstery fabrics were delicate brocades, horsehair, silks and satins with delicate flowers and stripes.

Sheraton 1751-1806

Sheraton lived from 1751 to 1806. He was the first designer to introduce concealed

HEPPLEWHITE

SHIELD BACK CHAIR

SHAVING MIRROR

SERPENTINE FRONT

Hepplewhite's favorites. He made many card, end, coffee, dining and side tables.

The Hepplewhite chairs are small, delicate and unusually graceful and usually have shield or camel backs. Within the backs he designed urns, Prince of Wales plumes and wheatears. Other backs included the oval, the interlacing heart and the wheel. The legs were straight, slender and tapering and might be square or round. The chairs often had upholstered seats. The sofas and settees had backs that repeated the chair backs.

Hepplewhite's other pieces included beautiful sideboards, dressing tables (with heart shaped mirrors), roll topped writing desks, washstands, secretaries, clock cases, four poster drawers, panels and compartments. Sheraton's pieces were characterized by rectangular forms. The fronts of his sideboards combined curved segments with straight lines in contrast to Hepplewhite's curved or serpentine fronts.

Sheraton chairs were delicate in line. Chair backs were rectangular in shape with vertical balusters, latticed bar work or ornamental splats between the upper and lower cross rails. Chair arms were delicate and had a continuous sweep out of the front legs and into the back. Chair legs were straight and tapering and terminated in a spoon or spade foot.

Sheraton used inlay, painting and multicolored marquetry. He often bleached and dyed woods for the marquetry. His favorite motifs were swags, festoons, urns, cameolike panels and latticework. He used mahogany, satinwood, sycamore and tulipwood. If pieces demanded upholstery he used delicate fabrics and colors.

Sheraton is well known for his Pembroke tables, his tripod base screens, his lattice door bookcases and his swan neck pediments.

SHERATON

SECRETARY

Victorian 1837-1901

The Victorian period from 1837 to 1901 was a hodge podge as far as design is concerned. It was a mixture of Gothic, Turkish, Venetian, Egyptian, Louis XV and Empire. Some of the pieces, such as chairs, tables and love seats, had a homey charm, but the styles in general were uncomfortable.

The principal woods used were black walnut, mahogany and rosewood. Carved decorations took the form of roses, buds and fruit. Wood pulls in the shape of fruits or pear drops replaced metal. Painting and mother-of-pearl were popular decorations also.

Chair backs were usually spoon shaped and the popular rose carving decorated chair and love seat frames. Many chairs were tufted and upholstered with plush or horsehair. Other popular pieces were drum shaped tables, terraced corner tables, whatnot stands, candle stands and drop leaf tables with center pedestals.

Most of the criticism is based on the over abundance of furniture and decoration during this period. Many of the individual pieces of furniture in correct surroundings are interesting and comfortable.

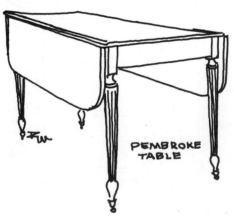

PEMBROKE TABLE

with gold and decorated with fine scaled flowers, animals and landscapes.

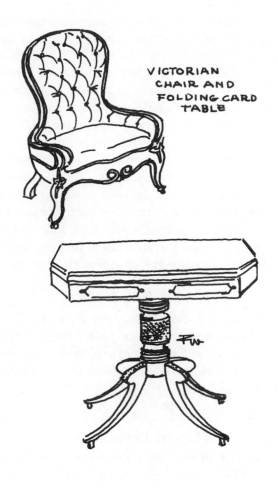

VICTORIAN CHAIR AND FOLDING CARD TABLE

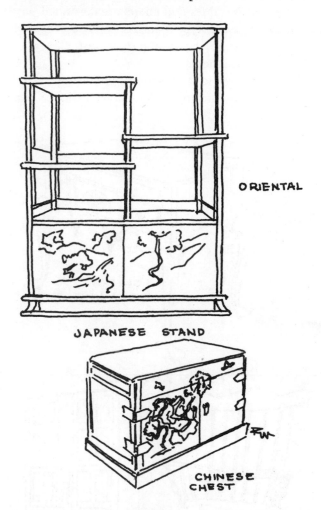

ORIENTAL

JAPANESE STAND

CHINESE CHEST

Oriental

Chinese furniture is rare since the requirements are few. Surface decoration in lacquer and decorative painting is important. Simple coffers and chests stand on low bracket bases ornamented with intricate metal mounts. Tables and stands are low, usually with turned-in scroll-like feet. Ceremonial chairs have flat surfaces with elaborate carving or inlay on flat surfaces. Dragons, flowers, landscapes with figures, and geometric borders are employed.

Japanese life requires but little in the way of furniture even as the Chinese. Chests and cupboards are usually built in with sliding panels for doors. For sleeping and sitting, mats are rolled on the floor. The rare tables are low and portable. Furniture is lacquered and highly polished. The lacquer is frequently flecked

American

In the main American furniture followed the designs current in Europe. The early furniture of the colonies shows the Gothic-Tudor influence.

Chests and cupboards had distinctly rectangular panels. Tables at first of the trestle type soon gave way to box styles and simple drop leaf types. Desk boxes, Bible boxes, forms or stools and a few crude beds made up the furniture. The woods at hand were used and these consisted of pine in great abundance, oak, birch and maple. The wood was left natural and aged to beautiful soft colors.

The Pennsylvania area shows the influence

185

of German, Swiss and Dutch peoples and the furniture has a distinct Medieval flavor. Chests, cupboards, tables and chairs are decorated with naive peasant type paintings. The wheel of fortune, tulip, heart and four leaf clover are typical ornaments.

Highboys, lowboys, chests, upholstered chairs with spiral turnings, elementary cabriole legs,

LOW BOY
QUEEN ANNE STYLE

EARLY AMERICAN

WINDSOR COMB BACK

SHAKER CUPBOARD

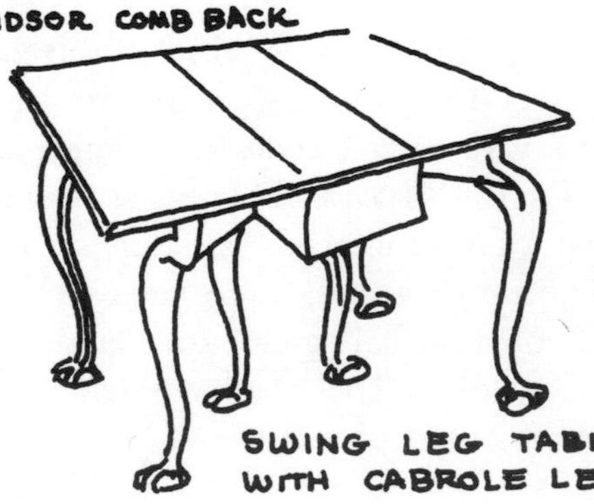

SWING LEG TABLE
WITH CABROLE LEGS

carved shells and pendants, and inverted cup shapes in walnut were typical of the 17th century.

The 18th century brought the Queen Anne and Rococo influences. Cabriole legs, shell carvings, pad or animal feet, Rococo curves and most of the other ornaments popular in England were used by the furniture makers.

The Windsor chair was a development of the Colonial furniture makers. Stools, chairs, benches, chests and cabinets made in pine, maple, hickory, oak, apple or cherry began to show the native talent. Beds with short posts, ladder back chairs, wagon seats, rocking chairs and writing chairs are all uniquely American.

Federal Period 1780

The natural movement away from the English during and immediately after the war and the turn toward the French is evident in the furniture. However, it was not long until the designs of Adam, Hepplewhite, Shearer and Sheraton became popular.

Duncan Phyfe 1790

Duncan Phyfe based his designs on Sheraton. His earlier work was in mahogany and his later work in rosewood. The lyre motif was characteristic of his work. This appeared in chair backs and table bases. His delicately carved lines in reedings and flutings combine with light carvings of leaves, plumes and animal motifs. He also used shells, bound arrows, pineapples, birds, lions' heads, eagles. Large areas on chests and drawers were veneered with beautifully grained mahogany in a V-shaped pattern. Hardware was used extensively in the form of metal or ormulu tips on legs, brass eagle finials on desks and mirrors, and metal lion masks and rings as drawer pulls.

Southwest America

The Franciscan monks left their mark on the southwestern section of America. Hand hewn leather-backed chairs, oak refectory tables and finely carved painted beds show their influence.

186

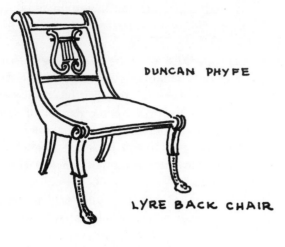

DUNCAN PHYFE

LYRE BACK CHAIR

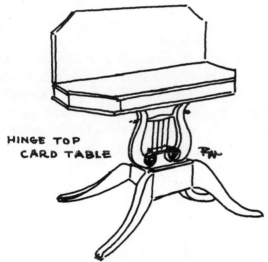

HINGE TOP
CARD TABLE

pattern and color harmonies, but also with the general feeling of the play itself. The furniture is an important part of the over-all design and must be treated as such rather than as a completely divorced element. It must be chosen carefully. In some instances furniture more than any other element provides the audience with clues about the actors, their aesthetic taste, their conflicts, their emotional patterns.

The furniture may be chosen to harmonize

MODERN FURNITURE

Modern

Each age has its modern furniture. The current age is no exception. Today's modern moves toward extreme surface simplicity. It combines functionalism with relatively small scale and surface beauty of the natural material.

It is possible to combine elements of various periods. Careful matching in regard to scale, harmony of line and desirable textural feeling are essential.

Furniture and the Stage Setting

The furniture used in a stage setting must be integrated not only with the other factors of design, including the general mood and atmosphere, scale of the various units, over-all texture

187

with everything else on the stage (setting, costumes, rugs, pictures and actors) or it may serve as an element of conflict. The stage may be deliberately divided into areas to show the difference between the varied characters by the furniture they choose and use. Single units of furniture may be used to attract attention deliberately, to serve as focal points. If this is done it should be done carefully and with motivation. The jarring note of an obviously mismatched piece of furniture can be extremely disturbing to the members of an audience and unless it is planned deliberately it should be avoided. Choose furniture carefully.

Furniture — General Information

Certain information of a general nature may be helpful to the crew working on the stage furnishings. It may be necessary at times to make slip covers, upholster, repair broken furniture, remove stains or even manufacture simple pieces of stage furniture. The information here will be basic, general and rather sketchy. More detailed information may be obtained from the books listed in the bibliography.

Cleaning Wood Finish

If furniture gets sticky wash it carefully with a solution of mild soap and water. Dry the area thoroughly and then polish.

Water stains may be removed by carefully rubbing the area with water to which has been added a couple of drops of ammonia. The area should then be dried carefully and polished.

Alcohol stains can be removed with alcohol or turpentine. Dry the surface thoroughly and polish.

Heat or burn stains will leave a white ring which can be removed with oil of camphor. After this has dried polish the surface.

Cleaning Upholstery

In order to prevent the upholstery from becoming soiled it is advisable to keep the furniture covered with muslin, sheets, blankets or even paper when it is not in use. It is also advisable to instruct actors, stagehands and visitors that furniture is to be used only by the actors and only when it is on stage during the running of the scene for which it has been procured. This will minimize the danger of soiling and staining both the fabric and wood.

If upholstery is generally soiled it may be cleaned with any of the regular soapless furniture shampoos.

Grease may be removed with carbon tetrachloride, benzine or a commercial solvent.

Blood may be removed with several applications of raw starch paste.

Chewing gum may be loosened with benzine or carbon tetrachloride.

Mud may be brushed off if allowed to dry.

Candy may be washed off with soapy water and then the area should be wiped thoroughly with a cloth wrung out in clear water. Avoid letting the water penetrate the fabric too deeply.

Fresh oil base paint may be removed with turpentine. Water mix paint can be removed with soapy water. The soap should be removed with a rag moistened with clear water and then the surface should be rubbed with a dry cloth. If turpentine is used the last traces of turpentine should be removed with benzine.

Powdered cleaners that are on the market will clean some of the soil from upholstery.

Upholstery and Slip Covers

If a piece of furniture is to be completely recovered it is easiest to remove the old upholstery and use the pieces as patterns for the new material. If this is done carefully the various pieces can be labelled as they are taken apart and the new pieces put together in the same order.

Slip covering or upholstering a piece of furniture which previously had no upholstery may seem to be a difficult job to tackle but for anyone who has simple sewing skill it is fairly easy. A little courage and faith in one's abilities will help, but no property crew member ever lacked these traits.

Inexpensive cloth or newspaper may be used for practice purposes. This should not be used as a pattern for cutting the finish upholstery cloth, however, since it will probably not retain its shape. The pieces will fit much better if the final cloth is cut to fit. Cut pieces to fit the various surfaces of the piece of furniture with about an inch to spare all of the way around for seams and strength. If the seam is too close to the edge it will tear or pull out easily. If the piece of furniture is symmetrical it is possible to turn the cloth upside down; if not it will be necessary to use a different procedure and mark the seam areas with pins. The pieces of cloth are cut to fit (with one inch to spare), pinned to the chair, and pinned together where there are to be seams. Cushions should be removed so that the material on the inside of the back and sides can be designed to fit down under them. The seams may then be sewn and the cover is finished. It will take considerable careful work if a professional looking job is to be done, but for stage use one need not be as careful as when doing a piece of furniture for display in the home.

Welting

Welted edges, which usually give much better finish to the piece of furniture, can be put on the upholstery. Cotton cord of the desired circumference is placed in the center of a strip of the upholstery cloth about 2½″ wide. The cloth is then folded over the cord and the cord sewn into the fold. A zipper foot on the sewing machine will make it possible to sew a seam snugly against the cord. This is the welting strip. The two pieces of cloth that are to make the seam are then placed wrong side out so they are even with the loose edges of the welting strip. Using the zipper foot the two pieces of material with the cording strip sandwiched between are sewed snug against the cord. When this is turned right side out the seam will be covered by the bead of the welting.

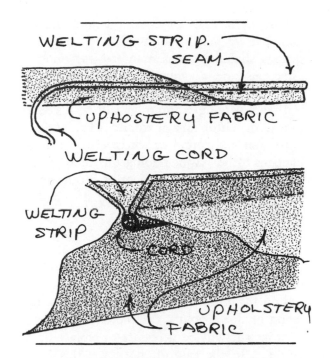

Soft Seats

The springs are frequently too soft on stage furniture. An actor who sits in a chair or sofa sinks too low and is ungraceful while sitting and struggles when he tries to rise. A board or piece of plywood placed under the cushion will distribute the weight over the entire spring area and give the seat more firmness.

Sagging Seats

Sagging seats on chairs, sofas or other pieces of furniture may be caused by loose springs, loosened webbing or lumpy padding. The chair may be turned upside down to check the webbing. A light dust cover may protect the bottom, but this can easily be pulled loose to inspect the webbing. It may be that the webbing can be tightened without disturbing the upholstery at all or it may be necessary to remove the muslin covering under the cushion and even some of the padding. The webbing may then be tightened and securely tacked.

If the springs are causing the trouble they can be retied. When this is done a strong hemp twine should be used and the springs tied to one another and to the frame. An inspection

189

will show how this was done before and the same pattern may be followed in retying. The springs should be tied straight across in both directions and diagonally in both directions. The padding can then be replaced.

If the padding is lumpy it will be necessary to take the entire area apart and redistribute the horse hair and cotton or whatever the padding happens to be. When doing this, as when doing any reworking of a piece of furniture, try to replace the parts so that they are in their original positions.

Broken Dowel

Sometimes furniture joints come apart or are broken. Most arms, legs, aprons, backs and ties on furniture are fastened with mortise and tenon or dowel joints. If the dowel or tenon is broken it will be necessary to replace or repair it. In the case of the dowel this is not too difficult. The broken pieces can be removed by drilling with a bit slightly smaller than the piece of dowel. This done the remainder of the dowel can be chipped out with a pocket knife. Pieces of dowel can then be cut to replace the broken ones. These should fit snugly into place. If the holes have been worn it might be advisable to redrill the holes a sixteenth of an inch larger in diameter. Be certain that the dowel is the correct size and length. With a pocket knife slice a thin strip off the dowel. Coat the piece of dowel with wood glue and push it into place in one side of the joint, then push the other part of the joint over the dowel. The sliver that was sliced off the dowel will allow the excess glue to seep out. Otherwise pressure of the glue at the ends of the dowel might crack the boards. Pressure should be applied while the glue is hardening. A large clamp, heavy cord tourniquet, or some other device can be used for this purpose.

If a tenon is broken it may be necessary to replace the entire board. Or it might be possible to mortise into the broken tenon side of the joint and then fashion a small block of wood

that will slide into both the old and new mortises. The grain of the key should run across the joint, and the key should be glued into place in the manner suggested for the dowel.

Building Simple Furniture

Simple pieces of furniture such as benches, stools, tables, ottomans, dressing tables, desks and footstools can be made in the shop if necessary. Such utility furniture can be made from white pine and various thicknesses of plywood.

For simple construction it is advisable to avoid complex joints and stick to butt, mitre

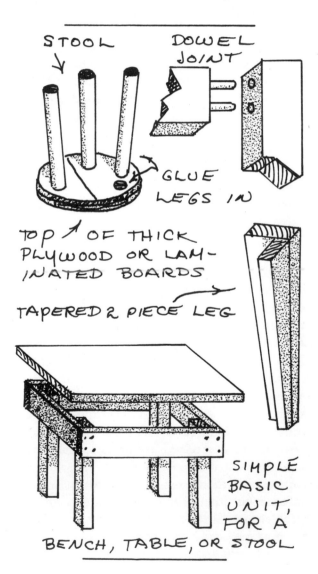

STOOL   DOWEL JOINT

GLUE LEGS IN

TOP OF THICK PLYWOOD OR LAMINATED BOARDS

TAPERED 2 PIECE LEG

SIMPLE BASIC UNIT, FOR A BENCH, TABLE, OR STOOL

and plywood reinforced joints such as those used in making flat frames.

Coated nails or screws with or without glue will probably work best for fastening the joints. The glue will make the connection more substantial but is not always essential.

Plywood in Construction

Sheathing plywood is relatively inexpensive and in thicknesses from 5/16" to 3/4" can be used wherever it is possible to fasten through the thickness of the material. It is not practical to fasten into the plies of the edge grain since nails or screws will tend to pry the thicknesses apart. Plywood is strong for tops and panels especially. With plywood it is possible to have an unbroken area as large as 4' x 8'. If regular 1" boards are used it is necessary to cleat several boards together side by side to get this same area. The cleated section is usually heavier and not as smooth as the plywood surface.

General Construction

Most of the utility pieces can be constructed in about the same way. Basically they will consist of legs that are fastened at the top inside of the corners of a rail frame. Over the rail frame, and usually projecting out beyond an inch or so all of the way around, is the top.

Rail Frame

The rail frame is composed of boards on edge secured together at the corners with glue, nails, screws or all three. If the legs are to extend straight down, the ends of the boards will be cut square. If the legs are to cant, or slope out slightly, the ends of the boards will be cut on a slight angle. The legs are usually fastened snugly into the insides of the corners of the rail frame. Fastening into the leg from both sides of the corner, if possible, will make the corner and leg more substantial and durable. In order to fasten the leg more easily it is advisable to clamp the leg and board of the frame to be nailed with a "C" clamp. This will hold the two pieces together securely while the nail-

ing or screwing is done. The size lumber used for the rail frame will depend upon the general design and style of the piece. Usually 1" x 4" will do.

Post Legs

Legs for utility furniture may be made from rectangular stock (1" x 3", 1" x 4", 2" x 2", 2" x 4", 4" x 4"), from round stock (dowel, closet poles, round stair rail stock), from pipe and flanges, or from two pieces of 1" board fastened together edge to edge usually with the piece that butts up edge wise being 3/4" narrower to make the leg measure the same on both of the right angle sides. The legs may be straight or tapered. The tapered leg gives a more graceful finished appearance.

Slab Legs

Slab type supports or legs are made either from one solid slab the width of the space between the front and back rails or from a hollow slab made up of two thin sheets of plywood or wall board with thickness spacers sandwiched between them around the exposed edges. Slabs may extend straight down, may cant outward

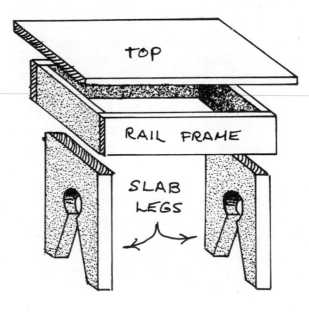

to provide a wider base, may have a split bottom or may have simple patterned open work cut out of them.

Top

The top will usually project out beyond the rail frame by at least an inch all around and may project out even more. If the top is to support but little weight it may be composed of thin plywood. If it is to support great weight it may be composed of either heavy plywood or planks. A thickness edging around the top will aid in projecting greater thickness than the top actually has.

Patterns for Furniture

Patterns or ideas for furniture may be obtained from magazines, books, photographs, sketches or pieces of real furniture. A little experience will aid one in simplifying the original design and duplicating only the essentials of the basic design.

Surface Decoration on Furniture

Simple pieces of furniture may be altered by adding surface decoration of one kind or another. Many materials can be used. Plastic Wood, gesso (a mixture of powdered glue and plaster), papier-mâché and other plastic materials can be used to build up areas on the surface. Applique pieces can be cut from plywood, cardboard, Styro-Foam, aluminum, felt, linoleum, or Plastic Wood and can then be glued, nailed or stapled to the surface. Rope, string, twine, electrical cable, iron and aluminum wire are other materials that might be applied to the surface. The surface may also be painted with a flat coat, stippled, wood grained, marbleized, patterned or decorated. Surface textures can be obtained by using a coating of glue and then brushing, dusting or blowing flock, sawdust, shavings or any other material onto the sticky surface. The furniture may be coated with gilt paint, enamel, fluorescent or aluminum paint, glitter (on a glue, varnish or bronzing liquid base) or shellac.

* * * *

Beg? Borrow? Steal? Buy?

Procuring furniture for use on stage may be a problem in almost any community, even for the wealthiest theatre. It is impossible to have stock furniture that will fit every production. It is possible for an organization to gather up a few standard pieces that can be used for rehearsal and for general all-around utility purposes. But there always comes the time when it is necessary to start out looking for items needed on a specific stage setting. Where does one look?

Furniture stores dealing in new furniture, old furniture, second hand stores, antique shops, junk shops, the homes of friends of the institution, clubs, lounges of the institution, offices, rest rooms — all of these may be places from which furniture may be obtained. It should be understood at the very beginning that there is great danger that the pieces of furniture will get damaged in transit, while being shifted on the stage or while being used by the actors. It is therefore always necessary to realize that it may be necessary to repair or replace any damaged goods. This should be understood by both the borrower or renter and the owner. With the assurance of care in handling the possibility of permission to use the furniture will be much greater.

While in the theatre the furniture should be kept clean. It should be picked up and taken to the stage only when absolutely needed and returned just as soon as possible after its use has been concluded. Complimentary tickets, if possible, a courtesy program note and a thank you note when it has been returned will all help make it possible for a repeat in the future.

Building a furniture "morgue" is valuable to any continuing theatre organization. Occasional purchases, acceptance of gifts (and gifts will be more likely to come if people know that the furniture is needed), and reclamation of discarded pieces will all be means of acquiring new pieces.

12

Electricity

"What is electricity?" is always a startling question to the novice contemplating his first wiring job, and the answer is rarely completely satisfying or wholly revealing. Fortunately, in order to light a simple stage production it is not necessary to become an expert in the field of electricity. However, it is helpful to know a few of the basic general facts about electricity in order to understand the operation and maintenance of stage electrical equipment and to be able to handle simple wiring projects adequately and efficiently.

VOLTAGE—The source of power in most of the electrical equipment used every day is the dry cell battery of the flashlight or portable radio, the wet cell battery of the automobile, or the generator of the local power plant. These various sources of electrical energy build up a pressure or force which can cause tiny charged particles called electrons to flow along a wire. The unit of pressure is the volt and the number of volts between two terminals is the voltage of the generator.

The ordinary flashlight battery is rated at 1½ volts. When two flashlight batteries are stacked end to end the voltages are added together 3 volts are produced. Most flashlight bulbs are designed to be burned at this voltage. Automobile batteries are usually rated at 6 volts or 12 volts, depending on the model of the car, and the lights, horn, starter, radio and all other electrical equipment in the car are designed for this same voltage.

Most homes and stages are equipped with 120 volt power lines and so, as would be expected, most stage lighting fixtures and home appliances are rated at 120 volts. Vacuum cleaners, refrigerators, waffle irons, electric shavers and most light bulbs are designed for use on 120 volts. Certain appliances which use a large amount of power, such as electric stoves, water heaters and clothes dryers, are designed to use 240 volts. To get this voltage a third wire must be brought into the building from the power company's lines.

Every piece of electrical equipment must be used only with the voltage for which it is rated. If the applied voltage is below the rated value the equipment will not operate; lamps burn dimly and motors will not start. If the voltage is too high the equipment will probably go up in smoke. A small percentage of leeway is allowable in selecting equipment for use at a certain voltage. For instance, it is perfectly all right to connect a lamp rated at 110 volts to a 120 volt power line, but a 6 volt lamp would burn out instantly if connected to either 110 or 120 volts.

CURRENT—It was stated that voltage represents a pressure or force which tends to make electrons flow along a conductor. This flow of electrons is called an electric current. Current and voltage are not the same and should not be confused with one another. Currents are measured in amperes (amps), one ampere representing the flow of 62,250,000,000,000,-000,000 electrons past any given point in a circuit each second. Don't be alarmed by this number. It will not be encountered in this book again.

POWER—Power is the rate of flow of energy in an electric circuit and it is measured in watts or in larger units called kilowatts. (One kilowatt is equal to 1,000 watts.) It is the power consumed which determines the amount of light given off by a lamp, the amount of heat given off by an electric stove or the horsepower output of an electric motor. Power is not the same as voltage or current, but is closely related to both by the following equation:

$$\text{Power} = \text{Voltage} \times \text{Current}$$
$$\text{or}$$
$$\text{Watts} = \text{Volts} \times \text{Amps}$$

In addition to a voltage rating most of the equipment used in stage lighting also has a power (or wattage) rating. These wattage ratings are very useful for they allow the technician to compare lamps which burn on different voltages. For instance, a 100 watt 6 volt lamp gives off just as much light as a 100 watt 120 volt lamp and the operating cost is the same for both even though the 6 volt lamp requires 20 times as many amperes.

Lamps are rated in watts and dimmers are usually rated in watts, but fuses, electric wires and cables, switches and connectors are rated in amperes. Therefore, it is often necessary to convert wattage ratings into current ratings, This is easily done since the power equation can be rearranged in the following way:

$$\text{Current} = \text{Power} \div \text{Voltage}$$
$$\text{or}$$
$$\text{Amps} = \text{Watts} \div \text{Volts}$$

With this form of the equation it is easy to find the current in any circuit if the wattage and voltage are known. For example, find the current in a 60 watt 120 volt lamp.

$$\text{Current} = 60 \div 120 = \tfrac{1}{2} \text{ ampere}$$

A 60 watt 6 volt lamp would have a current of $60 \div 6 = 10$ amperes

Other examples using the power equation will be given later in the chapter.

RESISTANCE — Every substance resists the flow of electrons to a certain extent, and this resistance is measured in Ohms. The resistance depends upon the character of the material and its cross sectional size. In general a thin wire, for instance, has a higher resistance to the flow of electricity than a larger one and consequently will carry less current.

The current which will flow through a resistance is given by Ohm's law which states in equation form:

$$\text{Current} = \text{Voltage} \div \text{Resistance}$$
$$\text{or}$$
$$\text{Amperes} = \text{Volts} \div \text{Ohms}$$

This means that in a circuit connected to a certain source of voltage the higher the resistance the lower will be the current. Some dimmers use this principle to reduce the current through a lamp, thereby reducing the light out put.

Whenever current flows through a resistance, heat is produced and this is why electrical equipment usually gets warm or hot when in use. Sometimes this heat is useful, as in the filament of an incandescent lamp or in an electric stove, but at other times the heat is not wanted. It wastes energy and can be a fire hazard if it gets out of control.

CONDUCTORS AND NONCONDUCTORS — It has already been stated that all materials resist the flow of electrons to a certain extent. In general the substances used in electric wiring may be classified as conductors or nonconductors. Silver, copper, aluminum, brass and most other metals resist the flow of current the least and are referred to as the conductors of electricity. These are the materials used for wire and contacts on electrical instruments. Porcelain, rubber, glass, wood, cloth and paper resist the flow of electrons almost completely and so are used for insulation, or covering, of the conductors.

WIRING SYMBOLS—Before proceeding further with this discussion it will be helpful to

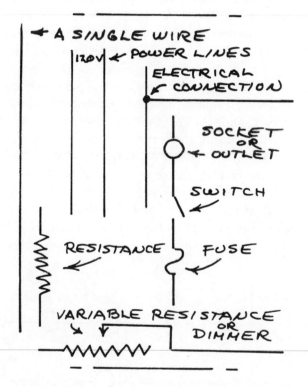

describe briefly and illustrate the symbols that are used in drawing electrical circuits.

Wire—A single wire or electrical conductor is indicated by a single line.

Power Lines—Parallel lines with a numerical indication of the voltage between them will be used to designate the power lines.

Electrical Connections—Two wires connected together are indicated by one line meeting another and the point of meeting indicated by a heavy dot. If the dot is missing it will be assumed that the wires are not connected.

Socket—A socket, outlet or an instrument that need not be specifically designated may be shown by a circle with appropriate wire connections—a wire connected on each of two sides.

Switch—A switch is shown as a break in a wire. A little lever section of the wire represents the break.

Fuse—A fuse is shown by an "S" curve in the line.

Resistance—A resistance in the circuit is shown by a zig-zag pattern in the line.

Variable Resistance—A variable resistance or theatre dimmer of the resistance variety is shown by one line terminating in a zig-zag pattern. An arrow above this leads into a continuation of the line. The arrow shows that the length of the resistance can be varied.

These are the symbols that will be used most frequently in drawing simple wiring diagrams. Other symbols may be needed; if so, they will be described when they are used.

ELECTRIC CIRCUIT—In order to have a flow of current it is necessary to have a closed circuit; that is, it is necessary for the current to flow around in a loop or circuit that returns to the point of origin.

FLASHLIGHT CIRCUIT—A flashlight may be used to show how a simple electrical circuit operates. The battery represents the generator; it is the source of power. When the switch is pushed on, contact is made between the lamp socket and the side of the flashlight case and the circuit is closed. The voltage or electrical pressure of the battery forces electrons to flow from the base of the battery, through the case, up through the bulb and back down to the button on the top of the battery to complete the circuit. The conducting case of the flashlight in this instance is a part of the electrical circuit. When the switch is turned off the contact between the case and lamp is broken so that no current flows through the circuit.

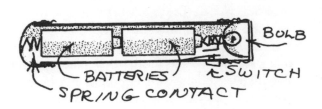

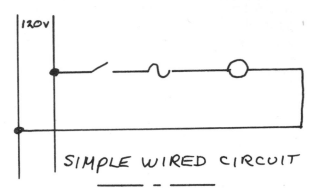

FLASHLIGHT CIRCUIT

SIMPLE WIRED CIRCUIT

SIMPLE WIRED CIRCUIT—A simple electrical circuit is similar to the operation of the flashlight. Several of the symbols already shown are used together to form the completed loop. Included here is a source of power, a switch, fuse, socket and wires connecting all of these units together.

DIRECT AND ALTERNATING CURRENT—In the wiring system of the flashlight, or of an automobile, the flow of current in the closed circuit is constant in one direction, from negative to positive. This is referred to as a direct current. There are some commercial electrical power plants that produce direct current. However, since most power plants serve large areas and must send power to distant points, it has been found that a pulsating, or alternating, current is more practical and efficient. In the alternating current system the current alternately travels in one direction and then the other. Most systems employ 60 cycles, which means that there are 60 pulses of current in each direction every second. Direct current is designated by the letters D.C. and

alternating current by the letters A.C. Practically all stage lighting equipment except arc lamps will work on A.C., but only resistance type dimmers can be used on D.C. Many arc lamps require direct current and rectifiers are used to convert A.C. to D.C. for this purpose.

TYPES OF CIRCUITS—Basically there are two types of circuits that are used frequently for simple stage wiring: parallel and series. Almost all wiring consists of one or both. For the present explanation it may be assumed that there are two wires representing the power source.

SERIES CIRCUIT—A series circuit is, in a sense, one continuous closed line of switches, wire and outlets. A single wire can be used and wherever an outlet is desired the wire can be cut and each of the ends fastened to one contact of the outlet. In order for the circuit to operate it is necessary to have something operating (a lamp or other electrical device) in each outlet. The circuit is not closed until contact is made through all of the sockets.

PARALLEL CIRCUIT—The parallel circuit consists of a continuation of each of the two lines of the power source. If the two wires are laid out in a line parallel with one another it may be explained that outlets are placed between the two wires so that the current flows

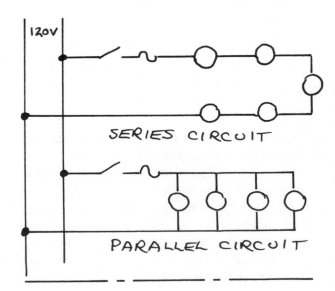

SERIES CIRCUIT

PARALLEL CIRCUIT

from one wire to another through each individual circuit. In the series circuit the current runs through one outlet before reaching the other and so on to the end of the series.

CHARACTERISTICS OF A SERIES CIRCUIT—Current flows in one straight path through several units as if flowing through a continuous wire. The voltage applied to the whole circuit is equal to the sum of the component parts. If there are two lamps of the same wattage and voltage each receives one half of the voltage. If there are three lamps each receives one third of the voltage. If there are four each receives one fourth and so on. As the voltage diminishes so also does the brightness of the lamps. The resistance of the circuit is equal to the sum of all of the resistances. And finally the amount of current flowing through the circuit is the same throughout.

CHARACTERISTICS OF A PARALLEL CIRCUIT—In a parallel circuit the current flows through several individual circuits or paths. Each unit is connected from one line voltage wire to the other. The voltage of each of the parts is the same as the voltage of the supply line. Adding more outlets does not diminish the voltage. The current flowing from the voltage source is equal to the sum of the currents flowing through the individual outlets.

USE OF PARALLEL WIRING—Almost all electrical outlets are wired in parallel so that the maximum voltage and maximum efficiency can be utilized from each individual circuit.

USE OF SERIES WIRING—Most switches are wired in series with the outlets since it is necessary to interrupt only one wire in order to stop the flow of current in a circuit. Turning off a switch is in principle the same as breaking or cutting one of the wires of the circuit.

FUSES—Fuses, or safety valves as they might be called, are also wired in series with the outlet. The fuse is designed so that it will allow only a specified amount of current to flow through a circuit before the fuse wire will heat enough to melt and break the circuit. Again, as with the switch, it is only necessary to interrupt the flow through one wire of the circuit so only one wire need be fused to shut off the flow through the entire circuit when the fuse "blows out."

Inexpensive sets of Christmas tree lamps are wired with eight lamps in series because it takes less wire to make a loop with a single wire than to make a loop of the same size with two wires. The lamps, or bulbs, are designed to burn with the lowered voltage ($120 \div 8 = 15$ volts). If the ordinary Christmas tree lamps designed to be burned at 120 volts are used in one of these circuits they will burn only very dimly. If, on the other hand, the 15 volt lamps are placed in a 120 volt circuit they will burn out immediately.

In rare cases where instruments having voltages lower than 120 are to be wired into a circuit it is necessary to have a transformer (see next paragraph) or to wire enough of the units in series to make the total of 120 volts. As an example, the use of 26 volt sealed beam lamps may be cited. In order to determine how many will be needed it is necessary to divide 26 into 120. The answer is about 4.6. It would be necessary to use either 4 or 5. If one wishes brilliance and is not disturbed about the lamps having a shortened life it is possible to use 4. If, however, the brilliance is to be sacrificed for long life 5 will be wired in series.

TRANSFORMERS—It is often desirable to have more than one voltage available for special purposes on the stage. With alternating current it is possible to use a simple transformer for this purpose. Usually the transformer is built with fixed voltage input and output capacities so that it can be used only for the special purpose for which it was designed. As its name implies, the transformer is used to transform power from one voltage to a higher or lower voltage. A transformer has two sets of terminals—one set called the primary would normally be connected to a 120 volt A.C. source and the other set called the secondary would be connected to the equipment requiring a different voltage (probably 6 volts for bells, buzzers, low voltage lamps, etc.) If the secondary voltage is lower than the primary voltage, the secondary current rating will be greater than the primary current rating so that the power equation is satisfied.

Primary Power = Primary Voltage × Primary Current

Primary Power = Secondary Voltage × Secondary Current

Primary Power = Secondary Power

WIRING SYSTEM—The wiring system of a building starts where the service lines come in from the street. These lines are large enough to carry the total power that will be consumed

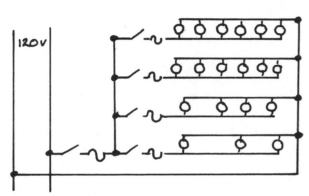

SIMPLE WIRING SYSTEM WITH MASTER AND 4 CIRCUIT SWITCHES

on the premises. Where they enter the fuse or control box they pass through a master switch and are then fused to carry that specified amount of electrical current. Wires of smaller current capacity are connected to the main fuses and then pass through smaller fuses having the same capacity as the wire. These become either individual circuits that extend out to the outlets or are branch circuits that are further broken down into smaller circuits. Usually the final break down is made as near to the place where the power is to be used as possible in order to economize on the amount of wire needed to complete the circuits. The capacity of each circuit is determined by the size of the wire that leads to it and the capacity of the fuse should not exceed the capacity of this wire.

120 VOLT WIRING SYSTEM — Where the 120 volt system is used throughout the building two wires enter the meter. One is covered

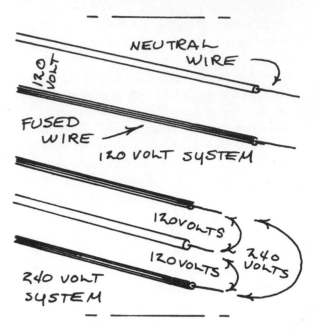

with white insulation and the other with black. The white wire is the neutral. The black wire is the one that is fused and switched throughout the system. Other wires of varying sizes

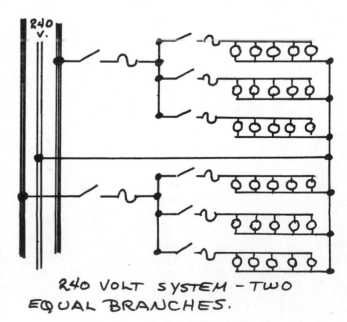

240 VOLT SYSTEM - TWO EQUAL BRANCHES.

connected to these two extend throughout the entire wiring system.

240 VOLT WIRING SYSTEM — Where the 240 volt system is employed three wires enter the meter. One is covered with white insulation; this is the neutral. The other two are fused. On the stage there is rarely any 240 volt equipment. If there is, the two dark wires are connected to it. For ordinary purposes the system is divided in half. One of the dark wires and the white one are connected to half of the branches and circuits while the other dark one and the white one are connected to the other half of the branches and circuits. This system is—or should be—fairly well balanced so that each half of the system carries approximately half of the total power load of the system.

SHORT CIRCUIT—When an electric circuit takes the path of least resistance and jumps across from one wire to another because of faulty insulation without first going through a lamp or other appliance, a short circuit or simply a "short" is said to exist. Usually the short will cause a fuse to burn out. If the circuit is overfused there is danger of extreme heat at any point in the short circuit which may cause a fire. The short circuit is a menace and as soon as there are clues that one exists — sparks, fuses blowing out or undue heat — a thorough inspection should be made to discover the trouble.

PRACTICAL APPLICATION OF THE POWER EQUATION—Now that circuits and fuses have been explained here are a few examples of how the power equation is used.

1. The wire in a certain 120 volt circuit is heavy enough to carry 15 amperes safely but no more than 15 amperes. (A) What is the wattage capacity of the circuit? (B) What size fuse should be used?

Ans. (A) Power = Voltage × current
Power = 120 × 15
Power = 1800 watts

No more than 1800 watts can be used at one time on this circuit.

Ans. (B) Since the wiring can carry only 15 amperes, a 15 ampere or smaller fuse must be used. A larger fuse might allow the wiring to overheat and cause a fire.

2. It is desired to connect three 1000 watt 120 volt spotlights in parallel to a single circuit. What must be the current capacity of the circuit wiring and fuse?

Ans. 3 × 1000 = 3000 watts, the total load
Amps = Watts ÷ Volts
Amps = 3000 ÷ 120 = 25

The wiring and fuse must be rated to carry at least 25 amperes. The fuse must not have a higher rating than the wire.

3. A dimmer is rated at 550 watts, 110 volts. What should be the circuit current capacity and the fuse capacity?

Ans. Amps = Watts ÷ Volts
Amps = 550 ÷ 110
Amps = 5

The circuit should be fused at 5 amperes in order to protect the dimmer. Most stage circuits will carry 15 amperes without overheating, but a 15 amp fuse in this circuit would be too high.

* * * * *

Although this discussion of electricity and electric circuits is brief it will suffice as an introduction to stage electrical work. The chapters that follow will provide information concerning practical applications of the basic ideas expressed in these few short paragraphs.

BORDER PATTERN

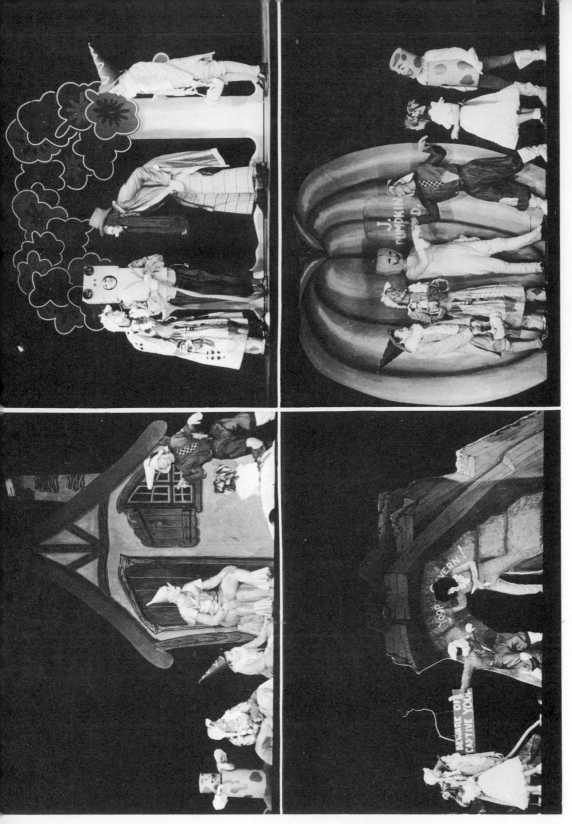

The Patchwork Girl of Oz. Small contoured book units that require a minimum of bracing are here space staged against black drapes.

Lighting Equipment

Stage lighting has become one of the major factors of production in the theatre. Equipment and facilities for lighting vary tremendously from one theatre to another so any listing must be fairly general, yet inclusive enough so that one desiring to make purchases and improvements may know what is available.

Tools

A limited number of tools are essential in the stage electrical department. Screw drivers, pliers and a knife are the major tools that will be used constantly.

SCREW DRIVERS—It will be convenient to have a set of varying width and length blade screw drivers. There are times when a long handled screw driver is convenient and times when only a short handled one can be used. Screw drivers for electrical work should have wooden or plastic handles and the width and

thickness of the blades should fit the screws of the electrical connectors.

PLIERS—Although regular snub nosed general utility pliers may be used for stage lighting purposes there are a number of varieties that are more practical.

Long nosed pliers, with or without cutting edges in the jaws, are useful for shaping the ends of wires before making connections with screw contacts on outlets. These are also useful for reaching into narrow apertures. Long nose pliers are available in 5″, 6″ and 7″ lengths. The 6″ length is a good general purpose size.

Side cutting pliers have rugged jaws and cutting edges. They are extremely useful and practical for electrical work since they can be used to cut almost any size of wire and their jaws grip firmly for pulling, bending and twist-

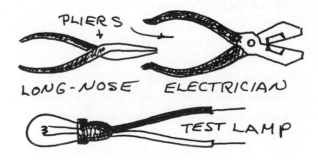

201

ing. They are available in lengths from 5″ to 9″. The 8″ size is large enough for most work.

Oblique cutting pliers are convenient to use if a great deal of wire cutting is done. Heavy side cutters can be used for most of the same work.

Insulation of pliers—When pliers are being used for electrical work it is a good idea to cover the handles with friction tape to insulate them and prevent shock to the operator.

CUTTING TOOLS—A knife is needed for removing the insulation from wires. Any type of sharp knife will do. If all of the work is being done on a work bench a paring knife will do. Usually a rugged pocket knife or a sheath knife with a belt case is more convenient to use if it must be carried around on the stage.

SCISSORS—A medium sized pair of scissors will work best for cutting color media.

WRENCHES—Most of the spotlights, floodlights and clamps have set screws that must be adjusted. Although pliers will work for loosening and tightening these, a crescent wrench will do the job better. An 8″ wrench is large enough for most of the nuts on lighting instruments.

PIPE WRENCHES—If there are "pipe stands," "trees" or "battens" on which lights are to be hung it may be necessary to have a pipe wrench. A pipe wrench has adjustable jaws with "teeth" so that it will grip the smooth surface of pipe and enable one to tighten or loosen a connection. A 12″ pipe wrench will be large enough for light jobs; 16″ or 18″ pipe wrenches will handle almost any pipe that will be used.

SOLDERING TOOLS—An electric soldering iron, small blow torch or cartridge type torch are convenient for heating wire and connectors for securing with solder. Often permanent connections need soldering in order to insure a sound contact.

SOLDER—It is advisable to use resin filled rather than acid filled solder for making electrical connections.

TEST LAMPS—A testing device consisting of a socket and lamp and pieces of insulated wire a few inches long extending from the socket is a convenient device for testing electrical circuits. The wires are touched to the contacts of a line. If the lamp glows, the line has voltage; if not, there is no voltage. By using the test lamp in various places along the circuit it is possible to trace the position of a faulty connection. Test lamps may be purchased or easily assembled in the lighting shop.

LABELS FOR EQUIPMENT—Electrical material, spotlights, cables, panel boards and swatch cords frequently need labels for rapid identification as to size, length, capacity, use, etc. Tie-on tags or regular bandage adhesive tape may be used for this purpose. It is easy to write on these and fasten them onto the object needing identification.

Light Bulbs or Lamps

LAMPS—The electric lamp, frequently referred to as a light bulb, is one of the most important elements in illumination. It consists of a number of parts. The globe is a sealed glass container. It may be evacuated or con-

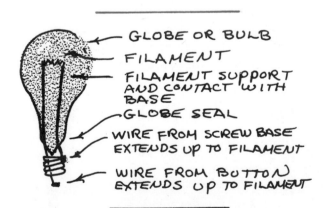

tain any of a number of gases, usually inert. Most of the common lamps are gas filled. The glass may be clear, frosted inside or out, made of stained glass, dipped in color or may be partially silvered on the inside or outside to create a reflective surface. Inside of the globe, glass supports or stems extend up from the base. Through these are wires which connect, one on each end, to the filament. The filament is a high resistance, high melting point wire that becomes white hot when the electric current is forced across it. The base of the bulb consists of two contacts separated by an insulation cement used to fasten the base to the globe. If it is a screw base lamp one of the wires fastened to the filament extends down and is fastened to the screw base while the other wire is fastened to a brass button at the tip of the base.

LAMP TYPES AND SHAPES — When lamps are ordered it is necessary to designate the shape of globe, type and size of base, voltage and wattage. The shape of the bulb is designated as follows: candelabra—C, flame—F, globular —G, ordinary lamps either pear shaped or modified pear shaped—A or PS, tubular—T,

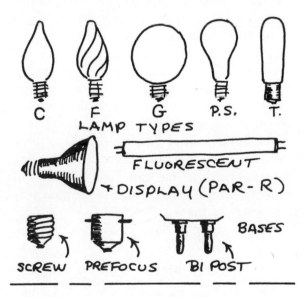

sealed beam display lights in the outdoor variety with heavy glass globes—PAR-38, display lights with indoor type globes—R-40, and long fluorescent tubes. The fluorescent lamp differs from the others and will be discussed later.

SIZE OF BASE — There are six commonly used sizes of lamp screw bases: candelabra, in-

termediate, medium, ad-medium, mogul and 3-lite (for lamp fixtures). Medium screw base is the type usually used in the home.

TYPE OF BASE—Although the majority of lamps have bases that simply screw into the socket there are other special varieties used extensively in the theatre. Prefocus is a variety of base designed to place the filament in a specific predetermined position. These are used in spotlights. The twist lock type of base is turned a quarter turn to lock it in position after being placed in the socket. The bipost base is another type of prefocus lamp that fits an instrument with the filament facing in a specified direction. The bipost has two connector prongs that are pushed into a special connector device.

LAMP SOCKETS—The receptacle portion of the lamp socket conforms to the size and type of lamp base to be used in it. The socket itself is made of insulation material and has contact screws for a pair of lead-in wires. There are numerous varieties of receptacles. Those used most often around the theatre will be the pendant variety that is supported either by hanging on the electrical cord or supported by a tubular conduit such as that of an ordinary floor lamp or table lamp; the porcelain socket that can be mounted on a flat surface; the sign socket that unscrews so that it may be mounted in a hole on a metal sign. The sign socket sandwiches the sheet metal with one half the porcelain on one side and the other half on the other side.

Fluorescent Lamps

Fuorescent lamps will undoubtedly be used more extensively in the future for stage lighting because of their high efficiency, long life, illumination characteristics and because it is now possible to partially control them with dimmers. The fluorescent tube differs from the regular incandescent lamp in many respects. The main difference lies in the fact that the incandescent lamp light comes from a heated filament while the fluorescent tube contains gas that is caused to glow by the current that passes from the contact at one end of the tube to the contact at the other end. Wiring of the circuit for the lamp differs, too, since it contains a ballast specifically designed for a certain wattage lamp.

Fluorescent lamps may be used for any general illumination. Footlights, striplights and especially cyclorama lights might be made from units of this type. The fact that the tube provides a line of light rather than a point makes it possible to eliminate many shadows that come from numerous points of light in a striplight section.

Electric Wire

The major conductors of electrical circuits are the sections of wire extending from one controlling unit of the system to another. There are basically two types of wire: the solid com-

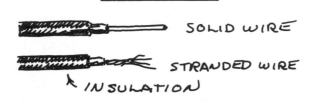

posed of a single wire and the stranded composed of a number of small diameter wires twisted together to form one conductor. Single strand wire is used for permanent installations and is relatively inflexible while stranded wire is flexible and is used for cords that are moved about a good deal. Theatre cable is composed of stranded wire.

SIZE OF WIRE—As suggested previously the cross sectional size and substance from which the wire is manufactured will determine the load carrying capacity of a wire. Copper is a good conductor, relatively plentiful, and is used throughout most electrical systems. A standard has been set up so that the capacity of a wire can be determined from its size number. The smaller the number the greater the capacity of the wire. The "load" indicates the amount

of current that can be safely carried continuously over the wire without danger of heating which might cause disintegration of the wire.

SIZE OF WIRE AND LOAD CAPACITY—Rubber covered cable is listed as follows:

#18 wire—	7 amps—	840 watts
#16 wire—	10 amps—	1200 watts
#14 wire—	15 amps—	1800 watts
#12 wire—	20 amps—	2400 watts
#10 wire—	30 amps—	3600 watts
# 8 wire—	40 amps—	4800 watts
# 6 wire—	55 amps—	6600 watts
# 4 wire—	70 amps—	8400 watts
# 2 wire—	95 amps—	11,400 watts
# 1 wire—	110 amps—	13,200 watts
# 0 wire—	125 amps—	15,000 watts
#00 wire—	145 amps—	17,400 watts
#000 wire—	165 amps—	18,800 watts
#0000 wire—	195 amps—	25,400 watts

LOAD—All electrical equipment has a load capacity that should not be exceeded. This capacity is listed in amperes (amps) or watts. If it is listed in amperes it is necessary to multiply by 120 to get the wattage capacity (using the formula $P=EI$) assuming the circuit has 120 volts. The process is reversed to determine the amperage from the wattage. If the capacity rating for a circuit is not listed on the switches, door of the box, control board or elsewhere it will be a good idea to have an electrician check over and label the entire system. Overloading of circuits will at the least burn out fuses or "kick" off circuit breakers and at the most may start a serious fire.

INSULATION ON WIRE—Wire used for conducting electric current is covered with nonconducting material or insulation. The insulation varies according to the capacity and specific use of the wire. Wire leads for instruments that are likely to heat considerably such as heaters, waffle irons and spotlights have a special asbestos fiber insulation. Most other wires, including theatre cables, have a rubber covering on the outside and various impregnated thread and compositional materials between this and the individual rubber covered wire on the in-

204

side. Usually there are two conductors within a cable so that both wires needed to complete a circuit can be handled as one.

WIRE SPLICES—When wires are connected or spliced together the ends of the wires should be carefully bared of insulation without cutting the individual strands. The ends to be connected should then be carefully twisted together. If they can be twisted back upon one another the connection will probably be stronger and if a spot of solder is put on the electrical contact will be even better. The solder is easily applied. Heat the joint with a soldering iron or small torch. As soon as it is hot enough touch the end of a piece of resin core solder to the wires at the joint so that it will melt and run in between the strands. It will take but a moment for this connection to cool. Soldering is especially important if the connection is permanent or semi-permanent. The connection is then covered first with a piece of rubber tape and then wrapped liberally with electrician's tape. The beginner might find it advisable to complete the connection of one wire of the pair through the taping stage before even beginning the other one. It is extremely important to insulate the wires from one another wherever there is a chance for a short circuit ("short").

"SHORT"—A "short" in a wiring system is a short circuit, which means that the electric current selects the easiest and shortest connection to complete a circuit. It is easier for it to flow across to its neighboring wire of the circuit if there is a bare section on both wires than it is for the current to flow through a lamp where it has to do work. Most short circuits are prevented by carefully insulating all connections.

INSULATING MATERIALS—Electrician's tape or friction tape should be used to cover bare wires. It is even better to cover them first with rubber tape and then electrician's tape. This provides an insulation similar to that on the wire. There is a special "scotch" tape that can be used to serve both purposes. It is more expensive than electrician's tape but sometimes the convenience is worth more than the added cost. There may be times and places where tape cannot be conveniently used so a substitute must be found. Sometimes exposed contacts are in an awkward place for taping. If they are small it may be possible to melt some sealing wax and drip it onto the connection. Sealing wax may be obtained from most stationery stores. Sealing wax has a fairly low melting point so it cannot be used where there is much heat or it will melt away. It is also inflexible when cold so it cannot be used on a joint that will be bent and twisted.

STAGE CABLE—Flexible two conductor electrical cord is cut into sections and used as extension cord or cable on the stage. A single cable, which may be any capacity and any length, is fitted with a connector on each end. One end is fitted with a female connector with no exposed contacts while the other end is fitted with a male connector with exposed prongs.

Plugs and Connectors

The connector is a device for connecting two stage cables together. The connector consists of two parts: the male, which is the portion with two prongs, and the female, which is the portion into which the male is plugged or connected. In ordinary home use the male is connected to the end of a cord on a light fixture and the female is the wall receptacle. The parts of the connector have matching contacts and by plugging the male into the female one is in fact extending the length of the power line. The male portion of the connector is *always* connected to the instrument or *load* and the female connector is *always* connected to the *line* or power source.

TYPES OF CONNECTORS—There are several types of connectors used on the stage. Among them are the following.

STANDARD CONNECTORS—The plugs ordinarily used around the home are standard connectors. These will carry only limited loads and they are connected by pushing into a standard receptacle. Some of these can be connected to lightweight utility cord without the use of a screw driver.

Twist Lock Connectors—The twist lock has two prongs with a short extension on one side. After it has been pushed into place it is twisted about a quarter turn which locks it into

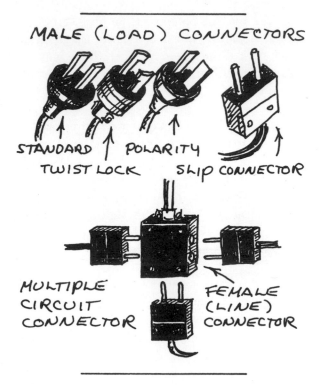

MALE (LOAD) CONNECTORS

STANDARD · POLARITY

TWIST LOCK · SLIP CONNECTOR

MULTIPLE CIRCUIT CONNECTOR

FEMALE (LINE) CONNECTOR

place. Twist locks are somewhat heavier than standard plugs and are excellent for stage use since they cannot be disconnected easily by accident.

Polarity Plugs—There are times when a plug must be used that can be inserted in only one specific position. Polarity plugs with mismatched prongs are used for this purpose. They either have one large and one small prong or they have one prong at right angles to the other prong.

Multiple Prongs—Sometimes it is necessary to have connectors with more than two prongs so a multi-prong connector is used.

Slip Connectors—Slip connectors are used on most stages. The round prongs are mounted in blocks of bakelite for the male half

and metallic sleeves are mounted in similar blocks for the female half of the connector. These are designed for heavy duty use and will withstand a good deal of abuse.

Floor Pocket Plugs—Floor pocket plugs may be of the slip connector variety or any of a number of other designs. Many of the heavier ones consist of a block of bakelite with a copper or brass contact plate on either side. These slide into pockets that have holes with similar copper plates on two sides to make the contact.

Jacks—Jacks are sometimes used as plugging devices. The jack may be used as a single or multi-wire connector. If it is a solid brass or copper rod an inch or more in length with an insulated handle to cover the wire connection it is probably a single conductor jack. If the rod is broken near the end with a segment of insulation it is undoubtedly a double pole conductor. Swatch panels in some interconnection systems use jacks.

Fuses

The fuse is a safety device placed in the electrical circuit to prevent overloading which may result in damage to the wire or the instrument wired into the circuit. The ordinary fuse contains a link or wire of fairly low resistance, low melting point metal. As soon as the load on the line exceeds the capacity of the fuse the link will heat and melt, thus breaking the circuit.

Screw Base Fuse—The screw base fuse

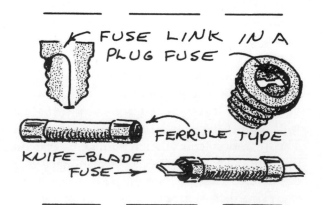

FUSE LINK IN A PLUG FUSE

FERRULE TYPE

KNIFE-BLADE FUSE →

fits into an ordinary socket. This type fuse is available in sizes up to 30 amps.

FERRULE CONTACT FUSES—Ferrule contact type cartridge fuses are available up to about 60 ampere capacity. These are made in renewable link or one time fuses. With the renewable type it is possible to unscrew the ends and replace the fuse strip.

KNIFE BLADE FUSE—The knife blade fuse is a cartridge fuse with heavy copper plate contacts on each end which make the contact in the receptacle. Knife blade fuses range in size from about 70 to 1000 amps.

CIRCUIT BREAKER—The circuit breaker is an automatic switch type fuse. An overload or short causes it to trip off automatically. The trouble must be corrected before it can be permanently switched on again. The circuit breaker insures against over-fusing a circuit.

Lighting Instruments

There are a few factors that should be considered when any type of lighting instrument is being selected for possible purchase.

1. *Size.* The physical measurements of the instrument should be known. Will it fit into the space where it is to be used?

2. *Shape.* Is it shaped so that it will be convenient to handle? Shape may be important if the instrument is to be in an exposed position where it will be readily seen by the audience.

3. *Weight.* Is it as light in weight as possible? Aluminum may be used by the manufacturer to cut down the weight of the instrument.

4. *Flexibility.* Can the instrument be used for varied purposes and in various places? The burning positions of the lamp may be checked to be certain that it will burn efficiently in the desired positions.

5. *Sturdiness.* Is it ruggedly built so that it will withstand rough handling?

6. *Convenience.* Can it be easily mounted and rigged? Can it be mounted in various ways — pipe, stand, tree, batten?

7. *Accessibility.* Is it easy to service? Can it be easily cleaned? Can the lamps be easily replaced?

8. *Ventilation.* Will it operate without undue heating? Is it ventilated without at the same time allowing undue light spill?

9. *Efficiency.* Is it as efficient or more efficient than similar instruments? Does it have a good reflector surface? Is the lamp positioned carefully in regard to the reflector and lens (if it is a spotlight)?

10. *Color holder.* Does it have a well designed color holder? Is it easy to mount the color media? Will the color frames stay in place when the instrument is mounted in the positions where it will be used?

Lighting instruments used for the illumination of the acting area of the stage may be classified under four headings for convenience: striplights, floodlights, sealed beams and spotlights.

Striplights

Striplights, as the name implies, consist of a series of units mounted side by side. Striplights may be employed as footlights, overhead borderlights, cyclorama base and overhead lights, backing lights and sometimes, when mounted vertically, as side lights.

The simplest striplight consists of a series of sockets mounted side by side on the wall, floor or a movable board. Plain lamps, colored lamps or display lamps may be screwed into the sockets.

A more complex striplight may be built by adding a reflector trough built of wood, sheet metal or aluminum. Large size eave troughs may be used for this purpose. When the reflector is added the efficiency of the striplight is increased and the amount of spill light is minimized.

Commercial striplights composed of a series of socket-reflector-color media units placed side by side provide for more efficiency and flexibility of operation. These may be purchased in various length sections and with various sized reflectors for lamps of from 40 to 500 watts. If the strip is to be close to the surface to be lighted, for instance footlights on a small stage, it is more advantageous to have closely grouped reflectors and lamps, especially if red-blue-green combinations are used so that the color mix will be close to the strip. With large units, obviously the color mix is farther out from the individual lamps to the point where the beams from the lamps intermingle. If the striplights are to remain in place at all times

SOCKETS MOUNTED ON BOARD

EAVE TROUGH REFLECTOR

STRIP WITH INDIVIDUAL REFLECTORS AND GLASS ROUNDELS.

the length of the sections is immaterial. But if the strips are to be moved about on the stage and used for varied purposes and if they are to be stored while not in use, it will probably be advisable to get sections that can be handled rather easily. Some strip sections are available in 5′ or 6′ sections. The length of the sections depends to some extent upon the size of each reflector unit. If the three color system is to be used it is also advisable to get strips that are wired in three circuits so that the individual

colors can be controlled separately by switch and dimmer.

FOOTLIGHTS — Although striplight sections are used as footlights, frequently the footlights are designed so that they can remain in place. Disappearing type footlights are convenient since it is possible to fold the sections down into the floor if they are not needed for a production.

INDIRECT FOOTLIGHTS—An indirect type of footlight is available that is placed with the socket side toward the stage and a mirrored surface on the side toward the audience. This makes it possible to diffuse the light more before it reaches the actor since it increases the distance the beams of light travel by a few inches. Even a few inches can make a difference here.

FLOURESCENT TUBE FOOTLIGHTS — With the rapid advancements that have been made in the development of fluorescent tube lighting equipment, practical striplights may soon be made with these tubes. The tubes will give even surface illumination and may be practical for footlights and cyclorama lights. The tubes are available in colors and at least partial dimming is possible. Tubes, providing as they do lines rather than points of light, might reduce shadows usually present when footlights are used.

Floodlights

Although floodlights usually have rather large wattage lamps—500, 750 or 1000 watts —they may be almost any size. A flood is used for over-all stage illumination. Basically a floodlight is a simple reflector housing equipped with a socket, lead in wires, color frame holder and frame, and a mounting yoke. For small wattage lamps the housing can be made of wood and shaped like a small box with one side removed. Or a 5 gallon cooking oil can (available at restaurants) can be used if one side is removed and a socket is mounted in the bottom. The inside of the reflector may be coated with white or aluminum paint. White will provide a high diffusion reflective surface

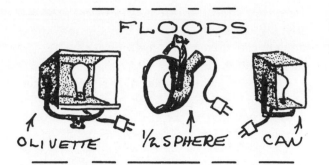

FLOODS

OLIVETTE   ½ SPHERE   CAN

which is largely non-directional. Sheet aluminum, available at "do-it-yourself" counters, can be used to make a reflector.

COMMERCIAL FLOODLIGHTS—A variety of floodlight types are available from theatrical supply houses. These range all the way from box shaped Olivettes (a type that has been used for many years) to spherical reflector floods that are probably more efficient. Since the flood is used primarily for over-all lighting its requirements are simple. It should have a lamp housing with a high diffusion reflective surface which may be white or silvered; it should have a substantial color frame holder and frame; and it should have a yoke mounting that will allow it to be rigged on a pipe stand, tree, pipe or batten. Most floodlights are relatively inexpensive.

Reflector Lamps (PAR38 and R40)

Electrical stores sell lamps for display purposes that are self contained spot or flood instruments. The PAR38 and R40 Reflector lamps are probably used more frequently than any other size. The PAR38 lamp is made of pyrex glass and will withstand considerable punishment. It is designed for indoor or outdoor use. The R40 series, on the other hand, is made of thinner glass and should be used indoors only. The number designates the diameter of the lens across the face of the lamp in eighths of an inch. R40's are therefore 5′ in diameter and PAR38's are 4¾″ in diameter. These are the numerical designations for the 150 watt Reflector lamps. Reflector lamps are

available in other wattages (75, 200, 300 or 500 watts), some of which have other number designations.

A theatre with a scant budget and no equipment might start with Reflector lamps as a basis for a lighting system. The lamps are efficient and easy to use. Part of the inside of the glass is silvered to provide a highly reflective surface and the front of the glass is designed to serve as a lens to distribute the light. The flood type tends to spread to a fairly wide beam while the spot type tends to restrict the light to a narrower beam.

Reflector lamps may be obtained with clear or colored glass. The color is baked onto the glass and is quite permanent. Unfortunately, the range of colors is somewhat limited but the variety is sufficient for simple lighting.

A number of devices can be purchased or manufactured to use with Reflector lamps. Some of these follow.

SWIVEL SOCKETS—Home made swivelling devices can be made. Two short pieces of 1″ x 3″ boards about 10″ in length may be hinged together at one end. Fold the two boards together flat and drill a hole through the two about an inch and a half from the unhinged end so that an adjustable bolt can be passed through both of them. The bolt can

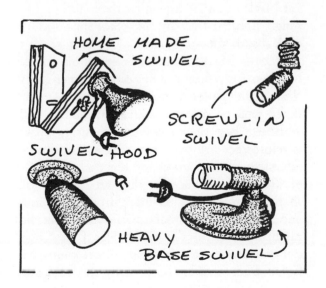

HOME MADE SWIVEL

SCREW-IN SWIVEL

SWIVEL HOOD

HEAVY BASE SWIVEL

be fastened securely to one of the boards by threading the nut down tight. This is the board that will be fastened in place wherever the unit is to be mounted. Cut a slot down toward the hinge for about 3″ in the other board. The socket can be mounted below this slot. If the bolt is long enough it will be possible to adjust this light to shine in almost any position by tightening or loosening a wing nut that is placed on the bolt after it goes through the socket board. Although this is a makeshift affair it will work fairly well.

Various types of swivel sockets and swivel units can be purchased from electrical shops. Some are available attached to "bullet" shaped housings. The housings will cut out some of the spill light, especially if they are fairly long so that the lamp mounts down inside of them. There are permanent swivels mounted in strip sections, screw in swivels, clamp on swivels, bolt down swivels and swivels with bases that will stand on the floor. The type purchased will probably be determined by the position in which they will be used.

LOUVRES—Louvres are concentric rings that fit into the housing in front of a reflector unit. They are designed to cut some of the spill (or extraneous) beams that fall outside the area to be lighted. To be effective the rings should have an inch or more of depth and be painted flat black. If they are shiny their surface will reflect light; if they are flat black their surface will absorb the spill light.

HOME MADE HOUSINGS — Home made housings for reflector lamps can be rather easily made from gallon cans. Paint, syrup or any other type of can that has a pry off lid will work the best since the edge of this type can is reinforced. A two piece sign socket can be mounted in the bottom of the can and 2′-0″ of asbestos cord and a plug attached. "U" shaped hangers can be made from strap iron and fastened to the sides of the can. The lid might be adapted as a color holder if the center can be cut out and a fastening device contrived. Color frame holders can easily be fashioned

from thin strap iron or the strap steel used for packing cases. Color frames to slip into these holders can then be made from cardboard, tin or aluminum.

FUNNELS—Unfortunately it is not possible to change the area coverage of reflector lights without devising a special mechanism. Funnels can be made for this purpose from 5″ stove

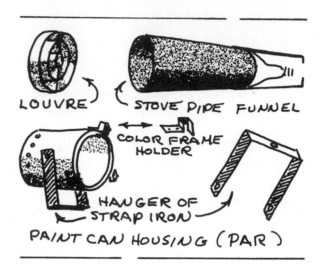

LOUVRE
STOVE PIPE FUNNEL
COLOR FRAME HOLDER
HANGER OF STRAP IRON
PAINT CAN HOUSING (PAR)

pipe. It is possible to make adjustable funnels by having inner and outer sleeves so that one will slide inside the other. Spill light that falls outside the area that needs lighting can thus be partially restricted and the light area increased or decreased in size. A funnel 2′-0″ long can be used where it is desirable to have a pin spot.

Reflector lamps have many uses on larger as well as smaller stages. They can be used for special effects, for footlights, striplights, backing lights and cyclorama base lights. They are inexpensive, efficient, easily obtainable and should not be overlooked as stage lighting equipment.

Spotlights

The most important light units on any stage are the spotlights. Although reflector lights can be used in place of regular spotlights they are never quite as effective where complex lighting effects are desired.

Basically the spot is a directional light and consists of:

Lamp housing with vent holes to cool the lamp but covered by baffles to prevent undue spill light.

Focusing device to change the size of the area lighted.

Reflector.

Support or hanger.

Lens or lenses.

Shutter, cutoff and iris devices (sometimes).

Frequently spotlights are loosely classified as large (if they are 1000 watts or more), standard (500 to 1000 watts) and baby (100 to 500 watts).

Several factors should be borne in mind concerning the selection and use of spotlights.

A spotlight gathers light rays from the lamp and redirects them so that they travel almost parallel to one another. The rays that cannot be redirected are absorbed by the blackened inside of the housing.

A spotlight is used where concentrated light is desired in a restricted area.

A spotlight operates more efficiently if it is close to a subject than if it is at a great distance from the subject.

The beam of light is hottest when the lamp is fairly far back in the housing and the beam is narrow.

There is a correct burning position for the lamps of almost all spotlights and the instrument should be positioned so that the lamp will be in this position for greatest lamp efficiency.

Spotlights should not be operated over long periods of time unless they are absolutely required. Spotlight lamps have relatively short burning lives and are expensive.

The spotlight is designed to capture a maximum number of the light rays emitted from the lamp and by means of a reflector and usually one or more lenses to bend those rays so that they pass through the front of the instrument in lines that are almost parallel. The ideal spotlight would make it possible to have evenly distributed light or a hot center and fading toward the edges of the area being illuminated and would make it possible at the same time to light either the maximum or minimum sized area desired on any stage. Since the ideal light has not been—and probably will not be—developed it is necessary to have a variety of instruments to achieve all of these desired effects. These instruments differ in many respects, including the shape and size of the housing, reflectors, lenses and lamps. These elements and their variations will be discussed first and then some of the general types of spotlights will be considered briefly.

REFLECTORS—The lamp in the spotlight is usually backed by a mirror surfaced reflector to project as many of the beams of light forward as possible.

Spherical Reflector—The spotlights that have been used predominantly have a spherical reflector. It is a mirror surfaced portion of a sphere designed to be placed in a fixed position in relation to the lamp so that it will capture the rays of light that are projected to the rear

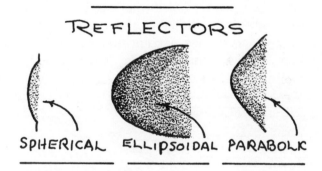

REFLECTORS

SPHERICAL   ELLIPSOIDAL PARABOLIC

by the lamp. With this type of reflector the rays of light from the lamp that strike the reflector and the ones that pass directly toward the opening in the front of the instrument are projected to the stage. The other rays are absorbed in the interior of the spotlight housing.

Ellipsoidal Reflector—The spherical reflector just mentioned is relatively small, surrounding as it does just a portion of the lamp. The ellipsoidal reflector is much greater in area. The lamp projects into it through a hole. The reflector extends around the lamp and projects considerably forward. This reflector captures many of the light rays that would be absorbed by the blackened interior of a spherical reflector spotlight.

LENSES—Most spotlights have a lens or a lens system in front of the lamp to bend the rays of light into approximately parallel lines as they leave the spotlight.

Plano-Convex Lens—The plano-convex lens is used on the majority of spotlights. This type of lens in cross section is flat on one side and curves outward on the other. Lenses are available in varying diameters and focal lengths. A given spotlight is built for one diameter but it is possible to get varying focal length lenses of this diameter. The focal length may be determined by allowing sunlight to pass through the lens. The straight rays of light from the sun are bent as they pass through the lens. The point at which they converge is the focal point and the distance from this point to the lens is the focal length of the lens. Theoretically a point source of light placed at the focal point will, when passed through the lens, be sent out in straight lines. However, the filament of the lamp is larger than a point and irregular in shape, so when used with the lens at exactly

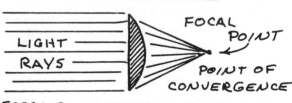

FOCAL POINT OF PLANO-CONVEX LENS

the focal point an image of the filament will be projected. In use the lamp socket on an adjustable slider is allowed to slide from slightly in front of the focal length to a position a fraction of an inch from the lens.

Long Focal Length Lens—The long focal length lens is thinner than the short focal

length lens and can be used in a spotlight where it is desirable to cover only a small area..

Short Focal Length Lens—The short focal length lens is thicker than the long lens and

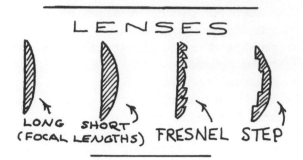

can be used where it is desirable to cover a wide area with a spotlight.

Step Lens—The step lens is a plano convex lens with a regular convex side. The plano, or flat side is partially carved out in "steps" to make the lens thinner which in turn reduces the weight, and cuts the light absorption of the lens.

Fresnel Lens—The Fresnel lens is a "step lens" with some of the characteristics of the plano-convex lens, but without its great thickness. The surface of this lens is composed of a series of concentric curved sections, each section having approximately the same curve as a plano-convex surface of the same diameter. Since the concentric breaks allow the curve to start again it is possible to reduce the maximum thickness of the lens appreciably. Reduction in the thickness of the glass reduces the danger of breakage from sudden heating and cooling, and reduces the amount of light lost by the absorption of the thick lens. The Fresnel lens is made of pyrex glass which will withstand greater heat than the optical glass of the plano-convex lens. Although the Fresnel lens is more efficient, at the same time, it usually has more diffusion qualities than the plano-convex lens.

Spotlight Types

With these few facts in mind, it is possible to

describe briefly some of the general types of spotlights available. In many instances the types of spotlights are known, by those who possess them, as "Leko", "Kleiglite" or some other trade name. There are many companies that make instruments that are similar in nature. So here the general type will be named rather than the trade name of the instrument of one manufacturer.

PLANO-CONVEX LENS SPOTLIGHTS — The standard spotlights that have been used most universally have plano-convex lenses and spherical reflectors. They are a general purpose spot light and may be used for area lighting. The beam is sharp edged and tends to have a hot

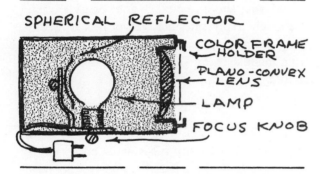

center and at times there is chromatic aberration around the edges of the lighted area. (Chromatic aberration is a colored "rainbow" effect at the periphery of the beam of light.) Usually they are less expensive than either the ellipsoidal or the Fresnel lens spotlights.

FRESNEL SPOTLIGHTS — The Fresnel spotlight gets its name from the Fresnel lens employed. Ordinarily it has a spherical reflector.

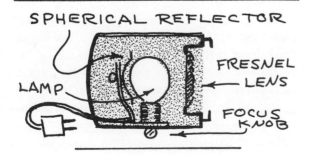

It is highly efficient, produces a soft, even beam of light with a fairly wide spread. Its tendency toward slight diffusion makes it better for use on stage than from the house positions since the diffusion tends to spread the beam.

ELLIPSOIDAL SPOTLIGHTS—Ellipsoidal spotlights have, as the name implies, ellipsoidal reflectors and they usually have one or more plano-convex lenses. This is a highly efficient light with a well defined beam. Many ellip-

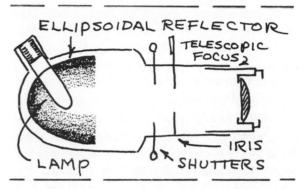

soidal spotlights are available with a telescoping lens mounting for increasing or decreasing the beam spread, with shutters to shape the beam and with an iris to diminish the size of the beam. Ellipsoidal spotlights are excellent for front of the house and other long throw use. Beam or balcony lights of this nature can be shaped by means of the shutters to fit the rectangular shape of the proscenium. Ellipsoidal spots give a sharp, well defined beam.

REFLECTOR SPOTLIGHTS—There are some spotlights that have no lens, or at least no lens that serves to bend the light rays. These may be referred to as reflector spotlights.

Parabolic Spotlights — The giant spotlights that sweep the sky to announce that a new supermarket is opening are of the parabolic variety. This is ordinarily a long focus spotlight with a shallow housing. A reflector is usually placed in front of the light source in order to eliminate the wide spill light. The light emitted from this instrument is all reflected light. These ordinarily have high watt-

213

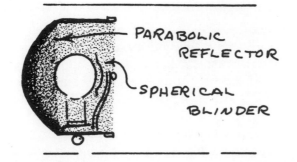

PARABOLIC REFLECTOR

SPHERICAL BLINDER

age lamps—or even carbon arcs—as the illuminant and are for long throw use.

Reflector Floods—The reflector floodlight is not as efficient as most spotlights as an area light, but it is widely available in electrical supply stores since it is used for outdoor yard lighting, display lighting, service station lighting and other general illumination. There is no focusing device on this light, but when equipped with deep louvres a certain amount of concentration of the beam is achieved.

THROW—When choosing a spotlight it is important to consider the distance the instrument will be from the object or area it is to illuminate. This is referred to as the "throw".

It is difficult to set specific standards, but the following suggestions might be helpful in selecting instruments to try out.

250 watt	15′ throw
500 watt	25′ throw
750 watt	35′ throw
1000 watt	40′ throw
1500 watt	50′ throw
2000 watt	60′ throw

In order to determine relative efficiency, throw, spread and adaptability to a specific situation, the lighting instruments should be mounted side by side, if possible, and compared with one another. One feature of a spotlight may make it superior to a similar spotlight for any one situation. The amount of light falling on an area can be measured with a photographic light meter.

Spotlights should be chosen for the features desired. If maximum illumination is desired they should be chosen for efficiency. The amount and evenness of the beam can be checked with a photographic light meter. If a small area or "pin spot" is desired the instrument should be checked for efficiency when the area coverage is small and it should also be equipped with an iris or shutters, or possibly with both, in order to facilitate in diminishing the area coverage. If a spot with a hot center is desired it should be checked for this quality. If smooth, even illumination across the area is desired—and this is the quality that will usually be the most desirable in regular area lights— this should be checked with the light in position where it will be used. Long throw, short throw, image projection, weight, ventilation, construction, servicing and mounting are other factors that should be taken into consideration. Although many salesmen are honest in evaluating their equipment, it is advisable to test the equipment side by side before making a purchase.

Instrument Supports

In order that spotlights can be focused correctly and remain in focus it is necessary to have strong, well anchored supports. Some of the various types of devices of this nature are as follows:

1. PIPE BATTENS — Pipe battens may be suspended from the flies on a rope or counterweighted flying system. When lights are mounted it is usually advisable to have or contrive some type of counterweighting so the rigged batten can be raised and lowered easily for focusing the spotlights. Pipes may be mounted permanently on walls, ceilings or elsewhere for this same purpose.

2. LIGHT STANDS—There are several types of bases used on stands. These are crow foot, solid base and caster base. *Crow foot* bases, which have three or four feet extending out at the bottom, are light in weight and frequently the legs are mounted so that they can be folded up against the upright pipe for storage or transportation. The *solid base* is composed of a heavy cast iron disc threaded in the center to

receive a pipe upright. The *caster base* is equipped with casters so that it can be easily moved around on the stage. Sometimes the casters have locks so they will not roll when positioned.

All light stands should be substantial enough to support the weight of the lights that will likely be mounted upon them. They should have substantial bases and should be capable

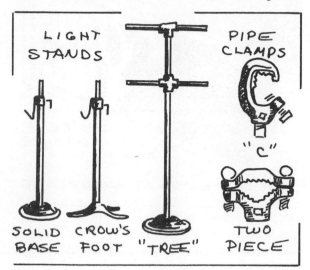

of storage and maneuverability on the stage where they are to be used. They should have telescoping sections that will allow them to be raised as high as desired for the specific stage.

3. TREES—Trees are light stands equipped with projecting arms on which lighting instruments may be mounted. These require a broad, heavy base that can be securely anchored.

4. TOWERS—A light tower may be made up with a wooden or pipe framework. It is frequently mounted on a caster base for maneuverability. Light towers should be designed for the individual stage so that they can be conveniently maneuvered and stored when not in use. For operation they should also—if tall and designed for many lights—have platforms for operators to stand on while focusing and repairing the lights.

Mounting Clamps

Instruments are mounted to the supports by means of "C" clamps or two piece clamps. The "C" clamp easily hooks over a pipe after which a set screw is adjusted to lock it against the pipe. The two piece clamp is composed of one toothed piece that fits on one side of the pipe and another piece that fits on the other side. A bolt at either end is used to tighten the jaw sections together and hold them firmly against the pipe. The "C" clamp will work very well where the lighting instrument hangs straight down from the batten. Where it is necessary to cinch the clamp up tight to hold the instrument support out at an angle the two piece clamp is probably better.

Image Cut-Off and Shaping Devices

Auxiliary devices may be mounted on some spotlights for cutting off or shaping part of the beam. These consist of two or four-way cut-offs with sliders that may be moved in across the beam, iris dissolvers that may be opened or closed like the iris of a camera, and "barn doors" (hinged doors) that may be partially or completely closed like a set of double doors. The funnel is another device of this nature.

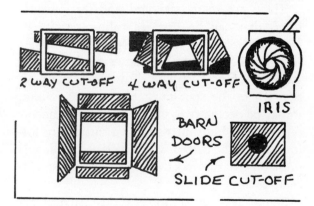

This is a long tubular contrivance, similar to a section of stove pipe. If the funnel is adjustable in length it is possible to cut out spill light and obtain a small pool of light that is almost without any halo spill area. The inside of the funnel should be painted flat black.

Special Lighting Devices

There are special lighting devices that should

be discussed. These are: follow spots, and projection instruments.

FOLLOW SPOTS — Musicals, variety shows, operas and ballet productions frequently make use of follow spots to accent the action of the moment. Although there are times and places where this can be accomplished with ordinary spotlights usually a more intense spot is desired so special instruments are used.

The follow spot will ordinarily be placed in the front of the house somewhere. It may be at the back of the auditorium, back of the balcony, front of the balcony or at one side of the balcony. Its greater distance from the stage requires that it be a long focal length light with cut-off or iris controls, or maybe even both. It should be capable of being pinned down so that it covers no more than the upper half of the human body. Usually it will be used to illuminate an entire person or a small group, although there may be times when it is desirable to open it up and cover the entire stage. Sometimes it is used wide open and then as a number starts it is pinned down onto a single person.

There are many standard and special spotlights that can be used as follow spots. In fact, any spotlight that will provide a higher illumination than the ordinary stage lights will serve in a pinch. If the throw from the position where the spot must be operated is long it may be necessary to obtain a special incandescent spot of high intensity or a carbon arc follow spot. The carbon arc, if well designed, will probably be the most effective and most efficient to use.

Some lighting companies manufacture excellent carbon arc follow spots with ellipsoidal reflectors.

LINNEBACH PROJECTOR — The Linnebach projector is basically a shadow projector, hence it is most effective when the screen upon which it is projected is light in color value and receives very little illumination other than the illumination from the projector. A Linnebach projector can be built quite easily. It consists

of a concentrated filament lamp, the filament being as close to a point source of light as possible; a housing painted black on the inside; and a cut out slide proportioned for the desired image to be projected. The entire instrument

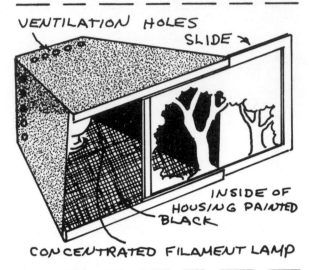

can be designed for the specific projection situation. Since the light shines out in a pyramid form with the lamp as the apex and the screen upon which the image falls as the base, it is easy to compute the desired width and height. The formula for computing this is as follows:

$$\frac{\text{Size of the slide}}{\text{Size of the image}} = \frac{\text{Distance of slide to the lamp}}{\text{Distance of the image to the the slide}}$$

The height and width are computed separately, using the same formula. When making the slide it may be necessary to distort the cut out in order to compensate for the distortion that will be caused by projection from a high, low or side angle. A little trial and error work will aid in making this compensation. The housing for the projector can be made from sheet metal or wood and the slide or cut out can be made from cardboard, metal or wood. If wood is used for the housing, asbestos paper can be pasted on the inside of it to reduce the fire danger. Slides can be made from sheet plastic and painted with special plastic paints if colored projections are desired. The flammability of all the materials used in the instru-

216

ment should be carefully checked, especially if a large lamp is employed.

The Linnebach projector will give unrefined definition and will be most effective where relatively bold effects are desired. If more defined images are desired it will be necessary to use a projector with a lens system.

Metal slides for ellipsoidal spotlight lens systems are available to project "cut-out" patterns.

SLIDE PROJECTORS—Photographic or painted slides can be projected onto a backdrop or screen on the stage by means of a lens projection machine. If the area to be covered is relatively small a regular slide projector or stereoptican can be used. If, however, the image is to be much larger, it may be necessary to use a projection lens system that fits onto a regular spotlight. This may be rented or purchased from almost any stage lighting supply house. By means of this type projector any image that can be photographed or drawn can be projected onto a background. As with the Linnebach projector, the best effect is obtained when the screen area is light in value and when the image projection is the highest illumination that falls upon that surface. Usually a fairly high intensity lamp is needed in order to project a desirable image for stage use.

MOVING PROJECTIONS—Special effects machines are used where it is desirable to have special moving effects such as clouds, rain, snow, flames or water falls. This machine is similar to the slide projector in that it contains a lens system, but it also has a large disc that is rotated by means of an electric or clock motor. Since machines of this nature are expensive to purchase, only the completely equipped theatre is likely to have one as regular equipment. It is usually more advisable to rent the machines when needed and obtain the specific effect desired. Most of the large theatrical supply houses have projectors and discs available for rental.

At this point it should be stressed that projections are effective only if they are not washed out by the other lights on the stage. Acting area lights cannot be allowed to fall upon the surface and even high value spill light should be restricted from the surface upon which the image is projected. Snow and rain effects from a moving effects machine are worthless if the sky is brightly lighted with strips and floods. So if the stage is brightly lighted it will be just as well to forget about ever trying projections.

Lighting Controls

Dramatic productions of today require careful and complete control of all of the lights on the stage. Control boards have become structurally complex and their initial cost is so large an item in the total budget that unfortunately the board is expected to last almost as long as the theatre building itself. And although most of the equipment built today is durable and should have a long practical operating life, there is a limit to how long it will last and continue to operate efficiently. It is therefore extremely important that the best and most practical type of equipment be purchased when the controls are installed. A basic knowledge of the various types of dimmers available may help in determining which is the best for any one situation.

Dimmers

There are a number of general types of dimmers that can be used in the theatre. Among these are the following:

1. SALT WATER DIMMER—The salt water dimmer is primitive, crude and obsolete, but a short description of it may help to explain the basic idea of all resistance type dimmers. This dimmer is composed of a jar of water and two electrodes (metal plates), one at the bottom of the jar and the other rigged so that it may be raised and lowered in the jar. One wire of the circuit is cut and the dimmer wired in series. One side of the cut wire is fastened to the electrode in the bottom of the jar while the other is fastened to the electrode that is to be raised and lowered. The load, probably a

lamp in a socket, is placed in the circuit. The movable electrode is placed just under the surface of the water and salt is added to the water until the lamp barely begins to glow. It will then be found that the light may be brightened by lowering the electrode and dimmed by raising it. When the electrodes touch, the lamp will come on bright, probably with a sudden jump. The resistance of the circuit is determined by the height of the column of water and by the amount of electrolyte (salt) present. This dimmer is practical for experimental purposes and for dimming light loads when there is no other device available.

2. RESISTANCE DIMMER—The basic principle of the resistance dimmer is similar to that of the salt water dimmer except that wire of high resistance and high melting point is used in place of salt water. The electric current flows through the wire. As more and more of the wire is introduced into the circuit it becomes more and more difficult for the current to flow. In actual practice, a long piece of wire of diminishing size and increasing resistance is mounted in a vitreous enamel base. Periodically along the wire, button contacts are fastened. By moving from contact to contact along the resistance wire it is possible to tap off an increasing or decreasing amount of electric power. With a slider device it is possible to gradually brighten or dim an incandescent lamp by moving from contact to contact up or down the scale. In both this type of device and the salt water dimmer the energy lost by dimming is dissipated in heat. In the salt water dimmer the water is heated and in the resistance dimmer the entire instrument is heated.

Resistance type dimmers have several disadvantages. The two major drawbacks are: loss of energy dissipated in heat and lack of flexibility (since a certain capacity load on the dimmer is necessary for it to operate successfully). The only places where resistance dimmers should be used at all in new installations are in buildings where only D.C. current is available or in small remote control units used as part of the control equipment of other type dimmers.

3. AUTO TRANSFORMERS—The auto transformer type of dimmer is the least expensive of the more efficient variable capacity dimmers. This is a device for tapping off any desired voltage. By moving a slider — either with a rotating knob or sliding contact—which may be done manually or with motors—the operator is able to tap off any desired voltage from zero up to the top voltage of the line. This type of dimmer will operate satisfactorily with any size load from the tiniest wattage to one of the total capacity of the dimmer. The auto transformer is efficient since it taps off just the voltage that you wish to use. It dissipates much less energy in the form of heat than the resistance dimmer.

Auto transformer dimmers are available in many sizes and under numerous trade names. They are available in both rectangular and radial shapes. Some are available with a single heavy duty winding but several sliders so that a single unit can operate as if it were several individual dimmers. Auto transformers may be operated manually or may be equipped with motor driven sliders so that they can be operated from a remote control board. The variable load capacity makes this an extremely useful dimmer. It can be incorporated into light boards to produce a workable, efficient control system. The heavy duty, large capacity dimmers are probably better than the smaller ones since their windings make them more durable than the ones with smaller wire windings.

Auto transformer dimmers of from 300 to 5000 watts are frequently used as circuit controls on small and medium sized stages. Large stages will usually require nothing smaller than the 2000 watt or 4000 watt sizes.

4. REACTOR DIMMER — The simplest reactance control works somewhat as follows: a coil of insulated wire is placed in series with the load (lamp). A movable iron core is then rigged that can be thrust into the center of the coil. An opposing force is thus set up in the core causing a lowered voltage in the coil and consequently the dimming of the lamps. As

the core is removed the voltage increases and the lights brighten again.

Another method of dimming similar to this uses a second coil instead of a movable plunger. A small direct current flowing through this second coil is able to control a much larger alternating current which flows through the main coil and the load. By adjusting the direct current with a small rheostat similar to a small resistance dimmer, the intensity of a lamp connected in series with the main coil can be controlled. This type of dimmer is well adapted for remote control, but it is often rather slow acting, fast changes of light intensity being impossible to achieve. As with the resistance dimmer, only a limited range of load wattages can be connected to a reactance dimmer; if the load wattage is too small it cannot be dimmed.

5. ELECTRONIC CONTROL—The electronic controls employ electronic tubes. These tubes, called Thyratron tubes, are remotely controlled by small rheostats or dimmers in the control board. The flow of current in the tube controlled by these small rheostats in turn causes large currents to flow in the lighting circuit. The tube acts as a valve to control the current flow.

The various Thyratron control and reactance control dimmers are being mass produced which should bring the price down within the range of many theatres that have found them too expensive to consider in the past. Although the electronic dimmer bank is a little more bulky than the auto transformer, it can be remotely controlled so it is possible to mount the dimmers in an out of the way corner under the stage or auditorium. The controls for the dimmers are compact and require only a small space. An added advantage is the plug-in unit being offered by at least one manufacturer. When something goes wrong it is possible to plug in another unit while the defective one is being repaired.

Control Boards

Dimmers, together with switches and fuses, are mounted in a convenient framework for efficient operation. In a simple board all of the equipment is directly controlled and mounted close to the acting area. In more complex systems it is found advisable to have the dimmers mounted in a room away from the stage and have the controls mounted in a position where the operator is able to see the stage.

Basically the control board is similar to a simple tree in its wiring structure. A trunk line comes in to the board. This is the source of power for the entire electrical system of the stage. There is a fuse box where it enters. This contains a Master Switch and Master Fuses. From here the wires branch off into groups of circuits. The groups have Master Switches and Master Fuses. Each unit of the group is then broken down into individual units which in turn have individual switches and fuses. When regular fuses are used they are mounted on the stage side of the line so that when it is necessary to change them the switch on the line side may be turned off first. Many times the switch-fuse combination is replaced by circuit breakers, which are automatic fuses that cut out when the circuit is overloaded.

In the most primitive control boards there are no dimmers. The circuits are merely turned on and off by means of switches. In this type of board, as in all of the more complex ones, each branch should be correctly fused so that it will carry not more than the rated load of the cable or wire leading to it. The total of the circuits should not exceed the load capacity of the wire leading to the Master Switch. The total of the Master Circuit should not exceed the load capacity of the group Master Circuits. And finally the total of the group masters should not exceed the capacity of the Grand Master and its line and fuses.

A simple board with dimmers may have the dimmers wired permanently into place or have some type of plug-in by-pass system so that a minimum number of dimmers can be used where they will be the most serviceable during a production.

The by-pass system allows the dimmers to be plugged in and used or allows the circuit to be used without the dimmer. A switch makes it possible to cause the current to flow through a dimmer or directly from the power line.

The plug-in system employs jacks, utility plugs, or some other type of connectors. The instrument can then be plugged in wherever desired. It may be plugged in so that it is operated by a switch or so that the current runs through a dimmer.

The system having dimmers permanently wired to specific circuits lacks flexibility. Although it is certainly superior to a board having no dimmers at all, at the same time it can be improved by rewiring and adding a simple plugging system to achieve flexibility and to allow the dimmers to be used on any of a number of circuits.

Interconnecting Devices

A variety of plugging systems are being used on control boards today. They are all designed to achieve the same thing in lighting — flexibility. A simple board may have only 3 or 4 dimmers that may be interconnected to 6 or 8 outlets. A complex board may have 50 to 100 or even more dimmers and twice as many outlets. The swatch cord system, push button selectors, slide contacts and other interconnecting devices are designed to accomplish the same thing. They make it possible to connect any dimmer to any outlet. Thus various combinations are possible, making the operation of the board more convenient and practical. This is similar to a telephone system where it is possible for a person to call anyone else in the system. This interconnecting system makes it possible to connect lights that work together near one another and to master control groups that need to dim or brighten at the same time.

SWATCH CORD CONNECTORS — A swatch cord system may have one end of the cord permanently connected and a jack or plug on the other end or the cords may be loose on both

ends so that both the line and load ends are plugged into place. This system gets rather complicated and messy, especially when there is much connecting across the board. The swatch cords get mixed up in one tangled ball.

PUSH BUTTON CONNECTORS—Push button connectors require the use of many contact buttons but certainly have much to recommend

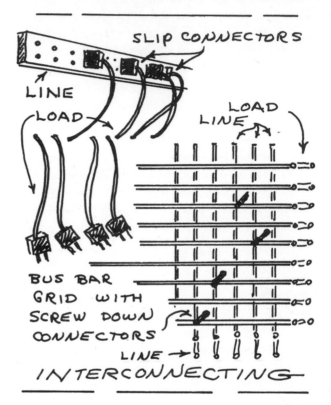

them for their simplicity of operation. For complete flexibility it is necessary to have a row of buttons equal to the number of stage circuits that can make contact with each dimmer circuit. In order to connect a circuit and a dimmer together it is merely necessary to push a button into place.

SLIDER TYPE CONNECTORS — Slider type connectors—and several use basically this type of device—reduce the number of contact buttons. The contactors are pushed along a slot until they make contact between the correct dimmer and outlet.

Any of these systems can be used. The con-

220

nectors should be heavy enough to withstand the wear of frequent use, should not arc enough to pit and stick and should be easy and convenient to handle. Compactness is essential if there are many outlets and dimmers; otherwise, the panel will take up too much space and be difficult to manipulate. The interconnecting panel can be placed beside the board or in a convenient place on the stage.

Remote Control

Remote control makes it possible to place the operator in a position in the auditorium where he is able to see the stage from the audience's vantage point. The orchestra pit or footlight position, the back of the auditorium and the face of the balcony are possible positions for an operational booth. The house position, wherever it may be, is highly recommended over any backstage position so that the operator can see the results of his lights. The only disadvantage is the distance separating him from the stage if anything goes wrong. A simple telephone system employing sound powered telephones will do wonders to correct this problem.

Dimmers — General

There is no inexpensive substitute for stage dimmers. This is one place where it is worthwhile not to skimp. Makeshift, inexpensive lights can be readily contrived and will be considered expendable, but the dimmer board, once installed, will be used for a good many years. A sizeable expenditure should be made at the time of installation in order to insure long and practical life for the control board. It should be purchased from a reputable company and should have guaranteed maintenance for a long enough period of time to insure its proper installation and operation.

When planning the dimmer board, considerable thought should go into the design. The controls should be as close together as possible for ease of manipulation. The controls should be grouped so that they can be operated effi-

ciently. And all of the mechanical parts of the board should move easily and quietly.

Color Media

Since the light from an instrument is almost always colored and rarely white, it is necessary to discuss color media rather briefly. Some of the various media and their characteristics follow.

1. GLASS—Glass roundels or color media are used especially in striplight sections. The glass is rather expensive and breaks readily if it is not handled carefully and so should probably be used only where the roundels will remain almost permanently in position. Roundels are available in deep colors and are far better where pure colors are needed than almost any other media. Most of the other media will fade while the glass is quite permanent.

2. CELLOPHANE — Cellophane is probably the least expensive of all color media. It is somewhat limited in where and how it can be used, but its cost somewhat compensates for its other weaknesses. It is flammable and so should not be used where it is in direct contact with the lamp or where an extremely hot beam of light will pass through it. Cellophane does not dry out and get brittle as soon as gelatine. The range of colors is limited and it is impossible to get deep values in many colors. The color tends to burn out with use.

3. GELATINE—Gelatine is the old standby and is probably used in more theatres than any other color media. Gelatine comes in a wide range of colors including all of the deep values and is nonflammable. The ordinary gelatine is soluble in water so cannot be used where there is a great deal of dampness. There are waterproof varieties but they are more expensive than the ordinary gelatine. For over-all use gelatine is probably still the best media.

4. PAR 38 AND R40 WITH BAKED ON COLOR—Par 38 and R40 lamps are available with a color media baked on the face of the lamps. The range of colors is rather narrow,

but the colors seem quite permanent and good almost for the life of the lamp.

5. COLORED FLUORESCENT TUBES—Fluorescent tubes that emit colored light are available. The range of colors is still not too extensive but there are red, yellow, blue and green glowing tubes available.

6. LAMP DIP—Special dyes are available for coloring the outside of the lamp globe. These colors will come off after extensive use, but for special purposes they will probably be useful, especially for small wattage lamps.

7. PLASTIC FILTERS — Numerous plastic filter media are on the market which are nonflammable and possess more durable dyes than some of the less expensive materials. Most of these are heavier than gelatine and, as indicated, are also more expensive. However, if they will outlast gelatine appreciably they will be well worth the additional cost in theatres where many plays are produced each season.

* * * * *

Although this seems like an extensive list of equipment it is by no means all inclusive. On the other hand, it is not necessary to have all of these items before a theatre can start operating. Items of this nature are accumulated over a number of years. Some of the devices may never be used while others will be used continually.

14

Lighting

Stage lighting in practice is the manipulation of color, light and shadow. Although the primary objective in any form of lighting is to achieve visibility other end results are also desirable when a play is being lighted. Either consciously or unconsciously the lighting artist attempts to: concentrate the audience attention, create mood and atmosphere, model forms and create dramatic design.

It has often been proved by experiment that hearing is dependent to a certain extent upon visibility. If members of an audience have difficulty seeing the action upon the stage they also have trouble hearing and understanding the dialogue. And obviously if they have trouble hearing and seeing they also have trouble following the action and story. Therefore, having sufficient light for visibility is of first importance in stage lighting.

By manipulating the quantity and distribution of the light on the stage it is possible to control the audience attention. In general, attention is drawn toward the point of higher illumination where there is a variation in light intensity. By subtly shifting the light during scenes it is possible to move the audience's attention from one area of the stage to another. In order to do this effectively the lighting operator must have complete control over every light on the stage.

The mood of a scene can be set by the amount and color of the illumination. There is usually a feeling of gayness when the illumination is in a high key and everything on the stage sparkles. On the other hand, low key lighting consisting of dim light and deep shadows will project a feeling of uncertainty, mysticism and fear. The mood of a scene as well as the mood of an audience can be controlled to a great extent by the proper handling of the color, intensity and distribution of the stage lighting.

The three dimensional qualities of form are revealed through the use of proper lighting. Subtleties of form are revealed by variations in the levels of intensity and variations in the color of the light. In nature the eye distinguishes the shape of objects by the slight variations in light values. Light strikes the object from all directions since it receives not only direct sunlight but also reflected light from every surface around it. Some areas will receive direct light, some high reflected light, others modified amounts of direct or reflected light. These variations in the quantity and quality of light

223

reveal the form to the eye. The stage lighting man can make use of variations in light intensity to reveal the nature of forms on the stage.

Light may be used as a design element on the stage. Surfaces may be lighted in patterns that come from regular or special lighting instruments. These patterns may be abstract or projections of photographic reproductions of real objects; they may be shafts of white light or interminglings of colored light forms. Light may be used in many ways to create all or part of the stage design. Evening and morning, summer and winter can all be suggested by the color and visible distribution of the light on the acting area of the stage.

Many or all of these effects may be used in lighting the stage for a production. The total effect of stage lighting enlarges the emotional impact of the total production. Lighting is used to assist the visual design, the emotional content and the physical movement of the play.

It is impossible to list a set of rules and say specifically "This is the way to light a play." There are too many physical variations from one stage to another. The lighting system for each stage must be worked out in terms of the relationship between the auditorium and stage, number and capacity of circuits, the type and number of dimmers and the size and arrangement of the various elements of the stage itself.

Basically there are two types of stage lighting. These types are actor illumination and shadow softening illumination. Ordinarily they are both used in lighting a stage.

ACTOR ILLUMINATION—Although a successful dramatic production consists of many elements fused together into a closely integrated whole, the actor almost always remains dominant. Consequently the major portion of the stage lighting is designed for lighting the actor and his realm of the stage. Spotlights are usually employed for this purpose. With the spotlight it is possible to concentrate a major portion of the light on a restricted area.

SHADOW SOFTENING—Although the major portion of the illumination from the spotlight will fall on the acting area each of the surfaces upon which this light falls will serve as a reflector and cause diffused rays to spill off in many directions. This spill light will tend to soften the shadows around the rest of the stage. Usually this isn't quite enough to "kill" some of the heavy shadows so a limited amount of additional general illumination is needed. This shadow softening light comes from strip lights, such as footlights and borders and from floodlights.

POSITION OF SPOTLIGHTS—The spotlights used for actor illumination will probably give the best results if they can be located in front and above the area of the stage they are to light. The angle of the light beam with the stage floor should probably not exceed 45°. If these lights are located on a low level and shine almost straight forward toward the stage,

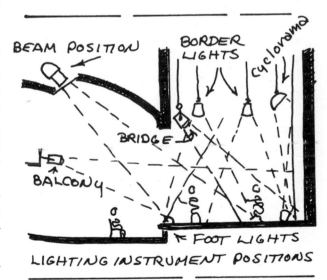

LIGHTING INSTRUMENT POSITIONS

large shadows of the actors will fall upon the scenery in the background. If, on the other hand, the angle is too steep the shadows under the eyes, nose and chin of the actors will be extremely heavy. An angle of from 30° to 45° will help modify both of these excesses.

STAGE AREAS—For convenience the stage is divided into areas for lighting. The size and number of areas will depend to a great extent upon the size of the stage and the size and number of spotlights available for lighting it. Ordinarily it is best to have a row of downstage areas and a row of upstage areas. If considerable depth is being used it may be necessary to have a third row or even a fourth row across the stage. The areas may be designated in terms of the stage directions accepted by theatre workers: upstage, downstage, right stage, left stage, right center, left center and so on. If there are spotlights in the auditorium they may have titles that refer to their relative positions. Lights in the ceiling are frequently referred to as "beam lights," those on the balcony as "balcony lights," those on the stage immediately behind the act curtain as "bridge lights." There are also "footlights," "border lights," "Cyclorama lights," "trees," and so on.

AREA LIGHTING PLAN—A small stage having a proscenium of 24' width or less may be lighted by having as few as 6 areas, 3 downstage and 3 upstage. The downstage areas are lighted, if possible, by spotlights located in the auditorium ceiling or beams. Each area should have two units focused on it. This

means that there will be at least 6 spotlights in this downstage position. These should be spaced so that there is approximately the same distance from the various lights to the stage area they are lighting. The two lights illuminating each area are placed so that their beams reach the area from different directions. If the 6 instruments are equally spaced across the beam the first and fourth may be used to light the stage right area, the second and fifth may be focused on the stage center area and the third and sixth may be on the stage left area.

NUMBERING THE ACTING AREAS — In order to further clarify the relationship between

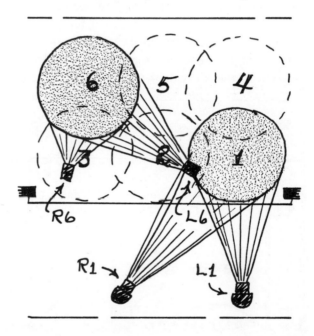

the acting areas and the lighting units it might be wise to number the areas. Looking at the stage from the actor's position, since the right (R) and left (L) directions are so located, number the down left area as "1", down center as "2" and down right as "3". The upstage areas will continue in the same order with up left as "4", up center as "5" and up right as "6".

SPOTLIGHT DESIGNATION—The spotlights may now be designated in terms of the area they light and the direction from which their beams reach the stage. Each area will have a

BRIDGE

← BEAMS →

225

right and left spot. Area "1" will have an "R1" and an "L1" and so on.

ALTERNATE POSITIONS FOR FRONT AREA LIGHTS—If there is no possibility for mounting beam lights it will be necessary to investigate other positions. It may be possible to mount them in high side windows, although the distance from the stage and the angle are not as good as for a beam position. Large chandeliers are other possible positions. If none of these possibilities will work it may be possible to rig ladder frames or tall flat frames in positions near the side walls and mount lights on these. If something like this is used it will be necessary to mask the supports so they are not too obvious. Sometimes towers of this nature can be rigged in the orchestra pit immediately in front of the stage, or even on the apron of the stage. However, the individual situation will have to

be studied carefully to determine the best place for mounting such lighting units so they will not seriously affect sight lines

BALCONY RAIL—Under most circumstances the balcony rail is the last solution to the problem rather than the first one because, as suggested before, lights mounted in this position usually are so low in elevation that when the actors move about on the stage they cast heavy shadows on the back wall of the setting. However, this position is better than having no

front lights. If spots are mounted here it might be advisable to use a larger number of smaller units rather than a few large ones so

that three or four from varying angles can be focused on a single area. In this way the back wall shadows will be minimized.

UPSTAGE AREAS—The upstage areas of the stage can best be lighted by instruments mounted behind the top of the proscenium arch immediately upstage of the act curtain. These lights, frequently referred to as the bridge lights, may be mounted on a catwalk or a batten

226

suspended immediately upstage of the act curtain or on towers upstage of the proscenium side walls. The overhead batten position is probably superior since it lessens the distance from the lighting instrument to the stage and enables one to get greater intensity than from the more removed side positions.

BRIDGE—The bridge spotlights are mounted and arranged in positions somewhat similar to those in the beams. Areas 4, 5 and 6 are lighted, each with two spots, one coming from the right and one from the left. So here again there are 6 spotlights.

If the stage is medium sized or large it may be necessary to increase the number of areas and consequently the number of spotlights. If the stage is also deep it may be necessary to have another bridge position part way upstage.

SIDE LIGHTING — In some instances side lighting may be used exclusively or for some areas. When used it is most effective if the beams are focused to shine across and slightly

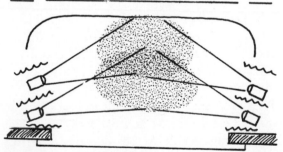

SIDE LIGHTING - SPOTS ARE DIRECTED SLIGHTLY UP STAGE

up stage. If the actor moves ahead of the beam his facial features do not receive the front light needed and unnatural shadows appear. Side lighting is probably more effective for ballet and modern dance than for legitimate drama. The bolder movement projects all right but subtle facial expressions need front light for the best effect.

AUXILIARY LIGHTS — The 6 beam and 6 bridge spotlights may be sufficient to supply the actor illumination on a small stage. For a

simple setting it is possible that the spots will provide enough illumination through their direct beams and reflected diffused beams from the floor and scenery to serve as both actor and shadow softening light. However, it will usually be necessary to have some auxiliary light from footlights, striplights and floodlights to serve the latter purpose. Using spotlights alone usually provides lighting that is harsh. The shadows are a little too heavy and the highlights a little too high. A touch of footlights to cut the eye socket, undernose and underchin shadows gives the face of the actor better definition. A touch of overhead borderlight helps cut any shadows cast by the footlights and softens the pool effect of spotlights.

Other lights are also necessary at times. There are various motivating or source lights used on the stage. Sunlight or moonlight shining through a window is affected by having a floodlight or flooded spotlight in a position offstage shine in through the stage window. Floor, table, gas or oil lamps may be placed on the wall, the mantel or on a table. These instruments, with extremely low wattage illumination, serve to indicate the source of the lights used on the stage.

BACKINGS — Areas off the setting (behind doors, windows, archways, and stairways), visible all or part of the time may also have to be lighted. These backing areas representing other rooms or the out of doors are frequently important to the action of the play and must be correctly lighted as a motivation for stage business or for the mood of a scene or to give credence to the lines of the play. These will be lighted in various ways depending upon their size and their position in relation to the setting.

Backings representing rooms are frequently lighted by placing a small striplight or floodlight immediately beyond the stage door so that it will shine upon the backing and also upon the actors as they enter. The position above the door provides face lighting for the actor and at the same time prevents awkward shadows from falling onto the backing. Of course the contrary is often desirable. The shadow falling into the room in advance of the entrance may be extremely important in a melodrama or mystery play, in which case a spotlight or floodlight should be positioned so that the body of the actor casts a shadow that precedes him into the room.

If the backing outside a door or window represents the sky it may be necessary to use two or more sources of light in order to get an even over-all illumination on the surface. Cross lighting from both sides, lighting from both top and bottom, or even lighting from

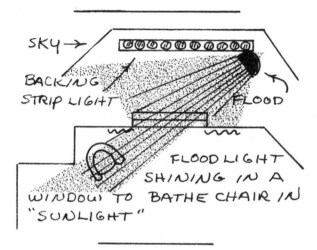

all four positions may be necessary. It may be desirable to represent dusk, morning, high noon or night on this surface. Using striplights from the bottom only and changing the color of the light may achieve some of these effects. Lighting from just the top may be a method of achieving other desired effects while combining the two will be desirable at other times.

FIRELIGHT—Indoor settings often have fireplaces. A fire on the grate indicates that it is cool or cold outside. The costumes of people entering from outside, the appearance of scenery outside a window, or the dialogue will usually be devices which with the condition and color of the fire will indicate the degree of coldness. The firelight may be the major moti-

vating source of light. Obviously it will not under ordinary circumstances actually be the only light used for the action. It may be at high intensity while the other lights are dimmed but usually it will need some help from beam and bridge. This light may be used for highly dramatic scenes and will, of course, usually be in dominantly warm colors: red, straw, amber and violet. At this point it must be recalled that colored light can have dastardly effects on makeup, costumes and other pigment-color surfaces; so the lighting colors should be handled carefully.

The firelight may be comparatively calm or have moving effects. This movement may be achieved in any of the ways suggested previously. Effects of this nature should be studied rather carefully to determine whether they add to or detract from the scene. Sometimes it might be advisable to start the scene with the moving flame effect and then diminish the flame activity as the scene begins to move toward a climax. At another time the flickering flames might be used to accentuate the movement toward the climax, increasing in tempo with the scene. This sort of thing must be adapted to the individual scene, director and production.

SWITCHES—Light switches on stage are always a problem. It is difficult to know how to handle the turning on and off of lights. This is something that must be rehearsed carefully and both the actor and the light operator must know just how it is to be handled. And once it has been set changes should not be made unless they are rehearsed carefully. Frequently it is better to have the control board operator handle both the switch on the motivating source light, a lamp for instance, and the acting area lights around it. In this way he is able to turn both on at once. The actor in this situation must be directed to place his hand on the switch as a cue for the lighting man and hold the position until the lights go on, or off, as the case may be.

Lighting a lamp or a fire should be handled in a similar manner. Real matches may be

228

used but the lighting process should be masked. When and wherever possible on the stage real flame lamps should of necessity be avoided to conform to fire ordinances. Torches, fireplaces, candles and oil lamps should be wired to either regular lighting circuits or flashlight batteries that are enclosed in the instrument itself.

SPECIAL LIGHT—Special lights are frequently needed on the stage besides the area lights. In fact some productions require that almost all of the lighting be done with "specials" rather than areas. In such cases the lights are focused so that they light only the table, the hat, the face of an actor, or a ghostly picture on a wall. Too many special lights may make the total job of lighting more difficult since the sheer number of instruments may suddenly "get out of hand." So it is usually advisable to start with area lights and then add a minimum number of specials. Specials may be mounted in strange and unorthodox places. Small units can be mounted about the setting, shining through windows, concealed in bookshelves, fireplaces, heavy picture moldings or in pieces of furniture, or they may be mounted in overhead positions above or at the side of the setting.

OUTDOOR SCENES — Outdoor settings on a stage have special problems of their own. To begin with there is usually more area to cover, including a large space of cyclorama sky. The acting area may be no larger than the area for a regular enclosure type of setting, but the open space around it may make it necessary to use more floodlights and striplights if there is supposed to be over-all sunlight or moonlight illumination.

The sky may be lighted from above and below with striplights or floodlights and striplights. The floor and overhead striplights will both usually need to be masked. This is more true of the floor lights unless the theatre is provided with a trough into which they are recessed. Ground rows as part of the scenic design will take care of this matter.

Usually the sky is lighted better with a large number of smaller units than with three or four

large units. The large units tend to provide hot and cold areas whereas the smaller ones can be located in positions somewhat more

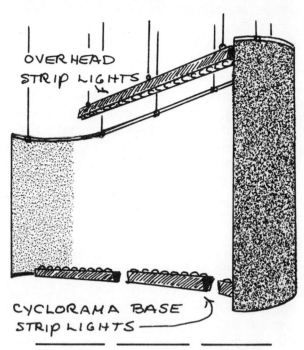

equidistant from the surface so that the entire surface is evenly illuminated. Striplights, floodlights or fluorescent tubes will probably serve best for cyclorama illumination.

SPACE STAGING — The process of staging productions with a series of levels as the only scenery and pools of light to locate an area as the space for the action of the moment is frequently referred to as space staging. The background for this type of production is frequently black drapes. The black velour will literally gobble up the light. If the costumes are light in value the problem of lighting is not too difficult. If, however, the costumes are dark in value it will be difficult to get enough light on the subjects to make them stand out from the background. Some side lighting or back lighting added to the front lighting will probably aid materially. Because of the absorbency of the black drapes, the areas for this type of staging will probably take more wattage than in productions where the background is light in value.

CYCLORAMA SPACE STAGING — Interesting effects can be achieved when a sky or other light background of a neutral nature is used since it is then possible to make use of silhouettes as well as front lighted subjects. Whenever the source of light is behind the actor he will stand out as a dark figure against a light background. Front area lighting with no cyclorama lighting will place him against a dark background lighted only by the spill light from the front spotlights. If side lighting is used it may be possible to make the cyclorama almost black out since the spill to the rear will then be minimized. There will be some spill but not as much as from front lighting.

CYCLORAMA COLOR EFFECTS—If the cyclorama is lighted with strips, floods or both of evenly distributed primary colors (red, blue and green) it will be possible to give the cyclorama, if it is light in value, almost any conceivable color by manipulation of the lights. Blues may be used for night. As dawn begins to break greens may be brought in and then gradually reds. The blue may be diminished allowing the red and green to mingle, producing yellow. The blue may be brought back in with the red to produce lavender. And all three may be brought up to produce white sunlight. Any combination may be tried. Sunrises and sunsets are rarely the same. It is worth experimenting to achieve the desired results. Color, especially on a cyclorama, can be used to great advantage.

PSYCHOLOGICAL COLOR IN LIGHT — Colored light may be used on a cyclorama to achieve psychological feelings. This must be studied rather carefully to be certain that the effect carries the correct mood. It may be that a blood red sunset in Macbeth will suggest the purge to come; that a deep blue or blue green will project the coldness of the Arctic; that intense yellow will project the heat of the Sahara; that surprise pink will suggest the glow of youth; that green will give the feeling of un-worldliness. It is usually worth while to try an effect and see if it is going to work. In the case of color it will be necessary to consider more than just the color of the light beams. Remember that the light beams fall on surfaces and that the final color effect is determined by the color of the light *and* the color of the surface.

DESIGNING WITH LIGHT—In the chapter on Scene Design there is some discussion of using light as the media for both color and form. This might profitably be discussed here also. Simple shadows, either of moving or stationary forms, can be used to advantage. Actors moving between the light and the background, especially if it is a cyclorama, can create a dramatic effect. The performer is lighted from the front with a single source of light

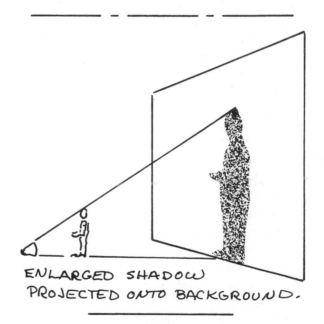

ENLARGED SHADOW PROJECTED ONTO BACKGROUND.

(usually one large floodlight from below so that a fairly sizable area can be covered) and he casts one shadow. The shadow will be large as he approaches the light and will grow smaller as he approaches the background until it becomes his size and he and the shadow merge into one. White or colored light may be used. The performer may be lighted from the sides without blotting out the heavy projected shadow since the light on his figure and the spill light will be shining across parallel with the front of the stage. As soon as front light is used the shadow begins to lose its intensity unless the front lights are focused low so they strike close to the front of the stage.

Stationary objects may be used to project shadows onto the cyclorama in somewhat the same manner. They are placed in a position between the source of light and the background so that part of the light rays are intercepted. Plants, flowers, cut outs, objects with distinguishable or indistinguishable shapes can all be used. The object will be chosen for the shape desired whether it is of a real or an abstract form. Projection may be from the front as suggested or from the side. The front light from below will give an upward widening distortion; side lighting will give a lateral and possibly also an upward distortion.

MULTIPLE SHADOWS — Multiple shadows will be projected if more than one shadow casting lighting instrument is used. Each unit will cause a shadow to be cast since the figure or object will cut the light from that instrument. A single dancer may have three definite shadows if there are three light sources close together. If the sources are widely separated they probably won't work out quite as well if it is desirable to have multiple shadows of about the same size and intensity.

COLORED SHADOWS — When two or more colored sources of light are used it is possible to get colored shadows. The colors on the surface of the person or object will be a mix-

SIMPLE PROJECTION OF PLANT

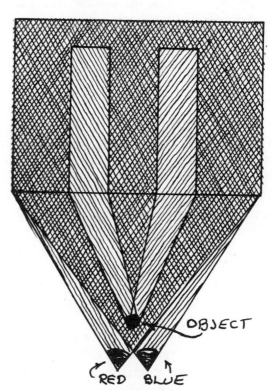

OBJECT

RED BLUE

COLORS MIX ON BACKGROUND
ONE SHADOW IS BLUE - ONE IS RED

SHADOW OF ABSTRACT FORM

ture of the colors if the units are close together but the shadows will differ in color. The form will create a series of shadows; each instrument will have a shadow cut from its beam. The shadow of each instrument will take on the mixed color of the other light sources. If red, green and blue lights are used, for instance, the shadow from the red light will appear to be blue green since only the red will be cut out; from the blue the shadow will be yellow since only the blue will be cut out; and from the green the shadow will be purple since only the green will be cut out. Multicolored foilage can be projected onto a cyclorama by shining various colored lights through the foliage of a house plant.

Color may be a significant factor in the projection of images. It should be chosen for the psychological effect desired and for its effect upon the colored pigment being illuminated or being used with the projection.

The type of projected scenery used and its effectiveness will be determined to a great extent by the physical structure and facilities of the building as well as the ingenuity, time and budget of the lighting technician. Effects such as those described above can be done with a minimum of equipment on a stage of almost any size and shape. A little experimenting will prove what can be done. The projecting light or lights can be located in the footlight position, off stage right or left from a low, medium or high level, part way up stage concealed in a scenic unit or under a platform, or almost immediately in front of the cyclorama. Of course if the stage has great depth, or if a cyclorama or backdrop is placed down stage leaving space at the rear, it is also possible to have rear projections. Rear projections are frequently far superior to front ones, but most theatre buildings lack the depth required for their use.

SHADOW PROJECTIONS THROUGH A BACKDROP — The rear projection may be achieved through a backdrop with portions painted with translucent paint and portions painted with opaque paint. The translucent sections will allow light to shine through while the opaque areas will hold it back. Other forms may be used in conjunction to cut off portions of the light. Even forms placed against the drop at the rear may be used to cast heavy shadows.

SCRIM LIGHTING—Scrim is frequently used on the stage to effect rapid changes. A pattern can be painted on a gauze or scrim drop and the surface will appear opaque as long as there is no light behind. As soon as light is brought

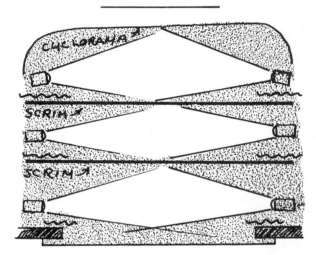

SCENES SET UP IN DEPTH BEHIND SCRIM—EACH IS REVEALED AS LIGHT COMES ON BEHIND IT.

up behind, the curtain will either disappear completely or fade into a dim mist. This is a place where fairly high angle front light and side light can be used to good advantage. Lights from straight front will usually spill through so much that objects behind the drop can be seen.

Scrim in depth can be used in a similar manner. Two or three drops may be painted and placed one ahead of the other with a playing space between them. As scenes are played in depth the lights are brought up on that area. It will then be possible to see back as far as the scrim behind the scene being lighted. When the scrim is to fade out it is better if the light is dimmed in front of it so that no halo or

232

ng for *Aladdin*. The rock structure above is partially covered with scrim. When lighted
the front it appears to be a solid surface but as the lights are brought up behind, the scrim
ns to disappear and the rear area can be seen as in the lower photo.

fuzziness will result. Obviously heavy thread weave materials, like camouflage netting, will become opaque in depth with more than two or at most three thicknesses between the actors and audience while material like theatrical gauze, sharktooth gauze, cheesecloth or marquisette might allow more scenes in depth. The main point to remember in using scrim is that visibility moves in the direction of the highest concentration of light.

FLUORESCENT EFFECTS — Objects painted with special fluorescent paints will glow when activated by ultraviolet light. The intensity of the glow is not as great as it first appears. It takes very little white light spill onto a fluorescent surface to destroy the effect of the ultraviolet light. If the fluorescent area is on a backdrop the acting area can be lighted from the sides with more success than from the front, that is, if the fluorescent patterns are not to be washed out by the actor light. Overhead beams used with such light should be aimed fairly straight down.

Ultraviolet lights usually provide low illumination since most of the rays are filtered out in order to get just the invisible ultraviolet wave lengths of light. Consequently it is important to have the light units as close to the surface activated by fluorescent paint as possible. The closer they are the brighter the glow of the surface. Ordinarily fluorescent paint-ultraviolet light effects are most useful for unusual or spectacular effects rather than for prolonged dramatic effects.

LIGHTING HIGH CONTRAST OBJECTS — If extremely light value objects are placed against a dark background almost the same effect as that of fluorescent paint may be obtained. The light values contain much white pigment so even the smallest light intensity is reflected from them while almost all of the light is absorbed by the dark background. This type of effect has advantages over the fluorescent effect since there is visible light so that actors can see their way around the stage and, of course, all objects that are not black will show to a certain extent. This last point may not be advantageous, however, since the desire is usually to have everything on the stage that is not coated with fluorescent paint disappear into nothingness.

* * * *

The above discussion is not intended to be definitive nor all inclusive, but rather is intended to present enough basic ideas to start the prospective lighting artist working with his medium. Imagination, a certain artistic sense and a great deal of hard work and inventiveness will help him to achieve the effects he needs for any given production. It isn't necessary to have elaborate equipment to achieve beautiful, stimulating light effects. On the other hand it is never advisable to stand in one spot and admire the lighting effects achieved by a lamp on the end of a drop cord either. Constantly try to improve both the supply of the lighting equipment in the theatre and the degree of artistry achieved with a minimum of effort. A hundred thousand dollars worth of fine equipment is worth no more in the hands of a lout than one PAR in the hands of an artistic soul.

15

Mechanics of

Design

A number of basic mechanical drawing processes will prove of value to the designer of stage settings. Among these processes are the planning and drawing of sight line sections, scaled floor plans, working drawings, simple and complex perspectives; and the planning and building of models of stage settings.

Sight Lines

The audience is one of the most important elements of the production. If possible the setting should be designed so that every member of the audience can see the action and scenic background of the entire play. This can be

accomplished by checking the sight lines carefully throughout the entire process of designing the stage setting.

SIGHT LINE FORMS—A scaled floor plan of the theatre, and a scaled drawing of the lengthwise cross section of the theatre, are needed for checking the sight lines. It is highly advisable to make a number of "ditto" or mimeographed copies of each section so that floor plans and elevations of projected stage settings can be drawn to scale directly upon these forms.

In order to place the essential portions of the plan on a single sheet of paper it is necessary to use a fairly small scale. A scale of ⅛″ = 1′-0″ might be suggested, but the scale will have to be determined by the measurements of the specific building.

The drawing need not include the entire building plan, but only the portions required to check the sight lines. The floor plan should include the entire stage area and at least the extreme end seats of the front row in the auditorium. In rare cases seats may be positioned

235

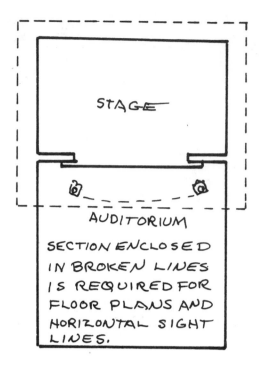

STAGE

AUDITORIUM

SECTION ENCLOSED
IN BROKEN LINES
IS REQUIRED FOR
FLOOR PLANS AND
HORIZONTAL SIGHT
LINES.

farther out to the sides of the auditorium; if so, then these positions should also be included.

The cross section drawing of the theatre, made to show the appearance from one side of the building split endwise, should include

BROKEN LINE SECTION NEEDED FOR VERTICAL SIGHT LINES.

the entire stage and enough of the auditorium to get the position of the lowest and highest seat levels.

HORIZONTAL SIGHT LINES—To check the horizontal sight lines the floor plan section of

the theatre is used. Lines are drawn from the extreme right and left seat positions of the auditorium. The line from the left seat extends up past the proscenium arch on that side to the back wall of the stage. The line from the right extends in like manner to the back wall on that side. The space between these two lines is the area of the stage that can be seen by all of the members of the audience. If the setting fits within this area the sight lines will be ideal horizontally. Actually, if the auditorium is extremely wide and the proscenium arch proportionately narrow, the sight lines will cut in so sharply that only a pie cut area will be left when the lines are drawn in. In a case like this designing becomes a much more difficult problem than in an auditorium where the block

IDEAL SIGHT LINE AREA

of seats extends out only as far as the width of the proscenium arch. But regardless of how wide or narrow the sight lines are, they must be checked on individual floor plans so that important portions of the setting aren't placed where they cannot be seen by sizable portions of the audience.

VERTICAL SIGHT LINES—Vertical sight lines may be checked by drawing a line from a seat in the front row across the leading edge of the stage apron and extending on to the back wall. This line will supply the critical upward angle. By drawing a line downward from the uppermost seat (in the balcony if there is one) in line with the lower edge of the grand drape and on to the back wall of the stage, the critical downward angle is determined. If the grand

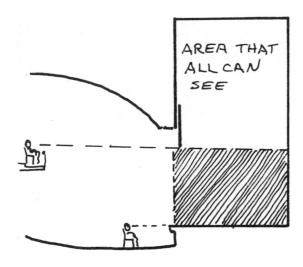

AREA THAT ALL CAN SEE

So another set of sight lines drawn from these same positions but in the opposite direction will indicate the areas that must be provided with some type of masking device to prevent the audience from seeing the backstage paraphernalia.

These sight lines should be checked carefully as the drawing of the floor plan and elevation proceeds. Even after the setting has been completed there probably still will be masking problems and some sight line problems, but

drape can be raised and lowered obviously this angle could change.

The four sight lines now computed are used to determine how far offstage in each direction and above the stage (on platforms) the action can be moved and still be seen by all of the members of the audience. These sight lines are all needed in designing the setting.

SIGHT LINES FOR MASKING — Another set of sight lines is needed to plan the masking for the stage. If each of the patrons seated in the critical seats, except that fellow away up in the balcony, looks in the opposite direction from the ideal sight line direction, he will see more than he is supposed to. These patrons will see off stage into the wings and up into the fly well.

PART OF AUDIENCE CAN SEE TOO MUCH OVERHEAD MASKING NEEDED

careful planning shows up most of these difficulties early enough that the director can foresee his problem.

SIGHT LINES AND THE SCRIPT—With the sight lines in mind, the script is studied carefully. Mechanical elements are noted: entrances and exits; the use of windows and fireplaces; business on stairways and platforms; references to elements of the stage or stage properties; manipulation of lights, draperies, windows, doors, fireplaces, stage properties; the use of furniture in stage business; movement of stage furniture; movement of the actors; important entrances and important actor stage picture arrangements. All of these factors and many others may affect the design of the setting.

After the script has been studied carefully, conferences should be arranged with all of the

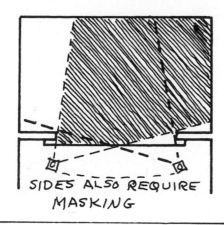

SIDES ALSO REQUIRE MASKING

other people involved in the production, but especially with the director. In these conferences preliminary plans should be worked out. These plans will be fairly simple and consist of

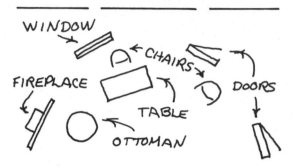

PRELIMINARY SKETCH WITH ESSENTIAL UNITS - APPROXIMATE POSITIONS.

determining the approximate positions and relationships between stage units, properties, furniture and major stage movements. After this conference it is time to begin devising possible stage floor plans.

Floor Plans

The floor plans drawn to scale (on the stage

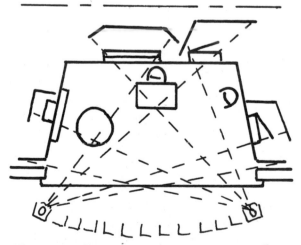

FLOOR PLAN - SIGHT LINES CHECKED FOR MASKING AND VISIBILITY

plan, at least to check sight lines) represent a view of the setting as seen from directly above. On this floor plan accepted symbols are used to represent architectural features. Walls appear to be lines. Walls on a floor plan of a home rarely go off on odd angles since architectural forms are more economical to build when they meet at right angles. However, on the stage, in order to improve sight lines and add interest to the design, there may be many strange angles.

The walls will be broken here and there by architectural units. Archway openings are shown as boxes to the rear of the wall showing the proportional width and thickness of the opening and the wall it is cut into. Doorways are drawn like archways except that the door and the direction it swings must also be shown. So the shutter (door) is shown part way open and attached at one side. Usually, to simplify

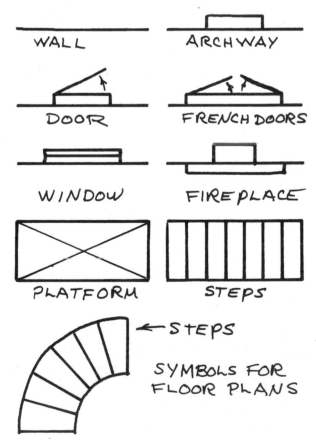

SYMBOLS FOR FLOOR PLANS

238

construction, the door opens offstage; and to help stage business and masking it is hinged on the upstage side. Windows are represented like archways with an extra line drawn through them lengthwise to indicate the sash in the frame. French windows or French doors will have one or two swinging sections like doors, depending upon whether they are single or double, and they probably will be labelled. A fireplace is shown with the position of the mantel indicated onstage and the firebox section indicated behind the flat. Platforms are shown by rectangles of the correct size and shape and each individual section will have diagonal lines drawn lightly across it to indicate the dimension lines of the unit.

The positions of steps in stairways are shown by a series of forms representing the width and depth of the individual treads. It is also wise to draw the major pieces of furniture in their individual positions. The form and approximate proportions of suggested units should be drawn so that stage business can be planned.

The various essential stage units can now be arranged in their approximate positions on the stage and the location of the walls of the setting drawn in place. Logical relationships as well as stage business relationships between the vari-

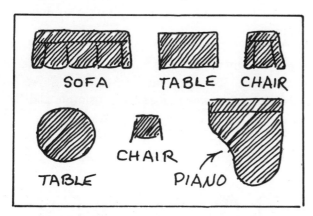

ous doors, windows, stairways, and fireplaces should be considered. The flow of stage movement is important to consider also when arranging these units. Furniture placement should be included in the floor plan so that this flow

can be more easily charted. The furniture should be drawn approximately to scale so that it is related to the rest of the stage equipment.

While all of this is being done the sight lines should be constantly checked to see that there is not too much blocking of entrances, action, playing area, furniture, and even important stage properties.

On the floor plan it will be necessary to indicate raised step and platform areas. These are functional devices. Sometimes only 2 or 3 steps are used to indicate an entire stairway. They are located so that the audience is led to believe that the rest of the stairs is beyond the wall or door that is conveniently next to them. In one play the step unit may be a place for stage business so it must be designed in dominance and in a good sight line position. An upstage area may be raised to set it apart from the rest of the stage, and to elevate the actors playing in that area so they may be seen above the furniture in the foreground. A jog is introduced into a wall in order to project the upstage portion of the setting onstage into sight lines, or it is designed into the floor plan to help brace and support a portion of a wall section, or a door, or a fireplace. Everything of this nature should be indicated on the floor plan so that it can be made useful to the director, the stage manager, the designer, and the builder of the setting.

After the floor plan has reached this stage, it is time to plan the backings, which are masking pieces placed beyond all of the openings to suggest other rooms, the out-of-doors, or just to block off the audience view beyond the setting. Sight line checks through the openings will help determine how much space must be covered by the backings. They can be drawn in position accordingly.

LABELING THE FLOOR PLAN — After the floor plan has been drawn to scale, complete with backings and approximate furniture, it is wise to label the wall sections. A system that works out fairly well is to start with the stage right return or tormentor (which is at the left

239

of the floor plan)' and letter it "A". The next wall section is "B" and so on around to the return on the other side of the stage. Usually it is advisable to skip the letter "I" since it looks so much like the number "1". The back-

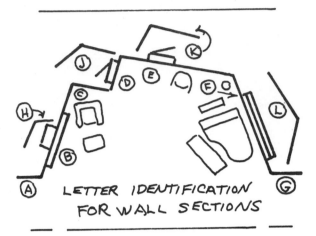

LETTER IDENTIFICATION FOR WALL SECTIONS

ings are lettered in a continuing sequence. This same system will be continued until the final setting reaches the stage and may even be used in setting up a stage shifting plan. It is a good idea to indicate on the floor plan areas that are elevated, such as platforms and steps. Each

FLOOR PLAN FOR ACT II THE FIRST TIME. SCALE ¼" = 1'0" G. SHY

SET, MAJOR FURNITURE BACKINGS, STEPS, PLATFORMS RETURN STEPS - DRAWN TO APPROXIMATE SCALE.

elevation can be shown by a number in a circle. The number indicates in each case the number of inches or feet off the stage floor. If the elevation from the stage floor rather than from another elevation is used fewer mistakes are made.

To clarify the floor plan for anyone who looks at it (especially for those who are not familiar with stage terminology) a legend frequently is included in a clear area on the paper on which the floor plan is drawn. The legend includes the symbols used, use of abbreviations and any further explanatory information needed. The scale used in drawing the floor plan and identification of this particular drawing (including the name of the production, the scene and the name of the designer) should also be shown on the floor plan.

Perspective Drawings

The floor plan provides only one simple view of a stage setting. It is rather difficult to conceive of the appearance of the stage setting unless one has the vivid imagination of an artist, architect or stage designer or the powers of a clairvoyant. So to arrive at a more tangible visual concept of the finished stage setting it is necessary to carry the drawing process a few steps further and make perspective drawings or simple models of the proposed stage setting.

The perspective drawing is usually made even though a model is also prepared. The drawing can be reproduced in color and prepared in such a way that it gives a simple audi-.ence impression of the finished product.

PERSPECTIVE — Knowledge of a few facts about perspective will make drawing easier. A

X REPRESENTS EYE POSITION OF VIEWER.

cube seen from various positions takes on differing appearances. If looked at from dead center the front is all that will be seen. If the eye is moved straight upward the front and top can be seen, but the far edge of the top will appear to be shorter than the near edge. If the eye is moved to one side while still above, three sides will be seen—the front, top and one side. If the eye is moved downward, again while at one side, the top will begin to disappear and soon only the front and one side will be visible. The eye may be moved into many other positions and the cube will continue to present still different combinations of sides.

If a row of objects of the same size and height are viewed from various positions their apparent heights and widths will vary. Objects that are close to the viewer will appear to be larger than those located at a distance. When

HORIZON

BASIC PERSPECTIVE - OBJECTS GROW SMALLER AND APPROACH ONE ANOTHER WITH DISTANCE

a row of poles are placed along a railroad track, the poles, the tracks themselves and the ties under the rails all seem to diminish in size as the eye moves along the tracks toward the

horizon. Finally they disappear as all of the lines converge at a point. This point is actually the vanishing point.

If a building is viewed from a position just beyond one end of the face, the side that can be seen extending away will appear to diminish

V. P.

FORESHORTENING OF SIDE WALL GIVES PERCEPTION OF DEPTH HORIZONTAL LINES LEAD TO A POINT AT HORIZON - THE "V. P."

in height as it approaches the far end. If the top and bottom lines are continued beyond the building they will converge and again a vanishing point will be located—the vanishing point for all of the horizontal lines of that building. The face of the building will appear to diminish in size, too, but the angle is not as apparent since we are looking at it almost head on.

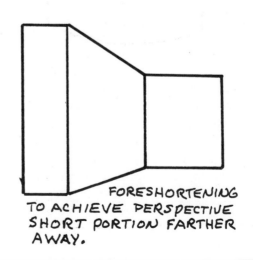

FORESHORTENING TO ACHIEVE PERSPECTIVE SHORT PORTION FARTHER AWAY.

241

Actually, the top and bottom lines if extended out, moving away from the viewer, will also converge, but the point of convergence will be at a much greater distance.

From this brief description it becomes apparent that objects at a distance seem to be smaller than near ones and if a rectangular flat plane is placed so that one edge is near and the other at a distance there will be apparent foreshortening of the surface as it moves away from the viewer. When reproducing this effect on paper, vanishing points (V.P.) are set up to aid in getting the correct angles.

BIRD'S EYE PERSPECTIVE — The bird's eye perspective is easy to draw, but it is not the most satisfactory type of reproduction. To see the stage setting as it appears in this conception the

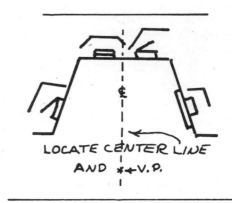

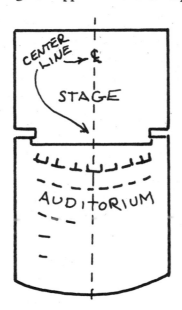

the stage. The center line (℄) is an imaginary line drawn through the center of the building extending from the back wall of the auditorium to the back wall of the stage.

From the VP lines are now drawn upward and outward through all of the corners of the

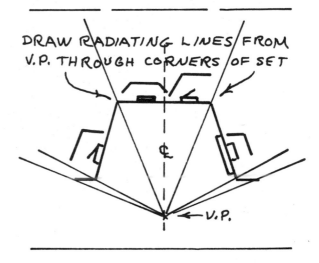

observer would have to perch himself in the thickness of the proscenium arch above the stage and look down. The distortion produced by this method makes the top of the setting much wider than the bottom.

In drawing the bird's eye perspective, as in all other perspective drawing, preparation of the floor plan is the first step. Then a vanishing point (hereafter referred to as a VP) is located a short distance below the front of the stage setting and on the Center Line (℄) of

setting, that is, all of the places where walls begin, end or change direction. These lines are extended a couple of inches above the floor plan lines.

The lines just drawn represent the vertical lines of the setting. After they have been drawn, a convenient height is decided upon. For the first elevation try two inches. Beginning with this height, on the left side of the setting draw lines parallel with the floor plan lines following across all of the lines of the setting to the final line projected from the right

242

side of the setting. This done, the setting in its bird's eye form appears. Doors and windows may now be drawn in a similar manner. Side lines are drawn up from the VP and the

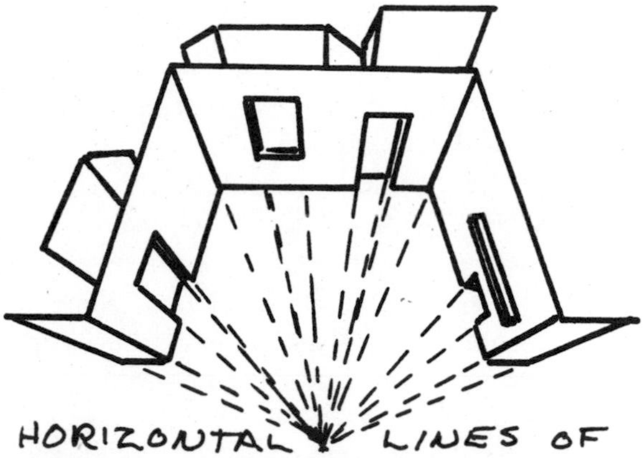

HORIZONTAL LINES OF TOPS OF FLATS PARALLEL WITH FLOOR PLAN LINES

tops and bottoms are drawn parallel to the base line on the floor plan. Furniture is drawn in a similar manner. This type of drawing may be completed with any detail that is to be included in the setting.

The finished bird's eye perspective is a means of rapidly drawing a rough impression of a stage setting. An angular type drawing that requires no VP may also be drawn. This reproduction has distortion, too, and is viewed from a position never assumed by any of the members of the audience. This might be called the pin rail projection.

Pin Rail Projection — For the pin rail projection, draw a floor plan. Now from each of the wall break points draw a line up and out on an angle of 30 to 45 degrees (choose any angle, but use the same one throughout). These lines will be parallel to one another. After the lines have been drawn, a height is determined for the flats; here actual scale can be employed and the top lines drawn across the flats parallel to the lines of the floor plan. Doors, windows and other units may be drawn in a similar manner.

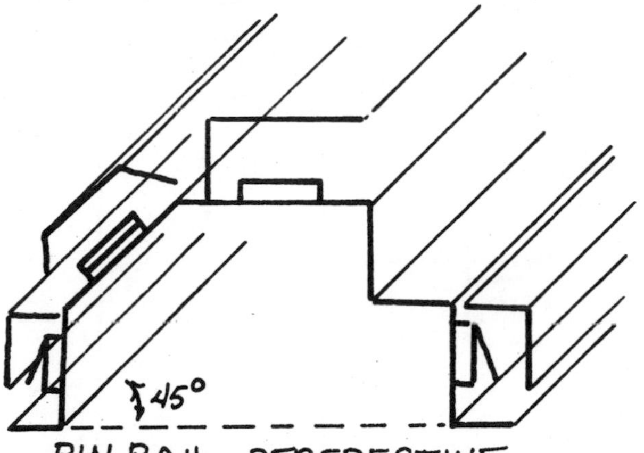

PIN RAIL PERSPECTIVE LINES EXTEND UP FROM FLOOR PLAN ON 45° ANGLE

The pin rail projection gives an angular view of the setting as it might appear from the pin rail above and to one side of the setting. This projection has an advantage over the other types

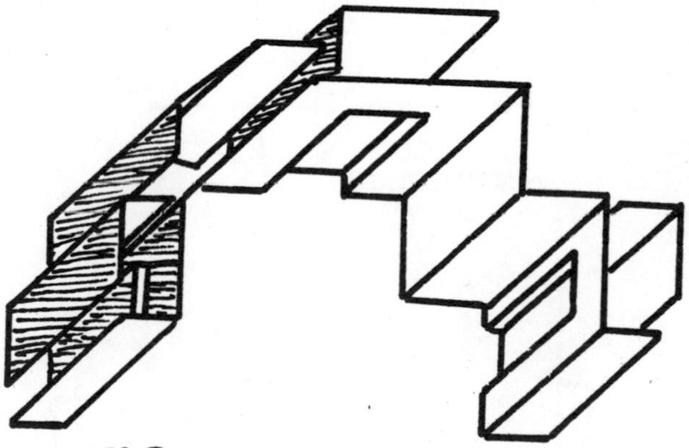

TOP LINES ARE DRAWN PARALLEL WITH LINES OF FLOOR PLAN.

of drawing since it is possible to draw everything to scale. Of course, one side of the setting is seen from the rear rather than from the front, but if it is desirable a view from the other side could also be drawn. This is almost as simple to draw as the bird's eye view and is probably more satisfactory.

ONE POINT PERSPECTIVE — The regular perspective system is more difficult to handle

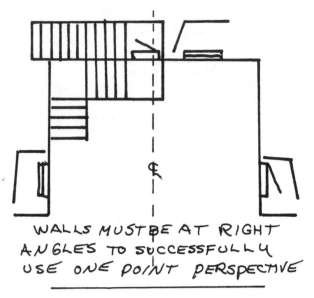

WALLS MUST BE AT RIGHT ANGLES TO SUCCESSFULLY USE ONE POINT PERSPECTIVE

than either of the other methods of reproduction suggested, but the result is more in the nature of an audience view.

The one point perspective system may be

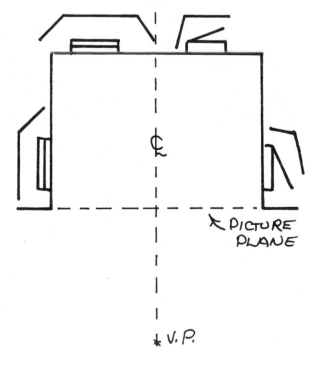

used as long as the walls of the stage setting are at right angles to one another and parallel with or at right angles to the curtain line.

The perspective drawing is started from the scaled plan. For the first step in the process of drawing, locate a vanishing point (VP) on the center line (₵) the equivalent of half way back in the auditorium. This point represents the position of the eyes of the patron seated in the center of the auditorium. Actually the position of any seat could be used, but this one will be the average view. The VP located will be used to determine the relative positions of the vertical lines and the foreshortening slope of the horizontal lines of the walls of the setting as they extend away from or come toward the audience.

For convenience, and to keep the scale exact, on some portion of the drawing the setting will

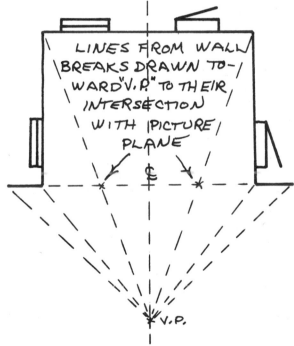

LINES FROM WALL BREAKS DRAWN TOWARD "V.P." TO THEIR INTERSECTION WITH PICTURE PLANE

be drawn as if it were flattened out along the line of the tormentors of the setting parallel with the curtain line. For convenience this will be referred to in the descriptions to follow as the *picture plane*.

To get the relative positions of the vertical

244

lines of the stage setting, lines are drawn connecting the VP and the breaks in the floor plan that indicate inside or outside corners in the walls. These lines need only be drawn from the corners to their points of intersection with

farther back in the auditorium. For the scene designer the best position is probably about 1/3 the height of the flats.

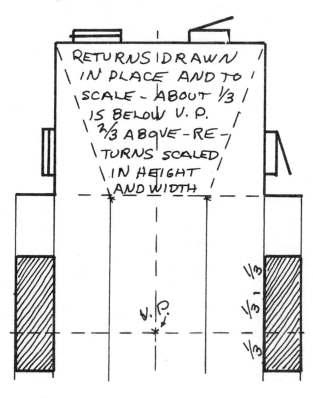

the picture plane. From the picture plane they are dropped straight down, at right angles to the curtain line. These lines are drawn so that they extend down below the VP.

The measurement to scale from tormentor to tormentor should be the same as it is on the floor plan.

Next in the drawing process, the height of the setting should be determined. And at this point in the process it is also necessary to determine the distance from the floor line to the VP. The members of an audience seated on the ground floor will view the stage from any of a number of eye levels ranging from even with the stage floor to a level about half way up on the stage scenery, depending upon whether they are seated in the orchestra or

If the flats are to be 12'-0" the VP for the plan shown will be about 4'-0" above the floor line, or above the bottom of the setting. A line is therefore drawn parallel with the curtain line and 4'-0" below the VP. This line need only extend across the lines that have been dropped down from the sides of the tormentors since they are the only portions of the setting that extend down to the picture plane. The tops of the tormentors may now be sketched by drawing a line parallel and 12'-0" above the one just drawn. This done, the tormentors will be completed and should measure, by scale, 12'-0" high and the width indicated by the floor plan.

The side walls adjacent to the tormentors may now be drawn. The vertical lines already have been dropped down into their positions. To draw the top and bottom lines, which will approach one another as they are drawn toward the center of the picture (because the wall sec-

245

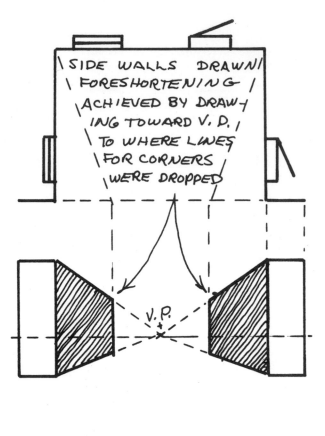

SIDE WALLS DRAWN
FORESHORTENING
ACHIEVED BY DRAW-
ING TOWARD V. D.
TO WHERE LINES
FOR CORNERS
WERE DROPPED

V.P.

tion moves away from the viewer and appears to be shorter as it moves upstage), lines are drawn from the top of the tormentor toward the VP and from the bottom of the tormentor toward the VP until they reach the point of interception with the next vertical line or wall break. This done, the two side walls are drawn in their correct positions.

Since the back wall is parallel with the footlights, it may be drawn straight across from the interception of the corner vertical and horizontal lines just completed.

The walls are now completed and other structural units, such as doors and windows, may be

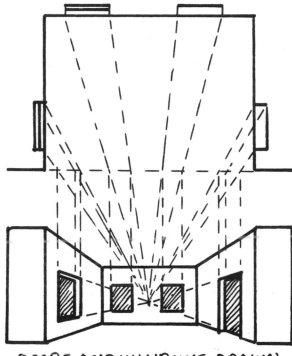

DOORS AND WINDOWS DRAWN AND LOCATED USING V. P.

BACK WALL AND
PICTURE PLANE
ARE PARALLEL
IN THIS PLAN
SO BACK WALL
IS DRAWN
STRAIGHT
ACROSS

drawn in a similar manner. First they are located on the floor plan. Then the relative positions of the vertical lines are located by drawing toward the VP to the picture plane, after which they are dropped straight down into position. The height of such units is measured on the tormentor since this is the only place where true scale may be measured. Then the measurement can be taken around to the correct position by following the process of using the VP.

PERSPECTIVE USING THREE OR MORE POINTS — If the side walls of the setting are raked, that is, if they move in on an angle, and if other wall sections are not parallel with or

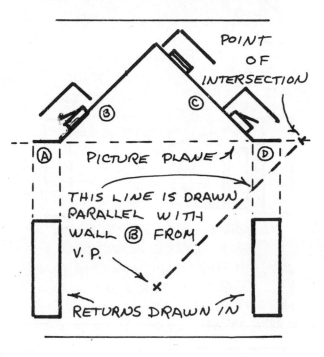

at right angles to the curtain line, it is necessary to add other vanishing points or the true foreshortenings of the walls will be lost. The process of drawing with three or more vanishing points is exactly the same as with the one point system through the step where the drawing of the tormentors is completed.

To minimize the distortion and foreshortening of wall sections a new vanishing point is introduced for each angle on the floor plan deviating from the square. If walls are parallel with one another they use the same VP and if they are parallel with the picture plane or curtain line they are drawn parallel with the top and bottom of the tormentors.

In perspective systems using more than one VP there is always a relationship between the original VP and any others. Each additional VP is located in terms of the original one.

To find the VP for a wall section that is

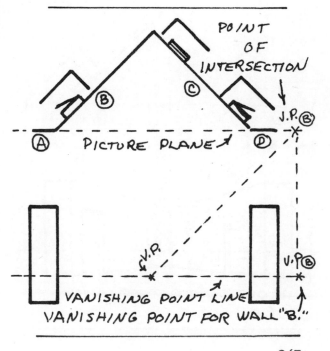

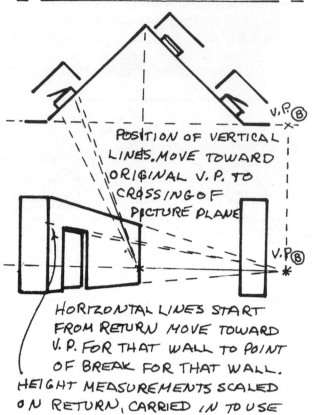

POSITION OF VERTICAL LINES. MOVE TOWARD ORIGINAL V. P. TO CROSSING OF PICTURE PLANE

V.P. B

HORIZONTAL LINES START FROM RETURN MOVE TOWARD V. P. FOR THAT WALL TO POINT OF BREAK FOR THAT WALL. HEIGHT MEASUREMENTS SCALED ON RETURN, CARRIED IN TO USE

PROCESS REPEATED WITH V. P. ©

raked on an angle, draw a line from the original VP toward the picture plane and parallel to the line of the wall. Stop the line where it intercepts the picture plane and then drop it straight back down at right angles to the picture plane until it intercepts a line drawn through the original VP and parallel to the picture plane. In this way there is a horizontal and vertical relationship between the new VP and the original one. All VP's located in this way are related to one another and to the original. Each VP should be labelled with the letter identifying the wall or walls with which it is to be used. The VP located in this manner is subsequently used to draw any horizontal line on that wall, be it baseboard, chair rail, top and bottom of a picture, door header, cornice over a window, mantel, window sill or shelf.

MODEL OF STAGE SETTING—A simple model of a stage setting can be made rapidly if squared paper is used. Paper with ¼″

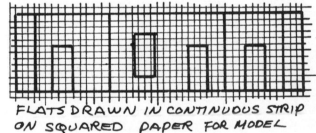

FLATS DRAWN IN CONTINUOUS STRIP ON SQUARED PAPER FOR MODEL

squares is probably as convenient as any other since a ruler can be used to do auxiliary measuring after the model has been completed.

The first step in making the model is to draw a front view of the flats transferring the sizes indicated on the floor plan onto the squared paper. At this time the height of the setting must be decided upon. If a relatively small model is desired a scale of one square equals one foot can be used. Begin with the stage right tormentor (the left side of the floor plan as you look at it—so begin on the left side of the paper and draw in the logical direction toward the right) and draw all of the sections

248

with each immediately. adjacent to the other on the paper. In case one piece of paper does not give enough length for all of the flats (and it probably will not) overlap and glue two or more pieces together to get the desired length. After the flats have been drawn—with doors, windows, fireplaces, pictures, moldings, etc. drawn in place—the strip may be cut out. Fold the strip where corners are indicated and place the finished product on the floor plan, or in a model of the stage, and the setting will be seen in its true form, proportion and shape. More complicated and complete models can be made from cardboard, matte board or similar material, and stage properties can be indicated by little cut out forms of blocks of wood. Even little figures to represent and scale actors can be cut out of pieces of cardboard and placed at

PAPER FOLDED AT CORNERS TO FIT FLOOR PLAN

various points on the stage. The model will make it possible to determine space relationships. Some of the directors and stage manager's problems might be solved before the setting reaches the stage if a model such as this is made and manipulated.

WORKING DRAWINGS—Selecting and processing the flats for an individual setting is made much easier if simple working drawings are prepared. If squared paper (preferably with quarter inch squares so that a ruler can be used with it to make more rapid calculations) is used for this purpose the drawing process is simple. Let one square equal 1'-0". Beginning with the stage right tormentor or return, draw the wall sections in sequence. Drawn in this way the

front of the surfaces is shown. If it is desirable to have both the front and back shown it is easy to turn the paper over, hold it up against a

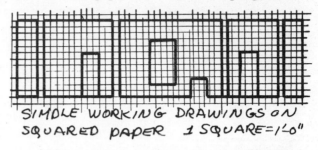

SIMPLE WORKING DRAWINGS ON SQUARED PAPER 1 SQUARE=1'-0"

window and trace the image that shows through. The detail can then be drawn on the flats to help in building, rebuilding and assembling them. Be careful to label in large letters which is the front and which is the rear view of the flats. The breakdown into flats may be indicated after the wall sections have been drawn.

When drawing the wall sections it is a good idea to leave a space a square wide between sections to show which areas may be fastened together later and which are to be hinged to make unbroken walls. On the drawing the sections should be lettered to conform to the lettering on the floor plan and then as the flats are "dug out" they also should be lettered. If the setting is complex, some type of checking system should be set up. The University of Utah system is to place a check on the drawing when a flat is found, cross the arm of the check when the wall section is assembled and ready to paint, and place a circle next to it when the section has been given a base coat of paint.

* * * * *

Although this discussion of the mechanics of drawing perspectives, floor plans and working drawings is not extensive it may be enough to start the designer in the right direction. Actually, every production a designer works on is a completely new project and new challenge and he continues developing procedures that make the entire job easier for him.

Jacobowsky and the Colonel (above). The size of the stage reduced with a double false proscenium. *The Green Pastures* (below). Contour flats in depth are here used with a platform.

250

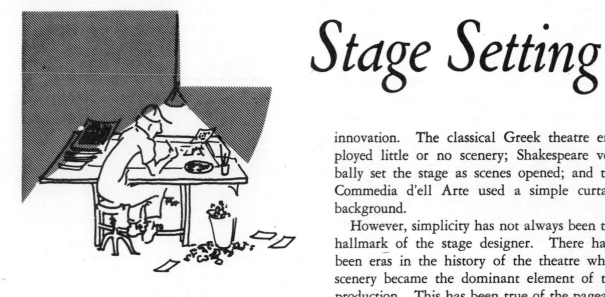

16

Designing the Stage Setting

"This is our doctor's house—Doc Gibbs; this is the back door. (Two arched trellises are pushed out, one by each proscenium pillar.) There's some scenery for those who think they have to have scenery. There's a garden here. Corn . . . peas . . . beans . . . hollyhocks . . . heliotrope . . . and a lot of burdock."

Thornton Wilder, in this portion of the opening speech of the stage manager is brilliantly setting the stage for his play *Our Town*. He is setting it in such a way that every member of the audience must be pleased or rebuke himself for his lack of mental imaginative artistry. By employing Wilder's method, stage hands, stage machinery and act curtains are replaced by a twist of the head, flash of the imagination and a flick of the eyelid. Poof! The set is changed.

Wilder's idea of dispensing with elaborate stage decorations is by no means a new or novel innovation. The classical Greek theatre employed little or no scenery; Shakespeare verbally set the stage as scenes opened; and the Commedia d'ell Arte used a simple curtain background.

However, simplicity has not always been the hallmark of the stage designer. There have been eras in the history of the theatre when scenery became the dominant element of the production. This has been true of the pageant stage of all ages; of the elaborate court masque of the Renaissance; of the melodrama of the nineteenth century; of the naturalistic theatre of the twentieth century; of the Hollywood motion picture productions and of the great television spectacles. The technicians of these theatres have employed literally wagon loads of scenery and machinery on their stages. Their machines have been used to make actors and scenery appear disappear, fly and sink into the floor. They have striven to outdo nature in depicting the great destructive forces of flood, fire, storm and war; they have striven to reach new and greater peaks of mechanical and spectacular beauty and grandeur.

In the contemporary theatre the designer usually tries to achieve a level of staging somewhere between the two extremes noted. He avoids both overabundance and poverty of scenery and stage effects.

FUNCTIONS OF STAGE SCENERY — Stage scenery may serve one or a number of functions. It may:

1. Serve as an enclosure for the action of the scene.
2. Serve as a motivating force for the action of the play.
3. Serve a purely decorative function.
4. Serve a symbolic function.
5. Serve as a reflective surface for light and sound.

The ordinary setting, especially if it falls into the category frequently referred to as a "box" setting, serves as an enclosure for the action of the play. It is in a sense a corral for the players and the very structure tends to define the space. It also serves to shut out distracting elements, elements that might be present just beyond the acting area such as actors waiting for cues, lighting units used to illuminate portions of the setting, and stray actors making cross overs behind the setting. When the *Our Town* style of production is employed it is impossible to accomplish these ends with the setting since there is no setting.

The various elements of the design may have specific use in the action of the play. This is more often true than not. In fact the designer usually begins his planning by placing doors, windows, fireplaces, stairways, platforms, trees, stumps and columns where they can be used to the best advantage for the stage business. At times the stage business may depend almost completely upon the manipulation of the actors by the setting. This practical and functional purpose of scenery is frequently the most important reason for its existence.

The elements of the stage design may be so arranged that they add beauty and interest to the production. Usually this visual beauty is enhanced by the actors and their costumes which also serve as a part of the scenery. Together the moving and stationary scenery present a pleasant picture. This is important even if the structure represented is a junk heap. There must be enough attraction to keep the audience's interest for the duration of the play.

Scenery may serve a purely symbolical function without being what one usually considers to be symbolism. The historical period, season of year, social level of the inhabitants and general mood may be symbolized by the elements of design and their treatment. Or abstract forms may be used to project specific moods and impressions.

And finally, scenery may serve as a surface from which sound and light may be reflected. An enclosure, setting, especially if it has a ceiling, will serve as a sounding board to help direct the sound into the auditorium, thus helping the acoustics of the hall — and many of them need all the help they can get. The painted surface of scenery also serves to reflect light, especially if it is painted in relatively high values of color. The light will be picked up and redistributed about the stage. If low light values are desired the setting can be painted to absorb light.

But whatever its function, the setting must be designed carefully and the design executed in such a way that it is functional, practical of manipulation upon the stage, and its composition pleasant and free from distracting elements.

Composition

Certain factors of art composition are important to the stage designer. He should be conscious of line, plane, mass, rhythm, symmetry, proportion, contrast, unity and coherence, in costumes, properties and scenery.

LINE—The simplest element of composition is the line. In theory line has only one dimension—length. However, it is the direction and apparent movement of the line that is important to the scene designer. He must be aware of the lines formed by moldings, tops of doors and windows, ground row forms, platforms and the flats of his setting. Certain general factors may be of value to him as he plans his setting.

252

A sharp, smooth line has smartness; a wobbly line may suggest indefiniteness and even carelessness; a curved line may have beauty and conformity; an angular line may suggest conflict.

gons and other flat surfaces. The plane has two dimensions—height and width.

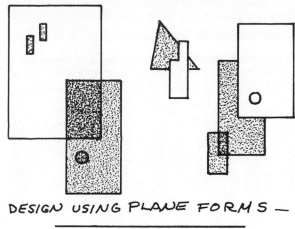

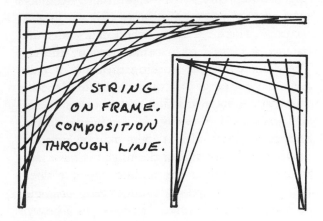

STRING ON FRAME. COMPOSITION THROUGH LINE.

DESIGN USING PLANE FORMS —

flict. Lines may lead into or out of the stage picture. They may lead the audience attention toward or away from the point of major conflict.

Simple, smart, abstract designs may be created by using lines exclusively. String, rope,

There are times when stage designs are composed of combinations of flat forms or planes with no attempt at three dimensional forms. Smart patterns can be created in this way for essentially abstract designs.

MASS—Usually planes are combined to form three dimensional forms known as mass. Mass forms have height, width and depth and seem to have weight which is somewhat absent in planes and lines. Practically every object in

SPANISH STREET SCENE. LINE DRAWING EFFECT USING TUBING AND WIRE. SUSPEND FROM GRID ON WIRE.

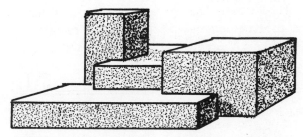

DESIGN THROUGH MASS. THREE DIMENSIONAL FORMS.

nature and every structure of man is in the form of mass. So when these objects are created on the stage the mass form is usually duplicated by using real or painted height, width and depth dimensions.

RHYTHM—Rhythm and movement are evident all about us. Life itself is composed of

pipe, rod, aluminum tubing or slats of wood can be arranged to make interesting patterns.

PLANES—Lines are combined to form planes or two dimensional forms such as squares, oblongs, triangles, circles, ovals, trapezoids, hexa-

253

complex rhythms: the rhythm of breathing, of the heartbeat, of footsteps, of day and night, of seasons, of the rotation of the earth and of the growth of plants. In design the repetition of forms similar or like and the flow of lines are

RHYTHM THROUGH REPETITION

examples of rhythm. Two factors concerning rhythm are important in design: having it and not overdoing it. Interest is achieved by repeating color and form, by the orderly flowing of lines and forms, and by the recurring of patterns and textures. But too much repetition results in monotony. Repeating exactly the same color, the same form, the same mass, the same line will result in dullness while the correct use of rhythm and variety will result in pleasure and excitement.

BALANCE—The operation of a seesaw may be used to demonstrate in part the matter of balance. A single weight placed across the

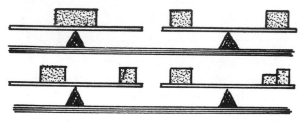

VARIETIES OF BALANCE

center of the seesaw will remain in balance. Two objects of equal weight will balance one another if they are placed on the board equidistant from the center. A large weight may

be balanced by a smaller weight if the larger is nearer the center or fulcrum. Two smaller weights together may balance a larger. Balance in a picture is achieved in a similar way. Weight, size, color, area—all of these elements may be used in accomplishing balance in the picture. There are times when deliberate unbalance is desired to project a specific feeling. The designer begins working in terms of balance as he arranges the floor plan for the setting and continues through the processes of design, execution, dressing and lighting of the finished setting. He balances a large area of grayed red on one side of the stage with a small amount of brilliant red on the opposite side. He balances textures by using similar ones on both sides of his setting. He balances a heavy

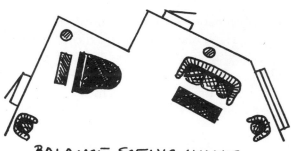

BALANCE SCENIC UNITS AND PROPERTIES.

weight on one side with an area of heavy color on the other. If he fails to balance his original design he can use pictures on the walls, pieces of furniture, boxes or whatever dressing materials are available to correct the imbalance. And, of course, if there is an apparent reason and motivation for imbalance, then that is what he strives to achieve in his finished setting.

SYMMETRY—Symmetry is in a sense a factor of balance. Perfect symmetry is achieved when the two sides of the picture are evenly and regularly balanced. When similar objects of the same weight or size are placed equidistant from the center of the stage the design is symmetrical. Informal symmetry is achieved by using dissimilar objects having the same feeling of weight, volume or color. Informal symmetry is usually more pleasant to the viewer than perfect symmetry. Perfect symmetry projects a feeling of orderliness in the extreme. Precision and mechanically developed aesthetic

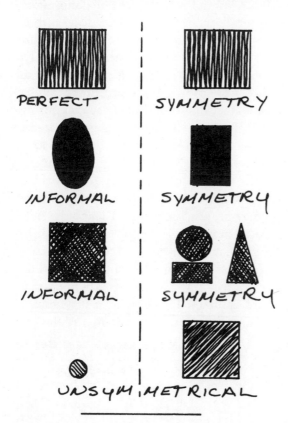

PERFECT | SYMMETRY

INFORMAL | SYMMETRY

INFORMAL | SYMMETRY

UNSYMMETRICAL

"taste" are suggested in this way. An asymmetrical design is unbalanced in one direction. This state of over and under balance may be deliberately used. When unintentionally employed it may be disturbing to the audience so it is a factor worth studying rather carefully before being employed.

PROPORTION — Proportion is important in theatrical design. This may also be referred to as scale. It is important to relate objects to one another in size, weight, color and form. A door 5'-0" high looks silly if all of the actors who use it are 6'-6" in height—unless there is a definite reason for this apparent abnormal relationship. A tall object will seem even taller if placed next to a short one and a short

object looks shorter when placed next to an extremely tall one. Actors may be dwarfed when playing next to tall scenery but seem like giants when playing in front of a short setting. If everything in the setting is scaled in the same proportions this relationship will be heightened even more. If actors are playing the part of insects in *Under the Sycamore Tree* or *The Insect Comedy* they seem small when scaled against a king sized tree trunk, but as soon as the stage hands walk on dressed in regular "man type" clothes the illusion is destroyed. This feeling for proportion is well shown in marionette productions where everything is scaled to the size of the marionettes. After a few moments the members of the audience begin thinking the figures to be of human proportions. At the end of the performance the

CORRECT SIZE RELATIONSHIP TO SHOW SCALE OF OBJECTS

operator climbs onto the stage and immediately the mechanical figures become tiny. The effect is startling but indicates how easily the eye may be fooled. Proportional relationship or scale

255

is extremely important in designing a stage setting. The designer should be constantly aware of this in planning his units of scenery and their relationship with one another, with the stage, and with the actors.

Openings for entrances must be proportioned for stage business at times. Hoop skirts, rapid

Units of scenery designed to be acted upon and designed to provide desired scale and proportion relationships between the actors and the setting.
Romeo and Juliet.

entrances and exits of mobs, movement of fencers, dancers whirling onto the stage—all of these require amply proportioned doors or archways.

CONTRAST—Contrast between the elements of the design may add to or detract from the total design. If deliberately planned, contrast between the sides of the stage or between the elements within a given stage unit may be of value. Frequently in a design where there are many rectangular forms one curved form is an interesting deviation. The same is true of a

setting that has a dominance of curved forms with a spot or two of recilinear forms. The contrast may be subtle or broad depending upon the effect to be achieved. Contrast of color, texture, general mood, mass, form and line is possible. Clashing colors might be deliberately used to startle or "jar" the audience and actors. Extremely rough and shiny surfaces might be used to achieve a feeling of contrast or conflict. The name character of *The Hairy Ape,* fresh from the stokehold of the ship, thrust into a clean, smooth, shiny atmosphere is completely out of his element. Tweedy suits might be out of place in a world of mirror surfaces. However, contrasts are needed. If everything in the setting has exactly the same feeling there will be a weak, sterile feeling to the whole. Tweed may be just the thing to make the mirror surfaces more interesting. A touch of brilliant color may touch off a large drab surface. Great contrast is desirable where a startling effect is desired; subtle contrasts where normal effects are desired. In the main it is advisable to have one dominant element in the design.

CONTRAST THROUGH FORMS

This element may be dominant because of its size, proportions, shape, color, dissimilarity, texture or pattern.

UNITY AND COHERENCE — Unity and coherence should be achieved when and where possible. Even if portions of the stage setting are dissimilar a certain amount of unity is desired. The stage setting should seem to fit together to make a whole. Too much dissimilarity is disturbing and calls attention to itself. There may be times when even this is desirable. If it is correctly planned then it is perfectly acceptable; if not, then it is probably distracting. Basic similarity of forms, patterns, colors, general style, mood and atmosphere, architectural period and scale are all essential if the parts of the setting are to be cohesive.

COSTUMES — Costumes, an important element of stage design, provide form, color, mass, rhythm, repetition, comparison and contrast. They are moving elements within the static stage picture that provide sometimes subtle, sometimes broad variations upon the original plan or theme.

The general structure and design of some of the elements of the scenery are largely determined by the structure, bulk, color, historical period, texture, movement and "feeling" of the costumes. There are times when the scenery is designed to fit the costumes and other times when the costumes are made to fit the scenery. More often than not the plan is a mixture of these two so that the elements dovetail into one another. Deliberate conflicts and harmonies are planned to indicate the relationships that exist between character and character and between character and setting.

The brevity of costume discussion in these pages is not intended to minimize the importance of this element of design. A more thorough, complete and informative body of information on this subject is to be found in the costume books that are listed in the bibliography.

Types of Settings

It has been suggested that a scene designer may use a poverty or a surfeit of scenery. It may now further be stated that there are many steps between these two extremes. Although there are no sharp lines of demarcation along the way, yet for convenience a number of types of settings ranging all of the way from simplicity to complexity of staging will be suggested. It is hardly necessary to say that these may be intermixed. The actual style or type of design used may be determined by one or all of the following factors: budget, physical facilities, style of stage direction, general atmosphere of the script, general audience character. In practice these will probably all be influential factors. However, in the finished design, regardless of style or form, there should be harmony, not conflict, among the playwright, the director, the actor, the audience and the scenic designer.

Projected Scenery

A bare stage with human forms moving into and out of pools of light can be extremely dramatic. Shadows cast on a background by

COMPOSITION OF HUMAN FORMS

the same moving forms can also be effective. There are occasions when no other scenery could be more desirable.

SIMPLE PROJECTIONS—Simple forms projected onto a background can also be effective. It isn't necessary to have complex equipment to achieve results of this kind. Giant palms can be the result of shining a spotlight through the stems and leaves of a potted plant. If the spotlight is on the floor the image produced in this way will be distorted and greater in size as it shines on the surface at a distance, but even this distortion can be valuable in some instances. Almost any form—china figurines, branches from trees, forms cut from cardboard or wood, rope patterns—may be used. This type of design will require some trial and error,

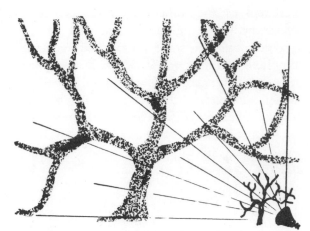

SIMPLE ENLARGED SHADOW
OF A SMALL OBJECT.

but in the theatre many of the best results come from this method of procedure. Every design is, in a sense, devised through trial and error. In some cases this process takes place on paper; in others it takes place in the scene shop or on the stage.

LINNEBACH PROJECTIONS — The Linnebach projector is essentially a shadow projector. The machine consists of a housing containing a large concentrated filament incandescent lamp. The front of the housing is equipped with a frame to hold a cut out pattern. When the lamp is turned on, portions of the beam of light are restricted or absorbed by the pattern on the front slide—the cut out. The resulting pattern which is allowed to fall on a surface at the back of the stage is basically a light and dark image. A certain amount of distortion may be eliminated by shaping the front of the box so that it conforms to the contour of the back wall. The pattern can easily be colored by introducing a color media to fill the open spaces of the cut out pattern. This colored effect may be enhanced even more by using a plastic slide which has a design painted on it with special plastic paint. Paint of this nature may be obtained from almost any hobby shop. Nonflammable plastic should be used if pos-

sible. The projector housing serves as a holder for the lamp and as a device to prevent spill light from spoiling the image. This piece of equipment, whether home made or commercially manufactured, should have adequate ventilation holes so that the heat may escape. The Linnebach projector is usually used for relatively broad effects. When used where other illumination is needed, that light should be directed so that it does not fall upon the projected image or it will be "washed out".

SLIDE PROJECTOR—Regular slide projectors with hand painted or photographic slides may be used on some stages and for some purposes. When this type of equipment is used it is possible to project extremely sharp focused images. However, unless it is possible to obtain a wide angle projector (with wide angle lens system) or possible to mount a projector in a position where it will have a long throw (at some distance from the screen surface) it is impossible to obtain a large image. If there is space at the back of the stage it is possible to use a rear projection on a translucent screen—a process much used in both motion pictures and television. When this type of projection is used the light falling on the other areas of the stage must be restricted. If too much direct or re-

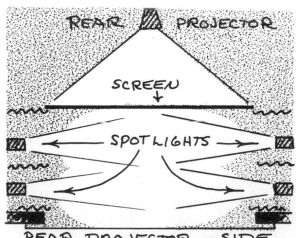

REAR PROJECTOR — SIDE
LIGHTING TO PREVENT
"WASHING-OUT" THE IMAGE

flected light falls on the screen the image of the projection will disappear. Although a regular picture screen surface will provide the most brilliant image when projections are used it is possible to get a fairly good image on almost any light colored surface. Scrim that is light in color value makes an interesting screen and introduces rather novel possibilities. As soon as the light is brought up behind, both the projected image and the scrim disappear.

Projected scenery when well designed and executed can be extremely effective. Although the process of building is minimal as far as the expenditure for supplies is concerned, yet the expenditure of time in working out an effective pattern or design and getting it projected onto the surface may be rather difficult and time consuming so this isn't something that should be left for the last moment. Experiments should be started early and continued until something satisfactory is achieved. Those who are easily discouraged probably should be dissuaded from trying this type of scenery—also those who are reluctant to spend time "fiddling around" and experimenting should keep away from it—but anyone who is anxious to try something different will have a wonderful time and come up with startling results.

In order to use projections one needs some type of lighting equipment, although nothing very elaborate, and some kind of background upon which to project the images.

Economy Staging

Almost all stages have some type of draperies or curtains used as a masking or enclosure for all of the miscellaneous lectures, recitals, concerts, meetings, movies and programs that invariably take place in the hall while it is not being used as a theatre. Many times when the budget is small, or nonexistent, the designer will have nothing but these draperies with which to work. Interesting things can be done with drapes alone, with drapes and a few odds

and ends, or with drapes and a few odd pieces of scenery.

There are many variations possible in rigging and handling stage draperies. They may be hung in folds straight down in rectangular panel sections; butterflied to form sweeping contours; rigged in combinations of one straight

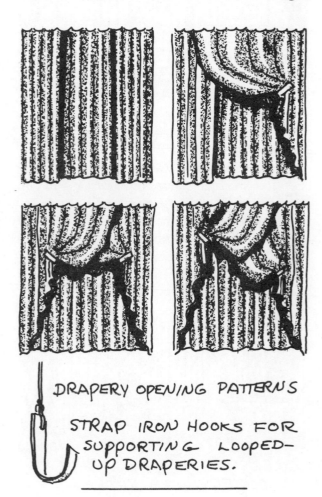

DRAPERY OPENING PATTERNS

STRAP IRON HOOKS FOR SUPPORTING LOOPED-UP DRAPERIES.

line and one butterfly; draped with one section high and the other section low; hung in one, two, three or even more swags or scallops; or hung on a half circle or full circle support so they form a column or tree trunk shape.

Scenery units such as doors, windows and fireplaces may be used in conjunction with draperies. If it is desirable to use pictures with this type of scenery the pictures may be hung

259

DRAPERY AND SCENERY UNITS

from the batten above rather than on the drapery itself.

Flats—plain, door, window, fireplace—may be placed behind draped-open curtains to add interest to the drapery setting.

Scenery units may be placed in front of the curtains. When possible these should probably be self supporting, self standing units rather than those which require bracing. In

SCENIC UNITS MAY BE USED FREELY WITH DRAPES.

fact, whenever possible scenery should support itself so that bracing may be held to a minimum. This is especially important when there are several settings in a production.

Screen type scenery units, faced on both sides and hinged with double acting decorative screen hinges, may be used to excellent advantage with this type of setting. The screen can have a scene painted upon either side and the scene

can then be changed by merely turning the screens around. One or more screens may be used. Screens of this nature may be made with

A screen used to suggest a hospital room in *All of the King's Men.*

two, three, four or even more sections and still fold into a pack that can be handled. If the bottoms have heavy furniture gliders they will move around easily and may rarely, if ever, have to be carried. By using several screens the entire stage can be covered and the effect of a box setting achieved. Many patterns and designs can be used on the screens. Decorative motifs that suggest nations and historical eras might be used as well as general patterns or colors to suggest mood or atmosphere.

If three scenes are needed when screens are used a trick that was devised for a production of *The Mock Doctor* (Fielding version of Moliere's *The Doctor In Spite Of Himself*)

260

A simple screen with a Chinese design motif
in a scene from *The Lute Song*.

might be used. Old over-sized window blinds that had been used in school rooms were obtained and cut so that they were as wide as the flats. Special holders were made from plumbers'

A PULL DOWN WINDOW SHADE
MAY BE MOUNTED ON TOP →

SCREENS MAY HAVE
ANY DESIGN PAINTED
ON THEM - DOUBLE ACT-
ING HINGES ALLOW
THEM TO FOLD BOTH WAYS

strap and the blinds were then mounted atop the screens. When the time came for the scene change the blinds were pulled down over one of the sides of the double faced flats. The scene painted on them was executed with a light stroke dry brush and lining technique so that the paint did not load on heavily and make the blinds difficult to roll.

Small drops to fit inside the curtained stage, cloth cut out patterns, pennants, spears, flags, colored rope, festoons of colored cloth and many other materials may be used with and on stage draperies. The limitations for this type of staging are set only by the stops on the designers imagination. If there is little with which to work then try to make that little work for you.

"Line Drawing" Design

Aluminum and thin-walled steel electrical conduit and aluminum or iron wire can be used to produce interesting and graceful design patterns for the stage. The tubes can be bent into graceful curves with a regular conduit "bender" tool or bent around a wooden circle-shaped template that has been securely fastened to a work bench. Straight pieces, long gentle curves, "S" curves, "C" curves, wavy forms, and many other shapes can be combined to produce abstract trees, bushes, flowers, buildings, or hills. Aluminum or soft iron wire can be used in conjunction with the tubing where more delicate lines are desired. Tubing and wire used in this way produces design forms that are similar to "line drawings" in art work.

Pieces of tubing and wire can be fastened together and used by themselves or they can be used as added decoration on flat frames, doorways, windows, furniture, or decorative screens. The tubing can be drilled and fastened with bolts, nails, or wire, or pieces may be lashed to one another with stove pipe wire. The aluminum wire can be fastened to tubing or other wire with string or stove pipe wire. It can be fastened to wood with staples.

Tubing and wire adapt themselves to designs

The secret compartment behind the fireplace is an important design element in *Shop at Sly Corner*.

for imaginative and fantasy type plays especially. These materials have a light "feeling" that can be used to produce flamboyant, rococo, and baroque qualities in design. Used in their natural color or painted in pastel or tint colors and placed against dark gray or black drapes or flats they produce handsome and striking design patterns.

Minimal Staging

Another type of staging might be referred to as minimal staging. This has many names, but in the main it is a type of staging in which everything is thrown out except the absolute essentials of the design. With a minimum of scenery quantitatively the designer suggests the flavor of the locale whatever it might be. If there are walls they are low except where large units like doors and windows are needed. As suggested before, there are many times when great height is unnecessary. Walls might be

MINIMAL SETTINGS WITH DRAPERY BACKGROUND

262

Simple set piece cut-outs for *Sing Out Sweet Land.*

only 6'-0" high around an upstairs or attic room except on the gable end. The garret room occupied by the orphan in the children's play *Radio Rescue* could be designed in this way, as could the upstairs bedroom in *Mary Poppins.* With this type of design pleasant effects can be achieved by having a portion of a room set in space. This portion contains all of the important essentials for the stage business.

The minimal type setting might center around the important unit of scenery: The oven in *Ladies In Retirement,* the fireplace in *Shop At Sly Corner,* the bed in *The Four Poster.* Of course when the production requires several

263

locales for its action it will be necessary to have several units to replace one another. The basic plan is to use only the barest essentials, but execute them well. The total effect should be one of scenic wealth rather than scenic poverty. Design, build, paint, mount and light the stage so that you project the feeling of completeness even though the entire setting consists of a single column.

Needless to say, this type of setting is ideal for variety shows where there are many short scenes or "black outs" since it allows scenery to be set up and struck rapidly. Many children's productions adapt themselves to this type of production. *Alice In Wonderland*—with scenes like the Duchess' kitchen in which the action centers around an outlandish stove, the Mad Hatter scene where an endless tea table is the main essential, the court room scene where the judge's stand is the essential element, the tree in which the Cheshire cat appears and disappears, and many other scenes where one small unit is essentially important—is an example.

The Patchwork Girl of Oz is another play in which there are many scenes but each requires only a small screen type unit to depict various places, such as the Voracious Tree, Jack Pumpkinhead's home, the Cave of Yoop, the Woozey's cage, the throne room. Many adult plays fall into a pattern much like this, too. *Of Thee I Sing* has many scenes but for the most part a single dominant idea can be used for each. The hotel room, which is a smoke filled campaign party headquarters, needs only a simple suggestion of a room with a symbol to suggest the party. The president's office requires a double desk and some symbol to suggest "Love", the party slogan, upon which the candidate was elected. The speakers' stand for the convention scene needs the names of the states on poles and a speakers' rostrum loaded with microphones. The Atlantic City Board Walk judges' stand for the bathing beauty scene needs nothing but a pennant decked platform with some semblance of a canopy for a background. The Senate chamber where Throttlebottom finally finds his job needs only an oversize desk so that he will seem as lost as he always is in the play.

The Green Pastures is another play requiring many settings, most of which can be small. The Lord's office, the dining room in Noah's

THE LORD'S OFFICE - GREEN PASTURES
SMALL BOX SET BEFORE DRAPES.

home, the tree in the Garden of Eden, the garden where the Lord talks to the flowers, the street lamp under which the young sinners are shooting craps, Noah's Ark and Moses' cave are a few of the scenes.

Small scenes of this nature may be made as booked flat units or built as screens to make them self standing. In order to make them easier to shift around on the stage the bottoms can be fitted with furniture gliders. Portions of the surfaces on these units can be blocked out by painting them the color of the background or they can be made with contoured irregular tops and sides, or they can be left basically rectangular and painted contour patterns can be applied to achieve the feeling of irregular forms. There are times when this process is more satisfactory since it requires less time and material in the building stages and the flats are immediately ready for reuse without having to remove the contour edges.

Units of this nature can also be made from drops. A drop need not fill the entire stage

264

laterally or vertically. Piano wire may be used to extend from the top of the drop up to the overhead masking so that it seems to stand in space. Drops may be shaped on the top by building contoured batten sections and may be cut to shape on the sides to a certain extent if the shaping is planned to avoid flap over and curling.

Functional Staging

There are times when the designer has no desire to describe the place of the action but does want to indicate it graphically. He desires to use units that have specific physical feeling of mass. He wants to differentiate between spaces on the stage while at the same time re-

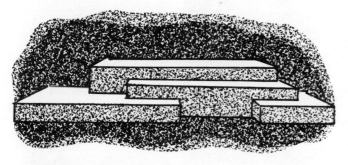

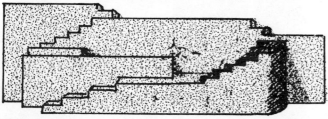

PLATFORMS – STEPS AND RAMPS.

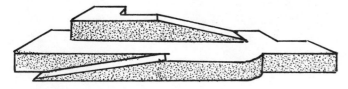

lating them to one another. The stage setting, consisting of platforms, steps, ramps and blocks, becomes strictly functional with no purposeless or decorative elements in the design. Careful

lighting then allows the designer to select any portion of the stage he desires for a given scene. He bathes that area in light while the rest of the stage remains in darkness. This lighted section is the place of the action. Later in the play other areas are used, people move up and down the steps, group themselves upon the platform, sit on the blocks. This is above all a setting in which the actor is the dominant figure. He is moving in space, facilitated by the functional elements designed for his use. The units may remain in the same position throughout the play or be moved into new positions giving new mass relationships, giving the director a chance to arrange people in new compositional arrangements. Norman Bel Geddes projected many settings of this nature. His designs for *Lazarus Laughed* by Eugene O'Neill, for a production of Goethe's *Faust* and for Shakespeare's *Hamlet* are in this style. Lee Simonson's designs for *The Tidings Brought to Mary* by Claudel and Toller's *Man and the Masses* were also designed in this general style. A school of design known as Constructivism evolved in Germany and was extensively developed by the Russian theatre, especially the Kamerny Theatre during the period immediately following World War I. The Constructivists carried functionalism to the extreme. They believed not only in using the elements that had practical functions, such as platforms, steps, ramps and slippery slides, but they made no attempt to conceal the structures of these elements. The legs and braces of platforms were there for one and all to see and so were many of the spotlights, flying lines and any other mechanical devices utilized in the production. This frankness no doubt led to an increase in the number of distracting features of the production.

The formal units utilized in most productions today are covered with muslin or canvas so that they are seen as mass and form rather than specifically as portions of a scaffolding. Most of the scenic designers desire even more description than they can project with the mere

265

Numerous steps and platforms provide many acting areas for *Romeo and Juliet.*

Formal Balance. The platforms are covered and decorated. *The Taming of the Shrew.*

267

BASIC SETTING

SCENIC UNITS ADDED AND—

CHANGED!

by facing it with stone forms; or it may be the deck of a ship by placing a portion of the ship's structure around it. In similar manner a step becomes a stairway or a rough hewn stone rise; a ramp becomes a hill, a stone slab or a river bank.

Basic Setting — Variable Plugs

A still more elaborate variation of the functional type setting carries it another step toward the theatrical type setting. The designer adds basic, if somewhat nondescript, architectural forms to his mass units. He may use a set of formal openings which with his basic platform structure remain intact throughout the play. During the course of many scenes he may fill these openings with various "plugs". These plugs may be draperies, wall sections,

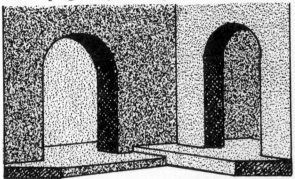

BASIC SETTING

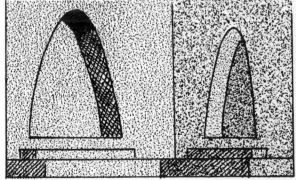

doors, windows, archways, battlements, portcullisses, hallways, fireplaces, thrones or any conceivable forms he desires. If the general flavor remains the same throughout the play, the permanent openings may have an oriental feeling for *Lute Song,* a Medieval quality for

forms they arrange on the stage for the actor's stage business. So after arranging the basic floor levels some background forms are designed to give the scene a little detail. A platform becomes a throne by placing an appropriate throne chair upon it; it becomes a judge's bench by erecting a facing across its front; it becomes a parapet by enclosing it with a battlement facing; it can be the edge of a cliff

268

The plugs behind the columns may be changed. *All of the King's Men.* The columns are flat surfaces with painted dimension.

An archway or proscenium rigged with plugs, drops, drapes, and scrim. *Lute Song.*

Macbeth, an Italian Renaissance character for *Romeo and Juliet,* an English Renaissance character for *Elizabeth the Queen,* a primitive design for *The Emperor Jones;* or the openings may have no specific character so that the general flavor may change with the inserts for *Marco Millions, Back to Methuselah, As You Like It,* or *Othello.* Lee Simonson's designs for *Marco Millions* graphically show the possibilities of this type of design.

Functional staging with formal openings, has possibilities for the complex production problem since it allows major changes through the use of smaller units. In order to change the entire picture appreciably it is not necessary to shift all of the scenery on the stage.

False Proscenium Staging — Modified Functional

In a sense staging with a false proscenium falls into the same category as the Basic Setting With Variable Plugs since a portion of the stage scenery remains intact throughout the entire production. Scenery behind or within the proscenium may take any form as long as its design is consistent with the basic mood and feeling of the proscenium. It may consist of flattage, backdrops, set pieces, or movable curtains that may be drawn to one side or both.

The proscenium when used can be placed far down stage so that the action takes place within and upstage of its confines or it can be moved further upstage so that it becomes more of a box type setting with a large movable section of back wall. If the latter method is employed,

FALSE PROSCENIUM AND DROPS

the proscenium becomes more like a giant picture frame without a bottom. The picture is then changed in the frame.

A combination of the two methods is also possible so that scenes can take place both in front of and within the archway stage. This of course makes it possible to change scenes behind while scenes are playing on the front stage.

If the proscenium is to be used so that much of the action takes place on the forestage area

Tracks — overhead and on the floor — for "sliding shutter" scenery on an outdoor stage. *The King and I.*

it will be advisable to design a wing or portal on either side of the proscenium with openings for entrances. These portals will also serve to help brace the proscenium.

A framework above and behind the proscenium supported by its own legs will be equipped with rigging for roll drops, backdrops, curtains or whatever type device is to be used.

It is possible to use one long continuous drop with scenes painted continuously one beside the

271

Movement toward realism but retaining simplicity of material and detail.
The Young Idea.

other in which case there should be sufficient space at either end of the track for the entire curtain to be stored. Another method allows

SMALL DROPS ON A SINGLE STRIP OF MUSLIN—ONE SCENE IN PLACE BEHIND PROSCENIUM—ONE IN "STORAGE" AT EACH END OF TRACK.

the curtains to be pulled on from one end and stored at the other with each wire carrying only one or two scene curtains. A third method would allow storage space for one curtain on each side of the stage. One curtain could then be stored on each end of a wire and pulled on stage for use, then pulled back into its own storage place and the other pulled in like manner from the other end of the wire and stored again at its own end of the proscenium.

A series of roll drops can be rigged on a support behind the proscenium and used to make the changes. The rigging mechanism and support for the drops will have to be more rigid, and probably heavier and more complex, in order to support the strain of lifting the drop.

The false proscenium type of staging will provide the designer with an interesting and flexible device for multi-scene productions. This method of staging may be a convenient way to handle the complex problems of touring productions.

Theatrical Settings

Most of the plays written today, as well as many of those written yesterday and the day before, literally cry for more than mere functionalism in their settings. They demand treatment that is theatrical. They innately require decoration to project the correct mood, atmosphere and environmental feeling. In order to fulfill this seeming need the designer becomes an architect, builder and interior decorator. In the previous types of settings listed, the designer described the environment of the play's action

272

in outline form only. In theatrical staging he begins to fill in the details. He describes it in one case with a duplication of reality—he uses the elements of the real structure or exactly duplicated facsimiles. Real moldings are applied to the walls, doors, cabinets and furnishings where needed; growing plants are installed in pots and planter boxes; expensive pictures are mounted in selective positions on the walls; furniture and furnishings to suit the exact period are provided; tables are set with the crystal, china and silverware required by the book of etiquette; correctly shaped and patterned rugs are placed on the stage floor; wall treatment as pictured in the history of decoration book is exactly duplicated on the walls. This is literally a real room, or a real exterior of a specific structure. Nothing is left to the imagination. This *is* a living room, circa 1910, complete to the last antimacasser and hair flower shadow box; it is the speakeasy of 1922; it is a Child's Restaurant in New York City in 1913; it is George Washington's study. This is the essence of decorative naturalism and it is theatrically effective. Extensive research must be done before the designer can do much beyond the floor plan of this type setting. He refers back to architectural magazines if it is in the 19th or 20th centuries. He may find his information in catalogues, history books, periodicals of the period, picture albums, home decoration books of the period, or any written work that will provide descriptions and illustrations of the style and period of the desired architecture and decoration. His desire is to duplicate as nearly as possible exactly what was used for this particular structure or portion of a structure. He must be a stickler for detail.

Equally effective theatrically is a variation on the above style of design in the direction of selectivity. The designer eliminates a few of the nonessential details but retains the basic important elements. In this way he retains the flavor of naturalism while at the same time moving a step back toward minimal staging. But by and large he is still remaining in the realm of theatrical staging. He retains the essentials without the clutter. Part or all of the moldings are painted rather than three dimensional; book cases are filled completely or partly with false book backs in place of the real thing; furniture suggests the period rather than duplicating it exactly; a table is set with a minimum rather than a maximum of silver, china and crystal; and rugs on the floor are there to deaden the actors' footsteps rather than to serve as a decorative part of the setting. This has the savor of naturalism without the frenzied braggadocio of exact, minute duplication. The majority of contemporary plays can be set in this style. They have this real, yet theatrical, quality.

The designer of theatrical type scenery begins with functionalism, the bare essentials for the stage business, and then he embellishes. He literally adds the seasoning, the sugar and spice, to the audience meal. His main cue for the design must come from the script, the style of action, the style of stage direction and the style of interpretation of the script. His spice may consist of salt, pepper and sugar, or he may move into the heady aroma of garlic, horseradish and ginger. He may remain in the realm of naturalism or may slip into the embellished world of romanticism and the artificial society of comedy of manners, or may enter into the biting but roisterous realm of satire. As he begins to move into this world he departs slightly from the real world. He becomes a bit tipsy, a bit flamboyant and a bit color happy. Elements of the Rococo and Baroque creep in and design becomes even more theatrical. Moods become gay and flippant. The scenery begins to smile with the audience. This is poking fun at realism without departing from it. Panels are enclosed by scroll work in place of stiff, formal moldings; furniture is gay and enchanting; lines are broken and free flowing; and colors are more dominant and talkative. Restoration comedies, comedies of manners and romantic comedies may well be staged in this way.

Staging of this nature must be handled with

273

Portion of a courtroom for *The Vigil*. Wood grain and molding details painted on a flat surface.

Skin of Our Teeth. Slight deviations from realism. A smattering of many architectural types
periods (above). And decadence suggested by the cut outs, the impending storm suggested
the background (below).

great care lest the scenery become an overpowering element. It may become another actor but its voice must not be so loud that the other actors cannot be heard. And as with other types of design it must conform in general flavor and feeling to all of the other elements of the production. Its degree of theatrical flamboyance must be innate in the script and in its interpretation.

The deviation from naturalism can easily move beyond the realm just described and over into an outer world—a world of extra sensory projection. Psycho scenic staging may result in designs that move away from the natural in any direction and any degree. Various devices may be used to suggest the inner life of the introvert or the outer life of the extrovert; the imaginary sight of the blind or hearing of the deaf; the visionary world of the dreamer or the mental world of the demented; the unstable world of the neurotic or the blank world of the dead. Almost anything within the realm of the imagination is possible of recreation upon the stage. Angular walls, endless tunnels, ever spiraling staircases, bottomless pits, growing trees, shrinking tables—all of these can be created.

Form and color may be used to project emotions and ideas. Abstraction of one or both of these elements may be difficult but challenging. The designer must try to use his elements so they can be universally interpreted by his audience or his abstraction will become a confusing element that attracts more attention than it deserves.

Varying degrees of abstraction are possible. The forms may be distorted but still recognizable. They may be twisted and contorted to seem other than what they actually prove to be. Or the designer may move completely into the realm of sheer form and color.

A mass through its size, position and relationship with other masses may be used to project mood and atmosphere without representationally describing any known form. In some respects this is a step that the designer passes

through in creating the representational types of design. He decides upon the correct juxtaposition of forms and the desirable colors to project his basic emotions. In abstraction he goes to the left and uses nonrepresentational form to achieve his final ends, whereas in representational design he moves to the right and creates familiar forms in familiar color patterns and arrangements.

There aren't too many occasions when the completely abstract design can be used. There are modern ballets that may be interpreted in this vein. And some of the plays of Eugene O'Neill, August Strindberg, George Kaiser, Karel Capek, Elmer Rice and Gertrude Stein move into this realm and can be treated wholly or partially in the abstract vein.

It is possible to intermix these styles whenever and wherever desirable. It is possible to use abstract elements of color or form in a setting that is basically representational or naturalistic and through the combination of elements to project moods and feelings that may not be achieved in any other way. It is possible also to add naturalistic clutter to a nonobjective setting in order to relate it to something familiar to the audience. However, when mixing the forms the designer must be careful that his ideas and units of scenery fit into a pleasingly coherent whole.

Shifting and Storage Space

During the course of the designing process the scenic designer will have to be constantly conscious of all of the settings for the production so that he can devise a shifting and storage plan if there is more than one setting. He must plan space for the setting that is in the acting area position, the settings that have been used for previous scenes and are now dead storage, and the scenes to come that are in live storage. Obviously the dead storage scenes are no longer important for this individual performance so the storage can be somewhat disorderly, but the live storage is extremely important. Usually scene shifts should be accomplished efficiently, rapidly and quietly. In order to do this it is necessary to plan with great care. Everything must be arranged to be moved easily and readily. Sometimes it is advisable

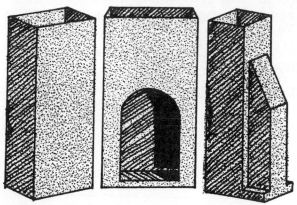

4 SIDED WAGON UNITS. USE TOGETHER, WITH FLATS, WITH DROPS, OR CYCLORAMA.

to fasten as many units together as possible so that there are just a few units to move.

Where and when possible it may be advisable to plan using special shifting devices such as wagons, revolvers, the flying system, jack-knife stages, self standing units, or any other device that may be convenient. Double faced scenery, small drops, screens, wings, three dimensional units with two, three or more faces may all be used. In fact, any contrivance that is convenient and helpful is usable if it is practical of manipulation and can be incorporated into the design without changing the basic plan.

Sets may on occasion be placed one inside the other. Then as one is used it is taken out and struck and the next one played.

It is advisable to be aware of all of the possible problems that are likely to arise when the scenery reaches the stage. It isn't possible to think of all of them, but careful planning will cut the last minute nightmares to a minimum at least.

The Design

The stage design may be executed in any medium (pastels, colored pencils, water colors or even oils) and on any surface (water color paper, pebble matte board, tracing paper, canvas, squared paper or even wrapping paper). The design can be beautifully or sketchily done. If the designer is to follow through and supervise the execution of his design he may by-pass many of the steps that must of necessity be taken when others are to reproduce the design in scenery. The major fact to bear in mind is that the finished product and not the steps along the way is the important element. Beautiful designs are useless if they cannot be transferred to muslin or canvas, and if they are not functional and practical when the transference has been completed. The design is complete only when it is on the stage, lighted and has actors performing in and around it. It must be an integral part of the production.

When it is necessary to make drawings and plans of details, short cuts and easy methods of procedure are welcome. Drawing on squared paper will save much time and provide easily translatable proportional relationships of objects and their parts. Impressions and sugges-

King Lear using four sided pylons mounted on wagons so they may be moved and rotated easily.

277

The Shop At Sly Corner. The shop of the dealer in antiques can contain countless stage property items.

tions are usually more valuable than skilfully executed mechanical drawings. Saving time on detail work of this nature will usually release more man hours for reproduction, dressing and lighting of the setting.

In planning the setting the designer must go beyond the mere mechanics of selecting flats of the correct size, putting them together, painting them and setting them up on the stage. He must be able to project the spirit of the play. To do this he employs the elements of form, balance, proportion, symmetry, texture and color. Through his setting he attempts to capture, by means of these elements, the mood and atmosphere of the production. He tries to capture the underlying spirit, translate it into design elements and then spread this on the surface of his scenery.

In setting *You Can't Take It With You* the designer captures the wild weirdness of a family where each member lives in his own hilarious private world; the immaculate cleanliness of *Craig's Wife* is stiff, cold, formal and precise; characters of *The School for Scandal* live in a beautiful, brittle, artificial, fragile, pastel world;

the violence and greediness of *Macbeth* is heavy, primitive and full of raw passion; anything may happen in *The Skin of Our Teeth* with its indefiniteness, yet the institution of marriage is shown as a great stabilizing force; *Peter Pan* has a light airiness that is exemplified by Peter in free flight. There is the usual clutter of a pawn shop about *Shop at Sly Corner,* yet there is also a feeling of foreboding and one feels that all is not as it should be. Maxwell Anderson inspires the designer of *Knickerbocker Holiday* with the jail cell where an inmate cut notches "bigger and bigger and bigger" until he cut one so big that he got out. *Star Wagon* dreams the actors back to a real past. *The Adding Machine* forcibly casts the hero into a horrible mechanical world.

Subtle or exaggerated elements of the design may suggest the spirit or general feeling. Gay, bright colors can be used to make one think of fun and laughter. Brilliant, rolling forms might suggest boisterous, noisy, farcical action. Deep values, heavy shadows and massive forms might suggest sombreness. Huge overpowering masses with upward lines might

278

iversity of Utah portable stadium stage made of tubular scaffolding units and a plank deck.
ic setting for *South Pacific*. Sliding shutters used to make the many scene changes required.
e of the spotlight poles is visible.

help to accent the basic idea of the smallness of man. Walls leaning inward, low ceilings and heavy colors pulling downward will help project the feeling of closing in, of claustrophobia. Green, dank colors, water stains and moss forms can suggest a stuffy, disease ridden atmosphere. Sharp, jagged lines and sharp contrasty colors can give a feeling of torture and constant injury. Unbalanced forms ready to collapse can help project the feeling of instability. The inevitable doom of depth, darkness and disaster can be projected through form and color. Warm colors and high light reflective surfaces combined with a feeling of openness can project warmth and sunshine. Hot, heavy colors will help develop the atmosphere of laziness and inertia. Cool colors, and stable forms can project a feeling of complacency and coolness. And sharpness of color, cleanness of line and simplicity of detail may suggest sophistication while careless use of the same elements suggests slovenliness.

The designer will need to learn the nationality, historical period and socio-economic level of the characters who inhabit the setting. A

thorough investigation and correlation of these factors will enable him to check the desired architectural features. It may be that a slight oriental flavor overlaid on American architectural units is needed to suggest that the setting is the home of a Nesei, an American born Japanese; whereas the home of native Japanese will have the clean, simple, uncluttered lines of Nipponese architecture. One from another land might be expected to bring along some minor decorative details so that regardless of where he lives there will be a slight mixture of the two styles of design: the homeland and the land of residence.

The character of architectural features, including doorways, windows, moldings, furniture, room proportions, materials, decoration and furnishings, should be studied carefully and then the salient features chosen for the setting being designed. The degree of conformity to exact details will depend upon the individual play and the style of the scenery and production. A single beautiful and appropriately styled column may suffice to suggest that this scene is in Greece, Rome or Egypt. An

279

archway may be designed to set the scene as China, Tudor England, Rome, Egypt, Peru or the land of Mohammed. Spaciousness and elaborateness of design will probably be used

Architectural units designed to project the mood and atmosphere of a time and place. *Romeo and Juliet.*

to suggest wealth and elevated position, while extreme simplification and space restriction will suggest modesty of means and position. The clutter and overabundance of color, furniture and knick knacks is typical of poor taste whereas the furbelows, tassels, heavy colors and gimcrack of Victorianism has a slightly different yet essentially the same flavor.

The designer will probably collect much material. In fact, he will probably scrounge around for old books, periodicals and pictures and will use them not only for the design of the moment, but will file them away for future

reference. But for any one design he will gather much more material than is needed. He will sketch details and general designs from it, absorb the flavor and try to digest it rather completely. Then he will try to tell his story with a few essential lines and details, allowing for clutter only when and where it is actually needed. Robert Edmond Jones, the eminent American designer, had great facility for this. His settings were economical of detail but wealthy in projectivity. Any designer would do well to study his work carefully.

Special Design Problems

There are theatrical productions that differ somewhat from the regular play performance. These should be discussed briefly. If the designer is working with Ballet, Opera, Arena Theatre, Outdoor Theatre or Touring Theatre he may encounter some special problems even though he is still working with basically the same materials, can design in the same styles and will have the same space and moving problems that he has with any other performance.

BALLET PRODUCTIONS—Ballet productions usually take place on one level. For traditional ballet, at least, the desire is for a large, unencumbered dancing space with several openings off right and left for entrances. Clear wing space for the dancers to begin and end their movement, beyond sight lines, is also desirable. The openings must be fairly wide to allow for the movement of the dancers and their costumes which are at times quite full. The choreographer will be the major consultant regarding the problems and requirements of a given program. He may be a traditionalist, in which case it will be necessary to refer to the original designs of the particular ballet. However, even if the original production is used as the basis for the design there is still a chance for considerable creativity.

In the main, because of its character and physical needs, ballet scenery will consist mostly of wings, backdrops and overhead borders. These needn't be conventional but may depart as far as possible from the traditional forms used for such stage elements. Basically the stage area should be clear and flat. It may be thought of as a lighted space occupied by the changing compositional forms of the moving dancers.

OPERA PRODUCTIONS — The production of opera presents its problems too and they differ somewhat from ballet requirements. However, there are frequently ballet interludes so the ballet requirements must also be borne in mind during the course of the designing process. Opera can be exciting or static and stodgy. Usually there is a conflict between the stage director who is intent upon movement and stage pictures and the musical director who is conscious only of singing perfection, and complete attention of the singer upon his direction during the performance which often results in a static performance. In order to please all of the people involved it is necessary somehow to plan a flat space for dancing and still have levels for manipulation of choruses near the musical director in the orchestra pit. Ordinarily there are relatively large choruses that must be herded onto the stage quickly and ushered out just as fast. This, of course, means that there should be an adequate number and arrangement of fairly large openings. It will be necessary to know all of the factors about the individual opera before any definite plans can be made. Then design in terms of the number of people in an individual scene, the amount of space needed for dancing, entrances and exits needed to get crowds on and off stage, and level arrangements needed to place choruses in positions where they can see the musical director.

ARENA STAGING—The arena stage is usually viewed from all sides. It is therefore necessary to design so that sight lines are not impaired regardless of where the individual member of the audience is seated. Furniture, hand properties and low platform levels become extremely important factors in the design. Suspended scenery, low partial walls, scrim walls, diaphonous architectural units, forms made of

wire, rope and string, lights and shadows, and painted floor cloths are all elements that the designer in the round may work with. If the room is so contrived it may be possible to shift the stage into different positions from play to play. It may be possible to run the stage along one end of the room, in a corner, diagonally from corner to corner, in two or more corners, at both ends, or almost any otherwhere. The variations are all but limitless in a flexible arena type theatre, but usually the audience is seated on more than one side so sight lines become a problem of more importance than in the regular proscenium theatre. Audience visibility, masking of off stage areas and doorways, baffles to prevent off stage light spill, careful arrangements of forms and lights to provide for fluid movement in all directions and careful execution of the scenic units so that they can pass close scrutiny of the audience that sits practically within the setting are all factors that must be considered very carefully.

OUTDOOR PRODUCTIONS—Outdoor productions also provide many headaches. Actually outdoor stages differ so greatly from one another that each has its own problems. The general problems of wind and rain, cold and heat, are more universal than any others and must be coped with in any outdoor theatre from the moment the project begins until it closes.

The wind is one unpredictable element that cannot be passed over lightly. A solid, permanent structure is the best solution to the problem. The next best solution is to have a solid framework to which movable flat scenery may be securely lashed. The third solution provides anchoring devices in the floor and floor that is securely anchored to the ground. Other convenient anchors are trees, permanent columns, pillars and pilons, stakes securely driven into the ground and heavily weighted wagons. Even slight gusts of wind can easily cause irreparable damage. A beautiful towering scenic structure can in a moment become a mess of tangled boards and shredded muslin. So when

Rectory scene for *Shadow and Substance*. Many items of stage dressing
will aid in projecting the correct mood and atmosphere.

out of doors it is advisable to never leave scenery unanchored unless it is lying flat on the ground—and even then the wind can whip it around.

Rain causes less damage than wind, ordinarily, although it can cause glue to loosen, paint to run, and muslin to pull completely out of shape. Water proof glue, paint that is at least somewhat impervious to rain and heavier covering material than muslin may partially solve these problems. Rubber latex, casein, or glue base paint (sprayed with a solution of formaldehyde after it has dried) may solve the paint problem.

When the weather is calm and beautiful outdoor theatre seems ideal, but as soon as the weather takes a turn so do the technicians' ulcers.

TOURING THEATRE — Touring theatre can be fun for those dreaming nostalgically about

it after it is over. But in the here and now there are packing, loading and unloading, repairing, setting up and striking problems that sometimes become almost insurmountable.

Scenery for touring should be built new if possible so that the flats will be relatively light in weight, sturdy and as impervious to rough treatment as possible. The size and proportions of the touring conveyance should be known so that scenery and props may be designed to pack and fit into the space neatly and easily. This will facilitate packing and unpacking. This will also aid in cutting down on the damage and repairs to the setting.

Scenery for the touring production should be designed so that it will brace and support itself as much as possible to hasten the setting up and striking process. The travelling company should attempt to be self sufficient scenery and property-wise so that there is adequate assurance that every item can be found when and where it is needed.

It is usually advisable to allow for expansion and contraction of the stage setting. Extra flats, a wide and narrow jog to fit in the same spot, places where portions of walls may be overlapped, are all devices that may prove handy when the set is being assembled on any one given stage.

If the problems of variable sized stages, loading and unloading, setting up and striking are considered carefully the touring problems may be cut to a minimum.

Conclusion

In general it is advisable for the stage designer to plan his scenery in terms of the specific problem at hand. The designer is planning one special production of a play. When that play was first designed it was treated in the same way, as a special production. The first designer had problems just as every designer who followed him in planning the staging for that particular play.

Most designers in the nonprofessional theatre plan their settings for one theatre, or one set of theatres. They must of necessity carefully study the facilities available on their stage and make these facilities work for them. They must also know the other raw materials of their art; know the characteristics of lumber, paint, muslin; know how to manipulate flats, drops, dimmers; in short know how to stage a play. The material of this text may point in the right direction by describing a few of the basic materials that have been used in the past and that are being used at present. The theatre technician should always be willing not only to use these materials and ideas but also willing to try new and unusual materials and ideas. New products are constantly coming into the building trades, display, lighting, and television

market that can be adapted to stage use. Materials need not be specifically manufactured for stage use before they can be taken into a theatre. In fact products that are manufactured for large commercial markets are usually mass produced and more economical to buy and use. The sealed beam PAR 38 and R 40 lamps are a good example of this economy. They were originally designed for window display use. Widely used they are produced in great quantities, hence are inexpensive. Many other products might be cited that have similar history. The designer should become aware of some of these products and try to use them, if they fit into his plan and design.

Ideally a designer should allow nothing to hamper his creative imagination. He should design freely in terms only of the total end result. Unfortunately however, there are other factors that enter in to hamper this freedom of design. The confines of the stage, the budget, the practicability of reproduction, the physical facilities of the stage, sight lines, and all of the other many and varied elements discussed previously must be carefully considered even before the creative work can begin. However, as stated from time to time, the conventions of the past and the shortcomings of the theatre plant should be employed rather than ignored and the designer's imagination should be tempered by thoughts of flats, paint and spotlights.

* * *

The stage designer is not an easel artist; he isn't a carpenter or cabinetmaker; he isn't a draper or upholsterer; he isn't an interior decorator nor lighting artist; he isn't an electrician nor a magician; he isn't a special effects man, pawnbroker or thief. Indeed not!!! He is all of them rolled into one. He has the aesthetic feeling of an artist and the scrounging ability of a junkman.

283

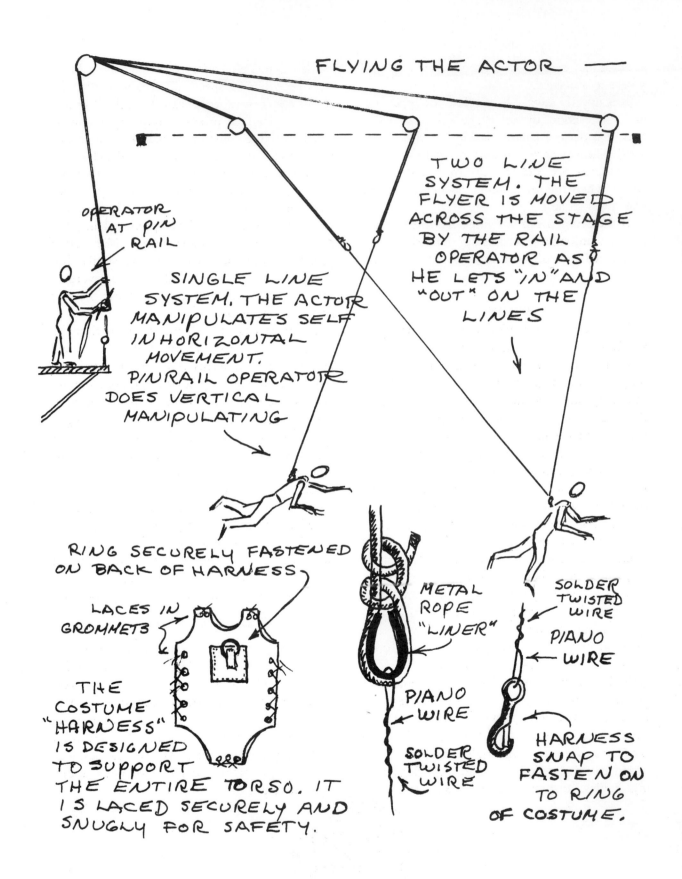

OPERATOR AT PIN RAIL

TWO LINE SYSTEM. THE FLYER IS MOVED ACROSS THE STAGE BY THE RAIL OPERATOR AS HE LETS "IN" AND "OUT" ON THE LINES

SINGLE LINE SYSTEM, THE ACTOR MANIPULATES SELF IN HORIZONTAL MOVEMENT. PINRAIL OPERATOR DOES VERTICAL MANIPULATING

RING SECURELY FASTENED ON BACK OF HARNESS.

LACES IN GROMMETS

THE COSTUME "HARNESS" IS DESIGNED TO SUPPORT THE ENTIRE TORSO. IT IS LACED SECURELY AND SNUGLY FOR SAFETY.

METAL ROPE "LINER"

PIANO WIRE

SOLDER TWISTED WIRE

SOLDER TWISTED WIRE

PIANO WIRE

HARNESS SNAP TO FASTEN ON TO RING OF COSTUME.

Appendices

SELECTED BIBLIOGRAPHY OF
REFERENCE BOOKS.

ARCHITECTURE

FLETCHER, BANISTER. *A History of Architecture.* New York: Charles Scribner and Sons. 14th Ed., 1948

HAMLIN, TALBOT. *Architecture Through the Ages.* G. P. Putnams Sons. New York, 1940

RICHARDSON, A. E. AND CONFIATO, HECTOR O., *The Art of Architecture.* London: English University Press, 1952

SEWALL, JOHN IVES. *A History of Western Art.* New York: Henry Holt and Co., 1953

STATHAM, H. HEATHCOTE. *A History of Architecture.* London, New York: B. T. Batsford Ltd., 1950

STURGIS, RUSSELL. *A Dictionary of Architecture and Building.* New York: MacMillan Co., 1901 (3 Vol.)

THORNE, MRS. JAMES WARD. *Handbook to American Rooms in Miniature.* Chicago: Art Institute of Chicago, 1941

THORNE, MRS. JAMES WARD. *Handbook of European Rooms in Miniature.* Chicago: Art Institute of Chicago, 1943

WASMUTH, GUNTHER, ED. *Wasmuth Lexikon Der Baukunst.* Berlin: Verlag Ernst Wasmuth A. G., 1929 (5 Vol.)

VIOLLET, E. *Dictionnaire Raisonne de L'Architecture Francaise.* Paris: Libraires Imprimeries Reunies. (10 Vol.)

ARMS AND ARMOR

..... *Handbook of the Severance Collection of Arms and Armor.* Cleveland, Cleveland Museum of Art, 1925

..... *Catalog of Military Goods.* Bannerman's 501 Broadway, New York

BOUTELL, CHARLES. *Arms and Armament in Antiquity and the Middle Ages.* London, Reeves and Turner, 1905

HAYWARD, J. F. *European Firearms.* New York: Philosophical Library, 1955

LELOIR, MAURICE. *Dictionnaire du Costume et de ses Accessoires des Armes et des Etoffes des Origines a nos jours.* Paris: Librairie Grund, 1951

YAMAGAMI, HATIRO. *Japan's Ancient Armour.* Board of Tourist Industry, Japanese Government Railways. 1940

ART COMPOSITION AND DESIGN

BISHOP, A. THORNTON. Composition and Rendering. New York: John Willey and Sons Inc., 1933

CLARK, ARTHUR BRIDGMAN. *Perspective. A Textbook and Manual for Artists.* New York: Bridgman Publishers Inc., 1936

GUPTIL, ARTHUR L. *Color in Sketching and Rendering.* New York: Reinhold Publishing Corp., 1935

EMERSON, SYBIL. *Design A Creative Approach.* New York: International Textbook Co., 1953

FELDSTED, C. J. *Design Fundamentals.* New York: Pitman Publishing Co., 1950

KAUFMANN, EDGAR. *What Is Modern Design.* New York: Museum of Modern Art. Simon and Schuster, 1950

RASMUSSEN, HENRY. *Art Structure.* New York: McGraw Hill Co., 1950

RATHBONE, RICHARD ADAMS. *Introduction to the Fundamentals of Design.* New York: McGraw Hill Co., 1950

SCOTT, ROBERT. *Design Fundamentals.* New York: McGraw Hill Co., 1951

WIGGINS, RICHARD G. *Composing In Space.* Dubuque, Iowa. Wm. C. Brown Co., 1949

COLOR

BURRIS-MEYER, ELIZABETH. *Color and Design in the Decorative Arts.* New York: Prentice Hall Inc., 1935

BURRIS-MEYER, ELIZABETH. *Contemporary Color Guide.* New York: W. Helburn, 1947

BUSTANOBY, JACQUES HENRI. *Principles of Color and Color Mixing.* New York: McGraw Hill, 1947

GRAVES, MAITLAND E. *The Art of Color and Design.* New York: McGraw Hill Co., 1951

GRAVES, MAITLAND E. *Color Fundamentals.* New York: McGraw Hill Co., 1952

GUPTIL, ARTHUR L. *Color in Sketching and Rendering.* New York: Reinhold Publishing Corp., 1935

JACOBSEN, EGBERT. *Basic Color.* Chicago: Paul Theobald, 1948

LUCKIESH, M. *The Language of Color.* New York: Dodd Mead, 1930

LUCKIESH, M. *Color and Colors.* New York: D. Van Nostrand Co., Inc., 1938

MAERZ, A. AND REA, PAUL M. *Dictionary of Color.* New York: McGraw Hill Co., 1930

MUNSELL, A. H. *Munsell Book of Color.* Vol. 1 and Vol. 2. Baltimore: Munsell Color Co., Inc., 1929, 1942

BOND, FRED. *Color, How to See and Use It.* San Francisco: Camera Craft Publishing Corp., 1954

JACOBS, MICHEL. *The Art of Colour.* New York: Doubleday Doran and Co., 1931

KING, JOHN L. *The Art of Using Color.* New York: The World Publishing Co., 1938

COSTUMING

BARTON, LUCY. *Historic Costumes for the Stage.* New York: Walter H. Baker Co., 1935

CHALMERS, HELENA. *Clothes On and Off the Stage.* New York: D. Appleton-Century Co., 1930

EVANS, MARY. *Costume Throughout the Ages.* Philadelphia: J. B. Lippincott Co., 1930

KOHLER, CARL, AND SICHART, EMMA VON. *A History of Costume.* Philadelphia: David McKay Co., 1928

KOMISARJEVSKY, THEODORE. *The Costume of the Theatre.* New York: Henry Holt and Co., 1932

RACINET, ALBERT C. A. *Le Costume Historique.* Paris: Firmin-Didot, 1888

WALKUP, FAIRFAX PROUDFIT. *Dressing the Part.* New York: F. S. Crofts, 1939

WILCOX, R. TURNER. *The Mode In Costume.* New York: Charles Scribner, 1947

WILCOX, R. TURNER. *The Mode In Footwear.* New York: Charles Scribner, 1948

WILCOX, R. TURNER. *The Mode In Hats and Head-dresses.* New York: Charles Scribner, 1946

LELOIR, MAURICE. *Dictionnaire Du Costume et de ses Accessoires des Armes et des Etoffes des Origines a nos jours.* Paris: Librarie Grund, 1951

CRAFT PROCESSES

GRISWOLD, LESTER. *Handicraft, Simplified Procedure and Projects.* Prentice Hall Inc., 1951, 1952

STEPHENSON, JESSIE BANE. *From Old Stencils to Silk Screening.* New York: Charles Scribner's Sons, 1953

DESIGN MOTIVES

ESTRIN, MICHAEL. *2,000 Designs, Forms, and Ornaments.* Philadelphia: Wm. Penn Publishing Corp., 1947

HORNUNG, CLARENCE PEARSON. *Handbook of Designs and Devices.* New York: Dover Publications, 1946

SPELTZ, ALEXANDER. *Styles of Ornament.* New York: Grosset and Dunlap, 1936

BOSSERT, HELMUTH. *An Encyclopedia of Color Decoration.* New York: E. Weyhe, 1928 (Color Plates)

GLAZIER, RICHARD. *A Manual of Historic Ornament.* London, New York: Batsford Ltd., 6th Ed., 1948

JONES, OWEN. *The Grammar of Ornament.* London: Bernard Quaritch, 1910

FURNITURE

ARONSON, JOSEPH. *The Book of Furniture and Decoration.* New York: Crown Publishers, 1941

ARONSON, JOSEPH. *The Encyclopedia of Furniture.* New York: Crown Publishers, 1938

BOSSERT, VON PROF. DR. H. TH. *Geschichte Des Kunstgewerkes.* Vol. 6. Berlin: Verlag Ernst Wasmuth. Gm. B. H., 1935

DERIEUX, MARY AND STEVENSON, ISABELLE. *The Complete Book of Interior Decorating.* New York: Greystone Press, 1954

DYER, WALTER ALDEN. *Handbook of Furniture Styles.* New York: The Century Co., 1918

LEE, RUTH W. AND BOLENDER, LOUISE T. *Fashions In Furnishings.* New York: McGraw Hill Co., 1948

JACQUEMART, ALBERT. *A History of Furniture.* London: Chapman and Hall, 1878

MILLER, EDGAR G., JR. *The Standard Book of American Antique Furniture.* New York: Greystone Press, 1950

THORNE, MRS. JAMES WARD. *Handbook to American Rooms in Miniature.* Chicago: Chicago Art Institute, 1941

THORNE, MRS. JAMES WARD. *Handbook to European Rooms in Miniature.* Chicago: Chicago Art Institute, 1943

SCENE DESIGN

BEAUMONT, CYRIL W. *Design for the Ballet.* London: The Studio Ltd., 1937

CHENEY, SHELDON. *Stage Decoration.* New York: John Day Co., 1928

CRAIG, EDWARD GORDON. *Scene.* Oxford: Oxford University Press, 1923

FUERST, WALTER RENE, AND HUME, SAMUEL. *Twentieth Century Stage Decoration.* 2 vols. London: Alfred Knopf, Inc., 1928

FRIEDERICH, WILLARD J., AND FRASER, JOHN H. *Scenery Design for the Amateur Stage.* New York: The Macmillan Co., 1950

HELVENSTON, HAROLD. *Scenery.* California: Stanford University Press, 1931

JONES, ROBERT EDMOND. *Drawings for the Theatre.* New York: Theatre Arts, 1925

JONES, ROBERT EDMOND. *The Dramatic Imagination.* New York: Duell Sloane and Pearce, Inc., 1941

KOMISARJEVSKY, THEODORE, AND SIMONSON, LEE. *Settings and Costumes of the Modern Theatre.* New York: Studio Publications, Inc., 1933

LAVER, JAMES. *Drama, Its Costumes and Decor.* London: The Studio Publications, 1951

MacGOWAN, KENNETH, AND JONES, ROBERT E. *Continental Stagecraft.* New York: Harcourt Brace and Co., 1922

NICOLL, ALLARDYCE. *The Development of the Theatre.* New York: Harcourt Brace and Co., 1948

OENSLAGER, DONALD. *Scenery Then and Now.* New York: 1936   ,

SHERINGHAM, GEORGE, AND LAVER, JAMES. *Design in the Theatre.* London: The Studio, Ltd., 1927

SIMONSON, LEE. *The Stage Is Set.* New York: Harcourt Brace and Co., 1932

SIMONSON, LEE. *Part of a Lifetime.* New York: Duell, Sloane and Pearce, 1943

SIMONSON, LEE. *The Art of Scenic Design.* New York: Harper and Bros., 1950

. . . . . *Theatre Arts Prints.* New York: Theatre Arts Magazine

ZINKEISEN, DORIS. *Designing for the Stage.* London: Studio Publications, 1938; rev. 1945

STAGECRAFT

BARBER, PHILIP. *The Scene Technician's Handbook.* New Haven: Whitlock's Book Store, 1928 (This is now a part of: GASSNER, JOHN. *Producing the Play.* New York: The Dryden Press, 1941)

BUERKI, FRED A. *Stagecraft for Non-Professionals.* Madison: University of Wisconsin Press, 1945

BURRIS-MEYER, HAROLD, AND COLE, EDWARD C. *Scenery for the Theatre.* Boston: Little Brown and Co., 1938

CORNBERG, SOL, AND GEBAUER, EMANUEL L. *A Stagecrew Handbook.* New York: Harper and Bros., 1941

HAKE, HERBERT V. *Here's How.* Chicago: Row Peterson Co., 1942

KRANITCH, FRIEDRICH. *Buhnentechnik der Gegenwart.* Verlag von R. Oldenbourg. Munchen, 1929

NELMS, HENNING. *A Primer of Stagecraft.* New York: Dramatists Play Service, 1941

PHILIPPI, HERBERT. *Stagecraft and Scene Design.* Boston: Houghton Mifflin Co., 1953

SELDEN, SAMUEL, AND SELLMAN, HUNTON D. *Stage Scenery and Lighting.* New York: F. S. Crofts and Co., 1930, rev. 1936

WADE, ROBERT J. *Staging TV Programs and Commercials.* New York: Hastings House, 1954

WADE, ROBERT J. *Designing for TV.* New York: Farr and Straus

WHITING, FRANK M. *An Introduction to the Theatre.* New York: Harper and Bros., 1954

STAGE LIGHTING

BENTHAM, FREDERICK. *Stage Lighting.* London: Sir Isaac Pitman and Sons Ltd., 1950

FUCHS, THEODORE. *Stage Lighting.* New York: Little Brown and Co., 1929

McCANDLESS, STANLEY. *A Method of Lighting the Stage.* New York: Theatre Arts, 1932

NELMS, HENNING. *Lighting the Amateur Stage.* New York: Theatre Arts Inc., 1931

RIDGE, C. HAROLD AND ALDRED, F. S. *Stage Lighting.* London: Pitman and Co., 1935

RUBIN, JOEL E., AND WATSON, LELAND H. *Theatrical Lighting Practice.* New York: Theatre Arts, 1955

SELDEN, S. AND SELLMAN, H. *Stage Scenery and Lighting.* New York: F. S. Crofts and Co., 1941

The designer may find the *Encyclopedia* Britannica, *Encyclopedia Americana,* and other similar general works of value. He may also find it helpful to thumb through the following periodicals:

The American Artist	Life
Better Homes and Gardens	National Geographic
House Beautiful	Theatre Arts
Holiday	

THEATRICAL EQUIPMENT DEALERS

COSTUMES

Brooks ....3 West 61st St., New York, N. Y.

Colorado Costume Co. ....1751 Champa St., Denver, Colo.

Eaves Costume Co., Inc. ....151 W. 46th St., New York (19), N. Y.

Manhattan Costume Co., Inc. ....1658 Broadway, New York (19), N. Y.

Salt Lake Costume Co. ....248 South Main St., Salt Lake City, Utah

Western Costume Co. ....5335 Melrose Ave., Hollywood, Cal.

Van Horn and Sons ....Philadelphia (7), Penn.

FABRICS

Antipyros Co. ....338 Berry St., Brooklyn, N. Y.

Art Theatre Equipment Co. ....155 W. 46 St., New York (20), N. Y.

Astrup Co. ....39 Walker St., New York (13), N. Y.

Cleon Throckmorton ....102 W. Third St., New York (12), N. Y.

Dazian ....142 W. 44 St., New York (18), N. Y.

Maharam Textile Co. ....170 W. 48 St., New York (20), N. Y.

Paramount Textile Mills ....34 Walker St., New York (13), N. Y.

Theatre Production Service ....1430 Broadway, New York (18), N. Y.

GENERAL THEATRE EQUIPMENT

Art Theatre Equipment Co. ....155 W. 46th St., New York (20), N. Y.

Grand Stage Lighting Co. ....23 Hubbard St., Chicago (10), Ill.

Northwestern Theatre Associates ....1000 Foster St., Evanston, Ill.

Theatre Production Service ....1430 Broadway, New York (18), N. Y.

LIGHTING COLOR MEDIA

Amplex Corp. ....111 Water St., Brooklyn (1), N. Y. (Colorbeam Lamps)

Brigham Sheet Gelatine Co. ....17-19 Weston St., Randolph, Vermont

Roscoe Laboratories ....369 Hudson Ave., Brooklyn (1), N. Y.

Paramount ....242 W. 27th St., New York (1), N. Y. (Cinabex)

Transolene Co. ....Barrington, Ill.

Note: Color media may also be obtained from most general theatre supply companies, from theatre lighting supply companies, and from motion picture supply companies.

LIGHTING EQUIPMENT

Ariel Davis Mfg. Co.	3687 South State St., Salt Lake City, Utah
Century Lighting, Inc.	521 West 43rd St., New York (36), N. Y.
Columbia Stage Lighting Co.	341 W. 47th St., New York (19), N. Y.
Cutler Hammer Inc.	Milwaukee, Wisc.
General Radio Co.	Cambridge (39), Mass.
Kliegl Bros.	321 W. 50th St., New York (19), N. Y.
Major Equipment Co.	4603 Fullerton Ave., Chicago, Ill.
Midwest Stage Lighting Co.	55 Wacker Drive, Chicago (1), Ill.
Otto K. Oleson Co.	Hollywood, Cal.
Strong Electric Corp.	94 City Park Ave., Toledo (2), Ohio
Superior Electric Co.	Bristol, Conn.
Ward Leonard Electric Co.	Mount Vernon, N. Y.

PAINT

Aljo Mfg. Co.	130 W. 21st St., New York (11), N. Y.
Alabastine Co.	Grand Rapids, Michigan
Gothic Colors Co.	90 Ninth Ave., New York (11), N. Y.
Glidden Co.	Cleveland (2), Ohio (Casein base paint)
A. Leiser Co.	48 Horatio St., New York (14), N. Y.
Luminall Paint Co.	3617 S. May St., Chicago (9), Ill. (Casein base paint)

PLASTIC MATERIALS

Arthel Display Plastics Co. ("Plastab")	Brookfield, Conn.
Ben Walters, Inc., ("Celastic")	156 7th Ave., New York (11), N. Y.

SOUND EFFECTS

Paramount Enterprises	242 W. 27th St., New York (1), N. Y.
Thomas J. Valentino, Inc.	150 West 46th St., New York (36), N. Y.

STAGE HARDWARE

Abbott Scrim Profile Co.	266 W. 44th St., New York (18)
Channon Corp.	1446 W. Austin Ave., Chicago, Ill.
J. R. Clancy Co.	Syracuse, N. Y.
Peter Clark	544 W. 30th St., New York (1), N. Y.

ADDRESSES

Additional addresses may be found in the *Theatre Directory* published by Bernard Simon, 1674 Broadway, New York (19), N. Y.

MISCELLANEOUS INFORMATION

Table of Equivalents.

144 square inches equals 1 square foot
9 square feet equals 1 square yard
12 dozen, or 144 equals 1 gross
100 pounds equals one cwt. (hundred weight)
1 board foot (bd. ft.) is a piece of board
1'-0" x 1'-0" x 1"
2 cups equals 1 pint
2 pints equal 1 quart
4 quarts equal one gallon
16 ounces (avoirdupois) equals 1 pound
8 ounces equals 1 cup
1 tablespoonful equals ½ fluid ounce
1 teaspoonful equals 1/3 tablespoonful

* * *

Stagecraft Material Measurements.

Fabric or textiles are listed by the lineal or linear yard, which means a running yard of the specified width.
Pipe is measured by its inside diameter.
Aluminum conduit is measured by its outside diameter.
Lumber is measured by the board foot.
Plywood, Masonite, and other wall board materials are listed by the square foot.
Nails are listed by the penny which originally referred to price per hundred but which now refers to the length of the nail. The sizes of nails increase with the numbers.
Screws are listed by diameter, length, head shape, and finish.
Bolts are listed by diameter, type, length.
Casters are listed by diameter of the wheel.
Hammers are listed by their weight and the type of head and claws.
Saws are listed by the type, length and number of teeth per inch.

* * *

Strength of Rope and Cable Material. The safe working load is listed.

Piano Wire.

13 gauge	....	250 lbs.
20 gauge	....	500 lbs.
26 gauge	....	900 lbs.

Manilla Rope.

¼"	....	130 lbs.
½"	....	400 lbs.
¾"	....	600 lbs.
1"	....	1450 lbs.

Braided cotton (sash cord), breaking strength.

¼"	....	450 lbs.
½"	....	1000 lbs.
¾"	....	1400 lbs.

Thinners and Solvents.

Water paint . . . use plain water or soap and water.
Oil paint . . . turpentine, kerosene, gasoline, brush cleaner.
Shellac . . . alcohol.
Lacquer . . . banana oil, lacquer thinner ,acetone.
Bronzing liquid . . . same as for oil paint.

* * *

Casting plaster and plaster of paris may be used for the same purposes. Casting plaster is usually obtainable in all lumber yards and is less expensive than plaster of paris.

* * *

Sal Ammoniac and Ammonium Chloride are the same.

* * *

Blocks and Block and Tackle Systems. Heavy objects may be lifted more easily if a block and tackle is employed. The mechanical advantage gained by using such a device is determined by the number and arrangement of the pulleys in relation to the load, the anchor and the operator. The friction of the rope moving on the wheel of the pulley and the friction of the pulley wheel on its axle are factors that cannot be ignored. Below is a list of the approximate advantages gained by using pulley or block systems.

1. One pulley. The rope is anchored above, passes up and over the pulley, (which is anchored above), and then back down to the operator. More energy is required to lift the object than when it is lifted without the pulley. Overcoming the friction adds to the strain of lifting. A 1000 pound weight would require a force of 1100 or 1200 pounds to lift it. The pull is downward, and there is no mechanical advantage.

2. One pulley. The rope is anchored above, passes down through the pulley and then back up again. The weight is fastened under the pulley and the operator pulls from above. A 1000 pound weight will require only half as much force as in the previous one pulley system. A 550 to 560 pound force will elevate the 1000 pound weight. The pull is upward and the M.A. is 2.

3. Two pulleys. The rope is anchored to the base of the top pulley, passes down around a lower pulley, and then up and over the top pulley and then down again. The pull is downward and the 100 pound weight will require a force of about 620 pounds to

lift it and overcome the friction of the pulleys. The pull is downward, and the M.A. is 2.

4. Two pulleys. The rope is anchored to the top of the lower block, passes up and over the top block, passes under the pulley of the lower block and then extends upward. 1000 pounds now seems to weigh about 420 pounds. The pull is upward and the M.A. is 3.

5. Double Block above and single block below. The rope is anchored to the top of the lower pulley, passes up around one of the upper pulleys, down around the lower pulley and back up around the other upper one, then back down. The apparent weight of the object is about 460 pounds. The pull is downward and the M.A. is 3.

6. Double block below and single block above. The apparent weight in this instance is about 350 pounds. The pull is upward and the M.A. is 4.

7. Two double blocks. The rope is anchored above, passed downward first and then in rotation through all of the pulleys. The apparent weight is about 385 pounds. The pull is downward and the M.A. is 4.

8. Two double blocks. The position of the lines is changed with the rope first anchored to the lower block. The apparent weight is only about 300 pounds. The pull is upward and the M.A. is 5.

It is to be noted that a loss of movement accompanies the gaining of the mechanical advantage. As the M.A. increases so also does the amount of rope that must be pulled so the movement on the object end decreases as the M.A. increases.

* * *

The Steel Square or Framing Square. The framing square is a valuable tool that has many uses. Ordinarily it is used for squaring the corners of flats or making marks across boards. It may be used for countless other computing tasks. Here are just a few of them.

1. Marking angles. Use the 12″ mark on one arm of the square and the number indicated on the other arm. Place the square with the 12″ mark at the junction of the lines of the angle and with the right angle of the square extending away from the point of convergence. The angle may be computed by drawing a line from the 12″ point toward the mark indicated on the other arm of the square.

12″ on one side and $1\frac{1}{16}$″ on the other for 5°
12″ on one side and $2\frac{1}{8}$″ on the other for 10°
12″ on one side and $3\frac{7}{32}$″ on the other for 15°
12″ on one side and $4\frac{3}{8}$″ on the other for 20°
12″ on one side and $5\frac{5}{8}$″ on the other for 25°
12″ on one side and $6\frac{15}{16}$″ on the other for 30°
12″ on one side and $8\frac{7}{16}$″ on the other for 35°
12″ on one side and $10\frac{3}{32}$″ on the other for 40°
12″ on one side and 12″ on the other for 45°

2. In order to draw the mitre angles for the corners of various frames use the following measurements on the square:
12″ on one side and $20\frac{21}{32}$″ on the other for a triangle (equilateral)
12″ on one side and 12″ on the other for a square
12″ on one side and $8\frac{23}{32}$″ on the other for a pentagon
12″ on one side and $6\frac{15}{16}$″ on the other for a hexagon
12″ on one side and $5\frac{25}{32}$″ on the other for a heptagon
12″ on one side and $4\frac{31}{32}$″ on the other for an octagon
12″ on one side and $4\frac{3}{8}$″ on the other for a nonagon
12″ on one side and $3\frac{7}{8}$″ on the other for a decagon

3. In order to find the center of a circle with a framing square lay the square on the circle with the corner at the circumference. Mark where the outer edge of the blades cut the circle and draw a line connecting these points. This line is the diameter. Draw another line in a like manner and the point of intersection will be the center of the circle.

* * *

The mitre cut angle for corners of various figures may be determined by dividing the number of sides into 180. This holds only if the sides are equal in length.
A triangle has 3 sides so the boards for mitres are cut at 60°
A square has 4 sides so the boards for mitres are cut at 45°
A hexagon has 6 sides so the boards for mitres cut at 30°

* * *

The hypotenuse of a right triangle is equal to the square root of the sum of the square of the two sides.

INDEX TO SUBJECT MATTER

ff. and following